*A*dventure Guide to

Ecuador
& the Galápagos Islands

Peter Davis Krahenbuhl

HUNTER

HUNTER PUBLISHING, INC,
130 Campus Drive, Edison, NJ 08818
☎ 732-225-1900; 800-255-0343; fax 732-417-1744
www.hunterpublishing.com

Ulysses Travel Publications
4176 Saint-Denis, Montréal, Québec
Canada H2W 2M5
☎ 514-843-9882, ext. 2232; fax 514-843-9448

Windsor Books
The Boundary, Wheatley Road, Garsington
Oxford, OX44 9EJ England
☎ 01865-361122; fax 01865-361133

ISBN 1-58843-346-3
© 2003 Hunter Publishing, Inc.

*This and other Hunter travel guides are also
available as e-books in a variety of digital formats
through our online partners,
including Amazon.com, BarnesandNoble.com,
and NetLibrary.com, as well as direct from the publisher.*

Cover photo: *Masked boobies, Galápagos Islands*,
Coral Planet Photography.
All other photos by author. Back cover photo: *Baños from above*.
Index by Nancy Wolff
Cartoons by Joe Kohl

Maps by Kim MacKinnon & Kim André, © 2003 Hunter Publishing, Inc.

www.hunterpublishing.com

 Hunter's full range of guides to all corners of the globe is featured on our exciting website. You'll find guidebooks to suit every type of traveler, no matter what their budget, lifestyle, or idea of fun.

Adventure Guides – There are now over 40 titles in this series, covering destinations from Costa Rica and the Yucatán to Tampa Bay & Florida's West Coast, Belize and the Alaska Highway. Complete with information on what to do, as well as where to stay and eat, *Adventure Guides* are tailor-made for the active traveler, with details on hiking, biking, canoeing, horseback riding, skiing, watersports, and all other kinds of fun.

Alive Guides – This ever-popular line of books takes a unique look at the best each destination offers: fine dining, jazz clubs, first-class hotels and resorts. In-margin icons direct the reader at a glance. Top-sellers include *The Cayman Islands, St. Martin & St. Barts,* and *Aruba, Bonaire & Curaçao.*

Rivages Hotels of Character & Charm books cover France, Spain, and Portugal. Originating in Paris, they set the standard for excellence with their fabulous color photos, superb maps and candid descriptions of the most remarkable hotels of Europe.

Romantic Weekends guidebooks provide a series of escapes for couples of all ages and lifestyles. Unlike most "romantic" travel books, ours cover more than charming hotels and delightful restaurants, with a host of activities that you and your partner will remember forever.

Cruise guides available from Hunter include *Cruising the Eastern Caribbean; Cruising the Southern & Western Caribbean; Cruising Alaska* and *Cruising the Mediterranean.*

Full descriptions are given for each book on the website, along with reviewers' comments and a cover image. You can also view pages and the table of contents. Books may be purchased on-line via our secure transaction facility.

■ Preface

If there is one bit of advice to carry on your journey it is to use this guide only as a reference, to help you explore and to expand your comfort zone. All too often travel guides and tours tend to "package" experiences, but then you miss half the fun. If it weren't for the mistakes I made and resulting experiences, this guide wouldn't have been written (at least not by me). Make it your own journey, wander and make travelers' mistakes, finding yourself in new and unexpected places, meeting new and unexpected people. Remember that adventure travel is experiencing life through new discoveries.

I want to thank first and foremost the bus driver who knew I had asked him to drop me off along the Pan-American Highway in Otavalo, but just kept on going. Otherwise, I never would have made it to the beautiful town of Ibarra and discovered the unanticipated beauty of a new-found place. I also want to thank the South American Explorers and the far-too-many-to-name organizations, tour operators, hotels, friends and acquaintances along the way who assisted and enriched my travels and my life. Finally, to my family and my love, Judith, thank you.

■ About the Author

Peter spent most of his childhood on the beaches of Oxnard, California. Favorite memories include surfing, baseball and family camping wherever Dad found big fly-fishing rivers. After chasing nature and being chased by "development," Peter completed his BA in Economics and Environmental Studies at the University of California, Santa Barbara. A global interest, particularly in deforestation and development, led him to pursue a Master of Public Affairs from Indiana University, concentrating in International Affairs and Environmental Policy. During this time, his Latin American travels and conservation projects began in Ecuador. As a result, he developed an Ecotourism company and joined The World Outdoors in 1997 as an adventure travel guide. He has guided in Ecuador, Cuba, Western North America and elsewhere. While researching and guiding in Ecuador, he met his beautiful wife, Judith, who has been integral to development of this guidebook. Peter now works in development at The World Outdoors and is Co-Director of Sustainable Travel International, a not-for-profit organization working to promote a more responsible travel industry. His dog, Shady, hates it when he travels, but she understands.

Contents

Maps

Introduction

Adventure Awaits

Picture for a moment a steam-engine train ride from the equatorial Pacific Coast into the second-largest mountain range in the world – the Andes! If that's not adventurous enough, hop onto the roof of that train for the experience of a lifetime. As the journey begins, notice the lush hillside vegetation shrouded in blankets of mist. This is a land of mangrove swamps, banana plantations, and coastal cloud forests; a land with the business heartbeat of a major Latin American political and economic center; a land of extreme material poverty that's rich in cultural beauty and pride. Experience the inquisitive gaze of local villagers and wave back to the children as you pass. The the scenery begins to change. The vegetation becomes sparse as the canyons deepen and narrow. The sunlight, as it strikes the high sides of the mountains, blends with the intense equatorial shadows.

Now it's time to climb up the side of a mountain. Another engine attaches to the train's caboose and you ascend a steep mountain gorge via countless switchbacks. This is *El Nariz del Diablo*, the Devil's Nose, and the experience is literally breathtaking. Hold on as your feet dangle not only over the edge of the train but over the surging river 1,000 feet below.

In the blink of an eye the Sierras emerge and the land transforms into a quilted checkerboard of farmland on rolling mountains. The characteristics of the people change as well, as cosmopolitan suits are replaced with traditional ponchos and Panama hats. The villagers break for a moment, still holding balls of wool or bundles of straw, to stare at you and the other fleeting strangers as you roll by. In each village you notice a slight difference in indigenous attire, signs of Ecuador's rich cultural history. You continue on, and later, as the sun sets, you contemplate tomorrow's journey: into the heart of the upper Amazon Basin.

South America

N

HUNTER PUBLISHING

NICARAGUA

COSTA RICA

PANAMA

GALAPAGOS ISLANDS

ECUADOR

VENEZUELA GUYANA SURINAME FRENCH GUINA

COLOMBIA

ECUATOR

PERU

BRAZIL

BOLIVIA

PARAGUAY

CHILE

ARGENTINA

URUGUAY

Pacific Ocean

Atlantic Ocean

FALKLAND ISLANDS

NOT TO SCALE

© 2003 HUNTER PUBLISHING, INC

Introduction

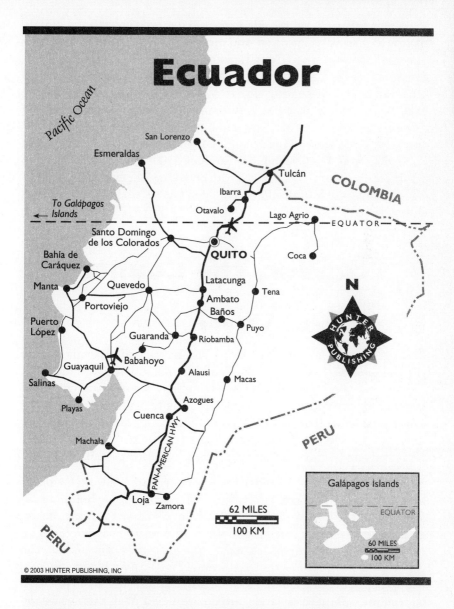

Ecuador

Pacific Ocean

San Lorenzo

Esmeraldas

Tulcán

COLOMBIA

Ibarra

To Galápagos Islands

Otavalo

Lago Agrio

EQUATOR

Santo Domingo de los Colorados

QUITO

Coca

Bahía de Caráquez

Latacunga

Manta

Quevedo

Tena

Ambato

Portoviejo

Baños

Puerto López

Puyo

Guaranda

Ríobamba

Guayaquil

Babahoyo

Alausi

Macas

Salinas

Azogues

Playas

Cuenca

Machala

PAN-AMERICAN HWY

PERU

Loja Zamora

62 MILES
100 KM

Galápagos Islands

EQUATOR

60 MILES
100 KM

PERU

N

HUNTER PUBLISHING

© 2003 HUNTER PUBLISHING, INC

■ World-Class Adventure

Simply put, Ecuador provides more biologic, geographic and recreational diversity than any other country in Latin America. You can experience the biological wonders of the Galápagos Islands, misty coastal cloud forests, the snowcapped jewels of the Andes, and the unparalleled diversity of the upper Amazon Basin. Add to this native markets and the beauty of the indigenous people, and you can imagine the adventure that awaits.

True adventure travel entails experiencing life through the simple beauty of discovery. To do so, you must expand your limits and open your arms to new encounters. Ecuador, a country that offers a cornucopia of rich, newfound experiences, is full of enchanting natural landscapes and welcoming smiles. Whether your goal is recreation, exploring pristine natural environments, or photographing the amazing variety of scenes, you will be delighted with the opportunities here. This is a land that gives back three times what you bring to it. So go now and take a chance. Challenge yourself, meet the people, try their food, and take a stab at speaking their language. The Ecuadorians will love you for it. And don't be surprised when you decide to return!

Ecuador, the Country

■ Adventure Overview

Charles Darwin rewrote the history of life on earth after his visit to the Galápagos Islands. Now the Ecuadorian mainland also lures adventure travelers, photographers, scientists, conservationists, and community developers alike. Ecuador is a hidden jewel that is slowly coming to light. The upper Amazon Basin, known locally as the Oriente, is a hotspot of biological diversity. It is truly one of the last places on earth where untouched primary rainforest still exists.

So, what exactly does Ecuador have to offer you? Well, pretty much anything you may hope to find. The Andes provide epic hiking, trekking, and mountaineering for all ability levels among spectacular Sierra scenery. Mountain biking in the high country is coming into its own as well, and horseback-riding opportunities throughout the country are as varied as they are scenic. For the avid birder, photographer, or botanist, Ecuador's cloud and rainforests, not to mention the unique Galápagos Islands, are unparalleled. Water activities top off the list, with snorkeling and diving off the islands. In the jungle there is boating by dugout canoe, as well as a rush of world-class whitewater rafting and kayaking. And all of this is within a day's travel from anywhere else in the country.

Like many Latin American countries, Ecuador is a poverty-stricken nation, but it also boasts peace and pride, a relatively stable political climate, and an extensive tourist and transportation infrastructure. Ecuador is among the pioneers of ecotourism and it continues to develop within the merging worlds of tourism, environmental preservation, and economic development. The time to go is now.

■ Location

Ecuador is located on the northwestern coast of South America. It covers approximately 104,550 square miles, plus the Galápagos. It straddles the equator on the Pacific Coast of South America and is bordered by Colombia to the north and Peru to the south and east. The Galápagos Islands form an archipelago over 600 miles off the coast of mainland Ecuador.

The name Ecuador is the Spanish term for the equator, the invisible line that divides the Earth horizontally in the Northern and Southern hemispheres and crosses the country (there is a monument near Quito, latitude 0°).

■ History & Politics

A view into the window of Ecuador's historical life is the first step in understanding and appreciating the beauty of this land.

Pre-Inca

Ecuador's earliest inhabitants lived in the Andes as hunters and gatherers, having arrived from Asia across the Bering Strait between 30,000 and 50,000 years ago. As agriculture developed, they settled in the fertile valley of the Andean Sierras. On the coast, related tribes with different dialects hunted, fished, practiced agriculture, traded and made war with each other, as well as with tribes of the highlands. Spear tips belonging to the earliest groups from as far back as 10,000 BC have been discovered. Though there is little evidence about Ecuador's pre-Incan past, by around 3,500 BC a fairly well developed culture known today as the **Valdivians** lived in the central coastal plain near what today is Santa Elena, along the south-central coast. Small earthenware figurines, most likely related to fertility rites and religious rituals within the Valdivia culture, have been discovered in this region and are on display in small archeological museums, as well as in Quito and Guayaquil. Other, more recent archeological sites exist in Esmeraldas and Manabí coastal provinces, and in the Northern Highlands.

In the fertile valleys of the Andes, meanwhile, several independent tribes evolved in more settled communities, ruled by local and regional chiefs and farming crops such as maize, quinoa, potatoes. In the Southern Highlands, they even utilized irrigation. As many independent tribes merged and evolved during this period, most early inhabitants lived primarily along the coast (the **Caras**) or in the highlands (the **Quitus**), though not much is known about possible cultures in the Oriente. These two groups merged into the **Shyri Nation** under the leadership of the coastal Caras, who were then in the Northern Highlands, and the Quitus, around the modern site of Quito. Another alliance by marriage united the Shyri Nation with the **Puruhá** of the Southern Highlands under the **Dachicela** lineage, while the Cañaris remained separate during the period of Inca arrival in the area around what is Cuenca today.

Inca Invasion

The Inca Empire dominated southern Peru – primarily the area around Lake Titicaca – as far back as the 11th century. By the 15th century, when the Incas began to expand their empire, the Quitucaras (from the Dachicela lineage) dominated the northern chain of Andean kingdoms in today's Ecuador, and the Cañaris ruled the south in the area around the beautiful modern-day city of Cuenca. The ninth Inca King, **Pachacuti Inca Yupanque**, meaning "Earthshaker," was primarily responsible for what eventually became 11 generations of Inca rule from as far south and Chile and Argentina and as far north as Ecuador and Colombia.

After years of resistance against Inca expansion under Yupanque's son Túpac-Yupanqui, the Cañaris and Incas settled "peacefully" in 1470. As the Incas proceeded north, the Quitucaras continued to resist for many more years. Eventually, the son of Túpac-Yupanqui, named **Hauyna-Capac** (meaning "rich and excellent youth"), was born of a Cañari princess and succeeded to the Inca throne. From this point forward the southern Incan culture in Peru began to merge with that of the peoples of Ecuador. Huayna-Capac, the 11th Inca King, expanded the empire further and reigned during a brief period of relative stability.

Inca-Ecuadorian Society

Though short-lived in Ecuador, the Inca Empire – particularly during Huayna-Capac's rule – had a profound effect on the Andean community and structure of life. The two cultures were relatively compatible, as Huayna Capac, who was fond of Quito, ruled with strength and reported wisdom. Traditional subsistence farming was complemented by agricultural advances from farther south near the capital of Cuzco, including new crops, expanded irrigation and the use of domesticated llamas. The people continued to use the land communally, with private allotments for family consumption. Under the Incas, however, the emperor "owned" the land by divine right and took homage and a portion of proceeds, mainly to support the largest army in the Americas and to provide personal comforts. Any resistance resulted in entire community displacement, and local inhabitants were sometimes relocated to far away lands in the empire and replaced primarily by Quichua-speaking groups from near Cuzco. This culture became the foundation for modern Ecuador's largest indigenous language group, the **Quichua**, who range from the Andes to the upper Amazon.

The Incas eventually subdued the resistant Quitucara and sacked Quito in 1492, although a peaceful alliance did not occur until Huayna-Capac married the daughter of the captured Quitu leader. Their son in Quito was **Atahualpa**. Huayna-Capac had another son, named **Huascar**, previously born of an Inca princess in the capital of Cuzco (and "rightful" heir to the empire). By now the Inca Empire included the Andean portion of Ecuador in what was known as Tawantinsuyu. Time was running out, though, even for the powerful Incas. According to the first Spanish historian, Father Bernabe Cobo, Huayna-Capac knew ahead of time that the ferocious Spaniards had "traveled across the sea in large wooden houses" and that they were on their way. But the Spanish sent messengers of death ahead of them in the form of smallpox and measles, and wiped out a significant number of native and Inca peoples, including Huayna-Capac. When he died around 1526, he left the empire to his sons, Huascar in the south and Atahualpa in the north. This division became a catalyst for the fall of the Inca Empire.

Brothers Divide as the Spanish Arrive

After their father (Huayna-Capac) died, a fratricidal struggle followed as Huascar declared war on Atahualpa. Huascar – born of pure Inca blood in Cuzco – claimed the empire, though he reportedly was a drunken, cruel and poor ruler. Atahualpa, though born of a "lesser" wife, was apparently a much more capable and benign ruler. Atahualpa sent his troops south from Quito to meet Huascar near Riobamba, where they fought. Initially captured, Atahualpa escaped and, with the aid of his father's loyal and capable generals, defeated Huascar. Ecuadorians today point to this conflict and victory as a source of pride and virtue over neighboring Peru.

Nevertheless, the Inca Empire was permanently weakened during the critical period of the Spanish arrival in 1532. Atahualpa, having recently defeated his brother, was recovering in Cajamarca in northern Peru when he heard the Spaniards were coming. Nobody knows why Atahualpa did not strike first with his still relatively powerful force. Historians theorize that there may have been confusion over whether these bearded creatures were gods or men, or perhaps a certain level of unconcern over such a small number of soldiers. In any event, Francisco Pizarro summoned Atahualpa and then ambushed him. Hidden conquistadors, who appeared more as deities than humans to the natives, fired upon and killed thousands of Inca soldiers and captured Atahualpa. With the natives' "Fear of God," the Spanish easily subdued the weakened empire. After Atahualpa was captured, he survived for a year by paying large ransoms, but eventually the Spanish saved his soul by baptizing and then executing him.

The Spanish then advanced toward Quito. Atahualpa's general – and modern-day Inca hero – **Rumiñahui**, resisted the Spanish for two more years, though the Cañari-backed conquistadors defeated them at a major battle near Chimborazo Volcano. Then, as the Spanish gained ground, Rumiñahui destroyed Quito rather than hand it over to the conquerors. In 1534 the Spanish rebuilt Quito, dubbed it *the Royal Audencia de Quito*, and proceeded to track down and execute Rumiñahui. Though there were other rebellions led by Inca leaders throughout the old empire, the Spanish were able to successfully murder, trick, seduce, infect with disease or breed out any further native resistance.

The Colonial Era

The era of Spanish rule was short-lived but perhaps the single most significant influence in shaping Ecuador of today. It took only 2,000

Spaniards to successfully murder tens of thousands of Amerindians, while subjugating almost half a million others. The rumors of gold and riches that fueled the colonization of Ecuador also sparked the first expedition through the Amazon to the Atlantic coast. In 1541, the Spanish General **Orellana** set out with 350 soldiers, 4,000 Amerindians and countless animals; he arrived a year later on the Atlantic coast with only 50 surviving men. Rather than gold, they found the danger, heat, and disease of the Amazon rainforest. Meanwhile, the coastal region became refuge to many natives that had escaped subjugation and persecution. African slaves, who were shipwrecked in 1570, heavily influenced the north coast. Mixing with native females, they evolved into a unique mixed black-Indian culture that remains prominent today.

In typical Spanish colonial fashion, the new rulers immediately introduced a feudal system of forced labor upon the indigenous people in the Sierras. The Spanish Crown alloted *encomiendas*, or enormous tracts of land, to Spanish settlers (*peninsulares*) in return for loyalty and riches extracted from the land and people. The natives were assigned a Spanish landowner and forced to work the land. In exchange, they received a small plot of infertile land to live on and the "protection" of their landlord. What they actually received were miserable living conditions, a forced religion, and obliged debt that would accrue over generations, thus reinforcing the system.

The ruling colonists lived well during this era. European arts and sciences were introduced to the area. Churches, monasteries, and colonial architecture sprouted throughout the region. The economy expanded, with textile production – again, via forced labor – and the introduction of cattle and banana farming. During this time, Ecuador became the seat of the Royal Audencia and Quito became an integral industrial component of the Spanish Empire. Meanwhile, the atrocious treatment of the natives that supported development of the economy and infrastructure resulted in many small but violent uprisings.

The Church, Haciendas & Recession

By the 1700s most surviving Amerindians were converted to Roman Catholicism. The Church grabbed its share of the Ecuadorian pie and expanded into the Oriente, becoming the region's largest single landlord. Thanks to disease and the ruthless forced labor, many Amerindians died, dramatically reducing the size of the "workforce." Private haciendas emerged during this period as the original landlords sold large tracts of land in exchange for a more favorable urban life. On the coastal plain the export of hardwood and cacao began with the help of slaves from Africa.

During the 1700s, recession was anchored to the sinking ship of Spain's troubled economy. This paralleled a growing unrest among the ruling class in Quito as they felt the effects of severe recession, especially as the Spanish crown tightened its grip in desperation. Meanwhile, Guayaquil had already established itself as an inter-American trade center. It was growing in strength, with liberal ideals of freedom and independence due to free trade. This was quite contrary to the controlled, conservative status quo. Indigenous voices, strengthened by the weakened *obraje* system (a form of indentured servitude) increased political instability during this time. By the end of the 18th century – partly as a result of the American Revolution, the arrival of progressive European ideas, and rise of national liberal intellectuals – this unrest began to show.

Independence

Major unrest in Ecuador developed primarily from the ***criollos***, Spanish descendents born in the new world, who were not allotted the benefits of *peninsulares* (original settlers). The first serious attempt at Ecuadorian liberation in 1809, though, was actually a case of Spanish loyalists rebelling against Napolean's recent French control over the (former) Spanish colony. While the movement was successful, it was also short-lived, and colonial troops regained control within a month. The stage, however, was set for independence. In addition to *criollo* unrest, the coastal city of Guayaquil became the new voice for liberation. The emerging middle class, born from cacao production and trade, joined the struggle for independence that was spreading across the continent. The leader was the Venezuelan general **Simon Bolívar**. Having declared Ecuadorian independence in 1820, his troops, led by lieutenant **José de Sucre**, joined the people of Guayaquil. For two years they struggled against the Royalist army, finally defeating them in 1822 near Quito on the Pichincha Volcano.

Ecuador's currency until September of 2000 was the Sucre, named after one of the liberators of Ecuador, José de Sucre. This currency was in place for over 100 years, until the US dollar became the official currency, though more remote areas of the country continue to think in terms of its national hero's namesake currency.

The Audencia de Quito was incorporated into Bolívar's vision of the Federation of Grán Colombia, which also included Colombia, Panama, and Venezuela. The Ecuadorians, however, were not as receptive to being subjected to yet another external power. The "state" of Ecuador was established and the federation quickly disintegrated. New boundaries were delineated in 1830, with Ecuador insisting on the same borders as the Audencia de Quito. Peru, to the south, argued that the new state could not claim such frontier demarcations. Thus began a long border dispute between Ecuador and Peru, although many believe it dates back much further, to the rivalry between the Inca brothers Atahualpa and Huascar.

Internal Strife & the Political Economy

Ecuador officially gained its independence in 1830 after it seceded from Grán Colombia. The country's troubles, however, were just beginning. Sharp political and economic divisions existed. In the north-central Sierras, the views of the conservative Roman Catholic Church and land-owning *criollos* conflicted with those of the agro-exporting middle class based in Guayaquil. The latter was heavily influenced by its contact with the outside world, and therefore adopted the more liberal views of the West. The different socioeconomic structures of the two groups – a colonial system of landlords and protectionism in the Sierras pitted against free trade and exports along the coast – made conflict inevitable. Meanwhile, the indigenous people were caught in the middle and lived under even worse conditions with their new landlords than under the Spanish crown.

By the 19th century, Ecuadorians were fed up with the ultra-conservative regime of the Old World. **José María Urbina** came to power in 1851 through a coup d'état as the voice of the liberal trade-bearing front and indigenous rights. Although he was influential for some time, the teeter-totter shifted back toward the conservative front as the country was on the verge of crumbling and unification seemed impossible. From 1860 to 1895, in fact, a period of ultra-conservatism and Roman Catholic "theocracy," founded by Urbina's nemesis García Moreno, reigned supreme. This was a major period in Ecuador's history, when puppet presidents where raised to maintain control and "elections" were rigged. Moreno pushed the development of Ecuador's economic integration internally as well as abroad. Meanwhile, the economic power of coastal Guayaquil, spearheading the Liberal front, continued to grow. In 1875 Moreno met his end by machete and the ensuing 20 years proved difficult for the weakened Conservative Party.

By 1895, internal party division (and new presidents seemingly every other day) provided the opportunity for the Liberal Party to take control with another coup d'état. Although only briefly in power, the anticlerical **Eloy Alfaro** became the symbol of Liberalism in the first quarter of the 20th century. With support of the **Liberal Party** (PLR), he promoted the separation of Church and State, rapid modernization, and indigenous land reform. On the coast, agricultural exports boosted the economy. As the Liberal influence grew, the conservative powers in Quito continued to decline. Alfaro worked to promote a more unified economy, encouraged primarily by US interests, for which he received strong nationalist criticism. To this end, he prompted the building of a railway line from the coast in Guayaquil to Quito in the Sierras. This successfully unified the two regions of the country, but also created the transportation infrastructure for the US to extract Ecuador's natural resources efficiently.

Unfortunately, Alfaro pushed the Church and landowners a bit too far by banning religion in schools and redistributing land. As the conservative landlords held on to their possessions and positions, indigenous life remained as it had during earlier times. The Liberals themselves also divided along religious lines and true democracy was not progressing, with the ongoing government takeovers and corrupt elections. Alfaro was eventually ousted by his own party and then murdered by pro-clerical supporters. Ecuador continued to be characterized by sharp political divisions and turmoil.

Modern Ecuador

The liberal front plunged into turmoil as soon as it had gained power. The powerful banking sector was founded upon a failing agricultural industry (cacao) and rising inflation from printing worthless money. And it was just as corrupt in elections as any prior party. World War I and international competition dealt severe blows to Ecuador's economy, which relied on export of the country's cash crops. The indigenous population suffered severely, while landowners diversified their crops to include bananas and rice. Plantation workers on the coast created organized unions and demonstrations. Simultaneously, the indigenous people of the highlands organized revolts, setting the stage for violent conflicts.

The onset of the **Great Depression** left its mark as demand for exports dropped, unemployment soared and a brief period of US-backed reform efforts followed. In 1932, as the Liberals were blamed for the sad state of affairs, a cloud of turmoil escalated into civil bloodshed. Out of the ashes rose Velasco Ibarra, a conservative with a populist façade, who became president in 1934 for the first of five times. His self-proclaimed dictatorship and military rule, however, did not go over well with the Congress, the people, or the army. He was ousted and fled the country several times over the next 40 years, only to return and regain the presidency each time. In 1941, a brief but intense war with Peru over national boundaries, and the ensuing unpopular settlement, added to Ecuador's instability.

The Conflict between Ecuador & Peru

For many years, Ecuador and Peru have been rather unfriendly neighbors, with border disputes flaring up many times during the second half of the 20th century. Several of these have resulted in considerable bloodshed, most recently in 1995. Historians argue that the rift dates back to independence in 1830, when the state of Ecuador declared the same boundaries as the previously Spanish-controlled Royal Audencia de Quito. Peru, to the south, was not quite as receptive to such frontier demarcations, and the two countries have been battling ever since. Some people, however, believe that the tension is rooted deeper, dating back to the rivalry between the half-brothers Atahualpa and Huascar just before the fall of the Inca Empire.

Recent maps of Ecuador display a large disputed area of land in the Oriente claimed by both Ecuador and Peru. Consisting primarily of relatively undisturbed rainforest, the disputed area would nearly double the size of Ecuador as it stands. The struggle came to a head in 1941 with a war between the two countries, after which the border was redrawn by the international community in Río de Janeiro to the advantage of the more powerful Peru. Ecuador continued to ignore these boundaries, as evidenced by Ecuadorian maps. Recently, however, the presidents of the two countries came together and signed a peace agreement, delineating final borders and hopefully ending future bloodshed.

The implications of both the dispute and settlement are far-reaching. They involve revenue from natural-resource extraction, access to the Amazon and its tributaries, ecotourism, colonization, and national pride. Although Ecuador has not received everything it desires, access to the Amazon tributaries within Peru is a part of the agreement.

Also, the benefits of border integration and trade can now proceed, as can massive foreign investment backed by the World Bank, the benefit of which is debatable.

Many Ecuadorians support the agreement, realizing that peace is the best alternative, but it is also a source of political strife for recent administrations. Voices from the coastal economic powerhouse of Guayaquil oppose the political agreement. So far, however, it has not been a major source of contention. The question of what will happen to this relatively undisturbed section of the Oriente remains open.

Military juntas and conservative regimes exchanged government control many times over the next several decades, with US-backed interests playing heavily in Ecuadorian politics. Ibarra came and went, with new rhetoric each time. A brief period of growth and stability occurred during the 1950s, due primarily to the prosperity of coastal agricultural exports such as bananas. Once those prices dropped, however, so did political stability. By the 1970s, Ecuador's military regime was well-practiced in the art of coups and military rule. This coincided with the discovery of **oil** in the Amazon region. Soon, oil revenues controlled by the state were flowing to the US and dominated all political decisions, creating wealth for one or two political puppets here and there, but abject poverty, as well as environmental and social desecration throughout the country. Some new roads and nice hotels were built, however.

For an in depth investigative journalist's first hand account of what happens when oil demands from the north clash with the Ecuadorian Amazon and its inhabitants, read Joe Kane's *Savages* (New York: Vintage Books, 1996). Having lived with the Huaorani Amerindians and experiencing most of the story firsthand, I highly recommend this book.

New modernization projects, funded by huge international loans, began to emerge. Free-trade agreements and interregional cooperation followed. Per capita income, the federal budget, social infrastructure and employment in the Quito-based public sector increased significantly. On the surface, Quito threatened to challenge Guayaquil as an economic powerhouse due to oil revenue, though the country as a whole was building its house on sand. Expectations far exceeded any realistic benefits for the majority of the Ecuadorian people as income and social inequality gap widened drastically during this period, inflation skyrocketed and the foreign debt mounted. Corruption and a bloody coup eventually forced enough pressure that the military allowed for a transition of power to a democratically elected government, a first in Latin America. Unfortunately, the 1980s began with party conflict, a speculative presidential death, drop in oil prices, the resultant debt crisis from massive loans during the oil boom, and a rekindled border dispute with Peru. And to top it off, the 1982/83 El Niño wreaked havoc on Ecuador's economy, infrastructure and on human life in the country. Ecuador spiraled downward with the rest of Latin America.

Ecuador was forced to depend on international lending institutions – such as the United States, the World Bank, and the International Monetary Fund (IMF) – for debt-rescheduling based on policy-adjustment programs. Measures to appease the IMF's credit rating, such as eliminating subsidies on basic necessities, drastically devalued the currency and decreased the purchasing power of the masses, further impoverishing them. Other recent adjustments include product diversification for export growth, privatization of state enterprises, and the encouragement of foreign investment. You can probably notice a socio-economic/political viscous cycle occurring here. Needless to say, little if any of this has manifested in real progress for any but the wealthiest Ecuadorians, while the intricate link between politics and economics continued to merge.

Ecuador Today

Ecuador continues to struggle with development under the constraints of massive external debts and inflation, rising oil prices, and a strain on its natural-resource base. Oil, shrimp, and bananas are the top three earners of foreign revenue, but all are nonrenewable and/or subject to fluctuating world prices. In addition, each directly injures tourism, the country's fourth most-important earner and arguably the only sustainable activity. Ecuador's immediate problems come from massive overpopulation and a rapid growth rate. With the highest population density in Latin America, the rural poor are flooding to ill-equipped cities and the Oriente. In the city, jobs are not available and the majority of Ecuadorians live well below the poverty line. In the jungle, they are devastating the land like swarms of locusts.

Recently, there has been quite a bit of tension related to issues that range from indigenous rites and social benefits to massive inflation and rising oil prices. Regionalism based on historical economic differences plays an enormous role, as do international influences. In 1999, Ecuadorian currency devalued significantly against the US dollar before leveling off. All of this has led to uprisings, strikes, and states of emergency throughout the country. Most recently, the spiraling Ecuadorian economy – with major bank collapses and instability leading to austerity measures – forced the government to adopt the US dollar on the eve of the new century as a desperate attempt at stability. This, of course, resulted in an uproar from the poor and dollarless rural and indigenous masses, and another brief coup occurred in early 2000. International pressures quickly intervened and the dollarization was completed. Meanwhile, stability measures continue, with mixed results. The major effort is to maintain the real value of the average Ecuadorian's purchasing power.

Despite the problems, the people of Ecuador remain hopeful and take great pride in their country. Most citizens are underemployed, but many of them work at more than one business activity. Quito remains safer than many Latin American and Western capitals and almost everyone is friendly to foreigners. Overall, Ecuador's position – as with most of Latin America – is precarious. It remains to be seen how the many variables involved will shape the future of the country.

■ Geography/Land

Ecuador, El Centro del Mundo, the "center of the world," is home to a great number of the earth's life zones. The **Andes Mountain Range**, which crosses the country from north to south, provides a dramatic array of topography. From the beaches of the Pacific Ocean, it is a short distance to Ecuador's highest volcanic peak (20,634-foot Chimborazo). Within the country's borders are mangrove swamps, coastal deserts, and tropical dry, cloud, and rainforests. In the highlands, agricultural land and cloud forests give way to *páramo* grassland and eventually volcanic rock and glaciers in the highest elevations. The *páramo* of the Andes is a unique ecosystem, a land of stunted growth, vast landscapes, and harsh weather extremes. Shrubs, tall grasses, and spongy plants complement fauna such as the Andean condor and "wolf" (actually, an animal related to the coyote) to create a place of haunting beauty.

The Andes divide continental Ecuador into the coastal lowlands (Costa), the highlands (Sierra), and the Amazon region (Oriente). The Galápagos archipelago constitutes the fourth distinctive region.

The **Costa** is located in the west, between the Pacific Ocean and the Andes Mountains, and consists of coastal lowlands and mountains.

Between the western chain of the Andes (Cordillera Occidental) and eastern chain (Cordillera Oriental) is the **Sierra Valley**, better known as the **Avenue of the Volcanoes**. The population here dates back to pre-Inca times, with Quito, Ecuador's capital, nestled in the valley at 9,320-foot elevation. The Sierra also contains 260 volcanoes, six of which are still active.

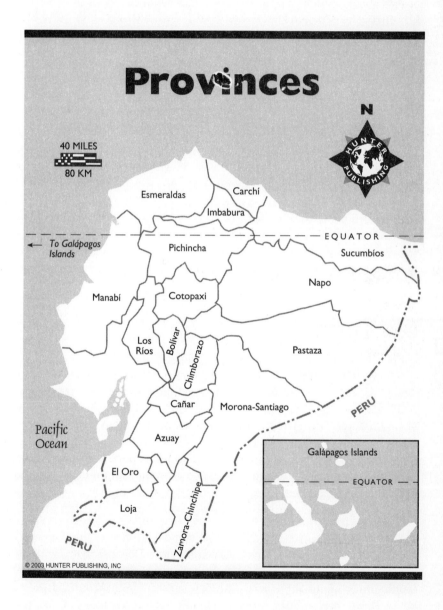

*The world's highest active volcano is **Cotopaxi**, which reaches 19,283 feet above sea level.*

On the eastern slopes of the Andes, melting snow and captured clouds from immense mountain volcanoes breathe life into the rivers that support the Amazon region. Better known in Ecuador as the **Oriente**, the Amazon region begins on these eastern slopes and covers the land with rainforest – sometimes referred to as the "green wall" – and some of the greatest biological diversity on earth.

*The **Napo River**, a tributary of the Amazon River, is the longest in the country.*

More than 600 miles off the coast of Ecuador are the **Galápagos Islands**, a protected and isolated archipelago. With 13 major islands, six smaller islands, and over 40 islets, the Galápagos Islands remain as fascinating to adventure travelers as they were to Charles Darwin in 1835. The Galápagos flora and fauna continue to evolve in unique surroundings on islands born of fire, separate from the rest of the world. Besides providing the most fascinating testimony to Darwin's theory of evolution, the Galápagos offer the experience of a lifetime for scientists, environmentalists, adventure travelers, and photographers alike.

■ Climate

Ecuador has four distinct geographic regions, each with a unique climate and environment. In fact, numerous microclimates are formed due to major weather patterns interacting with the extremely varied topography. However, Ecuador is generally cooler than most people would expect, considering it lies on and near the equator. Cold ocean currents and the high altitude of the Andes make temperatures pleasant throughout much of the year (though downright cold in the higher altitudes!).

The climate on the coast (e.g. Guayaquil) is warm, with temperatures averaging 76° to 90° F. The rainy season (December to May) is hot and very humid, with intense – though often brief – showers that typically occur in the afternoon. During El Niño years, December to January, rains can last for days and wreak havoc throughout the countryside, particularly along the coast. The dry season, from around June to early December, is less humid, though extremely foggy along the coast, with cooler temperatures and rougher seas. The north coast experiences more rainfall, and is comparable to Colombia, whereas the southern coast is a transition zone into the deserts farther south, due to the interaction between the cold Humboldt Current that flows north from Chile to Ecuador. And even though the southern coast is apt to get plenty of rainfall, its desert-like landscape is apparent in many areas.

The climate in the highlands varies according to the altitude. A subtropical climate prevails in the Andean valleys; at higher altitudes it is spring-like during the day, but cold at night. In Quito, the temperature ranges from 55° F at night to 78° F at noon, averaging 64° F year-round. Above 16,350 feet, permanent glaciers cover the highest peaks and temperatures throughout the higher elevations can be consistently chilly, with the wind often a factor. Generally, October through May is the rainy season, with rainfall picking up from February to April, though it can rain at any time. But this general rule varies, depending on which side of a volcano you are on. On the Eastern Range (Cordillera Oriental), for example, the weather along the western slopes that face the Sierra Valleys and Avenue of the Volcanoes may be quite different from the eastern slopes, where the climate is affected by the Amazon.

The Amazon region normally has a warm, humid and rainy climate. The average temperature varies from 72° to 80° F. It can rain at any time, and does, but generally rainfall is heaviest from around May through December. The effects of a downpour can transform a scorching hot day in the Amazon to one that is chilly and wet.

The Galápagos Islands often enjoy warm and dry weather, with an average yearly temperature of 85° F. The cool Humboldt Current and resulting "la garua" misty season kicks in around June in the Galápagos and on the Ecuadorian coast, with dry fog and chillier water temperatures. Days will be reasonably warm, but nights can be chilly, which – combined with rough seas – can make for an interesting evening cocktail out on deck. This may last through November. By December-January, air and water temperatures are quite warm, with tropical downpours common during this rainy season.

■ Flora & Fauna

 When it comes to flora and fauna, Ecuador's natural diversity is exceptional for a country its size. Located in the heart of the tropics and born of the Andean mountain chain, the country contains numerous ecological life zones, each unique and fascinating. Ecuador is one of the world's most biodiverse countries in terms of both flora and fauna.

So, what can you expect to see during your visit? It depends on where you go and what you are looking for. Much of Ecuador's wide variety of flora and fauna has already been catalogued. New species are constantly being discovered, though updated information is not as readily available as it should be. Research on how to preserve Ecuador's natural wonders is currently in a race with deforestation that threatens to destroy its heart. Learn about the flora and fauna of Ecuador. Explore, enjoy, and protect its natural habitats. Your contribution to conservation efforts can only help. See the *Addendum*, page 435, for more information.

Mammals

Monkeys

Picture a tropical rainforest and chances are the ever-playful monkey will be one of the first animals that comes to mind. Several species remain abundant here, including the howler, spider, and squirrel, to name a few.

If you spend the night in a pre-montane cloud forest for the first time, it may not be long before you leap out of bed to the thunderous roar of a male **howler monkey**. As competing troops forage through the treetops at dawn, they communicate with each other vocally from quite a distance. Shaking many a traveler out of deep sleep, the pre-dawn voice is unmistakable at close proximity. From far away their calls echo as if the forest herself were speaking.

Sloths

The tropical sloth is another commonly sighted Ecuadorian resident. If you see a motionless clump hanging from a branch, it's probably one of these sleepy, sluggish creatures. If you're out looking, you have a much better chance of spotting the diurnal three-toed sloth than its nocturnal two-toed relative.

Bats

While you're in the jungle, be sure to check out the pinnacle of your ecolodge's thatched roof. You may find a web of sticks and twigs up above, strategically placed to keep our winged rodent friends from resting near your bed. Believe it or not, bats are the most widespread, diverse, and numerous of Ecuador's mammals. In fact, true vampire bats live in the Ecuadorian Amazon. As dusk approaches, you may see them swooping, searching for insects via echolocation. And, by the way, the twigs under the roof don't work.

Tapirs

Less-developed sections of the upper Amazon Basin are still home to the pig-like tapir, an animal prized by indigenous people for its savory meat. One of the tapir's unique characteristics is its strong interest in swimming pools, where it can be spotted during many of its waking hours. A large mammal, the tapir is easy to hunt and therefore is quickly disappearing throughout the colonized areas of the Oriente.

Kinkajous

A favorite cloud-forest species is the nocturnal kinkajou, a member of the raccoon family native to South America. A good ear is all it takes to locate these evening fruitarians as they drop seeds from the treetops. If you shine your headlamp upward, the kinkajou will reflect back as two red, gleaming, peering eyes. Its prehensile tail allows it to hang from branches. In full view, the kinkajou appears almost like a cross between a cat and a monkey, with a thick, full tail and a curious, infant-like face.

Cats

 Your chances of actually seeing one of Ecuador's elusive predatory cats in the wild are slim. Among the cats are the **jaguar**, **ocelot**, **margay**, and **jaguarundi**, and, in the highlands, the **mountain lion**, locally known as puma. The small, secretive ocelot is beautifully camouflaged in shades of brown, black, and cream. Sometimes together, a male and female will hunt anything from birds and monkeys to frogs and fish. The even-smaller margay is sometimes referred to as the ocelot "copycat," colored in reddish-gray fur with black spots or streaks. Weighing only nine to 18 pounds and measuring just 32 to 51 inches in length, this natural acrobat can jump from ground to tree limb with little effort as it hunts rodents, rabbits, and birds. Margays particularly like to leap from high perches, even when they're not hunting!

These territorial hunters, particularly the big cats, represent the top of the tropical food chain and require large, intact tracts of land. Therefore, they serve as good indicator species, being among the first of the wildlife to feel the effects of deforestation and fragmentation. Although you may not see one in the wild (cats are nocturnal), know that they may very well be around. If you're lucky, your guide may even spot a paw print somewhere along the way.

Spectacled Bears

 A bear in the tropics? There is only one species of bear found in all of South America, and it lives in the higher-elevation cloud forests of Ecuador. The one-of-a-kind spectacled bear resides in isolated communities of moist, high-elevation forest. Vegetarian by nature, it feeds primarily on leaves and fruit. It has excellent eyesight and its name derives from the unique "mask" around its face. Endangered due to habitat loss, the spectacled bear today lives under protected status, primarily in private reserves.

Llamas

 Perhaps the most easily identifiable mammals of the high country are the Andean *cameloids*, including llamas and alpacas. Although not as abundant as in neighboring countries to the south, domesticated llamas reside in the country's north-Central Highlands. Since the introduction of sheep, wool in Ecuador – including that used in most of the sweaters produced for the Otavalo market – has come from sheep instead of llamas. The effect of sheep on the land, however, has been devastating. As a result, efforts are underway to reintroduce the llama to the Sierras.

River Creatures - Dolphins & Manatees

 A trip to the Cuyabeno Reserve (see page 41) would not be complete without catching a glimpse of the Amazon's freshwater dolphins. Of the region's two species, the more common pink dolphin appears with a pale, discolored skin in the waters of the deep jungle. They are often friendly enough to play near floating canoes and larger boats. The much slower Amazonian manatee can also be found in this region as it floats along the surface and grazes at the water's edge.

Birds

 For the avid birder, Ecuador provides an endless array of colorful and musical delights. If you're not a birder, watch out! A few hours spent with a good naturalist or bird guide, or even quietly on your own, will quickly make you a convert. With more than 1,550 species, or 18% of the world's total, Ecuador has more bird species per square mile than any other country in Latin America. Some 15% of the world's endemic species exist in the Sierra, on the coast, and in the Amazon.

For all of you birding enthusiasts out there, be sure to carry a copy of the recently released *Birds of Ecuador* field guide by Robert S. Ridgely et al. (2001).

For Galápagos birds and other wildlife, see pages 387-95.

Hummingbirds

Familiar to us all, but abundant in Ecuador, is the hummingbird. With more than 115 species ranging throughout the country, these magical creatures are the only birds on earth that can actually fly backwards. They are magnets of visual delight at most jungle lodges, cloud-forest accommodations, and high-country haciendas. Hummingbirds transect occupy many life zones and range in size from that of a thumbnail to a gargantuan 21 inches in the case of the giant hummingbird.

Toucans, Parrots & Macaws – A Rainbow of Flavors

Typical of the tropics are over 40 species of parrots and their cousins, the macaws. Their range in Ecuador is widespread, though they are not as common as in certain other coastal regions of Latin America. The bright-billed toucan is another symbol of the tropics that resides here. It is indeed a treat to follow its call and then spot one through the mists of a coastal cloud forest.

Hawks & Eagles – Predators in Flight

The **harpy eagle**, the largest eagle in the Americas, has an intimidating seven-foot wingspan. Preying on monkeys, sloths, small mammals, and other birds, a harpy in action is a magnificent, even intimidating, sight to behold. A monstrous presence, a full-grown harpy can pluck a large monkey right off the limbs of a treetop. There are also a variety of predatory hawks throughout the country. As a result, mixed flocks of different bird species often congregate in the forest canopy. By sticking together, their warning system for predators is much more effective and the chances that any individual will fall prey are much smaller. Don't be surprised if you spend hours in the jungle without seeing much of anything, and then suddenly are surrounded by a swarm of exotic birds. They are really gathering in a symbiotic relationship to maximize chances for survival.

Andean Condors

In and above the highlands of Ecuador lives the largest flying bird in the world, the Andean condor, with a wingspan of nearly 10 feet. The condor is an incredible – and incredibly endangered – species, with only a few hundred mating pairs remaining. You may spot one during an extended visit to the Sierras. Spending their time circling high in flight, they are scavengers that land to feed on carrión, but seem to be able to soar forever.

Carunculated Caracaras

Closer to the ground, particularly in Cotopaxi National Park (see page 168), is the carunculated caracara. Primarily black, this falcon has an orange-red face, a yellow bill and legs, and a white underside. It is one of the more commonly sighted birds in the *páramo* grasslands of the park. The caracara hunts small *páramo* rodents.

Reptiles & Amphibians

 From the 17-foot-long Amazonian anaconda to the brilliant poison-arrow frog, these unique creatures all call Ecuador home. In total, there are over 350 species of reptiles and 375 species of amphibians.

Crocodiles & Caimans

Among the notable reptiles in Ecuador is the crocodile, which lives in mangrove estuaries along the coast. Its smaller cousin, the caiman, is common in the Oriente. A night hike along water's edge or a silent canoe ride often provides ample opportunity to witness these special creatures. Floating motionless at the water's surface, their eyes reflect the beam of a flashlight as two red, glowing bulbs.

Fer-de-Lance Snakes

The most feared reptile in Ecuador is the deadly fer-de-lance snake. Camouflaged well within the cover of the forest floor, it has an arrow-shaped head and diamond patterns on its body. If you cross this snake's path, stop and back away very slowly. The fer-de-lance is nocturnal, so wear rubber boots on a night hike and try not to place your hands on tree trunks. Even if you are bitten, chances are it won't be enough to kill you; the snake would rather save its venom for prey. If it does inject a full load, however, start praying. Still, your chances of survival on a trek through fer-de-lance territory are much higher than gambling on the local public-transportation system. Very few people are ever bitten.

Anacondas

A favorite image of Ecuador is a group of half-naked natives carrying a monster-size anaconda. (This semiaquatic reptile can reach 29 feet in length!) In fact, the snakes have been eliminated throughout the more developed portions of their range, and the locals now dress in shorts and T-shirts. The anaconda is not often seen, but it's not uncommon in rivers and tributaries throughout the Amazon region, including areas where there is a tourism infrastructure. When they are sighted, they're usually sunning themselves on a beach along a river.

Frogs

Of the approximately 375 species of frogs and toads, most can best be seen at night after a heavy rain. The **poison-arrow frogs**, or dendrobates, are perhaps the most spectacular of them all, colored bright orange and green or red with black dots. Natives from throughout the tropics used to derive poison from the skin of these frogs for the tips of their hunting arrows. A good six-foot-long blowgun is strong enough to project these arrows quite a distance in order to drop monkeys, birds, and other larger game. Although relatively benign to the touch, the toxins can cause paralysis if they enter the bloodstream.

Other frog species include **tree frogs**, that never approach ground level, even though the young tadpoles require water to develop. The cup-shaped bromeliad plants, which catch and pool water, create a perfect mini aquarium-like habitat for the young.

Insects

 Imagine an electric-green ant-like creature almost an inch long, or a hand-size, hairy, purple bird-eating spider. Well, they're here. Insects – in all shapes and sizes – form the majority of species living in Ecuador. The number of different kinds of insects in the country is staggering. In fact, insect biomass far outweighs human biomass across the globe. And most of these species remain unidentified. These so-called "pests" are an invaluable component of forest development and survival, providing innumerable ecological services. Without these helpers, there would be no forest. Quiet solitude and close inspection of any forest in Ecuador will open your eyes to a fascinating new world of insect life. Just don't let a fire ant climb on board your body while paying them a visit. 'Ouch' doesn't even come close to what you will say when it bites!

Butterflies

Butterflies are the most radiant and sought-after of Ecuador's insects. With over 4,500 species, there are many beautiful colors, sizes, and species-specific aerial dances. The most stunning butterflies are the **blue morphos**, with a wingspan as big as an adult hand. Many travelers find themselves scrambling for the camera upon a first sighting, but this butterfly is as restless and fast as it is beautiful, and its electric-blue upper wings fold up to reveal a camera-shy camouflaged underside when resting.

Leafcutter Ants

Don't be surprised if you are walking along a forest pathway and come upon a micro-parade of leaves moving across the trail. Leafcutter ants are perhaps the most mesmerizing of the country's commonly sighted insects. Most people think that humans were the first creatures to develop agriculture on Earth. Ants, however, with their highly socialized community network, actually precede us by millions of years. They are also one of the strongest animals on earth relative to their body weight. These tropical insects cut and then carry upright pieces of leaf several times their own weight. Once at the nest, which can extend to 40 feet and hold up to three million ants, they chew the leaf and spit it out to grow a type of fungus for future community consumption. Their social (biological) hierarchy is relatively advanced for such a primitive creature.

Plants

 Ecuador is a haven for the botanist. In less than .02% of the Earth's surface, it contains 10% of the world's vascular plant species (25,000), more than all the plant species in North America combined. These plants' potential utility for human beings has barely been tapped.

Bromeliads

Along the slopes of Ecuador's cloud forests are a variety of bromeliads, along with plenty of orchids and moss. These epiphytes are often found attached to larger host trees, utilizing the anchor to grow upward in a cup-like shape and capture water. Some of the larger species can hold over two gallons of water, creating a natural aquarium. This provides habitat for frogs, insects, and other small animals.

Orchids

The Ecuadorian orchid family comprises as much as 11% of the world's total and 30% of Latin America's orchid varieties. Nearly one quarter of these are endemic, existing nowhere else on earth. Some of these orchids are used commercially and exported as houseplants. Baby ferns, pink in color until they begin to "grow up," can be found adorning the forest slopes and the canopy floor.

Mangrove Forests

Along coastal estuaries, mangrove forests form the basis of life for everything from marine animals to seabirds. Growing in brackish water and forming an interlacing root network, mangroves provide structure for soil in the shallows of coastal estuaries, as well as habitat for various marine organisms. Shrimp farming is the major threat to mangroves and there are currently only a few places left along Ecuador's coast where forests remain intact. Efforts to conserve the remaining forests however, are strong, as mangroves form the ecological foundation for these estuaries, which in turn affect the health of fisheries and marine systems farther out at sea.

Strangler Figs

The strangler fig "tree," actually a vine, is impressive, easily identifiable, and found throughout the tropics. It can be inspiring, if a bit eerie, to poke your head up a 100-foot empty space where a tree, once engulfed by the strangler fig, used to live.

The life cycle of a strangler fig is fascinating. A mature vine will produce fruit, which is then eaten by birds. After they're digested and passed through the bird's system, the seeds drop and become implanted near the bases of other trees. Eventually, the seeds put down roots and begin to grow up and around their newfound host trees. In time, they effectively block the host trees off from the sun. If the engulfed trees rot away, what is left is empty space, perfect for a good game of jungle hide-and-seek.

■ People/Culture

 Over 12 million people live in Ecuador today, more than 10 times the number of indigenous people estimated to have resided there during the Spanish conquest. The country has the highest population density of any South American nation, with around 100 people per square mile, though it also claims the highest percentage of Native Americans. Estimates of ethnic makeup vary; it is difficult to accurately quantify how many pureblooded Amerindians and mestizos (people of mixed European and Amerindian ancestry) there are. Some sources state the figures as mestizo, 55%; Amerindian, 25%; white, 10%; black, 9%; others (mainly Asian), 1%. If one considers less-than-pure Amerindian blood, the figures are closer to 40% Amerindians and 40% mestizos.

Spanish is the official language, though most indigenous people speak Quichua and live in the highlands. Among them, various subgroups have lived in isolation from each other for centuries and, consequently, speak different variations of dialects in regions near each other. The Quichua people can also be distinguished by region based on slight differences in clothing, a system introduced by the colonial landlords to identify the "peasants." The color of a poncho or the shape of a hat may identify a person from a specific region.

Some of the best-known highland groups are the **Otavaleos**, **Salasacas**, **Cañaris**, and **Saraguros**, with many of them now living in towns and cities. The largest population of rural **Quichua Amerindians**, at approximately 250,000, lives in communities in the province of Chimborazo. A few other small groups live in the Amazonian lowlands and include about 60,000 Quichuas, 40,000 **Shuar**, 1,000 **Huaoranis**, and 600 each of the **Cofan** and **Siona-Secoya** peoples. About 5,000 **Chachi Amerindians** live in the northern coastal rainforests around the Esmeraldas Province, and 1,000 **Tchatchilas (Colorado) Indians** live in the western lowlands. Each of these groups has its own language. Although these statistics may not mean much to you now, each of these unique peoples has fascinating histories and rich cultures that will come to life as you travel and learn more about them.

About 48% of the Ecuadorian population lives on the coast, while approximately 46% lives in the highlands, with the remainder in the jungle regions of the Oriente. With an annual growth rate of just over 2%, the population is set to double in 34 years, a significant fact, considering Ecuador already has the highest population density in all of South America. Nevertheless, this growth rate is much lower than it was several years ago. Life expectancy has topped 67 years for males and 72 years for females. At least 55% of the people live in urban areas; the remaining rural population is primarily indigenous. People living in the country are often referred to as *campesinos* (peasants or farmers); indigenous people are called *indígenas*. As with many developing countries, the income gap in Ecuador is stunning, and growing – a fact that becomes all too apparent in the urban centers. Nevertheless, the people here maintain a high level of dignity and pride, which is what makes this such a special place to visit.

■ Cuisine

 Ecuador is a country of diversity. From the Andes to the Amazon to the coast, its varied topography offers a delicious range of cuisine. As a staple, expect to find rice and/ or potatoes with most meals. *Aji*, or hot sauce, is served throughout the country with most meals and adds a bit of spice, but you may want to stick with the bottled hot sauce at the less tourist-oriented restaurants (to avoid potential health problems). **Bananas**, prepared in many ways, are served all over, and Ecuador remains the world's largest banana exporter. Commonly, a large, green banana relative called the **plantain** (*platano*) is cooked and served with typical dishes. And one of my favorites, the readily available **avocado** (*paltas*) often complements local cuisine.

On the coast, the more exotic dishes include seafood cooked in coconut milk, or *agua de coco*. **Ceviche** is a typical coastal dish, served as an appetizer or a light meal itself, with shellfish and seafood "cooked" or marinated in sliced onions, spices and lemon juice. In fact, it is the citric acid that "cooks" the seafood. Be careful though, as ceviche may include raw seafood and shellfish, which are not recommended because they can carry strains of cholera. Stick with restaurants that cater to the foreign traveler if you are uncertain. Other typical dishes you may see on a menu include ***camarones*** (shrimp), ***corvina*** or ***pescado*** (a sea bass or fish), ***conche*** (shellfish), ***langosta*** (lobster), and ***mixto*** (mixed seafood).

In the Andes potatoes and other tubers tend to replace rice as the staple side to any meal. ***Llapingachos*** are pancake-like potatoes generally made with onions and cheese and are a delicious accompaniment to any meal. Various potato soups, called ***sopas*** or ***caldos***, are also common, with some form of meat. The softened avocado in the soup is a wonderful touch. *Mais* (corn) and *quinua*, a type of grain, are also very important native dishes. *Quinua* is actually an extremely nutritious source of protein and fiber. Although sacred to the Incas, it is unfortunately being replaced in modern life with much less nutritious substitutes such as pasta and fast food. A typical Andean plate is the ***churrasco***, made with beef, veggies, potatoes and rice, a slice of avocado, and an egg. Another is the ***fritada***, which includes pork, *llapingachos* and usually corn or another side dish. If you are extremely adventurous, try ***cuy***, or roasted guinea pig. These "pets" were the staple meat supply in the Andes in pre-Columbian days and are still considered a delicacy by the common highland folk. Good luck.

Cuy is a type of guinea pig favored as a staple food source for centuries of indigenous families. In pre-Columbian and even pre-Incan times, cuy were raised in a penned-off portion of the kitchen and simply scooped up and "thrown into the pot" as needed.

In the Oriente, indigenous lifestyles incorporate more game hunting than elsewhere in local cuisine. Development and loss of habitat, however, have transformed local dishes into more agricultural and cattle-based. As along the coast, rice, *platanos*, and freshwater fish are common. Fried **catfish** are familiar and you may even have the opportunity to catch and cook your own **piranha**. Locally grown **fruit** is important in this region and makes a refreshing meal. Otherwise, tourist food is imported and usually combines international dishes with traditional jungle-grown cuisine.

■ Government

Ecuador is a Presidential (as opposed to Parliamentary), Unitary (as opposed to Federal) Republic. Its government is democratic, freely elected, representative and accountable in theory, though this is a far cry from reality. The government is divided into Executive, Legislative and Judicial Branches. The President is elected every four years, though very few have completed a full term. The President appoints provincial governors. A Congressional Assembly, elected by popular mandate, produced substantial reforms to the new constitution, which entered in force in August 1998. Now with 123 members, Congressional representatives are also elected every four years.

Except for the cabinet and provincial governors, the government is elected by free, secret, direct vote. Voting is a constitutional right for all Ecuadorian citizens and is compulsory for literate Ecuadorians under 65 years old residing in the country. Active members of the military do not cast their vote. Voting age is 18 years old. Voting is optional for illiterate and senior citizens (over 65) and the mechanism to cast votes overseas has not been implemented. Elections are organized and supervised by an independent agency, "Tribunal Supremo Electoral," that is not a part of the Executive Branch. It has special enforcement laws and is the final arbiter on electoral matters. Private citizens are called to "electoral duty" and serve during elections. Observers of political parties and international organizations may be present during vote counting.

■ The Economy

The Ecuadorian economy has historically been dominated by the agricultural sector, and by the export of a few specific commodities (cocoa, coffee, and banana). The economy underwent a significant structural transformation in the 70s when new discoveries made **oil** Ecuador's most important export commodity. The rise in oil exports fueled economic growth, and was accompanied by a sharp increase in government spending and employment, which was financed principally by external borrowing and oil revenues. From 1982 to 1987, the country experienced a slowdown as the economy was exposed to external shocks that affected Latin American nations generally throughout this period. The collapse of world oil prices in 1986 reduced Ecuador's oil export revenues by half. An earthquake in March 1987 destroyed a large stretch of the country's only oil pipeline. Oil now dominates the economy and creates severe socio-economic and political vulnerability related to the world oil market, agriculture continues to contribute significantly. The world's leading banana exporter, Ecuador also produces vast amounts of cocoa and coffee, as well as increasing amounts of roses and other flowers, fruits and vegetables. All said, the agricultural sector now contributes a bit under 20% to the GDP (oil fluctuates around 15%), and is a significant source of the country's employment. Shrimp farming dominates the fishing industry, another major contributor to export earnings, though in recent years it has been severely affected by massive die-offs at shrimp farms. Overall, exports average 35% of the GDP, which makes the country highly vulnerable to the world market and external fluctuations.

Tourism is the other major player in Ecuador's economy, ranking third or fourth in revenue, depending on your source.

The period from 1988 to 1992 was characterized by increasing oil export prices and reductions in government spending in real terms. Throughout this period, the government pursued a gradual stabilization policy. Despite this, inflation rose sharply, averaging 59.7% annually, notwithstanding intervals of relatively robust economic growth. In 1992 the government adopted a macroeconomic stabilization plan, supported by the International Monetary Fund (IMF). Inflation decreased from 60.2% in 1992 to 31% in 1993 and 25.4% in 1994; international reserves increased from a low of US$224 million in August 1992 to US$1.2 billion in December 1993 and US$1.7 billion in December 1994. The consolidated non-financial public sector deficit decreased from 1.2% of GDP for 1992 to 0.1% of GDP for

1993 and 0.2% of GDP for 1994, and GDP grew by 2% in 1993 and 4.3% in 1994.

Ecuador now has a diversified economy in which both the public and private sectors play important roles. Since 1992, the government has generally sought to reduce its participation in the economy. The State Modernization Law established a framework for increased private sector participation in the economy, particularly in sectors previously reserved to the state, starting with the sale of the national airline and cement company. The economic future lies somewhere between pleasing the international lending community with macro-economic stabilization plans (that often involve benefiting foreign investors), while addressing the effects of those policies on the average Ecuadorian. And the average Ecuadorian, historically, rarely hesitates to take to the streets.

Ecuador is the largest banana producer and third-largest shrimp producer in the world. Around 200,000 people are currently employed in the shrimp industry, which, interestingly enough, has been significantly affected by pollution runoff from the banana industry recently. Since the early 1990s shrimp farms have brought hundreds of lawsuits against the likes of DuPont, claiming that DuPont's Benlate fungicide and similar pollutants have devastated the shrimp industry and caused billions of dollars of damage. And this isn't taking into account the marine ecosystem damage. Dupont continues to spend large amounts of money in settlements and legal fees. What can you do to help? Buy organic.

Travel Information

When to Go

The best time to visit Ecuador is any time .... depending on where you plan to go. Geography and climate patterns vary considerably throughout the country. The hot, rainy season in the Galápagos coincides with the wet and relatively cold "winter" in the Sierras, as well as the less-wet season in the Oriente. The busiest travel time along the "gringo path" through Ecuador is June through August and around Christmas, both of which coincide with North American and European vacations. This also happens to be the best weather in the Andes, with cooler temperatures and rain picking up from around October through May. Any time is a good time to visit Ecuador.

The hot, rainy season along the coast generally occurs from late December/January to May. You will find the beaches full on the weekends during this period of nice weather and school vacations. Along the south coast, the middle and upper classes from Guayaquil flock to the shores, and in the north they generally visit from Quito and Colombia. Expect washed-out bridges and poor road conditions at this time of year, but unless it is an El Niño year, this is usually only a minor inconvenience. By June it may still be nice, but the Pacific Coastal mist, known locally as *la garua*, covers the land for the next several months. During this time the beaches are practically deserted, except for foreign backpackers.

The climate in the **Galápagos** is similar, with a warm, rainy season from January to April. The rest of the year is cooler and dryer, but again with the ocean mist. The roughest sailing months are August, September and October.

In the **Northern Sierras**, the cooler, rainy season begins by October. The coldest months are January through May, with a steady increase in rainfall from February to April. It is actually a bit chilly during this time, at least for an equatorial country. You'll need a sweater and rain jacket. It rained for eight continuous days during one of my recent visits to Quito, although the locals said that was unusual. June through September are the warmest and driest months in the Northern Highlands. Farther south, the dry season is more or less from August through January.

In the **Oriente**, the wet season runs from May through September, though heavy rains can fall year-round. And remember, in the jungle it's either warm and wet or warm and wetter. Surprisingly, the Oriente is not usually as hot as one might expect in the Amazon.

Getting Here

■ By Air

 Most foreigners arrive via Quito at the **Mariscal Sucre International Airport** (UIO/SEQU), which is the major tourist hub and gateway city. The other major international hub is **Guayaquil**, though this city is more business- than tourist-oriented. From the US, major airlines serving Ecuador are **American Airlines**, which uses Miami as the gateway city, and **Continental**, which flies through Houston. Some Latin American-based airlines may offer better rates by traveling through their associated countries, including **TACA** and **Copa**, based in Central America, and **SAETA**, the Ecuadorian airline. European-based airlines that travel to Quito include **KLM**, **Lufthansa** and **Iberia**. Online discount travel websites, as well as airline websites, usually offer better deals than calling the airlines directly or using a travel agent, though travel agents can help to insure that everything is handled properly, including services other than air. Round-trip fares average $850 from major US hubs, though prices can range from about $600-$1,600.

Be sure to call and reconfirm your ticket 48 hours before your departure, and arrive at the airport at least two, if not three hours before the scheduled flight. This will provide you with time to double-check that everything is set to go. It will also save you any hassles, such as losing your seat in case of overbooking. Also, if you prefer a vegetarian meal on your flight, don't forget to request one upon booking and / or when you reconfirm two days ahead of the departure.

Airlines Contact Information

Most major airlines are listed below. For a complete list, including other Latin American, European, Japanese, etc., visit www.ecuador-travel-guide.org/services/Airlines.htm.

When calling Ecuador from abroad, you must first dial the international access code (011), then the country code (593 for Ecuador), followed by the regional prefix (02 for Quito) and then the six- or seven-digit local number.

SAETA, the Ecuadorian airline for international flights and **SAN-SAETA** for domestic flights. Amazonas 1429 and Colón, Edificio España, Local #6, ☎ 2-2564-969, 2-2550-291, 2-2565005, 2-2565-008, 2-2502-706, 2-2502-715, Mon-Fri, 8:30 am-6 pm.

TAME, the major domestic carrier, also offers flights to some Latin American destinations. Amazonas 1354 and Colón, 2nd Floor. For international flights, ☎ 2-2221-494/495; for domestic flights, 2-509-382/83/84/86/87/88; fax 2-2554907. Mon-Fri, 9:30 am-1 pm and 1:45-5:30 pm. www.tame.com.ec.

TACA, Av. República de El Salvador No. 35 and Portugal, Quito, ☎ 2-2224-181; at the airport, 2-2451-924; in Guayaquil, General Córdova 1040 and 9 de Octubre, 9th floor of Edificio Banco de Préstamos, ☎ 4-2562-950; in Cuenca, Sucre 770 and Luis Cordero, ☎ 7-846-730. In the US, ☎ 800-535-8780. In the UK, ☎ (870) 608 0737. www.Taca.com.

LACSA, a Costa Rican Airline with connections through San José, Costa Rica. In Quito, 12 de Octubre 394, ☎ 2-2505-213/214/504-961/971, fax 2-2223-744, Mon-Fri, 8:30 am-6 pm. Airport, ☎ 2-2452-657. In the US, ☎ 800-225-2272. www.centralamerica.com/cr/lacsa/lacsa.htm.

American Airlines, for flights to and from the US and UK. In Quito, Amazonas 3 and Robles, ☎ 2-2561-144. Flight Information: ☎ 2-2528-166, Mon-Fri, 9 am-6 pm, Sat, 9 am-1 pm. Airport, ☎ 2-2434-610/653, fax 2-2434-612. www.aa.com.

Continental Airlines, for flights to and from the US and Europe. In Quito, Av. Naciones Unidas and Amazonas, Edificio Banco La Previsora, Torre B, 8th Floor, Office 812, ☎ 2-2461-485/6/7/8/9, fax 2-2462-119, Mon-Fri, 8:30 am-6:30 pm, Sat, 9 am-1 pm. Airport, ☎ 2-2461-493, 2-2461-494, fax 2-2461-492. www.continental.com.

KLM, for flights to and from Europe through Amsterdam. In Quito, Amazonas 3617 and Juan Pablo Sanz, Edifico Xerox. Reservations, ☎ 2-2455-233/550/551, fax 2-2435-176, Mon-Fri, 9 am-1 pm and 2-5 pm. Airport, ☎ 2-2432-088, fax 2-2432-089. www.klm.com.

Iberia, for flights from Europe via Madrid. Amazonas 239 and Washington. Reservations, ☎ 2-2560-546/7/8, fax 2-2566-852. Mon-Fri, 8:30 am-6 pm. Airport, ☎ 2-2431-708, 2441-509, fax 2-2431-711. www.iberia.com.

Lufthansa, for European flights via Bogota and Frankfurt. 18 de Septiembre 238 and Reina Victoria, ☎ 2-2508-396, 2541-300, fax 2-2224-844, Mon-Fri, 8:30 am-1:30 pm and 2-5:30 pm. www.lufthansa.com.

Flights from the US often arrive late at night, and the Quito airport can become fogged in after 10 pm. The airport closes up and the lights are all turned off at midnight. If the flight cannot land at Quito, it is diverted to Guayaquil where hotel rooms may quickly fill as a result (an overnight on the floor or on the plastic seats of the Guayaquil terminal happens more often than American Airlines will admit). As such, if you have to be in Quito on a specific day, book to arrive a day earlier if possible.

Getting Around

■ By Air

Many internal flights are with TAME, including those to the Galápagos, as well as major towns throughout the Andes, Oriente and along the coast. Other local airlines include SAN, the internal flight subsidiary of SAETA. Domestic flights are worthwhile, especially if you are heading deep into the Oriente and they are less expensive than flying direct to the Galápagos. Prices generally range from $40 to $120, depending on your destination. Flights to the Galápagos, on the other hand, cost $390 from Quito during high season, as the islands are 600 miles from the mainland. Ecuador's international airline, SAETA, and its domestic sister company, SAN, also offer flights between major cities and San Cristóbal Island in the Galápagos. You can make arrangements with other Ecuadorian carriers through travel agents in Quito. Quito's domestic terminal is adjacent to the international terminal. See airline contact information above for airline details.

■ Public Transportation

Ecuador's public transportation and travel infrastructure is fairly well developed. **Public buses** are frequent, inexpensive, and increasingly located around central terminals in each town. In fact, they are the easiest and most efficient way to travel around Ecuador. Buses are the main form of transportation for many Ecuadorians and, therefore, they travel to virtually every corner of the country. Each village, town and city will have easy access to bus transportation, whether it's in the form of a major bus terminal or by a dusty street-side general store. And, believe it or not, some buses are almost comfortable and clean. Roads are decent in most regions and long-distance travel is straightforward (sometimes made a bit too thrilling by "enthusiastic" bus drivers). Just make sure you know where to get off the bus so you can tell the driver where to stop.

Travel Information

Camionetas

Camionetas are trucks, mostly privately owned, that generally wait at local plazas or in the busy areas of smaller towns. Fares are in the same range as taxis, but *camionetas* are more durable in the backcountry. In addition, they are much more convenient than buses for taking you to remote areas and are very economical if you have a few people willing to split the cost. It is always a good idea to negotiate a price before the journey begins.

Taxis are a good way to get around in Quito and Guayaquil. If you're staying for an extended period, however, you may want to try and learn the bus system.

Guard your belongings in crowded big city terminals and on public buses.

■ By Boat

Where bus routes end, you have probably come to a waterway. At this point, boat transportation begins. This is particularly true around the northern coastal tropical forest region and throughout the entire Oriente. Waterway transportation is usually in the form of motorized dugout canoes. Although more expensive than buses, boats are also fast and efficient.

■ Hitching a Ride

In the more remote areas of the highlands, you can often hop in the back of a pickup truck and ride with the locals. This is a great way to travel and enjoy the spectacular scenery, as long as you don't mind the minor discomfort of a hard wooden seat. On the coast, trucks and open-sided bus-truck hybrids, called *rancheras*, sometimes substitute for a bus. Pay the driver whatever he asks, which should be only small change, usually similar to the bus fare.

■ By Rail

Once connecting the coast with the Andes, Ecuador's rail system was largely damaged by the 1997 El Niño and is often in disrepair, as the more efficient roadways have largely replaced its value. Now, it is more suitable for sightseeing than transportation. The Riobamba/Alausí line through the Devil's Nose runs several times per week and is a spectacular journey (see page 163 for details).

■ Renting a Car

Renting an automobile is an option that offers the flexibility of seeing the country at your own pace. Prices are the same as in the US or Canada. Be sure to check the condition of the car and insurance terms thoroughly. Keep in mind that driving in Ecuador can be crazy. And road conditions, especially in more remote areas, but also on the major thoroughfares, are poor and flat tires are a dime a dozen. A four-wheel-drive vehicle is recommended for many areas. See pages 76-77, *Quito and Vicinity*, and page 305, in the *Guayaquil* section, for specific rental information.

Many roadways in Ecuador are not only unmarked, but they may have no names other than "via a...," meaning "the way to...." Road conditions can be hazardous. Be cautious of other drivers, especially bus and truck drivers, and always expect that they will try to pass, even on blind turns. Still, driving in the Andean countryside is easy compared to the major cities.

What to Bring

Having spent years guiding tours, traveling and meeting other international travelers, I am the first to admit that everyone packs and prepares differently. Clothing, especially, is a personal thing. What works for one person may be unsuitable for another. The following, however, is a list of essentials.

■ Luggage

Bring one day-pack in addition to your luggage bag/backpack. This should be big enough to carry a water bottle, camera, raingear and any items that you may want to have accessible during the day.

An extra fold-up bag is good for any souvenir purchases you may wish to make.

■ Clothing & Footwear

 A trip to the Galápagos does not require as much as what's suggested below.

- Waterproof rain jacket and rain pants (Gore-tex, preferably).

- Long-sleeve thermal insulating shirt (for when the temperature drops). Preferably not cotton.

- A combination of mostly short- and a few long-sleeve shirts if you are going to the Oriente or Galápagos; or more long-sleeve and fewer short-sleeve if you are spending all of your time in the Andes.

- Two or three pairs of hiking shorts. Although shorts are considered inappropriate by traditional standards in the highlands – especially on women – they are tolerated on tourists at the beaches, in the Galápagos and in the jungle.

- Two pairs of trousers – cotton or nylon hiking pants or lightweight pants. Jeans are not recommended, though I always seem to bring a pair, as they are heavy, bulky, and take a long time to dry if they get wet.

- Enough undergarments and socks to get you through to the next wash. Socks should be non-cotton, quick-dry and warm for the Sierras.

- If you are spending time in the backcountry of the highlands, you will need more gear and layers, including a durable waterproof jacket, a fleece (warm synthetic mid-layer), and warm underlayers (long underwear made of synthetic material, such as polypropylene).

- Swimsuit.

- A couple of clothing changes for the evening (casual and compact).

- Hat with visor for rain and sun protection.

- Lightweight hiking boots, running shoes or cross-trainers that can be used for multiples activities.

- Comfortable shoes to be worn around town.

- Sport sandals.

■ Equipment

- Sunglasses with UV protection.
- Sunscreen with SPF 15 or higher (the sunscreen sold in Ecuador is generally poor).
- Camera (with film and extra batteries). In the Galápagos, one roll of film per day might not be enough.
- Travel alarm clock or wristwatch.
- Insect repellent for the jungle.
- Lip balm/moisturizer with UV protection.
- Toiletry kit (toothbrush, toothpaste, shampoo, brush).
- Hand lotion/skin moisturizer.
- First aid kit (aspirin, Band-Aids, personal medications, including prescription-strength anti-diarrhea drugs, eye drops, tampons). Be sure to keep prescriptions in the original bottle and carry the prescription with you.
- Foot care kit – moleskin or second skin, athletic tape, and a pair of small scissors.
- Binoculars.
- Guidebook (preferably this one), novel, journal.
- Water bottle.
- Small flashlight with extra batteries and bulb.
- Extra prescription glasses (if applicable) and a pair of glasses if you wear contact lenses.
- A strap (such as Croakies) to secure glasses to your head (especially important on the river).
- Plastic zip-lock and garbage bags (great for keeping dry things dry and wet things separate).

Customs & Entry

Foreign travelers need a passport that is valid for at least six months after arrival. You should always carry your passport with you during your visit. Upon arrival, you will receive a tourist card to fill out from the airline (prior to landing), which you should carry at all times. You will need it for stay extensions, passport checks and leaving the country. US and EU citizens are not required to have a visa for travel in Ecuador. Citizens from a few countries in other continents should inquire with their embassy. In addition to your passport and tourist card, you officially need a ticket out of the country, although Immigration officials rarely ask to see it.

It is always a good idea when traveling to photocopy the important pages of your passport and keep them separate, in case your passport is lost or stolen. Note that you are required by law to carry your passport with you at all times. On the back of the photocopy, list emergency phone numbers, as well as the numbers of travelers checks, airline tickets, and credit cards. It's also wise to photocopy your airline ticket and insurance policies. Keep these copies in a separate place from your travel wallet – back at your hotel, for example. Chances are you won't have to use any of these, but having them will make life easier if something gets lost. Leave additional copies of all of these documents, as well as your itinerary and any contact numbers, at home with a friend or family member.

If you are a student, be sure to acquire an International Student Identity (ISIC) card, as it may allow for discounts on airfares and at some hostels, museums and other attractions. For more information, visit www.istc.org.

Most flights to Quito from the US land late at night. Unfamiliar travelers will notice quickly upon entering the airport terminal that this is a whole new world. Take it in stride as you pull out your passport/return ticket/tourist card and pass through Immigration. You will probably be asked how long you want to stay (90 days is the maximum). Show them your tourist card, which they will stamp with the proper number of days, as well as your passport. Check to make sure the dates are legible and correct before leaving in order to avoid potential confusion later. After passing through Customs and picking up your luggage, catch a taxi to downtown and your hotel if you aren't being picked up. Taxis should not cost more than $3-$4, so make sure to ask before you hop into the cab, as Quito taxi drivers are notorious for overcharging, especially late at night.

Quito's Mariscal Sucre International Airport can become quite crowded. Keep an eye on your luggage at all times and be wary of unofficial baggage boys that start carrying away your bags for a tip without your asking. Note that there are official airport porters. If you allow a street porter to assist you, stay glued to his side and choose your own taxi.

Leaving Ecuador

Be sure to re-confirm your flight three days ahead of departure and arrive at the airport three hours before the scheduled departure for international flights. If this means leaving for the airport at 4 am, be sure to arrange a taxi the night before. Departure tax is US$25 and is payable in cash only when you check in.

Money Matters

■ Currency

Until recently, Ecuadorian currency was the **sucre**, which fluctuated drastically with the rise and fall of the oil and export markets. As of September 2000, the official currency has been the US dollar. In a few more remote and isolated locations, as well as smaller towns and villages, remnants of the sucre may exist (the last exchange rate was US$1 to 25,000 sucres). Note that it is very difficult to shop with or change bills of more than $20 due to counterfeiting.

The US dollar is a very touchy issue in Ecuador, as it represents the huge gap between the haves and the have-nots, as well as being perceived as the symbol of increased cost of living to the common Ecuadorian. Be sensitive to this. Be inconspicuous with money and modest in attire during your travels.

■ Your Money

Travelers checks are recommended if you are traveling with a good amount of money. American Express checks are the most common and can be exchanged at most major banks and high-end hotels. Change travelers checks in major cities and provincial capitals, including Quito, Guayaquil and Cuenca, as smaller towns may not have facilities to do so. Tourist-oriented towns, such as Baños, can also exchange travelers checks, but may charge more for it. Note that there are a few exchange houses, known as *casas de cambio*, left over from the days of the sucre, which can also exchange travelers checks quickly.

Credit cards – particularly Visa, MasterCard and, in some places, American Express and Diners – are readily accepted in most major tourist areas and at mid- and higher-level hotels. **ATMs** are readily available in the major cities, generally at the same banks that accept credit cards. Don't depend on ATMs, though, as they can be unreliable. Worse, when they are really hungry, they sometimes eat cards.

Bring travelers checks, rather than cash, and transfer checks to dollars in major cities as your trip progresses. A credit card is a great backup. It is always a good idea to split up your money in at least two different places. Always keep the majority of your funds, travelers checks and credit cards, along with a copy of your passport, back at the hotel in a secure room or safe deposit box. In addition, I always keep a few emergency bills in a zipper belt. Small bills are the best for spending money, but, whatever you do, don't carry anything loose in your pockets unless you are prepared to part with it.

■ Travel Expenses

Overall, travel in Ecuador is extremely inexpensive by Western standards. With persistent budgeting, it is possible to get by on $10 per day, although this means economizing at the very low-end hotels. The budget traveler does well on $15 per day and lives large at $25 per day. The latter will usually include comfortable and relatively nice accommodations, often with breakfast and possibly dinner. The mid-level traveler will do just fine at $25-$50 per day in the major towns, but expect to pay more at the nicer ecolodges and on package tours.

Prices for tour operators and outfitters vary, depending on the quality of the organization. At the bottom end, you'll pay $25 per day for a jungle excursion, including vehicle transportation, accommodations, and guide services. At this price, however, do not expect a licensed, top-quality, or even responsible outfitter. At the high end, an overnight mountaineering trip to the summit of a snowcapped volcano will cost about $200, everything included. All other prices for adventure and nature activities generally fall within this range. Galápagos excursions run $100-$200 per day for a five- or eight-day mid-range or mid-range-plus tour (classified as tourist to tourist superior vessels). Obviously, luxury-class tours cost more and economy-class vessels may run quite a bit lower.

■ Taxes & Gratuities

% Many of the more tourist-oriented restaurants include a 10% surcharge on the tab, and some even add an additional service charge (usually 5%), in which case you may not want to give an extra gratuity. A good rule of thumb for tipping in the service industry is 10-15%, whether it is in a restaurant, for a guide or for a boatsman. If you join a $50-per-day tour, it is perfectly reasonable to tip the guide $5 per person per day, usually a bit less for a driver. All of this, of course, is dependent upon quality of service. I find this particularly true with taxi drivers. If your driver is blatantly trying to overcharge for a fare from the airport to the hotel, then it is perfectly fair not to tip. If the driver is honest and helpful and uses the taxi meter, then a gratuity will only reinforce quality service and honesty.

Embassies	
Argentina	Edificio Río Amazonas, Av. Amazonas 477, between Roca and Robles, 5th Floor, ☎ 2-2562-992, fax 2-2568-177, Mon-Fri, 9 am-1:30 pm.
Austria	Veintimilla 878 and Amazonas, ☎ 2-2524-811, Mon-Fri, 10 am-12 pm.
Belgium	Juan León Mera 863 and Wilson, ☎ 2-2567-633, 2545-340, Mon-Thurs, 9 am-12 pm, and 2:30-5 pm on Mon and Wed.
Brazil	Amazonas 1429 and Colón, Edificio España, 9th Floor, ☎ 2-2563-086, Mon-Fri, 9 am-3 pm.

Canada	6 de Diciembre 2816 and James Ort, ☎ 2-2543-214, fax 2-2503-108, Mon-Fri, 9:30 am-4 pm.
Colombia	Colón 1133 and Amazonas, 7th Floor, ☎ 2-2228-926/2221-969, Mon-Fri, 10 am-1 pm and 2-5 pm.
Costa Rica	Calle Rumipamba 692 between Amazonas and República, ☎ 2-2254-945/2256-016, fax 2-2254-087, Mon-Fri, 8 am-1:30 pm.
Chile	Juan Pablo Sanz 3617 and Amazonas, Edificio Xerox, 4th Floor, ☎ 2-2453-327, fax 2-2444-470, Mon-Fri, 8 am-3 pm.
Taiwan	Rep de El Salvador 733 and Portugal, Edificio Gabriela 3, 2nd Floor, ☎ 2-4259-357, Mon-Fri, 8 am-12 pm, 2-5 pm.
China	Atahualpa 349 and Amazonas, ☎ 2-2458-337/2458-927, Mon-Thurs, 9 am-12 pm, 3-4 pm, Fri, 9 am-12 pm.
Denmark	Rep de El Salvador 733 and Portugal, Edificio Gabriela 3, 3rd Floor, ☎ 2-2437-163, fax 2-2436-942, Mon-Fri, 9:30 am-12:30 pm, 3-6 pm.
France	Embassy: Leonidas Plaza 107 and Patria, ☎ 2-2560-789, fax 2-2566-424, Mon-Fri, 9-12, 3-5; Consulate: Diego de Almagro 1550 and Pradera, Edificio Kingman, 2nd Floor, 2-2543-110, Mon-Fri, 9-12, 3-5.
Germany	Av. Patria and 9 de Octubre, Banco de Colombia Building, ☎ 2-2225-660/2567-231/2567-231 (after-hours emergency), Mon-Fri, 9 am-12 pm.
Great Britain	Citiplaza Building, 14th floor, Naciones Unidas and República de El Salvador, ☎ 2-297-0800, fax 2-297-0809, britembq@interactive.net.ec, Mon-Fri, 9 am-12 pm, 1:30-3:30 pm.
Ireland	Antonio de Ulloa 2654 and Rumipamba, ☎ 2-2451-577, Mon-Fri, 9-11 am, 3-6 pm.
Israel	Eloy Alfaro 969 and Amazonas, ☎ 2-2565-510/511, fax 2-2504-635, Mon-Fri, 8:30 am-4:30 pm.

Italy	Isla 111 and Humberto Albornoz, ☎ 2-2561-077, Mon-Fri, 10 am-12 pm.
Japan	Juan León Mera 130 and Patria, Edificio de La Corporación Financiera Nacional, 7th Floor, ☎ 2-2561-899, fax 2-2503-670, Mon-Fri, 9:30 am-12 pm, 2:30-5:30 pm.
Mexico	6 de Diciembre 4843 and Naciones Unidas, ☎ 2-2457-820, fax 2-2448-245, Mon-Fri, 9 am-12 pm.
Nether-lands	12 de Octubre 1942 and Cordero, ☎ 2-2525-461, Mon-Fri, 9 am-12pm.
Norway & Sweden	Pasaje Alonso Jerves 134 and Orellana, ☎ 2-2509-514/423, fax 2-2502-593, Mon-Fri, 9 am-12 pm.
Panama	Diego de Almagro 1550 and Pradera, Edificio Kingman, 3rd Floor, ☎/fax 2-2566-449, Mon-Fri, 9 am-2 pm.
Peru	Av. Rep de El Salvador 495 and Irlanda, ☎ 2-2468-410/411, Mon-Fri, 9:30 am-12:30 pm, 3:30-6:30 pm.
Switzer-land	Amazonas 3617 and Juan Pablo Sanz, Edificio Xerox, 2nd Floor, ☎ 2-2434-948 fax 2-2430-594, Mon-Fri, 9 am-12 pm.
Spain	La Pinta 455 and Amazonas, ☎ 2-2564-373/390/377, fax 2-2500-826, Mon-Fri, 9 am-1 pm.
United States	12 de Octubre and Patria, ☎ 2-2562-890, fax 2-250-2052, Tues-Fri, 8-11:30 am, 2:30-4 pm.

Health & Safety

Bugs and snakes are of minimal concern at most destinations. Accommodations will have **mosquito** nets where they are needed (tropical lowlands). If you are traveling in malaria-infested areas of the Oriente or lowland tropical forests along the western slopes, consider taking malaria pills, and remember that malarial mosquitoes bite at night. Wear long-sleeved shirts and long trousers (light and loose fitting) from dusk till dawn, as well as an insect repellent (with DEET). Although **snakes** are plentiful, there are only a few poisonous ones. They are rarely seen and hardly ever bite humans.

In the higher elevations of the Andes, especially if you will be climbing some of Ecuador's renowned volcanoes, **altitude sickness** is a very real issue. Altitude physiologically affects different people in different ways. Symptoms of Acute Mountain Sickness (AMS) include headache, nausea, loss of appetite, trouble with sleep, and lack of energy. To help prevent altitude sickness, you should always remain well-hydrated, gradually expose yourself to higher elevations, exercise moderately until you are acclimatized, eat a diet consisting of at least 70% carbohydrates beginning one to two days prior to ascent, and get plenty of rest. And remember that alcoholic beverages, caffeine, and aspirin tend to dehydrate you. If you are prone to altitude sickness or are concerned that it could be problematic for you, the prescription medication **Diamox** has been approved by the FDA for prevention and treatment of altitude sickness. Unless you are allergic to sulfa drugs, you may want to bring it with you, but be sure to check with your physician, as Diamox has potentially significant side-effects.

■ Vaccinations

Vaccinations are extremely important and should be addressed as soon as possible before traveling. Although they are not necessary for entry into Ecuador, the following are recommended.

Hepatitis A is the most common travel-related illness that can be prevented by vaccination. You can protect yourself with the antibody globulin or a new vaccine called Havrix. Check with your local clinic or physician for the latest developments.

A **yellow fever** vaccination is important if you are heading into the Amazonian rainforest or tropical coastal region (excluding the Galápagos Islands). This vaccination lasts 10 years.

A **typhoid** vaccination is recommended if you plan to spend a significant time in rural parts of Ecuador. It consists of two injections taken four weeks apart.

Most people get **diphtheria-tetanus** (DT), **polio** and **measles** shots while in school. You should get boosters for DT every 10 years, whether you are traveling or not.

Check with the Centers for Disease Control (CDC) in Atlanta for last-minute health updates on travel to Ecuador. ☎ (404) 332-4555 or www. cdc.org.

Travel Insurance

I never travel without travel insurance. Depending on the policy, it will cover everything from lost, stolen or damaged baggage and travel documents, to medical costs and medical evacuation from remote areas. If you are on a package tour, you can also purchase a policy that covers trip cancellation and interruption. Since 9/11, some policies even cover a certain level of terrorism, but be sure you are clear about exactly what is and isn't covered. I usually purchase an annual coverage plan, which is great if you travel a lot. Major reputable providers in the US include **Travelex** (www.travelex-insurance.com) and **Travel Guard** (www. travelguard.com).

■ Food & Drinking Water

Other than in high-end hotels and restaurants (which will give you bottles of water), drink bottled water or boiled rainwater only. The exception to this is in the Galápagos, where water is generally safe. If you are a backcountry traveler and will be depending on a filtration system, make sure that it is extremely effective, i.e., that it uses both mechanical and chemical methods of treating water.

Food quality on tours differs significantly from local cuisine. Salads and unpeeled fruit are normally the worst culprits for making you sick. Jungle ecolodges tend to cater the most to tourists with regard to food safety and appeal. When in restaurants, check around for how "gringo"-oriented it is. A good rule of thumb is that if a large percentage of the customers are tourists, it is probably safe. If, on the other hand, most are locals, be wary of salads and water-based salsas or other such items. Make sure water for hot drinks such as coffee has reached boiling. If in a more rural environment, make sure the food is cooked well. Undercooked meat, poultry or eggs are a sure way to become deathly ill from salmonella.

■ Toilets

Ecuador's plumbing is extremely poor. The quickest way to stop up any toilet is by placing toilet paper where you normally would... in the toilet. Always place it in the trash bin, unless you are at a high-end hotel or are told otherwise.

■ Security

In general, Ecuador is a safe place to travel, especially compared to its more notoriously dangerous neighbors, Peru and Colombia. Armed robbery is rare, although crowded places, such as bus stations, city streets or bustling markets, are breeding grounds for pickpockets. Assaults are on the rise in the more tourist-oriented sections of Quito. Take simple precautions to avoid being robbed. Stay alert and don't look confused or lost, even if you are. Thieves look for easy targets, such as tourists who carry a wallet or passport in a hip pocket. Leave the wallet at home. Keep a few loose bills and your passport in an inside pocket or, preferably, a body pouch or money belt.

Passport checks can occur at any time, though usually they are at Ecuador's entry and exit points, such as the airport or border crossings. There are also check points at provincial crossings. Be wary of "immigration agents" on the street if they are not in uniform or wearing an ID; refuse to show them anything until you are sure they are legitimate or make your way (with or without them) to the nearest police station. Note that sometimes immigration will "sweep" a popular tourist hang-out, such as a nightclub, to check passports. Just show them your documents and you will be fine.

■ Medical Facilities & Doctors

Most embassies can provide contact information for emergency and medical services, as well as recommended physicians. The larger and more modern the city, the larger and more modern the hospitals. Quito, Guayaquil and, to a lesser extent, Cuenca all have bilingual US- and Europe-trained medical professionals. Pharmacies and even clinics are readily available in most Ecuadorian towns, even smaller ones. In Quito they are everywhere, and some are open 24 hours. Look for an illuminated "Turno" sign outside. The pharmacy on 6 de Deciembre and San Ignacio (near Supermaxi) is recommended and is open 24 hours a day. Be sure to visit a doctor for the proper medication, though, and be wary of diagnosing yourself or taking the advice of a pharmacist. If you become significantly sick or injured elsewhere in the country, get to Quito or Guayaquil as soon as possible.

Major Medical Facilities

In Quito

Metropolitano (Av. Mariana de Jesús and Av. Occidental; ☎ 2-2431-520). Probably the best emergency facility, staffed by top professionals, but the costs are comparable to western countries.

Hospital Voz Andes (Villalengua 267, next to VozVoz Andes radio station, ☎ 2-2241-540) has an emergency room and is staffed by American, British and national physicians.

In Guayaquil

Clinica Kennedy (Av. del Periodista, ☎ 4-2286-963) caters to foreign visitors, with excellent emergency services and staff.

Doctors

The following doctors are recommended by British and American Embassies for quality, bilingual service:

Dr. Alvaro Dávalos. General Practitioner with specialization in tropical medicine. La Colina 202 and San Ignacio (near 6 de Diciembre and Colón), ☎ 2-2500-267/8, adavalos@pi.pro.ec.

Dr. Stephen Contag. Gynecology and Obstetrics. Medico Meditropoli, Av. Mariana de Jesús, across from Hospital Metropolitano, suite 109. 11 am-6:30 pm, ☎ 2-2267-972 or 9-709-670.

Dr. John Rosenberg. Internal Medicine. Foch 476 and Almagro (down the street from the Magic Bean). Look for MEDCENTER sign. ☎ 2-2521-104/2-2223-333/9-9447-237, jrd@pi.pro.ec.

Dr. Edward Jarvis and **Dr. Patrick Bullock**. Clinica Quiropractica Suiza 272 and Eloy Alfaro, ☎ 2-2460-306/9-721-503, jeovag@andinanet.net.

Communication

■ Telephone Service

 Overall, Ecuador has an adequate communications system. **Calling cards** work at specific public telephones to make international calls, but are not always reliable. There are also public phone **debit cards** that you can use at specific locations. The most reliable way to make international calls is through the **Andinatel** national phone company offices, located in all cities in the northern sierras and Oriente, and even in the smaller more remote towns. **Pacífictel** offices offer the same services in cities on the coast and Southern Highlands. There is always an operator there who will dial for you or give you tokens (*fichas*) to call yourself. Usually you will pay upfront for the number of minutes you want your call to last and will get a warning 30 seconds prior to the end of the time.

You can make national and international calls at most major hotels, or use a credit card to do so. Check on their charge policy though, or you may be paying for the call itself plus a surcharge. They shouldn't charge you on a time basis unless they are making a long distance call direct without the use of your credit card. You can call directly to an outside operator at no charge.

 *Connect with **MCI** in the US at ☎ 999-170, with **AT&T** at ☎ 999-119 and with **Sprint** at ☎ 999-171. To call Canada's **Teleglobe**, dial ☎ 999-175. ☎ 999-178 or 999-181 to connect to **British Telecom** in the UK.*

For several years now, the least expensive way to make international calls, at least from Quito, is through the Internet café **Net2Phones**. Rates are extremely reasonable, although the quality of the digital connection leaves a bit to be desired. You'll pay 20¢ a minute, rather than $1-$2 per minute for a regular telephone call.

Ecuador is in the process of privatizing its phone service. Recently, a digit has been added to numbers in Quito and Guayaquil (now seven in total). Plans to make all numbers seven digits are underway, but the timeframe is uncertain. Throughout the text, phone numbers include the regional prefix (similar to the US area code).

How to Call

When calling Ecuador from abroad, you must first dial the international access code (011), then the country code (593 for Ecuador), followed by the regional prefix (02 for Quito) and then the six- or seven-digit local number.

For example, to call Quito from the US, ☎ 011-593-2-2444-704. Note that when calling from abroad, you should drop the 0 in the regional prefix, so 02 becomes 2.

When calling from within Ecuador, use the full regional prefix if you are calling outside if your region. So, to call the above Quito number from Guayaquil, ☎ 02-2444-704. If calling locally (in this case, from within Quito), dial only the seven-digit local number (2444-704)

■ Internet Access

Internet access is readily available in cyber-cafés throughout Ecuador's tourist towns, providing an inexpensive and efficient way of communicating abroad. Internet cafés are a dime a dozen in Quito, and you can usually find one or two in less centralized towns as well, including Baños, Tena, and Cuenca.

■ Mail

There are post offices throughout the country, including the more remote and smaller villages. Registering important mail is recommended if you want to make sure it arrives safely at its destination, though this offers little security for important matters. For the most part, the Ecuadorian postal system is unreliable. Some vendors will send souvenirs home for you, but be cautious whom you trust, as many packages never arrive when sent this way. Using a shipping company is one of the most reliable options. There are several in Quito, Otavalo and other tourist-oriented towns. One reliable service is DHL, located in Quito, ☎ 2-2485-100, at Colón 1333 and República.

■ Newspapers

In luxury hotels everywhere you will find major international English-language newspapers and magazines. In Quito, there are a few good bookstores in the Mariscal District that will have the same. Ecuadorian newspapers include *El Comercio* and *Hoy* in Quito, *El Universo* in Guayaquil and *Mercurio* in Cuenca. There is also a Quito-based English publication known as *Q*.

Time Zone

 Ecuador itself is on Eastern Standard Time (GMT-5). The Galápagos Islands are on Central Standard (GMT-6). There is no Daylight Savings Time.

Electricity

 Current is 110 volts, 60 cycles, AC (the same as North America, but not compatible with Britain and Australia). Plugs have two flat prongs, as in North America.

Language

Spanish is the official language. English is spoken some within the business community and quite a bit in the travel and tourism industry. Some European languages, including German, French and Dutch, are spoken in the tourism industry as well, at hotels and with tour operators. You will gain the most out of your Ecuadorian adventure, however, if you learn Spanish before heading there and/or immerse yourself in a Spanish-language program upon arrival. Not only will this allow you to actually interact with Ecuadorians, rather than solely with other foreign tourists, it will open a whole new world, both to you and to them. For a list of recommended Spanish Schools and cultural exchanges throughout Ecuador, inquire with the South American Explorers Club (☎/fax 2-225-228, explorer@seac.org.ec).

■ Studying Spanish

Ecuador is teeming with opportunities to learn Spanish, whether you choose to take the formal route and study at a language school (perhaps living with a local family as well) or just prefer to learn through day-to-day interaction with locals. The Ecuadorian people are very patient with gringos struggling to express themselves in Spanish, especially in the more touristy towns. They'll appreciate your efforts and, at the end of the day, this will benefit you and them.

If you prefer a more formal classroom setting, there are inumerable language schools to choose from. Quito has dozens of schools, offering multiple learning options, ranging from courses of a week to several months. You can also choose between regular classroom-based courses or, if you prefer, one-on-one instruction. The latter could even be as informal as meeting in a local café or at your hostel and chatting for the afternoon. Prices and quality vary, of course, so check around, and don't commit to or pay for something that doesn't seem like an enjoyable, worthwhile learning activity. One school that has been teaching Spanish to foreigners since 1989 is **Amazonas Education & Travel**, Jorge Washington 718 and Av. Amazonas, Edificio Rocafuerte, Quito, ☎ 2-2502-461, info@eduamazonas.com, www.eduamazonas.com. They offer intensive courses (one-on-one or in small groups), as well as accommodation with Ecuadorian families.

Another option you might want to explore if you're on a budget is to arrange an *intercambio* or exchange. The way this usually works is that you swap conversation time with a local. If you meet for two hours, the first hour is dedicated to Spanish conversation, and the second hour to English. It's free and you can make a friend while you learn! On the downside, your partner may not be able to teach you the ins and outs of Spanish grammar in the same way a professional teacher could.

For a complete list of recommended Spanish schools and *intercambio* programs, inquire at **The Club** in Quito, at Jorge Washington 311 and Leonidas Plaza, ☎ 2-2225-228, quitoclub@saexplorers.org.

Women & Children Travelers

Ecuador is a relatively safe country for women. That being said, there are definitely areas in major cities where you should not walk around at night by yourself (this goes for men as well). Note that it is also easy to hook up with other foreign travelers while on the "gringo path." A minor irritation is the attention gringa women draw from Ecuadorian men, particularly younger guys in larger cities and more touristy areas. Machismo is a big part of Ecuadorian culture, and you may well find yourself walking down the streets of Quito as the center of attention from a group of men whistling and making kissing sounds. Ignore these advances, as addressing them in any way will encourage more. And don't feel that it is an assault only on foreigners; they do it to young Ecuadorian women too.

Of more consequence is the reputation, especially within the tourism industry, that gringa women are easy. This is unfounded for the most part, but lax social attitudes of some travelers haven't helped the situation. You may find yourself pursued by male Ecuadorian guides, for example. Once their actions border on harassment, be sure to notify the company management and the Ministry of Tourism. Please be aware that your actions and attitudes affect other women travelers.

Perhaps the most respected of all foreign travelers are women with children (and a wedding ring), as family is very important in Ecuadorian culture. You will discover the added bonus of extra help and friendliness from the locals. There is plenty to do in Ecuador for children and families. But don't forget this is a developing country without some of the conveniences of home, including abundant medical facilities and, in many cases, health and sanitation are not what you may be used to. But, if you come prepared, you will have a grand time with the kids.

Disabled Travelers

Ecuador is only just beginning to make accommodations for disabled travelers. As such, the infrastructure is minimal at best, with only the better hotels providing ramps and restrooms for the disabled. In fact, on a recent guiding trip, I found it difficult to rent a wheelchair even with advance notice. Nevertheless, the persistent traveler with minor disabilities will do just fine.

Gay & Lesbian Travelers

In 1998 the Ecuadorian constitution recognized "the equality of all before the law without discrimination against age, sex, ethnic origin, color, religion, political affiliation, economic position, sexual orientation, state of health, incapacity, or difference of any kind." This landmark move is progressive for Latin American countries and has since opened up a movement of relative openness within Ecuador, primarily in Quito's gay scene. Though machismo remains prevalent in Ecuador, the beginning of a gay support network is available in Quito. However, public displays of affection are asking for trouble. For the latest in gay-friendly bars, clubs, hotels, etc., visit http:// gayquitoec.tripod.com.

Holidays & Festivals

 ## January

January 1 - **New Year's Day**, Año Nuevo.

January 6 - **Three Kings Day** (aka Epiphany), Reyes Magos.

February

February 27 - **National Community Spirit Day**.

February/March

Carnival. The last days before Ash Wednesday and just before Lent, Carnival is the ultimate partying indulgence in Catholic Latin America, with Ecuador as no exception. Parades, waterfights and packed beaches are common during this time. Ambato, especially, is known for its *Fiesta de las Frutas y las Flores*, or Festival of Fruit and Flowers parade. Baños, as well, affords a great time if you don't mind getting "foamed" and drenched by hoards of children. In fact, most places will have a festive atmosphere. Although the actual dates change each year according to the religious calendar, Carnival celebrations always occur the weekend prior to Ash Wednesday.

Easter and Holy Week, Semana Santa. Parades, religious processions, and again, packed beaches, mark the festivities throughout the week of Palm Sunday, Holy Thursday, Good Friday, Holy Saturday and Easter Sunday. Many shops and merchants close during a good portion of the festivities.

May

May 1 - **Labor Day**, Día del Trabajo – more parties.

May 24 - **Battle of Pichincha**, La Battala del Pichincha. This national holiday recognizes the major battle in the war for independence from Spain in 1822. Celebrations are particularly exuberant in Quito, near where the battle was fought.

June

Corpus Cristi, celebrated on the ninth Thursday after Easter, is a hybrid religious festival/harvest celebration.

June 24 - **Saint John the Baptist**, known locally as Inti Raymi. Another example of the Spanish Roman Catholic Church blanketing their religion over an indigenous celebration, in this case that of the sun and summer solstice. The Northern Highlands are particularly festive during this time, especially Otavalo.

June 28-29 - **Saints Peter and Paul**.

July 24 - **Simón Bolívar's Birthday**. A public holiday with country-wide festivities celebrating El Libertador.

July 25 - **Founder's Day**, Guayaquil. A continuation of the previous day and Guayaquil's biggest party.

August

August 10 - **Quito Independence Day**, Día de la Independencia – a public holiday.

September

Throughout the Sierras, various festivals take place to commemorate the fall harvest.

September 1-15 - **Fiesta del Yamor** in Otavalo. This is Otavalo's main fiesta, with dancing, music and drinking, during the solar equinox, in which the *Pachamama*, or Mother Earth, is honored in preparation for the planting of new corn.

October

October 9 - **Guayaquil Independence Day**. Another excuse to have a public holiday and party big in Guayaquil for several days in conjunction with Columbus Day.

October 12 - **Columbus Day**, Día de la Raza (Day of the Race). Yet another public holiday.

November

November 1 - **All Saints' Day**, Todos Los Santos – a public holiday, commemorating all of the Saints of the Church.

November 2 - **All Soul's Day**, Día de los Muertos or Día de los Difuntos ("Day of the Dead") – a continuation of Todos los Santos, in which families visit cemeteries to pay their respects to deceased relatives, often bringing offerings of food, drink and flowers.

November 3 - **Cuenca Independence Day** – the largest fiesta of the year in Cuenca.

November 11 - **Latacunga Independence Day**.

December

December 6 - **Quito Foundation Day**, Día de Quito. Includes parades, dancing in the streets, bullfights, and chiva rides. A chiva is basically an open-air party bus. They typically have no sides; people pile inside or even onto the roof, and the bus drives around the more happening parts of downtown. There's often a live band on board, or just really loud music blaring from the stereo, to get everyone in a dancing mood.

December 24-25 - **Christmas Eve & Day**, Navidad.

December 28-31 - **Year's End Celebrations**. This holiday typically means big bonfires in the streets of most towns and cities, where life-size effigies – built to resemble prominent public figures, such as political leaders or TV personalities – are ceremoniously burned by the crowds, in a goodbye to the events of the preceding year. Another aspect of the evening is that the men dress up as 'widows' (tarty widows quite often, which can include some scary visions!) and hold up the traffic on all the main roads, wielding buckets and demanding money for the festivities.

Eco-Travel

State of the Environment

Ecuador's wealth of biological diversity is seriously threatened by human encroachment. The voracious appetite of unsound 'economic development' continues to consume the country's natural resources. In some

ways this trend resembles our own westward expansion across Europe and America. The two special problems in this case, however, are that (1) Ecuador represents the last of the planet's fortress of genetic diversity, and (2) this development is not helping most Ecuadorians in any way. In fact, economic development at the expense of natural resources increases the income distribution gap and the colonization of marginal lands.

Major threats to the remaining intact ecosystems include population growth and colonization, as well as the petroleum, cacao, coffee, banana, palm oil, shrimp, and cattle industries. These activities, in turn, are associated with the different regions of Ecuador: the coast, the Sierras (Andes), and the Oriente (Amazon).

■ Coastal Ecuador

Coastal Ecuador varies dramatically. From banana plantations, coastal mangrove swamps, and cloud forests of the western lowlands, the land transforms to the semi-arid desert-like plains of the south coast. In the northwest, a dense vegetation of the coastal rainforest dominates the landscape. In each of these areas, human impact has significantly altered the lay of the land.

Tropical Dry Forest

From the coastal town of Portoviejo south to Peru, the semi-arid plains once provided vital habitat for tropical dry forests. Much of this has disappeared, along with a large number of plants, animals, and endemic species. Population growth and a heavy investment in trans-

portation infrastructure from the 1960s and 70s paralleled a growth
in oil exploration and land cultivation for export products. Currently,
a small percentage of these forests are protected in areas such as
Machalilla National Park. Here, coastal scrub, deciduous trees, and
cacti meet the Pacific Ocean.

Mangrove Forests

Ecuador's mangrove forests, once plentiful in every far north and
southern estuary along the coast, have been damaged by the shrimp-
farming industry. These incredibly productive "swamps" are the life-
support system for the coastal marine ecosystem. Mangrove forests
provide habitat and nutrients for the entire food chain, and the trees'
roots provide structure and organic soil for other coastal marine
plants. They also provide habitat for fish and other marine life, as
well as the only nesting sites for a variety of seabirds.

Mangrove Deforestation

The rate of mangrove deforestation for shrimp farming currently threatens Ecuador's entire coastal ecosystem, including other fishery species that do not live directly in the
mangrove estuaries. It also affects the subsistence liveli-
hood of local people. Ironically, the shrimp-farming industry is also destroying itself, as it relies upon shrimp larvae
caught from natural stocks in tidal estuaries. In addition,
an incredible volume of "unwanted" aquatic wildlife entan-
gled in the nets is destroyed. Disease in shrimp farms also
cuts into profitability. While the productivity of shrimp
farming and the affected ecosystems continue to decline,
hard-currency profits go directly to Western investors.
Meanwhile, a few jobs are created for the locals, but wages
are meager. It is well worth visiting some of the remaining
intact mangrove ecosystems. The marine wildlife is abundant and efforts to preserve these areas are increasingly dependent on the collective voice of tourists and conservation
organizations. Supporting places like Bahía de Caráquez'
organic shrimp farm – the first in the world – will also
greatly benefit responsible economic growth.

Tropical Wet Forests

The western rainforests near the north coast and the Colombian border continue to provide habitat to some of the most diverse species in all of Ecuador. Regionally, this area receives even more rainfall than many parts of the upper Amazon Basin, and bird life is prolific. Many sections have been transformed for agricultural development, but such places as the Cotocachi-Caypas Ecological Reserve still provide protection for large expanses of these biologically rich areas.

We lose over six million acres of mountainous cloud forest cover, globally, every year. This is 1½ times faster than the global rate of tropical deforestation. Ecuador contains seven million acres of cloud forest, an area that provides virtually all of the water for local villages and watersheds. Farmers annually cut down 126,000 acres of this total, or 1.7%, per year. In one particular Ecuadorian cloud forest, studies revealed that in a six-month period, the vegetation gathers one million gallons of water by intercepting Pacific Ocean mists. Over the same period, a comparable deforested area converted to pasture collects 100,000 gallons. Deforestation has resulted in the drying up of entire watersheds in many regions.

A few stunning forests remain intact and they are more than worth visiting. These places are renowned for their birding, wildlife viewing, and photographic opportunities, which provides an economic alternative for locals. Several coastal cloud forests continue to provide habitat for spectacular animals such as the howler monkey and jaguarundi, as well as the kinkajou, blue morpho butterfly, and a fabulous array of bird species.

■ The Sierras

With the exception of private nature reserves, intact forests in the highlands of Ecuador are few and far between. Agricultural use of this land dates back to pre-Inca times in the earliest settled communities. The Andean countryside is now a quilted checkerboard of agriculture. Regardless, the snowcapped volcanoes of the Sierras are awe-inspiring. And the *páramo* grasslands on the slopes of the mountains remain relatively intact and are fascinating places to visit. National parks such as Cotopaxi continue to protect native flora and fauna in these areas.

Today's major threats to the human and natural environment include litter, pollution, and refuse from major urban centers, along with untreated sewage effluent in the main watersheds. In addition, steady

Eco-Travel

population growth is forcing human encroachment into the *páramo* grasslands of the steep Andean slopes.

■ Amazon Deforestation & Development

Deforestation in Ecuador's upper Amazon Basin is severe and wide-spread, arguably the most significant and scariest threat to the biological integrity of this planet. Some estimates put the rate of deforestation at close to 151 acres per minute, or 1,170 square miles per year. At this rate, the rainforest has less than 15 years left. Much of the Oriente remains somewhat intact, although fragmentation is significant and poses the greatest threat to biological preservation in the region. The destruction of the rainforest parallels development of the oil industry from the 1970s and is accelerating despite conservation efforts.

The pattern of modern devastation began with the discovery of oil. Roads were built through the forest, backed by heavy foreign investment. Historically, the oil industry gave little consideration to environmental and cultural consequences, although this is changing. The next stage is colonization. As the country's population continues to expand without a stable socioeconomic structure to support it, the government encourages people to take free land in the Oriente if they properly "utilize" it.

Once the access roads are built, colonists create the most permanent long-term damage, with uncontrolled forest cutting and agricultural practices incompatible with the productive capacity of the region. Soil nutrients become exhausted within a few years, resulting in continued agricultural expansion. This, combined with ongoing colonization, exacerbates deforestation at an exponential rate.

Fortunately, integrated conservation and development programs that include sustainable forest-product development, education, and ecotourism are helping a bit. Ecotourism is viewed by many as being on the forefront of sustainable economic activities and a major tool for community development. As a traveler visiting these areas, you have the opportunity to promote a strong incentive for preserving the remaining areas.

Reserves & National Parks

Ecuador has 25 areas classified as protected, including eight national parks, eight ecological reserves and a combination of national recreation areas, biological or fauna reserves and a geobotanical reserve. The head agency in charge of these areas is the Ministerio del Ambiente (Interior), within the Ministry of Agriculture Department. Previously, the National Park Service, INEFAN, administered the parks, though the most useful information is now available through the Ministry of Tourism (formerly CETUR). Main offices are located in major cities and towns and are listed in the *Visitors Information* section of each destination chapter.

Each park is different when it comes to tourism infrastructure, the quality of trails, and the quantity and quality of information available at visitor centers. In addition, there are numerous private reserves throughout the country, many of which were acquired by national and international nongovernmental organizations to preserve areas rich in biological diversity. Often, they work in conjunction with local communities on development projects that include ecotourism.

There has been discussion of privatizing Ecuador's national parks, though that is unlikely to happen in the near future. As ministries continue to shuffle about, phase out, and be created, there is some confusion as to the future of current national parks. Protected areas vary considerably with regard to enforced regulation and state of the environment. Much of this has to do with their particular location as it relates to colonization and industrial interests such as oil and timber. One thing, however, is for certain: These special places are incomparable and will continue to depend on the voice and dollar of the ecotourist.

Eco-Travel

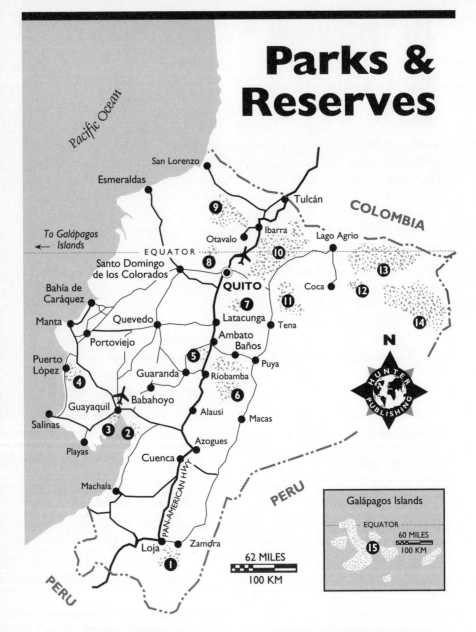

Parks & Reserves

1. Podocarpus National Park
2. Manglares Churote Nature Reserve
3. El Salado National Park
4. Machalilla National Park
5. Chimborazo Nature Reserve
6. Sangay National Park
7. Cotopaxi National Park
8. Mindo Nature Reserve
9. Cotacachi-Cayapas Nature Reserve
10. Cayamba-Coca Nature Reserve
11. Sumaco Nature Reserve
12. Limoncocha Nature Reserve
13. Cuyabeno Nature Reserve
14. Yasuní National Park
15. Galápagos Islands

Adventure & Outdoor Activities

▪ Hiking, Trekking & Mountaineering

The Andes of Ecuador are home to world-class hiking and mountaineering. From the leisurely morning hike to climbing the highest active volcanoes in the world, the opportunities are virtually endless. There are numerous well-marked trails, particularly in the more popular national parks and nature reserves. Ecuador's cloud and rainforests offer spectacular wildlife viewing and photography.

Many hikes are on easy, self-guided trails, while even more require overnight expeditions, a knowledgeable guide, hearty lungs, and a pair of rubber boots (in the tropical forests). For the more adventurous mountaineer, technical gear and experienced guides are required. Climbers should read Rachowiecki, Thurber and Wagenhauser's *Climbing and Hiking in Ecuador* (from Bradt Publications, 1997).

If you plan to visit the Sierras, be aware of altitude sickness. It is a very real and dangerous risk, particularly when hiking and climbing the volcanoes. In Cotopaxi, for example, the parking lot below the refuge is at well over 15,000 feet. Make sure you acclimatize for several days before attempting any of these hikes. Drink quite a bit of water and avoid drinking alcohol and coffee during this period. If you develop a headache or dizziness while hiking, stop climbing immediately, rest, and then make your way downhill.

▪ Rafting & Kayaking

Expert kayakers from North America are just beginning to discover what a few select people in Ecuador have known all along... that there are epic white-water opportunities here. The eastern slopes of the Andes breath life into the rainforest of the Oriente and provide numerous rafting and kayaking opportunities in the process, from slow paddles through virgin jungle to Class V white-water excitement. Some of the smaller waterways are so remote that they have not yet been tried. Many, however, are easily accessible and can be experienced with one of the country's few quality outfitters.

Although there are rafting opportunities in the Sierras along the western slopes with outfitters based out of Quito, water quality is often poor as a result of proximity to urban centers. Your best bet is to head out toward the Oriente. Be particularly leery of rafting outfitters based in the resort town of Baños. Some of them have no right to be on the water. The upper Amazon region around Tena offers the best commercially accessible whitewater (see page 359, *Central & Southern Oriente*, for more information).

■ Horseback Riding

 Experiencing Ecuador on horseback is a great way to view the country, especially in the Sierras. The habitats you can visit are as varied as the hiking and biking trails. Outfitters are plentiful in many areas, and are often simply locals with horses. Prices can be very reasonable, but many Ecuadorians do not maintain the same standards with their animals as we do. You will pay according to the quality you receive. When hiring a local, feel free to mention something that could be improved in order to attract more tourists, but be considerate. Often people cannot afford to care for their animals the way we expect them to be cared for at home. Many guest haciendas, too, have horseback-riding facilities; these are listed throughout this book.

■ Mountain Biking

 Bicycling in Ecuador is just starting to become popular among both locals and tourists. In the Ecuadorian Andes, there are epic mountain biking opportunities that haven't even begun to be tapped into. There are a few good tour operators and bike shops in Quito that provide information and guiding services. Baños, the gateway between the mountains and the jungle, has been a popular center of bike rentals for over a decade now. Many of these bicycles, however, are of questionable quality, and there are great opportunities throughout the rest of the country. Many hotels in the main tourist towns also rent bicycles.

■ Birding, Nature Viewing & Photography

 Currently a prime destination for professional photographers and naturalists, Ecuador is home to virtually anything you are looking (or listening) for. Dugout-canoe rides in the Oriente provide seldom-witnessed exhibits of nature at its finest. A predawn rise and hike through a fog-laden cloud forest will amply reward the avid birder. Whether it is the tropical coastal rainforest, the Andes, or the Oriente, there are numerous unbelievable destinations. All it takes is a bit of exploration and a good guide.

The best wildlife and bird guides are usually locals and most likely community members that grew up in and around a particular area. They may not know the scientific names of certain birds, but they will locate them well before anyone else. Complement this with a biologist, ornithologist, or photographer on a well-organized tour, and the opportunities are endless. The best places for wildlife viewing, birding, and photography are throughout the more pristine areas of the Oriente, coastal cloud and rainforests along the western slopes, and the cloud forests of the highlands. The Galápagos Islands, of course, are unparalleled and easily accessible. See specific chapters for more detailed regional information.

■ Cultural Tourism

 This is what makes Ecuador so special. You will be surrounded by the country's extreme ethnic diversity as you visit different parts of the country. How much you choose to immerse yourself in the culture will largely define your experience here. Community-focussed ecotourism projects are the way to really get the most out of your trip. This is particularly true in the Ecuadorian Amazon and rural highlands.

■ Island Excursions in the Galápagos

 The Galápagos Islands are what put Ecuador on the map of world-class travel destinations. No trip to Ecuador would be complete without an excursion to the islands. It should be noted, however, that it will add considerably to your travel budget, as airline tickets from Quito cost nearly $400 during peak season, and the least-expensive five-day tours cost almost as much. There is a broad range of quality in cruise vessels and guide services, so it really depends on what you are looking for. Fortunately, there are countless travel agencies in Quito that can provide a variety of options tailored to your budget and travel parameters. See *Chapter 13, Galápagos Islands* for detailed information on tours and the islands themselves.

Tour Operators & Guides

Tour operators in Ecuador vary across the quality and price spectrum. You get what you pay for, so be sure to research the company well. Ask for references and a contract of services provided for what you are paying. Be sure that the company and guides are licensed, though this does not insure quality. Other than recommendations in this book, a good source of recommended tour operators and guides is with the South American Explorers Club in Quito (☎ and fax 2-225-228, explorer@seac.org.ec). Note that though Quito-based and sometimes foreign-owned tour operators may offer the highest quality services, the most genuine experiences and benefit to local communities are had with locally operated community-based ecotourism projects, discussed in the appropriate sections within this book.

Eco-Rating

Throughout this guidebook, I have highlighted accommodations and tour operators that incorporate at least some elements of true ecotourism and sustainable travel. Under the *Where to Stay* sections of each chapter, note that certain ecolodges will be highlighted with a ☆ symbol to designate that it offers a standard of ecological responsibility. Lodges that incorporate renewable energy, recycle programs and environmental education are highlighted appropriately. Tour guides and operators whose primary goals include environmental preservation, promoting community development, local guide training and use of such guides will also be highlighted with the symbol. Any tours, packages and accommodations listed as Community-Based Ecotourism (CBE) projects rank at the highest level of responsible travel.

Quito & Vicinity

Welcome to Quito, the city of eternal spring, bridge to Ecuador's past, and your gateway city. Even if you are not much of a city person, this World Heritage Site has a certain charm to it. Nestled within the Avenue of the Volcanoes, the breathtaking backdrop blends with colonial architecture to create a truly unique surrounding. At 9,319 feet, Quito is Latin America's second-highest capital, after La Paz in Bolivia, and the main hub for Ecuador's tourism traffic. Visit

Quito not only because it's your gateway city, but because it is well worth spending a couple of days here. While running errands or searching among the hundreds of adventure-travel outfitters, spend some time enjoying the city's delights.

Located along a narrow stretch of land in the northern Andean Sierras, Quito is the main hub between the coastal lowlands in the west, the mountains, and the upper Amazon Basin in the east. From here, it is possible to fly or drive to virtually anywhere on the mainland. The Andes Mountain Range geographically divides the country in two from north to south, and the Pan-American Highway, which passes through Quito, stretches along this line. Daily flights leave for just about every major city, including Guayaquil, Loja and Cuenca, to the Galápagos Islands and to Coca and Lago Agrio, deep in the jungle.

You might expect any place near the equator to be scorching hot. Quito, however, is surprisingly pleasant, with a year-round spring-like climate. This is due primarily to its high altitude. The days are usually warm, with afternoon sprinkles or showers, and nights are cool enough to require a sweater.

Keep a raincoat close at hand from January to May – it never snows in the city, but weather is always a factor in the Andes.

Quito is laid out through the central Sierra Valley in a north-south direction and is nearly 22 miles long and 2½ miles wide. Pichincha Volcano forms the western edge of town and, to the east, a deep gorge and the Machángara River borders Quito. Beautiful colonial architecture stills exists throughout "Old Town" Quito, a bustling center of activity, where most of the working class live. Modern Quito, or the "New City," lies to the north of the old town. This part of the city is the center for commerce, shopping, embassies, and nightlife, as well as for all travel-related businesses. The airport and more affluent residential sections are also here.

History

 Dating back to pre-Inca times, Quito is named after the peaceful **Quitu** people of the Sierras. With the arrival of the **Spanish**, Quito, which was at that time under the control of the Incas, was destroyed. The Spanish rebuilt it in 1534 and claimed it as seat of the royal crown, the Real Audencia de Quito. During the ensuing period of colonial rule, haciendas, which often sat on estates that stretched for hundreds of miles, were built throughout the countryside, and the indigenous people were forced to practice Catholicism and to serve the Spanish crown through forced labor, in the land they had previously owned. It wasn't until the early 1800s that Ecuador regained its independence, with the definitive battle fought along the foothills of Pichincha Volcano, just outside of Quito.

The capital now boasts more than 1.2 million inhabitants, second only to Guayaquil. Quito is a major colonial city and continues to exude an air of European aristocracy.

Historically, there has been a major rift between Quito and her coastal counterpart, Guayaquil. "Money is made in Guayaquil and spent in Quito," goes the saying that typifies this division. While Guayaquil represents international trade and the export economy, Quito is a center of administration, the Catholic Church and colonial history. The city also symbolizes the continuing friction between Ecuador and Peru, dating back to when the Inca empire was split between Atahualpa and his brother, Huascar, in Cuzco. Read more about this on page 8 of the *Introduction*.

Flora & Fauna

The spectacular Sierras and majestic volcanoes dominate the region surrounding Quito. Checkerboard farmland and *páramo* – or sub-alpine – grassland dot the countryside in all directions. In small biological reserves are wet cloud forests, complete with prolific bird life and incredible species diversity. As the altitude increases, stunted trees fall prey to harsh weather extremes and habitat for wildlife decreases. Quito itself is a large colonial capital, with the surrounding areas converted largely to agricultural lands. Vegetation includes Spanish imports, but there is also a healthy selection of indigenous tropical species.

Getting Here

■ By Air

Quito's international airport, **Mariscal Sucre**, is located at the far north end of town. Daily flights are easy to come by and the major international carriers include American Airlines, Continental, and SAETA (the Ecuadorian airline), as well as KLM, Lufthansa and Iberia from Europe. From the US, the Costa Rican Airline TACA, as well as Copa Airlines from Panama, offer rates competitive with the US-based airlines. Numerous additional companies offer flights to other destinations in Latin America and across the globe. The domestic terminal is adjacent to the international terminal. See page 35 for airline contact information. TAME is the main carrier for domestic flights, and offers tickets to all destinations throughout the country. Airport information, ☎ 2-2430-555. From the airport, catch a taxi into town. It should cost less than a few US dollars.

Quito airport is known as one of the most difficult airports in the world to fly into. It is situated in the middle of a heavily populated city, and surrounded on all sides by steep, volcanic peaks. Only the very best, most experienced pilots fly this route. Planning seems to be ongoing for a new airport outside the city's boundaries.

Quito & Vicinity

■ By Bus

 The **Terminal Terrestre**, in the Old City at Maldonado and Cumandá, offers connections to just about everywhere in Ecuador. Dozens of bus companies, as well as their offices, plus shops and restaurants, are located here. There is also an information booth (☎ 2-2570-529). Buses are readily available to all major destinations throughout the day, particularly in the morning. Expect to pay the equivalent of about $1 per hour of driving time.

Getting Around

■ By Taxi

 Outside of Quito's comprehensive public transportation network, the easiest way to get around the city itself is by **taxi** – they're convenient and relatively inexpensive. You can taxi virtually anywhere in the city for just a few dollars. Here, as in many places throughout the world, taxis are yellow and obvious.

 *Drivers at the airport will try to overcharge, especially to incoming and confused gringos. In fact, the amount they charge seems to correlate with how late at night it is, how disoriented you appear, and how much Spanish you speak. Do not pay more than $3-$4 for a trip from the airport to downtown modern Quito (New City).*

Any time you take a taxi in Quito, ask your driver what the price will be before you leave, or make sure the taximeter (*taximétro*) is on. Late at night, calling a taxi is safer and more reliable. Try **City Taxi** at ☎ 2-2633-333 or **Taxi Amigo** at ☎ 2-2222-222/2333-333. Tipping drivers in Ecuador is not normal etiquette, at least not with Europeans; for me, however, it is a habit. I tip if the driver is honest with the price and offers exceptional service.

If you have the money and would like to check out the city this way, it is possible to hire a taxi for a few hours. Expect to pay up to $10 per hour. It may not be worth your time or money, however, if you're already planning to take an organized city tour.

Urban Quito

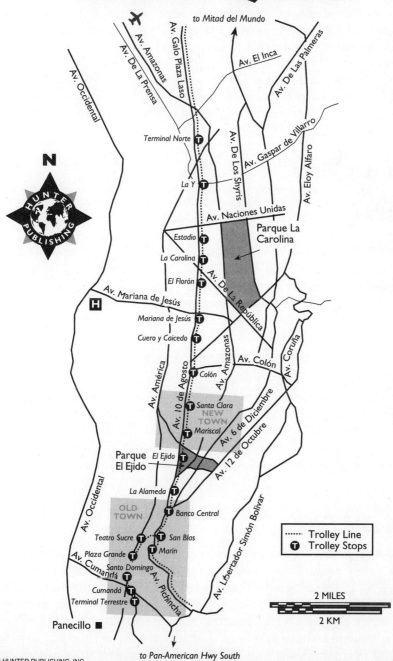

to Mitad del Mundo

Av. Galo Plaza Laso

Av. Amazonas

Av. De La Prensa

Av. Occidental

Av. El Inca

Av. De Las Palmeras

N

Av. De Los Shyris

Av. Gaspar de Villarro

Av. Eloy Alfaro

Terminal Norte

La Y

Av. Naciones Unidas

Parque La
Carolina

Estadio

La Carolina

El Florón

Av. De La República

Av. Mariana de Jesús

H

Mariana de Jesús

Cuero y Caicedo

Av. Coruña

Av. Amazonas

Av. Colón

Av. América

Av. 10 de Agosto

Colón

Santa Clara

**NEW
TOWN**

Mariscal

Av. 6 de Octubre

Av. 12 de Octubre

Parque
El Ejido

El Ejido

La Alameda

**OLD
TOWN**

Banco Central

Av. Occidental

Av. Libertador Simón Bolívar

Teatro Sucre

San Blas

Plaza Grande

Marín

Av. Cumandá

Santo Domingo

Av. Pichincha

Cumandá

Terminal Terrestre

Panecillo ■

to Pan-American Hwy South

...... Trolley Line
Ⓣ Trolley Stops

2 MILES

2 KM

Quito & Vicinity

HUNTER PUBLISHING

■ By Trolley

The double-length electric trolley – **El Trole** – is another fast, efficient, and very inexpensive means of transportation. It runs from the far north end of Quito near the airport directly to the southern extremes of Old Town along Av. 10 de Agosto. The trolley line operates from 6 am until midnight (10 pm on weekends).

Please be careful though – there are a lot of pickpockets. The trolley is probably best avoided if you are struggling with luggage or heavy backpacks.

■ By Bus

There are numerous **public buses** throughout the city that cost next to nothing, but they can be confusing and require a bit of research to use them effectively. The red and blue city buses run north and south along Amazonas, not to be confused with the red *selectivos,* which have various routes. Countrywide, buses travel anywhere there is a road, and then some. For a different view of the city, organized tours offer the opportunity to relax, see the sites, and free yourself from worrying about driving through the chaos of mad, runaway vehicles.

The New City, or *La Ciudad Nueva*, is where most of the modern amenities, inculding nice hotels, restaurants and cafés are located, though the historical highlights of Quito are in the Old City. Most travelers will find everything they require within walking distance of their hotel. Traffic is significant and it seems almost as though drivers speed up when pedestrians cross the street. Pay attention when crossing streets, but don't worry too much; just follow the locals and be ready to make a quick dash for the curb when necessary.

■ By Car

Unless you are extremely adventurous, driving around Quito is not recommended. Unless you are from New York, the drivers in this country, particularly the taxis, bring new meaning to the phrase "crazy driver." If you do decide to rent a car, most major international car-rental agencies, as well as few local ones, have offices in Quito. Prices range from $25 to over $100 per day, depending on the vehicle and length of rental. Of

Macaw, in the Oriente

Deforestation for agriculture & cattle in the coastal lowlands

A tapir in the Oriente, threatened throughout its Amazon range

Above: Horseback riding in the Pululahua Geobotanical Reserve

Below: Hacienda Guachala, one of the oldest, dating to the late 1500s

Above: Volcán Imbabura

Below: Market Day, Otavalo

Otavalo girls making sweaters for the market

course, better rates are given for weekly and monthly rentals. If you're heading into the backcountry, whether it's the Andes or the Oriente, be sure to rent a four-wheel-drive vehicle and make certain that insurance and mileage are included. Do a complete vehicle inspection ahead of time and note any problems. Check the spare and jack, as flats are common. Here's a list of rental agencies, most of which also have offices at the Hotel Colón, at Amazonas and Patria, opposite the Parque El Ejido:

Avis, at the airport, ☎ 2-2225-890.

Budget, Río Amazonas 1408 and Av. Colón, ☎ 2-2548-237 or 2-2221-814; at the airport, ☎ 2-2459-052 or 2-2240-763; at Hotel Colón, ☎ 2-2525-328.

Ecuacar, Av. Colón 1280 and Río Amazonas, ☎ 2-2529-781 or 2-2523-673; at the airport, ☎ 2-2247-298 or 2-2448-531.

Hertz, Veintimilla 928 and Amazonas, ☎ 2-2238-932; at Hotel Oro Verde, Luis Cordero 433, ☎ 2-2569-130; at the airport, ☎ 2-2254-257.

Premium, Orellana 1623 and 9 de Octubre, ☎ 2-2238-582 or 2-2552-897.

Visitor Information

The main artery of the central tourism and business district in Quito is Avenida Río Amazonas. This area is often referred to as New Town ("La Ciudad Nueva"). Most hotels are located around here, and it is just a matter of walking around a few square blocks to find just about anything you might need. Tour operators line the streets, while banks, ATMs and Internet cafés are plentiful. Restaurants and shops that cater to foreign travelers are also a dime a dozen. Photography stores, laundry facilities, and bookstores are all in close proximity.

Ecuador, situated on the equator, is often referred to as "El Centro del Mundo," the Center of the World, the place where the two halves of the world unite. At the crossroads of Avenidas J.L. Mera and Calama, just one block off Amazonas, is the area I call "El Centro del Gringo," where all traveler paths seem to join. Within a square block or two are numerous restaurants and hostels that cater to budget travelers, as well as Internet cafés, where it is cheap and easy to check and send e-mail or make international calls.

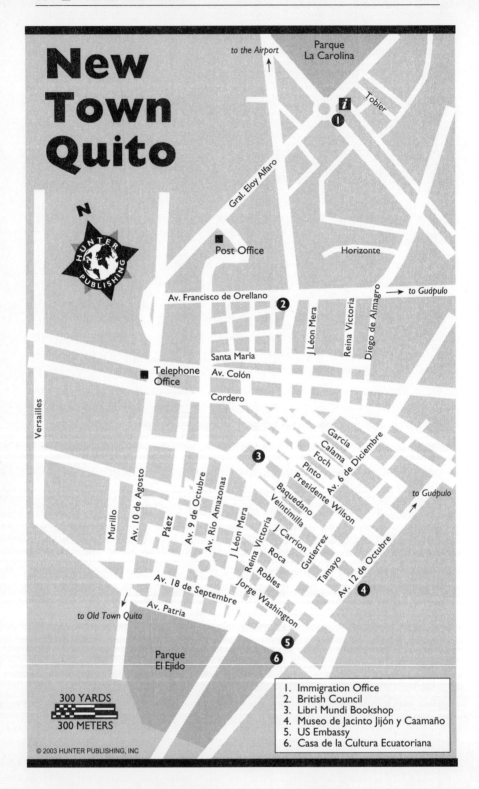

New Town Quito

to the Airport
Parque La Carolina
Tobier
i
1
Gral. Eloy Alfaro
N
HUNTER PUBLISHING
Post Office
Horizonte
Av. Francisco de Orellano
2
to Guápulo
J Léon Mera
Reina Victoria
Diego de Almagro
Santa María
Telephone Office
Av. Colón
Cordero
Versailles
García
Calama
Foch
Av. 6 de Diciembre
Pinto
3
Presidente Wilson
Baquedano
to Guápulo
Veintimilla
Murillo
Av. 10 de Agosto
Páez
Av. 9 de Octubre
Av. Río Amazonas
J Léon Mera
Reina Victoria
J Carrión
Roca
Gutierrez
Tamayo
Av. 12 de Octubre
Robles
4
Av. 18 de Septembre
Jorge Washington
to Old Town Quito
Av. Patria
5
Parque El Ejido
6

300 YARDS
300 METERS
© 2003 HUNTER PUBLISHING, INC

1. Immigration Office
2. British Council
3. Libri Mundi Bookshop
4. Museo de Jacinto Jijón y Caamaño
5. US Embassy
6. Casa de la Cultura Ecuatoriana

At night, this area is becoming increasingly dangerous for foreign travelers, and you can expect to be approached when it gets late. Reports of pickpockets and armed assaults are on the rise. Take a taxi after dark, even for short distances, unless you are with a group of people. In recent years, the state has added "tourism police" to the streets of this area, but that provides little assurance unless they are within sight.

The major embassies and consulates in Quito are listed on pages 45-47 in the *Travel Information* chapter.

■ Tourist Offices

The main **Minesterio de Turismo** tourist office (other than the one at the airport) is at Eloy Alfaro 1214 and Carlos Tobar, ☎ 2-2500-719/2507-555, ☎/fax 2-2507-564, www.vivecuador.com. The **Provincial Tourism Office**, Cámara Provincial de Turismo de Pichincha (CAPTUR), may be even more helpful, at Cordero and Reina Victoria near the Parque Gabriel Mistral, ☎ 2-2551-556. The **South American Explorers Club** is at J. Washington 311 and Plaza Gutiérrez, ☎/fax 2-2225-228, explorer@seac.org.ec, www.samexplo.org. This is a great place to track down updated travel information. The **British Council**, promoting learning opportunities and ideas exchange with the UK, including a language school and English-Spanish library, is located on Amazonas and La Niña (near Orellana), ☎ 2-2540-225, british4@uio.satnet.net. Open Monday through Friday. The **US Embassy** in Quito, ☎ 2-2562-890, after-hours, ☎ 2-2561-749, ☎/fax 2-2502-052, is located on the corner of 12 de Octubre and Patria. It's open Monday through Friday from 8 to 5.

■ Hospitals

The best hospitals in Quito include **Metropolitano** (Av. Mariana de Jesús and Av. Occidental; ☎ 2-2431-520). This is probably the best emergency facility, staffed by top professionals, and the costs are comparable to what you will pay at home. The other is **Hospital Voz Andes** (Villalengua 267, next to VozVoz Andes radio station, ☎ 2-2241-540). It has an emergency room and is staffed by American,

British and Ecuadorian physicians. For recommended physicians, inquire at the US or UK embassy or see the list in *Travel Information*, pages 45-47.

■ Post Offices, Call Centers & Internet Access

Though there are many post office branches in Quito, the main branch in New Town is located at Av. Colón and Almagro, open Mon-Fri from 7:30 to 5 and for the first half of the day on Saturday. There is also one at the airport. In the Old City, the main branch is on Espejo, between Guayaquil and Venezuela, and between New and Old Cities there is a branch behind the Santa Clara market at Ulloa and Dávalos.

The **Andinatel** office for international telephone calls in New Town is at 10 de Agosto and Colón, ☎ 2-2507-691 or 2-2509-025, and is open from 8 am to 10 pm. There are also branches at the international airport terminal and at the Terminal Terrestre (bus station).

Internet cafés abound in the New City, around Amazonas, JL Mera and Calama, offering easy and inexpensive communication options. And some of them serve up tasty dishes and drinks.

■ Banks

Banks vary in the services provided. Many change travelers checks, some offer ATM services, one may accept Visa while another works with MasterCard, either through an ATM or not. **Banco del Pacífico** has several branches. The main one is located on Naciones Unidas, between Amazonas and Shyris. There is another at Amazonas and Roca, and one in the mall El Jardín, on Amazonas between Mariana de Jesús and República. They change travelers checks (if you go later in the day, expect to wait in line) and accept MasterCard through the ATM machine. **Filanbanco**, at Amazonas and Robles, accepts Visa through the ATM machine and offers teller cash advances. **Banco de Pichincha**, at Amazonas and Colón, offersVisa cash advances. They also have a branch in the old city, near the Plaza de la Indepencia on Venezuela. **Banco Guayaquil** is on Colón and Reina Victoria, 3rd floor; they have a Visa ATM, with larger advances available through a teller. If

■ Maps

The **Instituto Geográfico Militar**, on Jiménez, near Parque El Ejido, sells the best topographic maps of Ecuador, which I refer to throughout this book (IGM maps). They are open from 8 am to 4 pm, Monday-Friday. To get there from 12 de Octubre, climb the hill on Jiménez, cross Colombia to Paz y Mino, go behind the military hospital, turn right and you're there.

Studying Spanish in Quito

Learning Spanish in Ecuador is a rewarding experience and being able to speak the language will afford you a great many opportunities to learn about the country, its people and its culture that you wouldn't otherwise have. Many tourists come to Quito just to study Spanish. There are numerous schools with various options for flexible schedules, from simply spending several hours per day with an instructor, to living with a local family and completely immersing yourself in the language. Check with the South American Explorers Club (☎ and fax 2-2225-228, explorer@ seac.org.ec) for recommended schools and instructors in Quito and elsewhere. Also see pages 54-55.

Touring & Sightseeing

■ Quito

 The city itself is filled with the wonders of history. When the conquistadors arrived here in hot pursuit of Rumiñahui in 1534, the Incan general – and last holdout against the Spanish – decided it was better to destroy the city and all of its secrets, rather than hand it over. After they had razed it to the ground, Pizarro's Lieutenant, Sebastián de Benalcazar, claimed the site and rebuilt Spain's seat of control out of the very ruins of the old empire. Little remains as evidence of pre-Columbian times, other than the stone foundations of the colonial city, most of which date to the 1700s. Though modern Quito has more of the comforts and amenities that foreign travelers desire, Old Town, or colonial Quito, offers a rich history and intriguing architecture, enough so that it has been deemed a World Heritage Site by UNESCO.

A Walking Tour

A great way to get a feel for Quito is a walking tour of the colonial section of town. The heart of it centers around the Plaza de la Independencia and includes architecture dating back to the mid-1500s. It is well worth spending a few hours exploring this unique area, wandering among the narrow, cobbled streets with their many plazas, churches, and museums.

Be forewarned that pickpockets have increased significantly over the last few years and are on the prowl for easy targets. Go in a group and stay alert. It would even be worth hiring a guide, both for added security and to gain a deeper appreciation of the area (see Tour Operators & Guides, pages 94-97). Leave your cash and credit cards at the hotel, don't carry an expensive camera or dress conspicuously. In fact, don't even bring a backpack, other than to carry water and souvenirs.

Once in colonial Quito, allow yourself to wander through history. Experience the religious influence of the Catholic Church as it mixes with ancient indigenous traditions and modern life. Colonial architecture, cobblestone byways and busy street vendors add to the ambiance. Remember, the sights and sounds are incredible enough, but the real adventure lies in the stories and history behind them. Learn well. The sites listed below are among the highlights and are relatively easy to navigate with a simple map, and even easier with a knowledgeable guide.

Plaza de la Independencia

This is a good starting point for a walking tour of colonial Quito. The Plaza de la Independencia is an attractive plaza, complete with palm trees, gardens, and a great view of the Virgin of Quito statue. There are plenty of benches on which to relax and watch the world go by. The

Old Town Quito

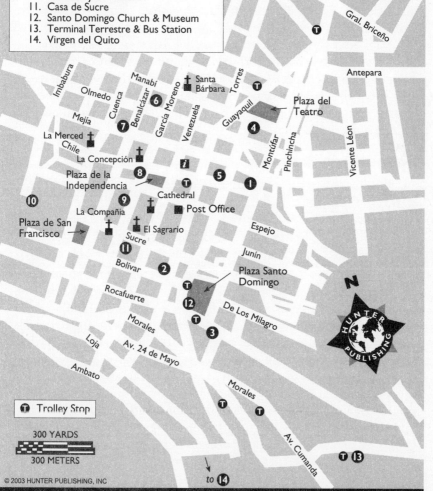

WHERE TO STAY

1. Viena Internacional
2. Real Audencia
3. Hotel Grand

● **OTHER SITES**

4. Teatro Sucre
5. San Agustin Church & Museum
6. Casa de Benalcázar
7. Museo Nacional de Arte Colonial
8. Palacio de Gobierno
9. Municipal Museum of Art & History
10. San Francisco Church,
    Monastery & Museum
11. Casa de Sucre
12. Santo Domingo Church & Museum
13. Terminal Terrestre & Bus Station
14. Virgen del Quito

Plaza del Teatro

La Basílica

$ Banco Central

Av. América

Av. 10 de Agosto

Gral. Briceño

Antepara

Imbabura

Olmedo

Cuenca

Benalcázar

Manabí

García Moreno

Santa Bárbara

Venezuela

Torres

Guayaquil

Plaza del Teatro

Vicente Léon

Mejía

Chile

La Merced

La Concepción

Plaza de la Independencia

La Compañia

Cathedral

Post Office

Montúfar

Pinchincha

Plaza de San Francisco

El Sagrario

Sucre

Espejo

Junín

Bolívar

Plaza Santo Domingo

Rocafuerte

De Los Milagro

Morales

Loja

Av. 24 de Mayo

Ambato

Morales

Av. Cumanda

T Trolley Stop

300 YARDS
300 METERS

N

to 14

HUNTER PUBLISHING

plaza covers one square block and is the location of the Presidential Palace and Cathedral. From here, you can stop and absorb a bit of history, but be aware of pickpockets.

Along the southwest edge of the plaza is the massive **Cathedral**, completed around 1565 and built of wood and adobe. The huge stone walls were erected much later, in the 1600s. Although less adorned than many of the other religious sites in Quito, the Cathedral is well decorated with works by some of Ecuador's finest early artists from the School of Quito. Historical plaques, presidential remains, and paintings reveal the city's rich and tumultuous history. The tower was added in the 20th century, and pictures of the construction period offer interesting insights. The Cathedral is open daily, except for a long midday lunch closure.

Situated on the northwest side of the plaza is the **Palacio de Gobierno**, or **Presidential Palace**, which was built in the 1700s and then later remodelled in the neoclassical style. Take note of the armed guards dressed in 19th-century uniforms (but carrying very modern semiautomatic weapons). You can enter the main courtyard, but that is all. The guards may not be smiling, but they didn't seem to mind my mother taking their picture. In fact, this is a great photo spot looking out over the plaza.

Plaza de San Francisco

As an alternative, this is another good starting point for a walking tour of colonial Quito. From here, you can visit the most interesting colonial churches, museums, and other buildings within just a couple of blocks in any direction. Each site is an amazing piece of the past in Ecuador's historical puzzle.

The plaza itself is a one-square-block cobblestone affair surrounded by typically whitewashed colonial buildings. While here, visit the impressive **Monastery of San Francisco**, which includes a remarkable display of churches, a school, a convent, and several courtyards. Construction on the buildings began in 1535 and was completed 70 years later. The site itself dates back to Inca royalty, having housed Huayna-Capac, his son Atahualpa, and Atahualpa's children before the city came crumbling down. You may wander through the magnificent church during services, but be considerate of the worshipers. You have entered the oldest church and largest colonial building in Quito. To the southeast is **Plaza de Santo Domingo**, with the church and monastery of the same name. The Plaza is located on Benalcazar between Bolívar and Sucre.

La Compañía

There are numerous churches, monasteries, and cathedrals in Quito, a testament to the influence of the Roman Catholic Church in Ecuador. La Compañía is by far the most ornate church in Quito and is a great source of pride for Quiteños. This church, built by Jesuits between the 17th and 18th centuries, took over 160 years to finish. It has been described as "Quito's Sistine Chapel," with awesome paintings on the vaulted ceilings and gold leaf-covered altars. The incredible amount of wealth required to create such a lavish manifestation of religion is obvious. It is easily one of the most magnificent churches in all of Latin America.

La Compañía is one block from the Plaza de la Independencia on Calle García Moreno.

Museums

Museo de Arte y Historia

While exploring colonial Quito, don't miss this museum, also known as the Municipal Museum. Inside you'll find an impressive collection of 16th- and 17th-century colonial art. The basement imprisoned the leaders of Ecuador's independence movement before they were executed in 1810. Eerie waxworks depict the somewhat disturbing scene of their murders.

The Municipal Museum is near the main plazas on Espejo 1147 and Benalcazar, ☎ 2-214-018; open Tue-Fri, 9-4, weekends, 10-4. There is a nominal admission fee.

Museo de Arte Colonial

Like the Museo de Arte y Historia, the Museum of Colonial Art includes an attractive display of colonial and religious art and furniture. The 17th-century building houses the work of some of Ecuador's finest painters and sculptors from the 16th to 18th centuries. This is a good museum to visit if you are an art or history enthusiast.

The Colonial Art Museum is a block from Independence Plaza at Cuenca and Mejia, ☎ 2-2212-297, open Tue-Fri, 9-5, and on weekends from 10-4. Admission is $3, with student discounts available.

Casa de Sucre

This is another museum worth visiting. It was once home to the Ecuadorian independence hero Antonio José de Sucre. The building has been nicely restored with antique furniture and includes a small museum and gift shop.

The Casa de Sucre is at Venezuela 573 and Sucre; ☎ 2-2952-860. Hours of operation vary. Admission is under $2.

The Guayasamín Foundation

World-renowned Oswaldo Guayasamín was arguably one of the most famous Ecuadorian painters. He graduated from the School of Fine Art in Quito as painter and sculptor, went on to exhibit all over the world, and was the recipient of a number of prestigious awards. His murals decorate the UNESCO headquarters in Paris, Barajas airport in Madrid and the Government and Legislative Palaces in his home-town of Quito. There is even an art museum dedicated to Guayasamín in Havana, Cuba. Sadly, he passed away in 1999, though his paintings are as popular as ever. Today, you can still find young Quiteño artists adopting his style and selling art throughout the country. The Guayasamín Foundation is at José Bosmediano 543, in El Batan, ☎ 2-2446-455, ☎/fax 2-2446-277. Open Monday-Saturday midday.

Casa de la Cultura Ecuatoriana

You can't miss the House of Ecuadorian Culture if you're anywhere near the Parque El Ejido, as it is a large, circular glass building. Inside are wonderful displays of indigenous musical instruments and traditional attire. The focus is on Ecuador, but other regions of the world are also included. A theater shows good international films (check the local and entertainment papers for schedule) and music is performed in the auditorium. This is the site of Ecuador's best museum, known as the Nacional del Banco Central del Ecuador, covering three floors and with numerous wonderful exhibits.

The museum is at Av. Patria and 12 de Octubre, ☎ 2-2565-808; 9 am-12:30 pm and 3-6:30 pm; admission $3 adults, $2 students. Guided tours in English are available.

Museo Jacinto de Jijón y Caamaño

Located nearby, in the library of the Catholic University (Universidad Católica) this museum has archeological exhibits, including pre-colonial and colonial artifacts and portraits. It is at Av. Patria and 12 de Octubre, open Mon-Fri, 9 am-4 pm, and Sat, 10 am-3 pm. There is a nominal entrance fee.

Museo de Ciencias Naturales

The kids will love this one. With a stuffed Andean condor to greet you, the Museum of Natural Sciences is a must for the natural-history buff or anyone unfamiliar with the region's flora and fauna. The comprehensive displays make it the best natural history museum in the country. Though not a huge museum, the fact that Ecuador has such a unique diversity of flora and fauna, spanning from the upper Amazon to the Andes to the Galápagos Islands, makes it truly one of a kind.

The museum is on Rumipamba 341 and Los Shyris, on the east side of Parque La Carolina, ☎ 2-2449-824. General hours of operation are Mon-Fri, 9-4:30, and Sat, 9-1; admission is less than $2, with student discounts available.

Vivarium

The Vivarium opened in 1989 as a center for research on amphibians and reptiles, and as a teaching facility to protect our endangered, scaled friends. It now features live animals such as boa constrictors, turtles, iguanas, and the deadly fer-de-lance snake.

The Vivarium is on Reina Victoria 1576 and Santa María, two blocks north of Colón, ☎ 2-2230-998, ☎/fax 2-2448-425, touzet@orstom.ecx. ec. Open Mon-Sat, 9-4. Admission is $2, and donations are appreciated.

Museo Amazonico

This is another worthwhile exhibit, geared toward protecting Ecuador's Oriente, through research on rainforest flora and fauna and education initiatives. Educational displays provide the opportunity to learn about the serious threats to what remains of Ecuador's Amazon basin.

The museum is at 12 de Octubre 1430 and Wilson and is open Mon-Fri, 8:30-6 (closed for lunch); ☎ 2-2506-247/2562-633.

Parks

There are many small and three main parks in the city, all of which offer a bit of green and escape from the surrounding traffic. From Old Town in the south, the smallest is **Parque Alameda**, offering shaded trees, an ancient observatory, and a statue in tribute to Simon Bolívar, the Venezuelan general that helped to liberate Ecuador from Spain.

Farther north, at the southern end of Av. Río Amazonas and bordering the main drag of New Town, is the larger **Parque El Ejido**, where locals relax and play on the weekends. It is a nice walk from downtown to the park, especially on weekends, when artwork is widely displayed and readily for sale. You'll see high-quality, high-value artwork, as well as less dramatic pieces. Fortunately, or unfortunately, depending on what you are looking for, it has also become swamped with tourist vendors selling everything under the equatorial sun. Step away from the booths, however, and the park remains peaceful and family-oriented, much as it always has been.

The largest of the main municipal parks, **Parque La Carolina**, is even farther north between Amazonas and Los Shyris, where República and Alfaro cross. Weekend activities include everything from kids monkeying around on the gym equipment to boating on a small lake. It is definitely a communal gathering place, something we don't often experience in North America. This is a great place to take the kids, but do not wander alone or in the remote parts of the park.

Quito's parks are not safe at night, or even during the day in sections that are remote and empty. However, if you are around groups of people and where the locals gather, relax and enjoy the day.

Public Spaces

Throughout your travels in Ecuador, and indeed in any Latin American country, you may notice that one common theme in any city or village is the central plaza or park. The importance of this public space as a driving social force cannot be overstated. It is a place of communing with friends, family and local residents; of relaxing under a shaded tree after church on Sunday; of romance; of gardens, benches, fountains and playing children. It is often an escape from the immediately surrounding busy streets and big buildings; And sometimes it is a place of local weekly markets.

Central plazas symbolize gathering and social pride, allowing locals to connect in ways that simply wouldn't exist without them. In Quito, they have evolved to enormous parks, complete with miniature lakes and playgrounds for children, but even in smaller towns and villages, these remnants of the colonial era remain. And they are often the best places to sit and absorb the local culture.

Vírgin of Quito

A great view of the city and surrounding countryside can be had at the statue of the Virgin of Quito on Panecillo Hill, or Cerro Panecillo. This landmark also provides for a good point of orientation from other sections of town. Note that Panecillo used to be a fairly dangerous hill to climb, as tourists were often assaulted in this relatively poor part of the city, but it is now guarded at the top and quite nice for an early morning panoramic photo. The statue of the Virgin looks minor from a distance but is quite impressive up close, especially as you climb the steps to the observation balcony. The kids will like it here. There are usually some souvenir and snack stands on the hill.

To get here, catch a taxi from anywhere in town to Panecillo Hill. Admission to enter the building is under $2, but views from the grounds are free and just as spectacular. There is a souvenir shop on the ground floor, but tacky trinkets are best avoided. There are public restrooms available across the parking lot; bring a few coins for the cleaning person, or for the person standing at the door pretending to be the cleaning person.

■ Around Quito

Guapulo Suburb

Where the flanks of the Andes form the main north-south boundaries of Quito, the Río Machángara cuts a deep canyon that forms the eastern border of the city. The relatively affluent Guapulo district is here, along Quito's mid-eastern edge. This area offers great views of the river valley below, as well as interesting urban sites, such as the **Basilica of Guapulo**, built during the colonial era in the 17th century. In addition to spectacular architecture and attractive décor, the basilica provided the foundation for Quito's renowned colonial art community. It is beautiful and well worth a visit.

El Mitad del Mundo (Equatorial Monument)

Don't forget to visit the "Middle of the World" during your stay; after all, it is the country's namesake and possibly the only chance you'll have to stand with one foot in the northern and one in the southern hemisphere. Lying just north of Quito, the equatorial monument features the equatorial line (of course), as demarcated by Charles-Marie de la Condamine and his French expedition in 1736. The paved area around the central monument has a bright yellow line that bisects the two hemispheres. The focal point of the monument is the **Museo-Etnografico**, a 98-foot-high multilevel museum topped with a giant brass globe. It has displays on the indigenous people of Ecuador that are as informative as they are interesting. Take the elevator to the top (if it's working) and then spiral your way down the many levels of exhibits.

Quito
& Surroundings

N

to Otavalo, Ibarra

Reserva Biológica Maquipucuna ■

Reserva Geobotánica Pululahua ■

Cochasqui ■

Tabacundo

Cayambe

Nanegalito

Calacalí

EQUATOR

Mindo

Pomasquí

Otón

Nono

Ascázubi

Calderón

El Quinche

Pichincha Mt ▲
15,728 ft/4,794 m

Zaruqui

Chiriboga

QUITO

Pifo

Mulauco

Papallacta Pass

Sangoiquí

Atacazo Mt ▲
14,642 ft/4,463 m

Pintag

Papallacta

Manuel Cornejo Astorga

Bosque Protector ■ Pasachoa

Reserva Ecológica Antisana ■

Tambillo

Alóag

Antisana Mt ▲
18,891 ft/5,758 m

Machachi

Corazón Mt ▲
15,708 ft/4,788 m

Sincholagua Mt ▲
16,053 ft/4,893 m

20 MILES

20 KM

Outside of the museum, wander around the park, which was modeled after a "typical" colonial town. In addition to restaurants, gift shops, and other tourist facilities, there is a huge model of colonial Quito, as well as a planetarium with regular shows. Note that the church within the park also has the yellow paint line running down its middle. Busloads of school children regularly visit the monument and park.

Solar Museum

In the nearby town of San Antonio is a small but impressive solar museum full of equatorial and solar exhibits. The showpiece is a solar chronometer that shows the precise time, day, and month of the year. Inquire with **Nuevo Mundo Expeditions** in Quito, as the museum is open only by appointment or as part of a prearranged tour.

To get there, head to San Antonio, less than an hour north of Quito on the highway to Mitad del Mundo. Ask at a tourist office for specific bus lines and schedules, as they may change (see *Visitor Information*, page 77). The museum is open Mon-Fri, 10-4, and weekends, 10-5. Admission is under $2.

A great way to visit El Mitad del Mundo is in conjunction with a trip to Pululahua Reserve (see page 98). Visit the ancient volcanic crater first for the best chance at good weather and great views – then see the equatorial monument on the way back.

Adventures near Quito

■ On Foot

Pasochoa Reserve

Less than an hour southeast of Quito, is a wonderful retreat within the nearest intact Andean humid forest reserve. Administered by one of Ecuador's most prominent conservation organizations, Fundación Natura, Pasochoa offers hiking opportunities at various levels of physical activity and a diverse range of interests for the birder and general nature enthusi-

Quito & Vicinity

ast. Numerous trails offer hikes from 30 minutes to eight hours in length. One trail reaches the summit of Pasochoa and takes about six hours to complete.

 Although a few of the trails are not too strenuous, you should spend at least a couple of days acclimatizing before attempting them. The high altitude and steep slopes can leave the average coastal resident quite short-winded.

Maps are available at the administrative entrance. See pages 98-99 for directions to the reserve.

Pichincha Volcano

Just west of Quito is Volcán Pichincha, the site of the historic battle that freed Ecuador from the clutches of Spain. It offers great views and a relatively strenuous, though not technically difficult, climb. Unfortunately, it has also been the site of attacks by thieves and armed bandits, so do not go alone. Check for recent reports from a local tour operator or the South American Explorers Club (☎/fax 2-225-228, explorer@seac.org.ec).

 Many of Ecuador's volcanoes are active and they make living in the Andes an adventure itself. After 339 years of dormancy, Volcán Pichincha became visibly active in 1998, creating a mushroom cloud near Quito and spreading a light blanket of ash over the entire city. Air traffic halted and there was brief concern over potential dangers of an eruption, though because of the crater's northwestern position, it is unlikely to threaten the city itself. And in November, 2002, El Reventador Volcano, 60 miles east of the colonial capital in the upper Amazon, created a cloud of ash 10 miles high that settled on the city and created a brief state of emergency. Much closer, Pichincha continues to rumble on occasion, a gentle reminder that nature has the last word.

Although Pichincha is still active and has recently dropped ash on Quito, experts do not expect any activity from it that would threaten Quito in the near future. The volcano has two climbable summits. **Gaugua Pichincha**, at 15,369 feet, is the lower of the two (but it's also the active one). Nevertheless, it does offer some spectacular views. To get there, take a taxi west out of Quito to the upper reaches of the city and start climbing via Cruz Loma. Allow about seven hours for the climb. Keep in mind that these poor suburbs can be dangerous. It is worth hiring a guide through a local outfitter (see pages 94-97).

The higher summit, **Rucu Pichincha**, at 15,676 feet, is the dormant cone and a bit farther away than its sister. Your best bet is to catch a taxi to the quaint village of Lloa. From the main plaza facing the volcano, follow the sign-posted road to the summit. It takes about eight hours to get to the refuge, where you can sleep and obtain water. Bring a sleeping bag and ask the caretaker if he will share his cooking facilities. The summit hike from the *refugio* is short, but the descent back to Lloa, which takes about three hours, is steep and strenuous. Once you are back on the main road in Lloa, walk down until you reach a fork. Wait for a truck to the outskirts of Quito, and catch a taxi from there.

Check around in Quito near Av. Amazonas for local outfitters or see the *Tour Operators & Guides* section below, pages 94-97.

■ On Horseback

Hoofing it through Pululahua National Reserve

Pulalahua offers perhaps the best riding within close proximity to Quito, as it is a massive reserve that is a world away from city life, nestled deep down in an extinct volcanic crater (see *Eco-Travel* section, page 98, for more details). Travel through geological history in this 4,000-year-old dormant volcano and witness human history with remains that pre-date even the Incas. For excellent horseback riding excursions in Pululahua, including deep gorges, dizzying views, thick cloud forest and local communities sunken at the bottom of a crater, contact the **Green Horse Ranch** in Quito, ☎ 2-2523-856, fax 2-2504-773, ranch@accessinter.net, www.horseranch.de. Bring warm clothing and rain gear. Lunch is provided on their one-day tours, and longer excursions are available in and around the crater. For the intrepid adventurer, Astrid at the Green Horse Ranch offers horse and trek trips of up to six days on the Mojanda Trail, complete with portions of a "nerve-wracking trail... through the most hallucinating and breathtaking landscapes you can possibly imagine." There are even longer trips of up to nine days.

■ On Wheels

 I wouldn't want to dodge traffic on a bicycle in Quito itself, but, once you leave the city, there is plenty of Andean countryside to explore by mountain bike or, for the more daring, by road bike. Check with local bicycle outfitters listed below for specific routes and guided tours or vehicle-supported travel.

Tour Operators & Guides

The following Quito-based outfitters specialize in various activities and different regions in Ecuador. Quite a few of them operate or arrange trips to the Andes, Amazon and Galápagos. Many other operators along Amazonas and the surrounding Mariscal District offer similar trips of decent quality. Check around to compare price and quality, ask for references, a written contract and use the South American Explorer's Club (☎ and fax 2-2225-228, explorer@seac.org. ec) for recent recommendations and reports.

Metropolitan Touring, Av. República de El Salvador 970 and Naciones Unidas, in the Hilton Colón, ☎ 2-2463-680, ☎/fax 2-2464-702, www.metropolitan-touring.com, smb@metropolitan.com.ec, is by far the largest and best-known tour operator in Ecuador, offering everything from cultural city tours to first-class Galápagos trips and responsible high-end rainforest excursions. They specialize in large groups.

On a much smaller scale is **Safari Ecuador**, Calama 380 and J.L. Mera, ☎ 2-2552-505, fax 2-2223-381; or Roca Pasaje 630 and Amazonas, ☎ 2-2234-799, ☎/fax 2-2220-426, admin@safari.com.ec, www.safari.com.ec. From the US, ☎ 800-434-8182. They specialize in volcano climbs and provide a wide variety of services, from one-day natural and cultural tours to multi-day jungle trips. Everyone that works for Safari, which is jointly operated by British and Ecuadorian owners, is friendly and knowledgeable. Climbing guides are certified by ASEGUIM (the Association of Mountain Guides of Ecuador).

Andisimo Travel, Av. 9 de Octubre 479, ☎ 2-2508-347, www. andisimo.com, tours@andisimo.com, offers climbing and trekking throughout the Andes. They also rent and sell climbing and outdoor gear. Other climbing/mountaineering outfitters include **La**

Companía de Guías, J. Washington and 6 de Diciembre, ☎ 2-2533-779, a top-quality ASEGUIM-certified company. Guides are very professional and speak several languages. This organization is at the high end of the cost spectrum for climbing, but is worth the price. **Surtrek**, in Quito at Amazonas 897 and Wilson, ☎ 2-2561-129, www.surtrek.com, info@surtrek.de, offers comparable expertise, is ASEGUIM-certified, and is well known for its climbing and trekking trips.

For trips into the Oriente, **Native Life Tours**, Foch E4-167 and Amazonas in Quito, ☎ 2-2505-158, 2-2550-836, or 2-2236-320, ☎/fax 2-2229-077, natlife1@natlife.com.ec, offers excursions on Río Aguarico and Río Cuyabeno. Ecuadorian-owned and -operated, the company is one of those "family feel" operations that is always a pleasure to recommend. They have three main, all-inclusive trips ranging in length from three to seven nights, with varying levels of private accommodations. Itineraries are varied to suit individual needs, and guides are professional and knowledgeable – the best bet for a budget-oriented, deep-jungle enthusiast.

One of the companies most sensitive to ecology and conservation is **Tropic Ecological Adventures**, Av. República E7-320 and Almagro, in the Edificio Taurus, ☎ 2-2234-594 or 2-2225-907, ☎/fax 2-2560-756, tropic@uio.satnet.net, www.tropiceco.com. Working with local groups, this professional outfit is about as responsible as they come. They offer top-quality trips into the jungle, work closely with local indigenous communities and are a good contact for community-based ecotourism projects in the Cuyabeno region. They are a great option if you want to visit natives while maintaining a high degree of cultural sensitivity.

Kempery Tours, at Pinto 539 and Amazonas in Quito, ☎ 2-2226-583, ☎/fax 2-2226-715, www.kempery.com, kempery@kempery.com. offers solid jungle trips in conjunction with the Huaorani, in and around the Cuyabeno Ecological Reserve. They also arrange Andes and Galápagos excursions.

The Ecuadorian-owned **Nuevo Mundo Travel and Tours**, Av. Coruña 1349, ☎ 2-2552-617, 2-2553-826, ☎/fax 2-2565-261, nmundo@uio.telconet.net, is very high-end, professional and conservation-oriented. Their guides are exceptional and they are at the pricey end of the market, but you get what you pay for. The company's president, Oswaldo Muñoz, is a founding member of the Ecuadorian Ecotourism Association and very personable. Nuevo Mundo specializes in cultural and natural-history tours to the Cuyabeno Ecological Reserve, deep in the Oriente, and organizes Andean treks, horseback rides, and Galápagos excursions. Other destinations include El Mitad del Mundo and the solar museum.

Also on the higher end is **Canodros**, at Av. Portugal 448 and Isabel de Aldaz, ☎ 2-2256-759, www.canodros.com, eco-tourism1@ecu.net. ec. Their specialty is the Galápagos Islands and the new, world-class ecotoursim jungle lodge at Kapawi Ecological Reserve (see page 378).

Klein Tours specializes in mid-plus to high-end custom group tours. With multi-lingual guides and their own vessels in the Galápagos Islands, this is a good company to travel with. They also offer various city tours in Quito and day-excursions to surrounding cities. In the jungle they offer several different luxury options, all centered around impressive ecolodges. They are located at Av. Los Shyris 1000 and Holanda, ☎ 2-2430-345, ☎/fax 2-2442-389, www.kleintours.com, ecuador@kleintours.com.ec.

Ecoventura has been around for awhile, at Colón 535 and 6 de Diciembre, ☎ 2-2507-408, from the US, 800-633-7972, www. ecoventura.com, info@galapagosnetwork.com. Specializing in the Galápagos Islands, they offer trips and services in other areas as well.

Ecuadorian Tours, Av. Amazonas 329 and J. Washington, ☎ 2-2560-488 or 2-2560-494, ☎/fax 2-2501-067, www.ecuadoriantours. com, ecuadorian@accessinter.net, is another highly respected outfitter offering various services, including Quito city and museum tours. They also participate in the Ecuadorian Ecotourism Association.

Angermeyers Enchanted Expeditions, Foch 726 and Amazonas, ☎ 2-2569-960, ☎/fax 2-2569-956, www.angermeyer.com, angermeyer@ accessinter.net or angerm1@ecnet.ec, offers various tours to the Oriente and the Andes, as well as Galápagos excursions.

Explorandes, at Wilson 537 and Diego de Almagro, ☎ 2-2556-936, explora@hoy.net, does just about everything. In addition to climbing and trekking, they offer rafting trips near Quito as well as jungle trips in the Oriente.

The German-owned **Ranft Turismo**, www.ranfturismo.com, ecuador@ranfturismo.com, offers tours to pretty much everywhere in Ecuador. I can't vouch for the quality of their organization, but they have a great website.

Quasar Nautica-Galápagos Expeditions, ☎ 2-2441-550, ☎/fax 2-2436-625, in the US, ☎ 800-247-2925, Carlos Montúfar E14-15 and La Cumbre, www.quasarnautica.com, qnautic1@ecnet.ec, offers luxury-class yachts and sailing vessels with excellent guide and crew services. Inquire about their diving tours. They also offer custom services for group travel to the Andes and jungle trips.

Pre-dating most Galápagos inhabitants is **Rolf Wittmer** of **Wittmer Turismo**, Mariscal Fosh E7-81 and Diego de Almagro, ☎ 2-2526-938, ☎/fax 2-2228-520, www.rolfwittmertiptoptours.com. His family offers tourist-level cruises and an economy-class sailing vessel. They will be sure to emphasize the early human history of the islands, as the owners' mother, Margaret Wittmer, was one of the earliest inhabitants of Floreana Island.

Galacruises, J. Washington 748, between Amazonas and 9 de Octubre, ☎ 2-2556-036, ☎/fax 2-2224-893, www.galapagosseaman. com.ec, seaman@uio.satnet.net, operate the comfortable mid-range vessel, *Sea Man*. Freddie the *panga* (boat taxi) driver is always good for a laugh and for evening island activities if you twist his arm.

For horseback riding around Pululahua Crater and Geobotanical Reserve, contact the **Green Horse Ranch**, ☎ 2-2523-856, ☎/fax 2-2504-773, ranch@accessinter.net, www.horseranch.de. Astrid Muller provides top-quality trips into the crater, as well as extended excursions of up to 15 days. Prices range from $50 to $65 per day.

For mountain biking around Quito, try **The Biking Dutchman**, Foch 714 and J.L. Mera, ☎ 2-2568-323, ☎/fax 2-2567-008, dutchman@ uio.satnet.net, www.bikingdutchman.com. They offer the best equipment with top-of-the-line components. Customized, full-package trips are available.

For tours, as well as sales, parts, repairs and general biking information, try **Biciteca y Renta Bike**, at Av. Brasil 1612 and Edmundo Carvajal, ☎ 2-2241-687. They also rent bikes.

See the *Tour Operators & Guides* sections in specific chapters for more information on tour operators to various regions, such as the Galápagos and the Oriente.

Eco-Travel

■ Reserves

Pululahua Geobotanical Reserve

 The **Pululahua Crater** is an excellent day-excursion from Quito. Just a couple of miles beyond the Mitad del Mundo monument lies this 8,250-acre reserve, protected primarily by the steep slopes of the extinct volcanic caldera. When the volcano collapsed in ancient times, it left an enormous cone over 1,000 feet deep. Agriculture dominates the flat and fertile crater valley, corn and sugarcane being the predominant crops. Moist Pacific winds from the west provide a variety of microclimates and blanket Puluhahua's slopes with thick native vegetation.

Visit the reserve early in the day for the best views, before the afternoon clouds engulf the crater. Views or not, the experience is breathtaking. There are two cones within the crater: **Loma Pondona**, the larger of the two, and **Loma El Chio**. A good way to see both cones is by driving along the rim, which offers magnificent views of the entire caldera, or you can take a trail down to the valley floor, where there are opportunities for bird-watching in the thick vegetation. It may seem like an easy descent, but don't forget about the return climb. Bring some water. You can also arrange for a tour from Quito in conjunction with a trip to the Mitad del Mundo monument. See *Adventures on Horseback,* page 93, for an exciting way to visit the crater.

Just a couple of miles north of Mitad del Mundo on the road to Calacalí is a marked turnout to the right that accesses the crater's rim. This is the entry point for most tour buses. Closer to Calacalí is a small, unmarked dirt road on the right, which is the entrance road down into the crater. It is obscure, as well as being a very rough road. Ask around or go with a guide. Admission is about US$5.

Pasochoa Forest Reserve

Pasochoa has one of the few remaining stands of native Andean humid forest. It's a private reserve just 45 minutes southeast of Quito. Although small (only 988 acres), it is a great place to find nature in close proximity to Quito and to try out that new set of high-altitude lungs. Pasochoa is one of the only areas near Quito with trails through relatively untouched forest and is a popular destination for environmental education programs. The reserve is located along the northern slope of the extinct Pasochoa Volcano (13,734 feet) and is home to abundant flora and bird life.

The reserve is managed by Fundación Natura, Ecuador's major non-governmental environmental organization. Entrance-fee proceeds go toward the protection and administration of the reserve. Weekends at Pasochoa are often crowded, and early mornings are best for the avid birder.

From Quito, there are two main ways to get to the village of Amaguaña, where the turn-off to Pasochoa Reserve is located. It is less than an hour from Quito by car. There are buses from colonial Quito, but you are better off taking a taxi (be sure the driver knows how to get there), or make arrangements through Fundación Natura for specific driving directions. Once in Amaguaña, a signed cobblestone road leads to the reserve entrance a few miles away. Locals can help point you in the proper direction. The entrance fee is $7. Camping ($3) and cooking facilities ($5) are also available. There's an information center with decent displays, a restroom, and picnic and barbecue areas. Take your trash with you when you leave. Fundación Natura's office in Quito is on America 5653 and Voz Andes, ☎ 2-2447-341.

■ Hot Springs

Papallacta Hot Springs

 Baños de Papallacta is a relaxing natural hot springs resort. I recommend going on a weekday, as the weekends are often pretty crowded with Quiteños trying to escape the city streets. The hot springs include several clean thermal pools surrounded by trees and greenery, which add to the overall feeling of escape. On a clear day, the views of the snowcapped Antisana Volcano are spectacular. Facilities at the springs include showers, a restroom, changing rooms, and a restaurant that specializes in farm-raised trout. The restaurant is nice, but the food is a bit overpriced and nothing to rave about. There is a good, moderately priced hotel here as well, the Termas de Papallacta Hotel, right next to the entrance to the baths. Papallacta is also a great place to wind down after a long journey from the Oriente before returning to the city. Visit www.goecuador.com/termas for more information.

Quito & Vicinity

To get there, take Route 28, the road from Quito, through Baeza and into the northern Oriente, which passes near Papallacta. Head 37 miles east of Quito and .62 mile from the road to Baeza. From the small town of Papallacta, turn onto the well-marked road west of town and meander up past the trout farm to the prominent entrance.

The Quito office is at Foch 635 and Reina Victoria, ☎ 2-2557-850, ☎/fax 2-2557-850. Admission to the developed facilities is about $3. There are lockers for personal belongings.

Where to Stay

ACCOMMODATIONS PRICE SCALE	
Unless otherwise noted, prices are per room, up to double occupancy. Some prices are per person, particularly with all-inclusive packages, but these generally include meals, lodging, guide services and other amenities.	
$	Under $25
$$	$26 to $50
$$$	$51 to $100
$$$$	Over $100

■ Old Town

 In colonial Quito, the **Hotel Grand**, at Rocafuerte 1001 and Ponton, ☎ 2-2210-192, is a family-operated establishment popular with budget travelers. This is a good place to meet a friendly Ecuadorian family and other backpacking travelers. Choose private or shared bath with basic, clean rooms. Amenities also include a restaurant and laundry service. Rates are about $10 per night. $

The **Hotel Real Audencia**, on the corner of Plaza Santo Domingo at Bolívar 220 and Guayaquil, ☎ 2-2950-590, ☎/fax 2-2580-213, is the best value in the old part of town. Clean rooms complement private baths with hot water, telephone, and TV. The dining room offers a fabulous view, and there is a bar on the premises. Rates average $15 per night. $

Comfortable and popular is the **Hotel Viena Internacional**, at Flores 600 and Chile, ☎ 2-2954-860. All rooms include private baths, hot water, and telephones. Simple amenities such as the restaurant and book exchange are adequate for inexpensive accommodations in colonial Quito. Rates average $15 per night. $

■ New Town

Budget Hostels

New Town (La Ciudad Nueva) has several small hostels that are ideal for the budget traveler. Many have dorm-style accommodations and some have private rooms. Make sure you bring earplugs if you are a light sleeper.

The **Residencial Marsella**, just east of Parque la Alameda at Los Ríos 2035 and Julio Castro, ☎ 2-2515-884, is popular with backpackers. This hotel is often full during peak season. Rooms vary considerably but generally are clean, with hot water. Check out the rooftop views. From here, it's not much of a walk to Amazonas and the main tourist facilities. Rates average $10 per night. $

For a mellow, enjoyable, and smoke-free (other than outside on the patio) budget hostel environment, try **Hostal El Taxo**, at Foch 909 and Luis Cordero, near Amazonas, ☎ 2-2225-593, www.hostaleltaxo. com, hostaleltaxo@yahoo.com. With new owners, you'll still find interesting characters floating around here, travel services, a kitchen, cable TV, a small library (it's hidden off the dining room – ask for directions!) and a lounge with a great fireplace. In the front yard, enjoy bamboo architecture and a new music stage with excellent acoustics. An attached bar/café with a wood-burning pizza oven complements the musical festivities. Rates average under $10 per night. $

☆ A great choice for those on a budget is **La Casa de Eliza**, at Isabel La Catolica 1559 and Coruña, ☎ 2-2226-602, manteca@uio.satnet. net, associated with Cerro Golondrinas Cloudforest Conservation Project. Eliza Manteca, who founded the project, offers several comfortable budget rooms, as well as laundry and kitchen services. The friendly staff will make you feel at home and help arrange treks through northern Ecuador. Rates average $10 a night. $

The popular **Magic Bean**, located at Foch E5-08 and Juan León Mera, ☎ 2-2566-181, magic@ecuadorexplorer.com, www.ecuadorexplorer. com/magic, is American-owned and centrally located. Although clean and often full, the atmosphere is a bit stiff. I would rather eat at its (excellent) restaurant than stay at the hotel. Don't be surprised when they show you photographs of the rooms instead of actually taking you to see them in person. Nevertheless, the place is tidy, secure, and, overall, good value. Rates average $10 a night. $

A recent renovation has received positive reviews at the **Crossroads Café and Hostal**, Foch E5-23 (678) and Juan León Mera, ☎ 2-2234-735, www.crossroadshostal.com, info@crossroadshostal.com. American-owned, this is one of the better budget choices, with locked storage space, shared baths with hot water, a good restaurant, garden and patio, kitchen access and cable TV in the lounge.

Bed & Breakfasts & Hotels

A very friendly, family-style B&B is the **Posada del Maple**, at Juan Rodriguez E8-49 and 6 de Diciembre, ☎ 2-2544-507, www.posadadelmaple.com, admin@posadadelmaple.com. The pleasant rooms are all different; several open up onto covered patio areas or meandering stairways. Rooms range in size from singles to quadruples and include private baths and hot water. Cable TV is offered downstairs in a common room, and additional social areas are located in the adjacent restaurant. This is a nice place to stay if you want to step up from the hostel category without paying too much more. Plan to spend at least $15 a night; breakfast is included in the price. $

Formerly known as Posada del Maple 2, the recently renamed **Hostal Alcalá**, at Luis Cordero E5-48 [1187] and Reina Victoria, ☎ 2-2227-396, www.alcalahostal.com, admin@posadadelmaple.com, is just a few blocks away and under the same management. Very clean and comfortable facilities complement modern rooms and a pleasant environment. Rooms vary from an eight-person dorm-style room with a shared bath, to doubles and a matrimonial suite. Thanks to a nearby disco, the Posada can be just a bit noisy on weekends, but the atmosphere and accommodations more than make up for it. Rates vary, but expect to pay at least $15 a night. $

One of the better accommodations for a great price is the bright **Casa Sol Bed-and-Breakfast**, at Calama 127 and Av. 6 de Diciembre, ☎ 2-2230-798, ☎/fax 2-2223-383, info@lacasasol.com, www.lacasasol.com. Owned and operated by an indigenous couple from Otavalo, Casa Sol offers a wonderful atmosphere in a charming building, just a couple of blocks from all the activity. Very clean and comfortable rooms are centered around a garden patio and have private or shared baths. Breakfast is included, as is access to a common reading room, a fireplace, and tour services. They also offer a shuttle service to and from the airport, but at $10, you're better off arranging a taxi yourself. Expect to pay at least $15 a night. $

The centrally located **Alston Inn**, at Juan León Mera N. 23-41 and Veintimilla, ☎/fax 2-2229-955 or ☎/fax 2-2508-956, www.angelfire. com/de/alston, alston@uio.satnet.net, is clean, friendly, and comfortable. Bordering on modern, it is somewhat lacking in character. The Alston is ideally located if you're looking to get oriented in Quito. Rooms include private baths, hot water, telephones, and TVs. Good value. Rates average $20 a night. $

In a quieter location is the **Hostal Sierra Nevada**, located at Jaoquin Pinto 637 and Luis Cordero, ☎ 2-2553-658, ☎/fax 2-2554-936, snevada@accessinter.net, www.hotelsierranevada.com/hostal. html. Clean and modern, the Sierra Nevada has the advantage of being situated on the quieter side of the main drag, Amazonas. There are 20 comfortable rooms and well-decorated but simple facilities, with an adjacent travel service specializing in climbing adventures. Additional bonuses include phone, fax, laundry and e-mail services, as well as gardens, communal areas and rooms with private hot water baths. Rates average $15 a night. $

Café Cultura, at Robles 513 and Reina Victoria, ☎ 2-2224-271, ☎/fax 2-2224-271, info@cafecultura.com, www.cafecultura.com, is a colonial home converted into a lovely hotel. British-owned, it's situated above a restaurant of the same name, with a garden patio that is a great spot for breakfast and afternoon tea. Rooms are quite comfortable. It's popular, so call ahead. Rates range from $25 to $50 per night. $$

Hostal Charles Darwin is a wonderful bed and breakfast with friendly Ecuadorian owners, located at La Colina 304 and Orellana (enter from 6 de Diciembre and Coruña), ☎ 2-2234-323, or 2-2529-384, ☎/fax 2-2529-384, chdarwin@ecuanex.net.ec. This B&B is set back a few blocks on a side street, away from the hustle and bustle of Amazonas. The modern but quaint rooms are part of a family home that centers around a lovely garden patio, perfect for enjoying a cup of coffee. Rooms have private baths, with plenty of hot water, and cable TV. Complimentary breakfast, including great coffee, freshly squeezed fruit juices and croissants. The owners are extremely nice and helpful (they don't speak a lot of English though). Call ahead, as the Darwin is often full with tour groups during peak season. Also, make sure the taxi driver knows how to get here before starting the fare on the meter. With rooms that run $25 to $50 per night, it is one of the better values. $$

A relative newcomer is **La Cartuja**, at Leonidas Plaza 170 and 18 de Septiembre, ☎ 2-2523-577/3721, ☎/fax 2-2226-391, cartuja@uio. satnet.net, www.hotelacartuja.com. It's located at the site of the former British Embassy. The young couple from Spain who own it has created a very quaint and pleasant B&B, complete with lovely, comfortable rooms and a Spanish-style garden patio. Restaurant, laundry and other modern facilities are also available. Expect to pay $25-$40. $$

Moving on up, **Mansión del Ángel**, at Wilson E5-29 and Juan León Mera, ☎ 2-2557-721, ☎/fax 2-2237-819, is an elegantly renovated colonial building. The French design is exquisite, and you may feel as if you are in a museum, rather than a hotel. It's brightly decorated, with antique furniture and lots of cushions, or fluff, shall we say. The patio upstairs is particularly nice. Amenities include full-size bathrooms with hair dryers and robes. Room prices run $50 to $100 per night. $$$

Among the less expensive of the "luxury" hotels is the **Hotel Tambo Real**, at 12 de Octubre and Patria, across from the US Embassy, ☎ 2-2563-824, ☎/fax 2-2554-964. It has 24-hour room service and, as with several of the top-end hotels, a casino. Room prices range from $50 to $100 per night. $$$

☆ **Hotel Sebastián**, with a European flare, is among the best values among the modern accommodations, at Almagro 822 and Cordero, ☎ 2-2222-400 or 2-2222-300, ☎/fax 2-2222-500, hsebast1@ hsebastion.com.ec. With 56 rooms, it has an intimate feel, and is priced well. The rooms, some with balconies and great views, have all the amenities of a luxury hotel without the extra fluff. Meals are good, purified water is safe to drink directly out of the tap, and organic food is served at the café and restaurant. Hotel Sebastián is popular with the better tour operators. Room prices run $50 to $100 per night. $$$

A comparable luxury hotel is the **Chalet Suisse**, at Reina Victoria 312 and Calama, ☎ 2-2562-700, ☎/fax 2-2563-966, www. hotelchaletsuisse.com, which includes a sauna and exercise room. I have not eaten in the restaurant, but the food is French, and the staff claims to have fed, among others, King Juan Carlos II of Spain, Princess Caroline of Monaco and various South American presidents – if that whets your appetite. As with many of the luxury hotels, you can spend money and gamble the night away in the casino, although this is far from Las Vegas. There are plenty of more exciting options in town. Rooms are in the $50-to-$100 category. $$$

The upscale **Hotel Colón Internacional** – a Hilton – is prominently located at Amazonas and Patria, opposite the Parque El Ejido, ☎ 2-2561-333 or 2-2560-666, ☎/fax 2-2563-903. The Colón is one of the largest luxury hotels. It is popular with Metropolitan Touring, Ecuador's largest travel agent and tour operator, as well as foreign diplomats and affluent Quiteños. The Colón has everything you could ever want in a hotel, from hair salon to massage parlor, swimming pool, exercise room, and even a discotheque. There's a coffee shop and the restaurants serve great food, but I have heard that the service is less than the best. The 450 rooms with views vary in price but start at $100. $$$$

Among the larger of the luxury hotels is the centrally located **Hotel Alameda Real**, at Roca Pasaje 653 and Amazonas, ☎ 2-2562-345, ☎/fax 2-2565-759, apartec@uio.satnet.net. Many of the big rooms have kitchenettes and balcony views. Additional amenities include a recommended restaurant, bar, café, and casino. It is highly regarded by upscale clients and, overall, is quite beautiful. Room rates start at $100. $$$$

Oro Verde was one of the reigning champions and a luxury five-star hotel, complete with high-end international eateries and stores, until unceremoniously dethroned by the monster new JW Marriott. Located at Orellana and Amazonas (you can't miss it), ☎ 2-2566-497, ☎/fax 2-2569-189, ecovq@uio.satnet.net, the Oro Verde has 203 rooms and 37 suites. Expect to find the upper echelon business clientele here. $$$$

A great luxury hotel away from the fast pace of Amazonas is the **Hotel Quito**, at Gonzalez Suarez 2500 and 12 de Octubre, ☎ 2-2544-600 or 2-2567-284, www.hotelquito.com, hotelquito@orotels.com. It features all the amenities of the best hotels, but is in a quieter part of town and offers a spectacular view. This is the place to go if you want to stay at a luxury hotel away from downtown. Rates start at $100. $$$$

Outside Quito

If you want to avoid the hustle and bustle of Quito and are in the vicinity of Pululahua Crater, try the nearby **Hostería Alemania**, situated outside of town just before the Mitad del Mundo (Equatorial Monument) on the road from Quito, ☎ 2-2394-243. It has comfortable rooms, a ranch-like atmosphere, and friendly owners. The restaurant serves an excellent trout dinner. Rooms range from $10 to $25 per night. $

Another nearby retreat is **San Jorge** (in the US, ☎ 877-565-2596; outside the US, ☎ 203-263-0705, www.eco-lodgesanjorge.com, info@ eco-lodgesanjorge.com). This is a recently converted 18th-century farm, located in the foothills of the Pichinchas, 10 minutes outside of the city and high above the valley of Quito. This beautiful lodge and nature retreat consists of 375 acres on the San Jorge Botanical Reserve. You'll find Spanish architecture, a relaxing atmosphere and attractive garden patios, along with 25 cozy rooms that include private baths and rustic stone fireplaces in each suite or cabin. There is a heated swimming pool, sauna, Turkish bath, hydromassage pool and a restaurant that offers both international and Ecuadorian cuisine. They can also arrange a variety of adventure excursions on foot, bike or horseback into the surrounding area.

Staying for Long?

If you are staying in Quito for any length of time, you may prefer to rent your own apartment or reside with a local family. Either way, Quito has plenty of great options. Check in with the **South American Explorers Club**, at G Washington 311, ☎ 2-2225-228, www.samexplo.org, explorer@ saec.org.ec. A home stay is nearly as cheap as a stay at the budget hostels, and it's much more social.

■ Camping

The **Pasochoa Forest Reserve**, managed by Fundación Natura, Ecuador's major non-governmental environmental organization, offers a nice getaway within close proximity to Quito. Camping is permitted in designated sites behind the Education Center and near where the trails begin. The fee to camp is $3 and cooking facilities in a simple hostel that also features bunk beds and showers cost $5. Pack everything in and out. See *Eco-Travel*, page 98-99, for more detailed information and how to get there.

Where to Eat

The vast majority of eateries in Quito are in the new part of the city. Those in the Old City tend to cater mostly to locals, and hygiene and quality can be dubious. Modern Quito, however, provides an array of international cuisine, particularly in the more tourist-oriented section of town near Amazonas. The best fine dining is found in the luxury hotels. Some of the area's new foreign restaurants provide better food and sanitary conditions than the local establishments, as they cater to the traveler and are the result of foreign capital. Still, there are a few good Ecuadorian cuisine options.

For good, typical Ecuadorian food and decent portions try **Mama Clorinda**, at Reina Victoria and Calama, ☎ 2-2544-362. Prices are very inexpensive by Western standards, and the staff is efficient and friendly. This is a great, centrally located option for the budget traveler. The *llapingachos* (pancake-like potato, onion and cheese patties) are particularly tasty.

Experience live music many nights at **Rincón La Ronda**, Belo Horizonte 400 and Almagro, ☎ 2-2540-459, a very up-market restaurant (they have a red carpet leading from the street to the door, and the host proudly wears a top hat and tails), serving top-notch Ecuadorian dishes. This place is popular with the more affluent locals and tourists. The service is second to none, and they have a nice selection of wines and liqueurs.

La Choza, at 12 de Octubre 1821 and Luis Cordero, ☎ 2-2230-839, serves good traditional meals in a nice setting. Prices are moderate to expensive.

If you happen to be in the Old City for lunch or dinner, **Cueva del Oso**, Edificio Pérez Pallares on Chile 1046 and Venezuela, ☎ 2-2586-623, is expensive, but well worth it. Serving traditional Ecuadorian food, La Cueva definitely caters to the more affluent crowd. Service is exceptional and the art deco interior is impressive. Try the *locro de papas,* a potato specialty.

La Bodeguita de Cuba, at Reina Victoria and La Pinta, offers the best Cuban food in the area. It's a bit pricey, but the atmosphere is nice and they have excellent live music, at least on Thursday nights.

For decent meat dishes try **Columbus**, on the corner of Amazonas and Santa María, ☎ 2-2540-780. The service is standard and they have tasty steaks and mixed grills.

A lot of the Ecuadorian-operated restaurants in Quito, particularly those that cater mostly to locals, are closed on Sunday evenings, and, while the more tourist-oriented places are open, they tend to get very crowded, so try to go out a little earlier on Sundays.

The Magic Bean, at Foch E5-08 and Juan León Mera, ☎ 2-2566-181 (see pages 101-102), is a staple and a personal favorite. They have a fairly wide-ranging menu, from jumbo breakfasts and delicious fruit juices and smoothies to dinner salads and sandwiches with home fries. Portions are big and there's great coffee to wash it all down. The outside patio is nice and relaxing, though it tends to fill up first. Get there before 11 am for breakfast.

If you're seeking vegetarian fare, the **Maple Vegetarian Café**, on the corner of Juan León Mera and Calama, ☎ 2-2520-994, is a clean choice. It has a variety of international dishes and claims that its food is organic. The quality of the food is decent, if a little inconsistent, and not too expensive. Although very popular, it is a bit overrated. Their "all you can eat" salad bar really means all you can eat in one visit with a small plate. I would also stay away from their garden burgers. Try one of their pasta dishes for a tasty, light meal.

Another favorite, and rightly so, is **El Holandés**, downstairs at Reina Victoria 600 and Carrión, ☎ 2-2522-167. The food is excellent, and there are various set dishes (that have not changed much over the years) offering Indonesian, Dutch, Indian, and Thai food, among others. The décor, with the exception of the misplaced neon Heineken sign, is also nice.

El Cafecito, at Luis Cordero 1124, ☎ 2-2234-862, serves good vegetarian dishes, excellent soups, and snacks on a nice patio. There is also a bar with a fireplace and a low-priced hotel upstairs by the same name. This is a popular spot among budget travelers.

Several of the new Internet cafés on Calama 413 and Juan León Mera serve tasty meals. **Papayanet**, ☎ 2-2561-192, serves great food, including salads, sandwiches, pizzas and pastas. The Buena Tierra (Thai chicken) salad gets a thumbs-up for presentation as well as flavor, and the brownie sundae takes the prize. They also do breakfasts.

If you're in the mood for Ecuadorian-style seafood, try **Las Redes**, located on Amazonas 845 and Veintimilla, ☎ 2-2525-691. Here you will find one of Quito's better *cevicherías*. Ecuador's ceviches are renowned country-wide and abroad. Made with marinated seafood, usually shrimp, they are easy to come by in Quito as well as along the coast. Expect to pay up to $10 at Las Redes, where the décor makes it seem as though you're in a giant aquarium.

Don't order ceviche in the cheaper local restaurants unless you want to spend the next 48 hours in the bathroom. But if the establishment caters predominantly to tourists, you can probably assume it'll be fine.

El Viejo José, Veintimilla 1254 and Páez, is a good, budget seafood restaurant operated by friendly folks from the coast. Food at this popular establishment is about half the price of that at Las Redes, and the service is good by Ecuadorian standards.

Su Cebiche, at Juan León Mera near Calama, may be overpriced, but their seafood is great. You'll dine among affluent Ecuadorians and foreign travelers. The patio in front is particularly nice for an afternoon lunch. Expect to pay around $10 for a meal and good service.

Italian food is always a good bet, and **La Gritta**, Santa María 246 and Reina Victoria, is popular, though relatively expensive. The same can be said for **La Scala**, Salazar 958 and 12 de Octubre. The **Ch'Farina**, Carrión 619 and J.L. Mera, is also very popular, but less expensive. Their food, including pastas and sandwiches, is good for the price – but don't expect thick-crust, American-style pizzas. Finally, **Ristorante Il Risotto**, Pinto 209 and Almagro, ☎ 2-2220-400, has been highly recommended by other travelers. Meals are reasonable at about $5 for a standard pasta dish.

For Chinese food, the ever-popular *chifas* (Chinese restaurants) are a good bet in Quito and in many of the smaller towns, particularly if you are hungry and don't want to take any chances. Most *chifas* also serve decent vegetarian, noodle, and rice dishes. Their prices are in the moderate range and quality is usually good. Two of the cheaper outlets are the **Hong Tai**, on La Niña and Yanez Pinzón, and the **Chifa Mayflower**, Carrión 442 and 6 de Diciembre. The Mayflower, especially, seems to be quite popular.

There are two excellent sushi establishments in Quito. The original, **Tanoshii**, is in the luxury Hotel Oro Verde, at 12 de Octubre and Cordero, ☎ 2-2566-497. The other, arguably the better of the two, is

Sake, ☎ 2-2524-818, at Paul Rivet and Eduardo Whimper. It was opened by the former sushi chef from Tanoshii, and has a great atmosphere and tasty food.

Having grown up in southern California, I am, admittedly, a Mexican-food snob. Therefore, I find that the options for good Mexican food in Quito, and Ecuador in general, are somewhat lacking. A few decent places have sprung up in the last few years, but most of them resemble Americanized Mexican-food establishments, or "Tex-Mex" joints.

El Sabor Mexicano, at Reina Victoria and 18 de Septiembre, is fairly authentic, with good food and live mariachi bands on the weekends. Prices are moderate. Across the street is **Tex-Mex**, ☎ 2-2552-790, a less expensive, American-style restaurant. I could not bring myself to eat there, although it looked fine. Try **La Guarida del Coyote**, Carrión 619 and Amazonas. It's moderately priced (around $10) and has been around longer than the other Mexican restaurants. The best Mexican food and margaritas are at **Red Hot Chilli Peppers**, on the corner of Foch and Juan León Mera. Try the sizzling chicken fajitas or the tasty (but proportionately small) nachos while you're reading many years worth of travelers' wisdom written all over the walls. This is also the place to go for a big-screen American football game. The restaurant is very small, however, and they're closed on Sundays.

Outside town, near the entrance to El Mitad del Mundo, **Equinoccio**, ☎ 2-2394-741, is a popular and relatively expensive restaurant that provides live music in addition to good food. Tour groups visiting the equatorial monument often eat lunch here.

Entertainment, Nightlife & Shopping

■ Nightspots

While Quito is no Río de Janeiro, there is plenty to do in the evening, and you're unlikely to become bored very easily, as long as you're willing to get out and about. Many of the popular night spots are concentrated around the Mariscal Sucre area.

A personal favorite is **Café Havana** on Juan León Mera and Calama. They have a DJ most nights and relatively cheap cocktails and beers. It's usually quiet earlier in the evening, but the dance floor fills up by around 11 pm. It's a popular haunt for tourists and locals alike, although last time I was there it was dead and it's generally hit-or-miss.

El Cafecito, at Luis Cordero 1124, ☎ 2-2234-862, has a cozy bar with a fireplace and is popular among budget travelers. Although they have a nice outside patio, it is often a bit too chilly later in the evening, and they don't have outside heaters.

The **Reina Victoria** is a British pub on Reina Victoria (surprisingly enough), 530 and Roca, ☎ 2-2226-369. They have a fireplace, dart boards and European beers, but the atmosphere is lacking. They also serve food, but it's not the best. A popular meeting place for British expats.

La Bodeguita de Cuba, at Reina Victoria and La Pinta, is a Cuban restaurant that blares with live, danceable Cuban music on Thursday evenings.

Arribar, on Juan León Mera and Santa María, is an ever-popular bar, with two levels, depending on what kind of atmosphere you're after. Downstairs they have loud European techno and dance music, with a pool table. It can get a bit rough here on the weekends. Upstairs is a quieter place for chilling out over a drink or two. They also serve tapas-style food and sandwiches.

Right around the corner on Lizardo García 662 and Juan León Mera, is **Mayo 68**, which offers a more intimate setting. This is a great *salsateca*, playing mostly traditional Latin dance and salsa music. If for no other reason, go there to check out the really good dancers. Get there early though – the place really is small.

El Pobre Diablo, Isabel La Católica and Francisco Galavis, ☎ 2-2222-4982, is another laid-back café/bar, serving snacks and sandwiches. They offer inexpensive cocktails, and good live jazz and blues music. Popular with college students.

I highly recommend a night out at **Seseribó**, Veintimilla and 12 de Octubre, ☎ 2-2563-598, one of the bigger and better night clubs in Quito. They're open from Thursday to Sunday, and have a cover charge. Very popular among the trendy young Quiteños, they play mostly Caribbean and salsa music. The dancing's great, especially if you can find a willing partner to teach you the moves. Drinks are expensive.

Quito & Vicinity

Varadero, on Reina Victoria 1721 and La Pinta, ☎ 2-2542-575, is a friendly Cuban bar/restaurant. They have fairly cheap cocktails, snack food and great Cuban music, often with live bands.

No Bar, on Calama and Juan León Mera is always crowded with young travelers and locals. The music is loud, and most people are there to drink. They play a good mix of Latin and American music.

■ Cinema

There are a number of very modern, multiplex movie theaters in Quito that show mostly Hollywood films, with some European and Latin American ones thrown in for good measure. More often than not, the English-language films have Spanish subtitles, but sometimes they are dubbed – so check in advance if your Spanish isn't great.

Cinemark at Plaza de las Americas, ☎ 2-2262-026, www.cinemark. com.ec, has multiple screens, and all the standard amenities. It costs $2.50, Monday-Wednesday; Thursday-Sunday it's $3.90 for adults, $3.75 for students and $3 for matinee shows.

Multicines in the Centro Comercial Iñaquito, on Amazonas and Naciones Unidas, ☎ 2-2259-677, has eight screens on two levels, and plenty of fast food restaurants. They also have international film festivals from time to time – keep an eye on a local paper such as *El Comercio*. They have a second location at the Centro Comercial El Recreo (get off the main trolley at the El Recreo stop). Admission is around $2.

The **Casa de la Cultura**, Av. Patria and 12 de Octubre, ☎ 2-2565-808, also shows foreign and independent films. Again, check the listings in the local papers, *El Comercio* or *La Hora*.

■ Shopping

There is no shortage of shopping in Quito, much of it revolving around street traders and stalls set up along Amazonas and in the main parks. The Old City is always bustling with traders, shoppers and street entertainers. Most of the goods on sale are for the locals – with everything from food, clothing and toiletries to electronic equipment and household items, such as clothes pegs and mops. It's great to wander along the streets on Sunday afternoon and just soak up the atmosphere. Be careful though, as pickpockets are known to operate here.

Most of the tourist shops are in the modern part of Quito, which has as many stores and shopping malls as most other cities.

The largest of the shopping malls is **El Jardín**, which is next to the Parque Carolina, on Amazonas, between Mariana de Jesús and Av. De La República. It is open Monday-Sunday from 10 am to 8 pm. Farther along Amazonas, at the Naciones Unidas intersection, is the **Centro Comercial Iñaquito**, or CCI. Opening hours are also 10 am to 8 pm. The **Centro Comercial El Recreo** is on Av. Maldonado at the El Recreo Trole stop. A smaller shopping center, **El Caracol**, is on Amazonas and Naciones Unidas.

For groceries and other basic supplies, there are plenty of corner stores in and around the main tourist area of Mariscal Sucre. There are also several national supermarket chains, which are more expensive, but are likely to carry everything you could possibly need. **Supermaxi** is the largest chain of supermarkets in Quito, with branches throughout the city. Find it in El Jardín, CCI, and El Recreo. **Mi Comisariato** is another supermarket chain with locations in many of the larger cities. There is one in the Quicentro shopping mall, just a few blocks from CCI, on Av. Naciones Unidas between Los Shyris and 6 de Diciembre.

If you prefer to shop in the open, with a little local flavor and better prices, check out the street markets. For **Mercado Santa Clara**, on Versalles and Dávalos, take the Trole to the Santa Clara stop.

Libri Mundi, centrally located at Juan León Mera N23-83 and Veintimilla, ☎ 2-2234-791, has the best book selection in the city, including Spanish, English, German, Italian and French books. Nearby, on the corner of Calama and Juan León Mera, is **Confederate Books**, with a wide selection of second-hand books, all economically priced, of course. Local and international newspapers can be purchased at newsstands along Amazonas Avenue.

Artesanías, or crafts, and souvenirs can be purchased from street vendors or at the many stores that line the streets of the Mariscal area. Shop around for the best quality and prices, however, as they can vary significantly.

Quito & Vicinity

The Northern Highlands

From Quito north to the Colombian border, the Andes provide spectacular views of rolling mountains, sparkling lakes, and tiny villages. Indigenous culture, passed down through the ages, is mixed with the colonial legacy. Renowned for their **handicrafts**, local communities offer everything from leather goods to Panama hats, wool sweaters, paintings, sketches, woodcarvings, pottery and stoneware, hand-

crafted jewelry and fine lace and embroidery. Travelers flock here to buy the quality crafts and goods hidden within the area's remote villages and sold at the world-renowned market in **Otavalo**, one of the largest and oldest indigenous craft markets in all of Latin America.

Arts and crafts are just one facet of this amazing region. With lower elevations, a milder climate, and less extreme weather conditions than the central Sierras, the Northern Highlands are ideal for outdoor activities. **Cayambe Volcano** and its surrounding lake-trodden countryside offer plenty of exciting opportunities to explore and play. And from Cotacachi Volcano, the western slopes of the Andes begin with the boundary of the **Cotacachi-Cayapas Ecological Reserve**, and include the emerald jewel of **Lago Cuicocha** set within. The ecological reserves in this region offer some of the least explored and perhaps most underrated natural treasures in the country.

The range of activities includes whatever you dare to dream up, from hiking and mountain biking to horseback riding and mountaineering. Whether you're an explorer or you just want to absorb the local culture, you will quickly realize why Otavalo and its surrounding countryside is one of the most visited regions in mainland Ecuador. What most people don't do, however, and what we encourage you to do, is to get off the beaten track and really experience the finest of the highlands.

North of Quito

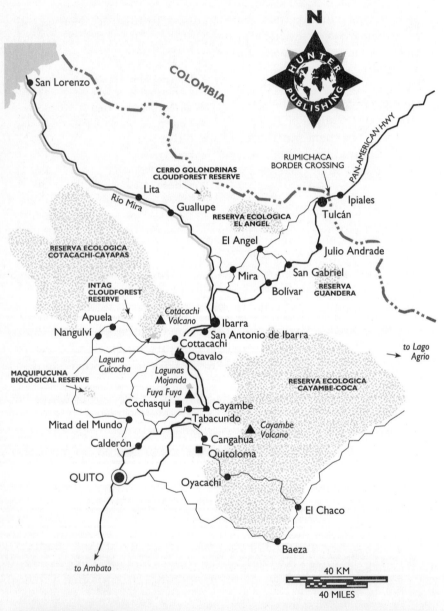

N

COLOMBIA

HUNTER PUBLISHING

PAN-AMERICAN HWY

San Lorenzo

RUMICHACA
BORDER CROSSING

CERRO GOLONDRINAS
CLOUDFOREST RESERVE

Lita

Río Mira

Guallupe

Ipiales

Tulcán

RESERVA ECOLOGICA
EL ANGEL

El Angel

Julio Andrade

RESERVA ECOLOGICA
COTACACHI-CAYAPAS

Mira

San Gabriel

INTAG
CLOUDFOREST
RESERVE

Bolívar

RESERVA
GUANDERA

Apuela

Cotacachi
Volcano

Nangulví

Ibarra

San Antonio de Ibarra

Cottacachi

to Lago
Agrio

Laguna
Cuicocha

Otavalo

MAQUIPUCUNA
BIOLOGICAL RESERVE

Lagunas
Mojanda

Fuya Fuya

RESERVA ECOLOGICA
CAYAMBE-COCA

Cochasqui

Cayambe

Mitad del Mundo

Tabacundo

Cayambe
Volcano

Calderón

Cangahua

Quitoloma

QUITO

Oyacachi

El Chaco

Baeza

to Ambato

40 KM

40 MILES

History

Otavalo and its surrounding communities are a highlight for anyone traveling through the province of Imbabura. For thousands of years the indigenous Otavaleños, using an ancient tool known as the back-strap loom, were expert **weavers**. In the mid-1500s Spanish colonists arrived to discover many communities trading products from the highlands with rainforest peoples of the Oriente. Realizing the amazing productivity of these Quichua people, the Spanish relentlessly exploited the Amerindians and forced the Otavaleños to weave while trying to survive in a feudal system of agriculture. Later, independence for Ecuador did little to change the Otavaleños' lives, as the new hacienda landowners continued the same system of slavery and forced them to work in sweatshops called *obrajes*.

In the early 1900s, the textile industry expanded rapidly, particularly weaving, with patterns that were introduced from Scotland. By the time the indigenous people gained freedom and land rights in 1964, the Otavaleños were expert weavers in an emerging world market. Since then, they have diversified their products for the tourism industry, and their goods can now be found all over Latin America, in the United States and Europe. They have become one of the most affluent indigenous groups in all of Latin America.

Native Apparel

During the period of forced labor and sweatshops, landlords required slight variations in clothing between the people of neighboring villages in order to distinguish their laborers. This tradition persists today, and the locals can easily recognize where people come from by observing their attire. Distinct patterns, different-colored shawls, a hat in a particular shape, even a hairstyle is all that is needed to distinguish a neighbor from an outsider. This customized attire has become a source of pride and cultural definition for Otavaleños and other native groups. Beautiful, long, braided hair on men is common, and clothing may include ponchos, felt hats, white pants, and rope sandals. On the women, you will see headdresses, embroidered blouses and shawls, and extravagant gold-colored bead necklaces.

Flora & Fauna

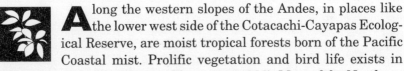

Along the western slopes of the Andes, in places like the lower west side of the Cotacachi-Cayapas Ecological Reserve, are moist tropical forests born of the Pacific Coastal mist. Prolific vegetation and bird life exists in these areas (see *The Western Slopes*, page 236). Most of the Northern Highlands, however, are given over to dairy farms, agriculture, and the cultivation of flowers for export to North America and Europe. Mt. Cayambe (18,933 feet), the third-highest peak in Ecuador, is home to *páramo* grassland and a snow-capped peak. The area surrounding the volcanic caldera of Lago Cuicocha offers a variety of dwarf trees, shrubs, and mosses. Wildlife consists of shrub-dwelling birds and other animals, as most of the area lacks forest cover. Flowering plants, especially orchids, attract a variety of hummingbirds.

Getting Here & Getting Around

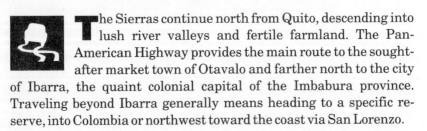

The Sierras continue north from Quito, descending into lush river valleys and fertile farmland. The Pan-American Highway provides the main route to the sought-after market town of Otavalo and farther north to the city of Ibarra, the quaint colonial capital of the Imbabura province. Traveling beyond Ibarra generally means heading to a specific reserve, into Colombia or northwest toward the coast via San Lorenzo.

From Quito, the highway stretches northwest through Calderón, then descends along the historically rich **Guayllabamba River Gorge**, before ascending again to the lush and productive valleys farther north. Passing through **Cayambe**, the gateway to the **Cayambe-Coca Ecological Reserve**, the highway reaches **Otavalo** within two hours from Quito. From there, numerous opportunities exist to explore the surrounding region, including indigenous villages, the town of **Cotacachi**, the **Cotacachi-Cayapas Ecological Reserve** and **Laguna Quicocha**. Heading back to the northeast, the Pan-American Highway reaches **Ibarra** and additional opportunities for exploring new areas. Continuing, the highway splits north to **Tulcán**, on the border with Columbia, or northwest toward the coastal town of **San Lorenzo**, also near the border.

■ Getting to Otavalo

Unless you're journeying toward a specific ecolodge or hacienda, most folks make a home base out of Otavalo and vicinity, which provides easy access to various day-long or longer excursions. Getting to Otavalo is as simple as heading north from Quito on the Pan-American Highway for a couple of hours. Very frequent buses make the trip from the Terminal Terrestre in Quito. Make sure the bus you choose actually goes into Otavalo or that the driver knows to stop for you along the highway, as many bus routes continue farther north. See the next page, for specific bus information.

By car, head north on the Pan-American Highway from Quito and continue past Laguna San Pablo, a small lake on the right (you can't miss it), a few more miles to Otavalo. Taxis from Quito are another alternative, particularly if you have a few people in your group. Expect to pay about $30. You can reach other sites in this region via the Pan-American as well. Note that the railway service from Quito to the north is currently suspended.

Visitor Information

■ Otavalo

Most tour operators and travel services are based in Quito, although Otavalo is now very traveler-friendly. Modern services in Otavalo such as banks, post offices, and communications are readily available within a few blocks of Poncho Plaza. Heading southeast along Calle Sucre from the southern corner of the plaza are a bank, an ATM, and at least one relatively new Internet café. The **post office** within the Municipalidad is situated across from the plaza on G. Moreno. The **regional tourism office** is located at Bolívar 8-14 and Montalvo. The **Andinatel telephone office** is on Calderón, between Jaramillo and Sucre. However, check the rates at the Internet café as well; they may be lower. The **Hospital** is on Sucre, just north of Poncho Plaza, ☎ 6-920-444.

Northern Highlands

The **bus terminal** in Otavalo is at Atahualpa and Ordonez, on the northeastern edge of town. Bus companies from Quito that go directly here, rather than dropping you off on the Pan-American Highway, include Trans Los Lagos, Trans Otavalo and Flota Imbabura. **Taxis** and *camionetas* are available at Parque Central (Moreno and Sucre) and the Plaza Copacabana (Atahualpa and Montalvo).

 A good amount of Otavalo information can be found at www.otavalo.com and at www.otavalo-web.com.

Festivals

If you happen to be around during the first week of September, Otavalo celebrates the harvest, or **Yamor Festival**, with a wonderful array of parades, music and general revelry. **All Soul's Day** (November 2) is another interesting time to visit many of the highland villages. On this day, locals make a pilgrimage to the cemeteries, to visit and honor deceased relatives and friends. They bring offerings of food and flowers, and families later gather at home for a traditional meal that includes *guaguas de pan*. These bread dough figurines (think Gingerbread Man) are in the shape of children (*guagua* is the Quichua word for child). They are washed down with *colada morada*, a delicious, thick blend of maize, cloves, orange, blackberries and other ingredients, served warm. Try it if you have the chance; its delicious! In the town of Calderón, just northeast of Quito, it is actually traditional to have this family meal among other festivities at the cemetery.

■ Ibarra

In Ibarra, the **post office** is on Salinas between Moncayo and Oviedo and the **Andinatel telephone office** is near Parque Moncayo at Sucre 4-56. For **banks**, try Banco del Pacífico, at Moncayo and Olmedo, Filanbanco, at Olmedo 11-49, or **Banco Continental**, at Olmedo 11-67. There are one or two others in the downtown area as well. The **Ministry of Tourism** office provides useful travel information, located upstairs at Olmedo 965 and Moncayo (open Mon-Fri, closed for lunch). The local **hospital** at Oviedo 8-24 is always open. **Buses** are spread out in Ibarra, as there is no central terminal. They tend to all be within a couple of blocks of the train station and Obelisk near the streets Guerrero, Velasco and Narváez.

■ Tulcán

Most services and hotels here are located near the Central Plaza at Suere and 10 de Agosto. Downtown is pretty compact, with the **Tourism Office** at Bolívar and Pinchincha, and the **post office** several blocks to the north on Bolívar, near Junín.

Touring & Sightseeing

■ Calderón

Calderón, a small village north of Quito on the Pan-American Highway, can be an interesting stop for the souvenir hunter. The people of Calderón are known for their tradition of making small figurines and other ornaments out of bread dough, intricate objects that make great gifts and Christmas-tree ornaments. If you're in the vicinity on November 1-2 ("Dia de Los Muertos"), check out the local ceremonies that incorporate the figurines as symbols of pre-colonial animal and human sacrifices (see *Festivals* on previous page). The figurines are also used to help decorate the community cemetery, but be aware that locals aren't particularly fond of pictures being taken during this time.

■ Cayambe

The pleasant village of Cayambe is most noted for the cheese-rich dairy farms that surround it and for the towering mass of **Cayambe Volcano** that dominates the scenery to the east. If ice climbing and crevasses aren't your thing, however, the surrounding countryside offers plenty of easier high-altitude hiking near the western edge of the **Cayambe-Coca Ecological Reserve**. See *Ecotravel*, page 139, for more details.

The town itself does not offer much for the foreign traveler, unless you are a big **chocolate** fan, in which case you can always visit the local Nestlé factory. The cheese and tasty biscuits are renowned here, and worth stopping for at one of the local factories. Cayambe is also known for its export flower industry, which is a major contributor to the national economy, but of little interest to the traveler. You will most likely pass through Cayambe on your way north to Otavalo or other highland destinations such as the Cayambe-Coca Ecological Reserve, with its endless miles of open *páramo*. A favorite destination just south of town is **Hacienda Guachala**, which has nice accommodations (see *Where to Stay*, page 144) and makes a great home base from which to hike or ride horseback in the surrounding region.

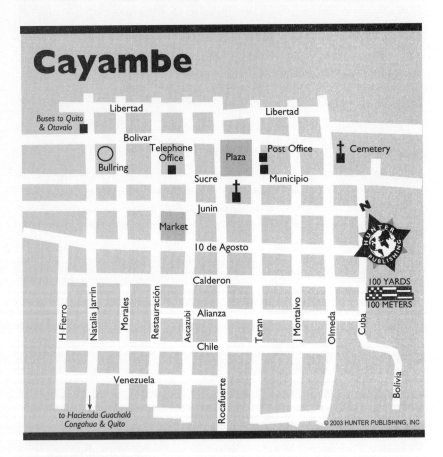

Cayambe

Libertad
Buses to Quito & Otavalo
Libertad
Bolivar
Telephone Office
Plaza
Post Office
Cemetery
Bullring
Sucre
Municipio
Junin
Market
10 de Agosto
Calderon
100 YARDS
100 METERS
H Fierro
Natalia Jarrin
Morales
Restauración
Ascazubi
Alianza
Teran
J Montalvo
Olmeda
Cuba
Chile
Venezuela
Rocafuerte
Bolivia
to Hacienda Guachalá
Congahua & Quito
© 2003 HUNTER PUBLISHING, INC

■ Otavalo

No trip to Ecuador is complete without a visit to Otavalo. The potential for collecting gifts and souvenirs from the town's (originally) pre-Incan native market is surpassed only by the beauty of its indigenous people.

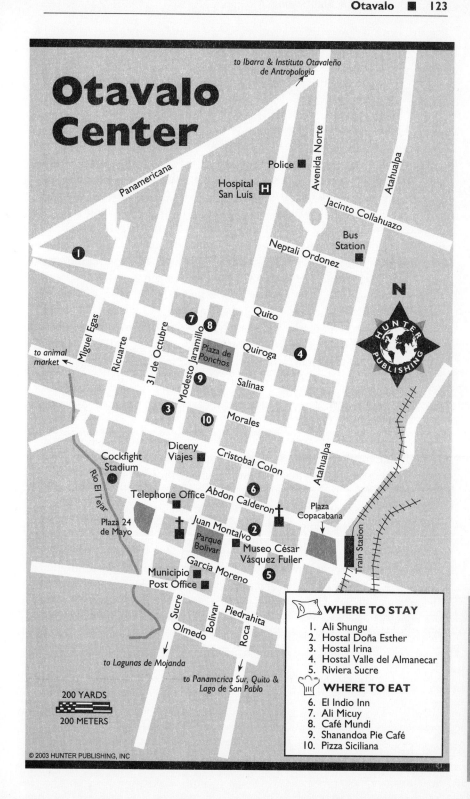

If you plan to photograph the Otavaleños, ask their permission first. Don't be surprised if they refuse. Camera-toting tourists and professional photographers have accosted them for years.

The **Saturday market** in Otavalo is the main attraction. It's become such a big event, however, that you may wish to see it on any other day of the week, when you'll find the same goods without the crowds. If Saturday is your day, try to arrive on a Friday night and go to the market early to beat the arrival of the morning tourist buses. The other aspect you will find only on Saturdays is the local market, catering exclusively to natives and selling everything from livestock, to food and daily necessities. This begins and ends earlier than the tourist market. If you're up for it, hike or catch a quick early morning taxi back toward the highway to the main livestock market – well worth the effort.

To guarantee a bargain at the market, shop early. The superstitious vendors are more inclined to cut a deal on their first sale of the day, in the belief that this will bring them good luck, and presumably lots of buyers, throughout the afternoon!

Poncho Plaza is the hub of activity for travelers in Otavalo. Here, you'll find everything from sweaters, hammocks, tapestries, and embroidered clothing to a variety of arts and crafts. The bargains are incredible! Expect to negotiate prices. Try not to bargain too hard, though, as differences in price often boil down to spare change for the tourist but may be a meal for the vendor. And during peak demand periods, the locals will not barter as much.

The Saturday market is one of the oldest, largest, and most renowned in all of Latin America. It originated when jungle goods from the Oriente were brought in to trade for items from the Sierras. During the colonial era, Spanish landlords exploited the indigenous expertise at weaving. Their skills have since been passed down and used to create products for today's tourist-oriented market.

The Saturday market has become such an enormous tourist attraction, that with the crowds you can also expect thieves and pickpockets to be strolling the plaza. Most of them migrate from Quito and they are good at what they do. If you look at all vulnerable (i.e., confused or toting too many dangling cameras, bags and purses), you'll be a target.

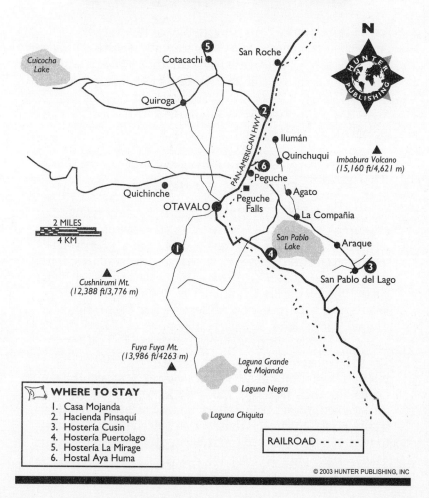

Otavalo Area

Cuicocha Lake

Cotacachi ⑤

San Roche

Quiroga ②

Ilumán

Quinchuqui

Imbabura Volcano
(15,160 ft/4,621 m)

⑥ Peguche

Quichinche

OTAVALO

Agato

Peguche Falls

La Compañia

2 MILES
4 KM

San Pablo Lake

Araque

①

④

③

Cushnirumi Mt.
(12,388 ft/3,776 m)

San Pablo del Lago

Fuya Fuya Mt.
(13,986 ft/4263 m)

Laguna Grande de Mojanda

Laguna Negra

WHERE TO STAY

1. Casa Mojanda
2. Hacienda Pinsaquí
3. Hostería Cusin
4. Hostería Puertolago
5. Hostería La Mirage
6. Hostal Aya Huma

Laguna Chiquita

RAILROAD -- -- --

Northern Highlands

Plaza Bolívar

Poncho Plaza and the market in general in Otavalo is geared primarily to the foreign traveler and is without question a tourist trap. For a change of pace, take a stroll and relax at Plaza Bolívar, on Sucre and García Moreno. It is much more tranquil, with shaded trees, quiet benches and locals that aren't caught up in the madness of Poncho Plaza. The centerpiece is a statue of Rumiñahui, who was the Incan general under Atahualpa. Rumiñahui was not only a key figure in the division of the Inca empire and the main force behind the resistance of the Spanish invasion, but he symbolizes the proud Otavaleno heritage with their ancestry.

A couple of **museums** are worth a visit around town. For local artifacts, musical instruments, and ethnographic displays of indigenous attire, be sure to visit the **Otavalo Institute of Anthropology**, located on the north side of the Pan-American Highway on Av. Sarances. It's open Tuesday through Saturday. Also recommended is the **Cezar Vasques Fuller Archeological Museum**, at Roca and Montalvo. Open Monday through Saturday.

Cultural Curiosity

Numerous indigenous villages dot the countryside surrounding Otavalo. The farther away you get from the market, the more traditional they become. On a prearranged tour from Otavalo you can visit several of these places, chat with the people in their homes, and watch the work that goes into the expert traditional craftsmanship that has been passed down over countless years. Each village is unique, specializing in a particular product. To watch the speed, accuracy and skill of the craftsmen is a real treat.

Try to be courteous by asking them directly before taking a picture, even if your guide says it's okay. These people have opened up their homes to you. Talk to them and ask them questions. Interact. You will be amazed at how much they would prefer to engage than act as sideshows for curious tourists. Give a little and you will leave this experience with at least one smile to remember forever.

To really experience the local culture, take a tour with a local operator into the surrounding villages to see the natives hard at work. Not only is it a culturally rewarding experience, but you will appreciate the labor that goes into your purchased goods. It's also a great way to experience life outside of market day. Each village in the region specializes in one particular product that is brought to market in Otavalo. For instance, one community may monopolize a certain type of poncho, while people in a neighboring village may work only on sweaters. For these and other local excursions, see the *Adventures on Foot* section, page132.

Otavalo is less than two hours north of Quito via the Pan-American Highway. Modern services are available in town. See *Visitor Information*, page 119, for details. From Quito's main bus terminal, there are many companies with service to Otavalo, but most of them will just drop you off on the highway, and that is assuming you are paying attention. Recommended are the bus lines **Cooperativo Otavalo** or **Cooperativo Los Lagos**, as they both will take you to the new bus station in town. A nice alternative is **Supertaxis Los Lagos** in Quito, at Asuncion 3-81, ☎ 2-2565-992. From your hotel, expect to pay under $10 for the trip to Otavalo in these Otavalo-bound shuttles.

■ Cotacachi

Less than an hour's drive northwest of Otavalo is the small town of Cotacachi, famous for the high quality leather goods produced there. It may be worth a quick glance if you're in the market for inexpensive leather. The surrounding area offers a few high-end converted hacienda-style accommodations, but the main attraction of this area is a specific portion of the **Cotacachi-Cayapas Ecological Reserve**, punctuated by the magnificent emerald crater of **Lake Cuicocha** (see pages 140-41). To get to the town, follow the Pan-American Highway nine miles north from Otavalo. Buses are frequent between the two towns, or you can catch a bus coming from Quito to the north, if you stand on the side of the main highway out of Otavalo (the Pan-American).

■ Ibarra

Ibarra is the provincial capital of Imbabura, a quaint colonial town that is home to over 100,000 people. With typical whitewashed colonial architecture, cobblestone streets, and pleasantly adorned parks, Ibarra is a relaxing change of pace from bustling Quito and Otavalo

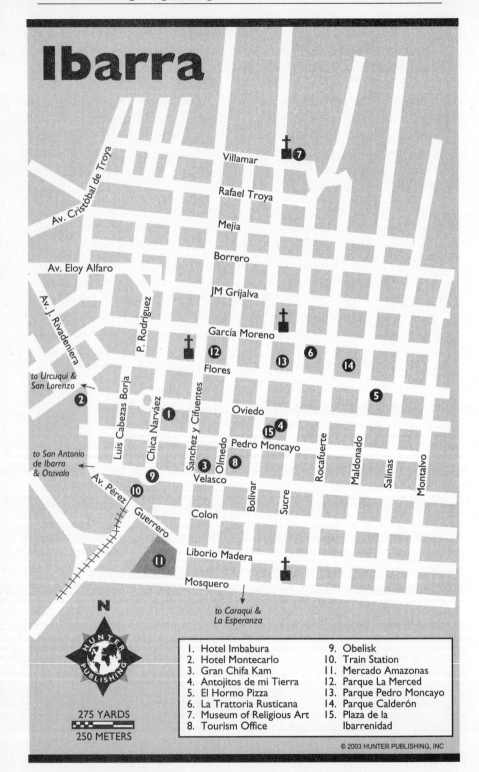

Ibarra

Villamar

Rafael Troya

Mejia

Borrero

JM Grijalva

García Moreno

Flores

Oviedo

Pedro Moncayo

Velasco

Colon

Liborio Madera

Mosquero

Av. Cristóbal de Troya

Av. Eloy Alfaro

Av. J. Rivadeniera

P. Rodríguez

Luis Cabezas Borja

Chica Narváez

Sanchez y Cifuentes

Olmedo

Bolivar

Sucre

Rocafuerte

Maldonado

Salinas

Montalvo

Av. Pérez

Guerrero

to Urcuqui &
San Lorenzo

to San Antonio
de Ibarra
& Otavalo

to Caraqui &
La Esperanza

N

HUNTER PUBLISHING

275 YARDS

250 METERS

1. Hotel Imbabura
2. Hotel Montecarlo
3. Gran Chifa Kam
4. Antojitos de mi Tierra
5. El Hormo Pizza
6. La Trattoria Rusticana
7. Museum of Religious Art
8. Tourism Office
9. Obelisk
10. Train Station
11. Mercado Amazonas
12. Parque La Merced
13. Parque Pedro Moncayo
14. Parque Calderón
15. Plaza de la
   Ibarrenidad

© 2003 HUNTER PUBLISHING, INC

on market day. Travelers in the north use Ibarra as a gateway to Ecuador's Pacific Coastal province of Esmeraldas, although there is not much to do here other than to get away and absorb the solace. The nearby university students, however, do indulge in evening activities during the weekends, providing a small spark of festivities if you are at the right place.

With the setting sun we rolled into what seemed to be an atypical town in the highlands, or at least not what I expected. Perhaps that is because we were not arriving where I expected to be. My first experience in Ibarra came as a result of sleeping on the bus at it passed Otavalo. What struck the most was the easygoing peaceful atmosphere and mix of Indian and Afro-Ecuadorian inhabitants, a bit of an anomaly in the Sierras. The setting sun punctuated the untouched antiquity of the place to create a real 'lost in time' ambiance. (Traveler's account)

Points of interest in Ibarra include two of the city's several attractive parks/plazas, the larger of which is the **Parque Pedro Moncayo**. Here you'll find the *casa cultural* and the cathedral. The smaller plaza, which is great for people-watching, is the Parque Penaherrara, better known as the **Parque de la Merced**. The **Church of Santo Domingo** (at the end of Calle Simon Bolívar; open Mon-Sat, 9 am-noon and 3-6 pm) contains a museum of religious art depicting interesting biblical stories. The entire downtown area is nice to stroll around in and has a good selection of restaurants and artsy cafés. The day market by the railway station on Cifuentes is also worth a browse.

Of archeological interest, the **Museo Banco Central**, at Sucre and Oviedo (open Monday-Friday, no charge) is well worth a visit. Exhibits provide insight and artifacts pre-dating Inca times, with descriptions in English and Spanish. South of town a mile (head down Bolívar, which turns into Av. Atahualpa) to the suburb of **Caranqui** and the **Museo Atahualpa de Caranqui** and **Plaza Atahualpa**. Thought to be the birthplace of the last great Inca King, Atahualpa, who lost his life to the Spanish, the plaza has remnants of Inca and Pre-Inca temples, as well as a small museum. The plaza also has a small market on Sundays.

■ San Antonio de Ibarra

A worthwhile local excursion, either from Ibarra or Otavalo, is this small village famous for its woodcarvings, just west of Ibarra on the Pan-American Highway. Most activity here revolves around the main square and along Av. 27 de Noviembre, including a few excellent galleries with a wide range of carved motifs. South of Ibarra a few miles is the quaint village of **La Esperanza**. In addition to bargain-price, high-quality leather goods, the village offers easy access to **Cubilche** and **Imbabura Volcanoes**. The trip to the top of Cubilche takes just a few hours from La Esperanza. The hike to Imbabura is a little more difficult and requires a very long day (over 10 hours), but is reportedly well worth the effort.

Ibarra is on the Pan-American Highway, less than three hours north of Quito by bus. Frequent buses head there from Quito and Otavalo; it's easy to flag one down along the side of the highway. From Otavalo, it is just a hop, skip, and jump by car or taxi. Buses begin and end along the western side of town, though at no specific terminal. They tend to wait around the train station on Juan de Velasco and farther west.

◼ El Ángel

Just over 19 miles north of Ibarra, at the village/military checkpoint or **Mascarilla**, the Pan-American splits. To the north is the old road to Colombia via **Mira** and **El Ángel**. The town of El Ángel is known to travelers primarily as the gateway to **El Ángel Ecological Reserve**. See El Ángel, *Eco-Travel* section, page 142.

◼ Tulcán

Alternatively, the main road to the north reaches Colombia via Tulcán. With a population of about 40,000, Tulcán is the capital of the Carchi Province and is the region's commercial center. This is due primarily to the fact that it is a border town with Colombia, and is only of interest to the traveler heading into Colombia or perhaps into El Ángel Ecological Reserve. If you're here, check out the cemetery, which is famous for its artistic display of topiary bushes. The renowned work began with a local Ecuadorian, José Franco, and still draws attention through his family's continued efforts. The cemetery is just north and a couple of blocks west of Ayora Park, away from the city center in the northwest corner of town. It is a bit of a hike (or short cab ride) from Independence Plaza and the hotels and restaurants downtown.

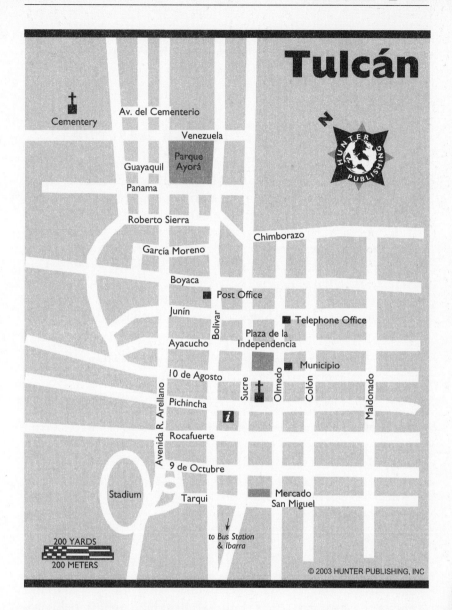

Tulcán

Cementery

Av. del Cementerio

Venezuela

Guayaquil

Parque Ayorá

Panama

Roberto Sierra

Chimborazo

García Moreno

Boyaca

Post Office

Junín

Telephone Office

Bolívar

Plaza de la Independencia

Ayacucho

Municipio

10 de Agosto

Sucre

Olmedo

Colón

Maldonado

Pichincha

Rocafuerte

9 de Octubre

Avenida R. Arellano

Stadium

Tarqui

Mercado San Miguel

to Bus Station & Ibarra

200 YARDS

200 METERS

© 2003 HUNTER PUBLISHING, INC

Northern Highlands

■ To the Coast

If you're not heading toward the Colombian border, the newest stretch of highway north of Ibarra veers to the northwest (at Mascarilla) and the lowland coastal town of San Lorenzo. The dramatic drop in elevation is a wonderful way to experience the radically changing habitat from the Andes down the western slopes to the coast. And the coast itself, just a short distance away, is a whole other world. But we'll save that for another chapter.

Adventures

■ On Foot

Cayambe-Coca Ecological Reserve

 With nearly a million acres of protected reserve that includes *páramo* (sub-alpine) habitat, Ecuador's third-highest peak, cloud forest, indigenous communities, hot springs, lakes, streams and sub-tropical forest along the foothills of the upper Amazon, there is plenty of hiking in Cayambe. In fact, you could never hope to explore it all, nor would you want to without a good tour operator, guide or solid backcountry skills. One great hike is on the route from **Oyacachi to Papallacta**, a town famous for its hot springs. Oyacachi itself is a little-known village that is becoming known as a hidden jewel for its therapeutic mineral springs, rich culture and as a gateway to the Amazon.

For the intrepid hiker, head down the **Oyacachi valley** toward El Chaco. A three-day trekking journey down the eastern slopes to the upper Amazon is a great adventure through cloud forest, waterfalls, rivers and mountain scenery. From Oyacachi, head east and downhill to the cemetery, from which you will come to an ancient stone trail that follows the Río Oyacachi all the way to El Chaco. Although a beautiful trek, it is not easy, with thick vegetation in some places and rivers that require crossing with a cable and harness. Inquire in Oyacachi for a local guide, or pre-arrange the trip with a Quito-based trekking outfitter.

There is also plenty of wide-open countryside within the *páramo* foothills of **Volcán Cayambe**. Other opportunities exist closer to the town of Cayambe, which has excellent views of the snow-capped namesake volcano. If you happen to be staying at **Hacienda Guachala**, for example, there is an excellent hike right from the hotel's front door and up the nearby mountain to the pre-Incan ruins of Pambamarca. With expansive views, this is also a good horseback ride if your lungs aren't quite adapted to the highlands yet, though its pretty steep in places. It is a straightforward route. Inquire at Guachala for horses, a guide or directions (see *Where to Stay*, page 144).

Other hikes and treks within the park include **Reventador Volcano** and **San Rafael Waterfall**, described on page 331, *Upper Amazon Basin*.

Tour Operators & Guides

Local guides are often associated with individual accommodations. Quito, however, has several quality outfitters that offer climbing excursions to Cuyambe, hiking around the region, and mountain biking, listed below and in *Quito & Vicinity*, pages 94-97. Otavalo also has local guides offering cultural excursions to nearby indigenous villages, hiking and horseback riding. There are also a few lodging options that have horses and bicycles for rent. Ask around.

Around Otavalo

Peguche Waterfalls & Surrounding Villages

Northeast of Otavalo are the villages of **Peguche**, **Lluman**, and **Agato**. By foot from town, these villages make for a pleasant afternoon hike in the countryside among rolling hills and beautiful streams. The people in this area are known for their abilities to weave and make other crafts. If you are walking along and hear the spinning of a wheel from inside, give a warm hello and you might be allowed to watch someone at work. Note that specific families have demonstration workshops and sell their work on-site, but the easiest way to find the best ones is through a local outfitter.

Las Cascadas de Peguche, a waterfall just south of Peguche, is a great side-excursion. A trail leads from the railway through the forest and to the falls, which is managed by Fundación Natura. It's a popular hike, and there may be a small entry fee at the parking lot. To get there, pick up a local map and directions in town, or use a guide a make a day of it in conjunction with visiting local villages.

For the **local villages**, follow the train tracks northeast from Otavalo. In a couple of miles you will reach the village of **Peguche**. The road to Peguche then continues on a couple of more miles to the village of **Lluman**. Alternatively, the village of **Agato** is due east of Peguche, where you can track down the best weaving and embroidery around.

Laguna San Pablo

Just southeast of Otavalo, and a pleasant day-hike from the town, is San Pablo Lake. Highlights of the walk from Otavalo to the tranquil lake include rolling countryside and great views of Imbabura Volcano. You can't miss it from the Pan-American Highway. Accommodations are available at San Pablo Lake for travelers who want to be near Otavalo but away from the hustle and bustle of the busy market town itself.

To get there, follow the paths leading southeast out of Otavalo from the railway station. The trails roughly parallel the Pan-American Highway. Once at the lake, follow the road around it and through the village of San Pablo.

Lagunas de Mojanda

The Mojanda Lakes, about 10 miles south of Otavalo, lie in the shadow of the towering **Mount Fuya Fuya**. This area, among high *páramo* habitat and jagged ridges, is great for hiking. Although the area is largely deforested, some native patches of woods remain in protected gorges and along the edges of cliffs. Numerous bird species – including hummingbirds – call this area home, thanks to a wide variety of flowering plants. Other wildlife in the region include white-tailed deer and *páramo* foxes. Andean condors are sometimes spotted soaring high above Fuya Fuya.

Laguna Grande de Mojanda, the largest lake of the three, is also known as Caricocha, or Man Lake. **Little Mojanda**, set behind the southeast corner of Caricocha, is also known as Huarmicocha, or Woman Lake. A third lake, beyond the southwest corner of Caricocha, is known as **Yanacocha**, or Black Lake. When the weather is good, it's possible to hike three hours from the lakes to the summit of Fuya Fuya, at 13,940 feet. The trip begins and ends with spectacular views of the beautiful *páramo* grasslands and the Cordillera.

To reach the lakes from Otavalo, hire a taxi ($5) or hike there along the dirt road from Otavalo to Lagunas de Mojanda. Ask for "el vía a las lagunas de Mojanda," or contact local tour outfitters (see pages 135-37). Camping is possible on the south side of Laguna Mojanda. There is also a very basic backpackers' refuge. Check with local outfitters on security issues. It's best to hire a guide.

There has been an increase in assaults on hikers in the vicinity surrounding Otavalo, including destinations listed above. Avoid hiking alone and be sure to leave your money back at the hotel.

Regional Tours

For regional tours, including hiking, horseback riding and trips to indigenous villages, the following tour operators and guides are recommended. In Otavalo, **Zulaytur**, at the corner of Sucre and Colón, ☎ 6-921-176, offers the best half- or full-day tours of local *artesanía* communities. Rodrigo Mora, the owner, is very knowledgeable and knows people in the surrounding communities; sometimes he has an English-speaking guide. Full-day tours costing under $20 per person take you into homes to experience working indigenous life. Zulaytur can also arrange tours on horseback.

Also in Otavalo, **Diceny Viajes**, Sucre 10-11 and Colón, ☎ 6-921-217, offers multilingual regional tours, including climbing. They are local and culturally sensitive. **Indy Aventura**, Salinas 305 and Sucre at Poncho Plaza, ☎ 6-923-611, also knows the region and all the major attractions listed above well.

In Ibarra, **Nevitur Cia Ltda**, ☎ 6-958-701, Bolívar and Ovieda, is recommended for guiding services throughout the region.

Imbabura Volcano

The prominent volcano, visible from Otavalo at 15,140 feet, can be climbed in a day, though it is a full day, with significant elevation change. The best route is to begin at La Esperanza, between Otavalo and Ibarra, and head up the obvious, well-trodden route. Although this is not an easy hike, the views more than make up for the workout. This is a good hike to acclimatize yourself before attempting climbs to some of Ecuador's higher peaks. Alternatively, some folks prefer to start at Laguna San Pablo.

Cotacachi Volcano & Lake Cuicocha

At Lake Cuicocha, hiking along the trail that circumnavigates the rim of the volcano above the lake is a great way to spend the day. It takes up to five hours to complete the easily navigable trail. The view from the rim is exceptional on a clear day. Various wildflowers and birds complement the scenery below and the Andean backdrop in the distance. Start early in the morning and hike counterclockwise for the normal route, particularly if you may not complete the entire loop. Lake Cuicocha forms the southern tip of the Cotacachi-Cayapas Ecological Reserve, which spans down the western slopes toward the Pacific lowlands. For specific directions to the lake and the reserve, see *Eco-Travel*, page 140.

El Ángel Ecological Reserve

Hiking and multi-day trekking opportunities exist in El Ángel, close to the Colombian border. They are described in the *Eco-Travel* section, below.

Trekking for Conservation: Cerro Golondrinas Cloud Forest Trek

North of El Ángel and west of the Colombian border town of Tulcán is the Golondrinas Cloud Forest Reserve, owned and operated by the Golondrinas Foundation. So far, Fundación Golondrinas has done an excellent job integrating ecotourism with community development and local participation, including trekking, agro-forestry, scientific research and environmental education for local school children. Offering two- to four-day treks that begin at 13,734 feet in Andean highlands, the route follows the western slopes through ever-changing ecosystems until you reach sub-tropical forest at 3,300 feet. All-inclusive packages include horses that carry most of the gear, while travelers have to carry only day-packs. Student discounts and volunteer opportunities are available. To make arrangements, inquire through the hotel **La Casa de Eliza**, located in Quito at Isabel La Catolica N24-679 (☎ 2-2226-602 or e-mail manteca@uio.satnet net/permaviajes@yahoo.com).

Serious Climbing

Cayambe Volcano

 Volcán Cayambe in the Cayambe-Coca Reserve is Ecuador's third-highest peak at 18,933 feet, and the highest point on the equator. The mountain, while magnificent, is very difficult to climb, and technical experience is an absolutely necessity if you wish to reach its summit. Just south of the town of Cayambe is an unmarked road heading east (via Juna Montalvo) for 16 miles to the *refugio*. The refuge is situated at a windy 15,696 feet and it can be quite chilly. From the refuge, the standard route to the left includes technical outcrops and crevasses, with risks of avalanche close to the summit. Quito-based climbing outfitters are recommended for guided services, or at least for information before attempting this climb.

Outfitters

For climbing, hiking and trekking outfitters based in Quito that operate in the Northern Highlands: **La Companía de Guías**, J. Washington 425 and 6 de Diciembre, ☎ 2-2504-773, is a top-quality ASEGUIM-certified outfit. Guides are very professional and speak several languages. This organization is at the high end of the cost spectrum for climbing, but is worth the price.

 ASEGUIM is the Ecuadorian Association of Mountain Guides, which licenses local guides who reach certain levels of skill and experience.

Surtrek, Amazonas and Ventimilla, ☎ 2-2561-129, offers comparable expertise, is ASEGUIM-certified, and is well known for its climbing and trekking trips. **Safari Ecuador**, Calama 380 and J.L. Mera, ☎ 2-2552-505, in the United States ☎ 800-434-8182, fax 2-2223-381, admin@safari.com.ec, www.safari.com.ec, is ASEGUIM-certified and specializes in volcano climbs, including Cayambe, trips to Otavalo, hiking, and mountain biking in the region. They are a good all-around company.

■ On Wheels

Mountain Biking

There is ample breathtaking countryside for the avid two-wheel enthusiast, including backcountry roads through indigenous villages and amid scenic mountain vistas. What's more, the slightly lower altitude and milder climate in this region makes it more accessible throughout the year than other parts of the country. Some of the same routes for hiking around Otavalo, are just as easily enjoyed on bike, which also allows for covering more distance.

One possible bike ride begins at the brim of **Cuicocha Crater Lake** – northwest of Otavalo – which is also a great hike around a beautiful emerald lake. From here, hop onto two wheels for a day of off-road-enchantment, through the dramatic Andean highlands, and into the town of Cotacachi, which sits at the base of the Cotacachi Volcano. Allow several hours to finish the ride, and remember to bring a rain jacket, just in case.

Outfitters

The Biking Dutchman, Foch 714 and J.L. Mera, ☎ 2-2542-2806, ☎ /fax 2-2568-233, dutchman@uio.satnet.net, www.bikingdutchman.com, pioneered mountain biking in Ecuador. They offer the best equipment, top-of-the-line components, and customized, full-package trips.

For renting mountain bikes in Otavalo, try **Taller Ciclo Primaxi**, at García Moreno and Atahualpa. Rental cost is roughly $5 for the day, and the bikes are in pretty good shape by Otavalo standards. Otherwise, ask around for the latest best options.

■ On Horseback

 In Otavalo, **Intiexpress**, at Sucre 11-06, ☎ 6-921-436, fax 6-920-737, has been recommended as offering scenic horseback rides into the surrounding countryside for up to $20. There are plenty of wonderful places in this region for riding. Many of the mid-level to higher-end accommodations, especially the haciendas, offer horseback riding excursions or horses for hire. See *Where to Stay*, page 144.

Eco-Travel

■ Cochasqui Archeological Site

 Heading north from Quito, the pre-Incan ruins of Cochasqui provide an excellent view of the Sierras and, in the distance, Quito. Although it's not as magnificent as other ruins in South America (or even in Ecuador), the site is interesting for its incredible history and is a good stop for archeology buffs. Built by the Cara natives before the Incas arrived, the site consists of numerous low-lying mounds and flat-topped pyramids overgrown with vegetation. The view suggests that the site's location may have been chosen for strategic purposes, although the pyramids themselves were most likely ceremonial in function and related to astronomical alignments. One particular mound, for example, suggests an enormous sun and moon calendar, which, although somewhat eroded, is easily explained by a guide. Several of the overgrown pyramids themselves represent constellations, including the Southern Cross, Ursa Major (Big Bear) and Scorpius. They were also most likely used as offerings for health, fertility and the like. One of the mounds once housed the skulls of slain enemy groups from the surrounding region. On-site exhibits also include a re-created pre-Incan indigenous hut. Local Spanish-speaking guides provide informative tours (bring a translator), and there is also a small and interesting on-site museum. It's appropriate to tip the on-site guides.

To get there, head north on the Pan-American Highway and take the left fork a few miles beyond the village of Guayllabamba. Turn left again just before the village of Tabacundo on a dirt road signed *Piramides de Cochasqui*, and head directly toward Tocachi and the Cochasqui Ruins. If you are not on a prearranged tour or driving yourself, catch a taxi from Cayambe and bargain with the driver. The round-trip journey should cost under $15. Open daily. Of course, you can also start in Quito.

■ Cayambe-Coca Ecological Reserve

The Cayambe-Coca Ecological Reserve, at 914,270 acres, is massive. Nevertheless, it is one of Ecuador's lesser known treasures, due largely to its lack of development and inaccessibility. Straddling the

Eastern Cordillera of the Andes, the region stretches east and down to the Amazon, offering *páramo* habitat, cloud forests, the country's third-highest mountain, natural hot springs and quaint indigenous communities. The Quichua community of Oyacachi is known for its natural thermal baths and is a gateway into the Amazon.

The ecological significance of the reserve cannot be overstated. More than 450 species of birds have been identified here. The endangered Andean condor resides in this region, as do abundant and diverse flora, including orchids, balsa wood, dragon's blood, ayahuasca and laurel. And this untapped reserve offers more to do for the outdoor and adventure enthusiast than one could ever hope to absorb in one trip. Stick with the experts for fantastic opportunities to hike, bike, ride horseback, mountain climb, or just relax and soak in the natural hot springs. See *Adventures*, page 132, for an excellent trek from Oyacachi east into the Oriente via Chaco.

The reserve itself is east of Quito and Otavalo and includes various life zones, from *páramo* in the highlands down to upper Amazon ecology. The reserve has various access points, most of which require four-wheel-drive and a good guide. To get there from Cayambe, take the road (to Hacienda Guachala), which veers east off of the Pan-American three miles south of Cayambe to the village Cangahua. After a drive of just over an hour, there is an entrance station to the park. In theory, it is open daily and is where you would pay the $5 entrance fee, but there's usually no one at the gate. A couple of miles beyond the entrance station is the village of Oyacachi. If you want to climb Volcán Cayambe, the refuge on the mountain costs $10. Another entrance to the reserve is on the road through Papallacta to Baeza via Papallacta.

■ Cotacachi-Cayapas Ecological Reserve

Near the town of Cotacachi, on the southern slope of Volcán Cotacachi, is the ancient **crater lake of Cuicocha**, meaning *guinea pig* in Quichua. Don't let the name fool you, as this is a truly beautiful lake, with great views and hiking. Cuicocha Lake is a popular weekend spot for both Ecuadorians and foreign visitors. The area has been developed for tourism and a fee is collected when officials are stationed at the entrance. A motorboat can be hired (about $2 per person) for excursions out to the middle of the lake and around the Yerovi and Wolf islands. You can't leave the boat, however, as the islands are protected for research and hiking on them is not allowed.

Much of the activity at the lake revolves around the former **Hotel Parador Cuicocha**, which is now a tourist facility with restrooms, a restaurant, and live music. It's usually open on weekends and during the high season, although I doubt if even the people who work there know exactly when it is going to be open, as things tend to change often in Ecuador. Hiking around the volcano rim that surrounds the lake is a great way to spend time in the outdoors (see *Adventures on Foot*, page 135, for more details).

To get to Cuicocha, follow the Pan-American Highway nine miles north from Otavalo to the little town of Cotacachi. From there, continue another 11 miles to Cuicocha (el vía a Cuicocha). A pickup (*camioneta*) or taxi can be hired at the market in Otavalo for about $8 and $15, respectively, one-way, less from Cotacachi, and generally takes about 20 minutes from Cotacachi. There are also buses that frequent Cotacachi from Otavalo.

■ Rumicucho Archeological Site

While these Inca ruins are less than magnificent, the view from the site is spectacular. Excavation and restoration efforts are proceeding slowly. The site is a couple of miles north of San Antonio, just off the main road; open weekdays, 9-3, weekends, 8-4; entrance fee is under $2.

■ Intag Cloud Forest Reserve

Beyond the entrance to Quicocha Lake lies the small private reserve of Intag, covering a modest 202 acres. Intag drops down the western slopes from 9,156 to 5,886 feet into lush cloud forest. The reserve, managed in conjunction with DECOIN, the Organización para la Defenca y Conservación Ecológica de Intag (www.decoin.org) offers a myriad of flora and bird species within close proximity to Otavalo and the Northern Highlands. A simple, all-inclusive lodge is associated with the reserve, which is popular with birders and university students. Groups only. For reservations, contact **DECOIN**, Casilla (PO Box) 144, Otavalo, Imbabura, Ecuador. ☎ 6-648-593, decoin@hoy.net.

Santa Rosa is the village closest to the reserve, on the road from Cuicocha (and farther back, Cotacachi) to **Apuela** (buses depart from Otavalo and Cotacachi to Apuela), where hiking is available in the

Northern Highlands

surrounding countryside, including the hot springs at **Nangulví** and pre-Incan burial mounds at **Gualimán**. Inquire with guides in Otavalo or locals in Santa Rosa or Apuela for exploring this area.

■ El Ángel Ecological Reserve

El Ángel is a giant sponge. The climate is cool and moist, with high humidity, allowing for the birth of water in the Northern Highlands. The rarely visited ecological reserve, located just northwest of the town itself in the Carchi Province, is closer to the Colombian border than any other major point of interest. The reserve, nearly 40,000 acres in size, offers a great opportunity to experience a well-protected, biologically diverse, and contiguous *páramo* habitat.

One of the park's highlights, the cactus-like *frailejones*, is actually a member of the daisy family and can grow to the spectacular height of 6½ feet. The reserve was originally created to protect the threatened endemic namesake, which was in danger of becoming extinct due to unsound land-use patterns and application of chemical fertilizers in the area. The region's high humidity combines with its altitude to create opportunity for the *frailejones* and other special life forms that make it an atypical *páramo* habitat. A number of other threatened plant and animal species exist here as well.

Hiking through the reserve as an accommodation based day excursion suits some travelers. Trekking for several days in the reserve, however, provides ample birding opportunities and a chance to see the endangered **Andean condor**, as well as **hawks** and the **caracara**. The reserve is also known to hold a population of the very endangered **spectacled bear**, the only known species of bear in South America. Other typical *páramo* fauna includes **white-tailed** and **páramo deer**, **páramo fox**, **puma** (mountain lion) and, as with most Andean regions, introduced **trout** in the lagoons and streams. Rivers and lagoons support local villages and travelers wishing to camp in the region (see *Camping* below). Among the lagoon highlights are the **El Voladero Lagoons**, nestled in a glaciated valley at 12,100 feet elevation. Between the various lagoons, you'll find thermal pools, broad vistas (when it's clear), healing waters, trout that grow up to three feet in length and an abundance of *frailejones* plants. Fishing is allowed and quite popular here.

Be sure to obtain permission to fish here from the Ministerio de Medio Ambiente office in the town of El Ángel, on Salinas and Esmeraldas.

El Ángel is about four hours north of Quito. There are a few access routes into the reserve. One main (paved) road is Ibarra-Mira-El Ángel; the other is Ibarra-Pimampiro-Bolívar-San Gabriel-Tulcán. For the former, the paved road from the town of El Ángel to Tulcán quickly becomes deteriorated. Follow it north about 10 miles to El Voladero, where you can park, as long as you know you are there, and follow the trail to nearby lagoons (under an hour, camping available). From Tulcán, you can hire a truck or hop on a bus that will take you to the beginning of the reserve's trail system and out to the El Voladero Lagoons. Inquire in town. Always bring a good map and preferably a local guide. Adventures into this region are often done in conjunction with the **Cerro Golondrinas Cloudforest Trek** (see page 136).

Guided Trips

For guided trips to El Ángel, try contacting **Neblina Forest** in Quito at Centro Comercial La Galería Local No.65; ☎ 2-2460-189, fax 9-703-939, mrivaden@pi.pro.ec. Weekly departures cost about $50 per person per day and require a minimum of six people. Guide services, tents, and food are included. Bring your own sleeping bag, rain gear, and rubber boots. The dry season between June and September is best.

■ Jatun Sacha & the Guandera Cloud Forest Reserve

The 2,590-acre Guandera Biological Reserve and Station was purchased in the 1990s by the Jatun Sacha Foundation. The project is dedicated to preserving one of the last intact inter-Andean valley forests remaining in this part of Ecuador. The land is important for its relatively high biological diversity for a forest at such high elevation. Named after a characteristic tree species of the northern inter-Andean forests of Ecuador, Guandera is also a center for research, education, and community service. More information and volunteer opportunities are available through Jatun Sacha and can be viewed online at www.jatunsacha.org or www.jatunsacha.org/english/guandera.html.

Where to Stay

ACCOMMODATIONS PRICE SCALE	
Unless otherwise noted, prices are per room, up to double occupancy. Some prices are per person, particularly with all-inclusive packages, but these generally include meals, lodging, guide services and other amenities.	
$	Under $25
$$	$26 to $50
$$$	$51 to $100
$$$$	Over $100

■ Cayambe

 Near Cayambe is **Hacienda Guachala** (www. haciendaguachala.com). Call for directions in Quito, ☎ 2-2563-748, Reina Victoria 1138 and Foch. This hacienda, nestled within the beautiful Sierra countryside, offers a wonderful experience. Remnants of past cowboy glories adorn the halls and walls of this giant ranch-style home. Comfortable rooms with fireplaces wrap around the hacienda in a giant S-pattern. Wandering through the premises is like taking a step back in time. In fact, Guachala claims to be the oldest hacienda in Ecuador, having been around since the late 1500s. Comfortable common rooms, a large dining hall, and even a covered swimming pool are all available. Perhaps most interesting is the large open courtyard alongside a colonial chapel. Hacienda Guachala also offers horseback riding and hiking tours at minimal cost. $$

■ Otavalo

Accommodations in Otavalo and its surrounding areas are generally less expensive than those in Quito. While the town is geared toward the Saturday market (with higher prices and hotels that fill on Friday nights), it can be a very pleasant and tranquil place to spend a few days during the week. Doing so provides the perfect opportunity to visit local villages and people, explore the surrounding countryside, or just relax in town and do nothing.

Hostal Irina, Modesto Jaramillo 5-09 and Morales, ☎/fax 6-920-684, hostirin@uio.satnet.net, costs just a few dollars per night. Located a couple of blocks from Poncho Plaza, Irina is definitely a backpackers' hangout, with low ceilings and a variety of shared and private rooms sleeping from one to three people. The rush of village activity can be enjoyed from a sideline seat at the adjacent restaurant. Water is hot 24 hours a day, and there's Internet access. $

For a much more tranquil and spacious setting, try the **Hotel-Riveria Sucre**, at G Moreno 3-14, ☎ 6-920-241, also under $5 per night. Away from the main market activity, this converted colonial home offers rooms on two levels and surrounds a covered patio on one side and an extended garden courtyard on the other. The common game room with books and a Ping-Pong table offers a well-needed break from a rough day of hummingbird watching in the courtyard. The garden is a great place to chat with fellow budget travelers. About the only thing to watch out for is the neighbor's rooster, which tends to crow at the crack of dawn. $

Also inexpensive are two renovated colonial houses – **Dona Esther**, on Montalvo 4-44, ☎ 6-920-739, which also has a great restaurant, and the **Valle del Amanecer**, at Roca and Quiroga, ☎ 6-920-990, recommended for its nice setting and friendly atmosphere. The former is nicer, but both are great budget choices and can help to arrange tours or point you in the right direction. $

Hostal Aya Huma, secluded near the village of Peguche in the hills above Otavalo, ☎ 6-922-663, fax 922-664, ayahuma@ibanet.net, is one of the better accommodations in the area. A nice 40-minute walk from town or a short bike or taxi ride, Aya Huma is a great little mountain retreat surrounded by handicraft villages. The people are friendly and the rooms, though small, are quaint, with private or shared baths and hot water. The restaurant serves tasty meals, vegetarian options and has live music on weekends. $

Hotel El Indio Inn, at Calle Bolívar 904, ☎ 6-922-922, fax 920-325, is a very clean and relatively modern facility, yet is still quite affordable. Centrally located, it offers a friendly staff and restaurant on the premises. Not to be confused with the less-expensive hotel of the same name, El Indio provides spacious, comfortable rooms surrounding an interior courtyard. This is good value if you don't mind a nontraditional atmosphere, catering more to the modern Ecuadorian family. Watch out on weekends, though, as it can become a bit noisy here. $

☆ **Hotel Ali Shungu**, Miguel Egas and Quito, ☎ 6-920-750, www.alishungu.com, alishngu@uio.telconet.net, offers the best deal within the town itself. The facilities are superb for the price and the atmosphere is filled with a love for the traditional Otavaleño life. If you are of their opinion, the American expatriate couple that owns this place is very friendly, though they won't work with tour operators. They have gone out of their way to support the local community. Double rooms with private baths are comfortably decorated. Larger suites can hold up to six people. A beautiful and spacious garden patio is out back and rooms open up onto a walkway that overlooks it. There is also a fabulous restaurant serving a well-rounded menu. On Friday nights (a two-night stay is required on weekends), experience the wonderful Andean *musica folklórica*, with a live group of local, talented musicians. $$

■ Otavalo Outskirts

Just a few miles northwest of Otavalo are the unique **Cabañas Troje Cotama** (Pan-American Highway Km 4, ☎ /fax 6-946-119). Set among native villages and with panoramic views, the facilities are built with traditional architecture in the original grain-barn style of the early haciendas. The rooms are in two cabins and include private bathrooms and hot water. Private fireplaces, comfortable furnishings, and spectacular views come with a healthy dose of peace and solitude. It's well worth a visit. Horses are available. Inquire about monthly apartment rentals. $-$$

☆ A step up in rural retreats is the **Casa Mojanda Mountainside Inn and Farm**, less than two miles from Otavalo on the road to Mojanda, ☎/fax 6-922-969, mojanda@uio.telconet.net, www.casamojanda.com. This family-operated establishment lies on 25 acres of farmland and forest, a couple of miles from Otavalo on the road to the Mojanda Lakes. With spectacular views and activities such as hiking, horseback riding, and mountain biking, Casa Mojanda is an ideal setting for the nature enthusiast. The adobe cabins, typical of traditional local architecture, include eucalyptus-beamed roofs and hand-formed red-clay tiles. Relax in the peaceful surroundings, complete with outdoor gardens, wonderful views, a library and social rooms. Live indigenous music accompanies evening festivities. A little pricey, but meals are included, which makes up for the difference. Rooms are less for one person. $$$-$$$$

■ San Pablo del Lago

Along the shore of San Pablo del Lago is the **Hostería Puertolago**, south of Otavalo along the Pan-American Highway at Km 5.5, ☎ 6-920-920, fax 6-920-900, efernand@uio.satnet.net. From here you can bike around the shoreline, take a boat onto the lake, or simply relax on the shore. The accommodations offer a warm setting with rooms that include private baths, hot water, phones, and TVs, as well as a restaurant with a grand view of the lake. $$$

Hacienda Cusin, also at San Pablo, ☎ 2-2918-013/316, fax 2918-003, hacienda@cusin.com.ec, www.ecuadorexplorer.com/cusin, is a wonderfully renovated hacienda on the southern outskirts of San Pablo del Lago. This is one of the region's oldest and largest haciendas. It has been completely redone to offer attractive and comfortable accommodations with an authentic atmosphere. Most of the handsome rooms include private fireplaces or are set back in separate cottages. Comfort abounds, with attractive gardens, a bar-side fireplace, and plenty of relaxing common-room facilities. The meals from their excellent restaurant can be added to the price of the stay, and horseback riding is also available. It's a great choice if you prefer top-quality ranch-style accommodations. $$$+

■ North of Otavalo

Along the Pan-American (and just beyond the turnout for Cotacachi), is **Hacienda Pinsaqui**, ☎/fax 6-946-116/7, www.pinsaqui.com, info@pinsaqui.com. Definitely one of the nicest establishments in this region for the price, Pinsaqui provides a cozy ensemble of rooms, each with antiques and a unique personality. The colonial flare here is obvious and the setting is truly grand, complete with dining, beautiful grounds and plenty of options for exploring the area at a relaxed pace. Breakfast included. Horseback riding is also available. $$$

■ Cotacachi

The granddaddy of luxury and elegance in the Otavalo region is the **Hostería La Mirage**, in Cotacachi, ☎ 6-915-237, fax 6-915-065. This beautiful, modern, hacienda-style facility is adorned with antique furniture and very attractive rooms, though some might think it a little too ornate. Each unique room offers comfort and elegance, not to mention a cozy fireplace. Located outside the village of Cotacachi, northwest of Otavalo, the hotel is part of a working farm and rests

Northern Highlands

among acres of flower gardens. The restaurant is probably the best in the region, but its popularity means it can get a bit crowded. Amenities are too numerous to list, but include an ornate solar-heated swimming pool and horseback riding excursions into the extensive rolling countryside. This is the place to visit if you are looking for a luxurious rural retreat popular with Ecuador's upper echelon. Rooms begin at $150. Breakfast and dinner are included. $$$$

■ Ibarra

If you want to get even farther away from Otavalo, **Hostería Chorlaví**, ☎ 6-955-777, fax 6-956-311, is farther north near the town of Ibarra (Pan-American Highway Km 4, south of town). A bit more traditional than some of the extravagant lodges listed above, the reasonably priced Chorlaví maintains an old hacienda atmosphere in a relaxed setting, with the added bonus of a pool, a hot tub and *musica folklórica* on weekend nights. It gets crowded with tour groups on the weekends, so reservations are recommended. Note that Ibarra is a much more tranquil city than Otavalo, with strong traditions and less tourist influence. $-$$

In Ibarra itself, all accommodations are very inexpensive for what you get. **Hotel Montecarlo**, ☎/fax 6-958-182, Av. Rivadeneira 5-63 and Oviedo, is on the high end at $25-$50 per night. Modern in style, Montecarlo offers an indoor heated pool, hot tub and sauna. Rooms have private bath, telephone and cable TV. $$

There are quite a few decent budget choices near the cross streets of Oviedo and Olmedo. Walk around for a bit and check out a few for the best fit. The most popular is **Hostal Imbabura**, at Oviedo 9-33 and Narváez, ☎ 6-950-155, fax 6-958-521. The rooms in the renovated colonial building surround a very nice courtyard, perfect for a casual breakfast or just lounging about. Clean shared baths, laundry service and a friendly, helpful staff add to the pleasant atmosphere. For the true budget traveler. $

■ Camping

Cayambe-Coca Ecological Reserve

Camping in Cayambe is generally done by those ascending the peak. The **Ruales-Oleas-Berge climber's refuge** offers quality facilities at $10 per night, with a fireplace, running water, toilets, and cooking facilities (bring a sleeping bag), as well as a resident administrator. Sleeps 37.

The three- to four-day trek from Oyacachi to El Chaco, heading east into the Oriente, requires camping in the reserve. Bring all needed supplies for complete self-sufficiency.

Lagunas Mojandes

Camping is available at Laguna Grande de Mojanda. Bring a tent, sleeping bag, food and water.

El Ángel Ecological Reserve

Campers enjoy trekking through the high altitude, humid reserve and often stay near one of several reserves, including Voladero, Potreillos, Crespo, and Pelado. See *El Ángel*, page 142, for specific directions.

Where to Eat

■ Otavalo

 The lodges in and around the Otavalo area usually have restaurants. Especially worthwhile are those at **Hacienda Cusin** and **Hostería La Mirage**, near San Pablo and Cotacachi, respectively (see *Where to Stay*, page 147). There are also a couple of good *peñas* in town (they offer live traditional folk music, *musica folklórica*, primarily on weekends). Walk around and listen for the music, or ask a local, as establishments come and go all the time. Keep in mind that some Otavaleños tend to get very drunk on the weekends after big sales at the market. Otavalo is sleepy throughout the rest of the week.

Shenandoa's pie shop, right along the southwestern edge of Poncho Plaza, serves delicious pie and ice cream dishes with coffee or tea. Get there early for the best selection. They serve simple breakfasts and lunch items as well (omelets, sandwiches and the like), but I've never made it past the midday dessert. Nearby is **Café Mundi**, on the plaza at Quiroga and Jaramillo, serving tasty meals, veggie dishes as well, at inexpensive prices. It's a good place to drink coffee, relax, and watch all the activity outside.

At the southern corner of the plaza is **Tobasco's Mexican Restaurant**, at the corner of Calle Sucre and Salinas, with decent food and an excellent bird's-eye view of the market from its upstairs patio. Opened six years ago by an American couple, the establishment was sold to Ecuadorians within the last few years. Although not as "Mexican" as it used to be, it is still a great place to hang out.

Ali Micui's, on the northern corner of Poncho Plaza, provides great, inexpensive food. Meat and vegetarian meals are offered, and the portions are large and tasty. The black bean soup and pasta dishes are especially good. Groups should arrive well before hunger sets in, as it's usually just a one-person show in the kitchen.

Geminis, located between Sucre and Bolívar on Salinas, has also been recommended by travelers for the great food, music and setting, though I haven't eaten there.

SISA, on Calderón between Sucre and Bolívar, upstairs (☎ 6-920-154), is one of the better restaurants in Otavalo. Great appetizers and traditional dishes complement a tasty international menu. On weekends there may be live music out on the balconies. Expect to pay a little more here, but it is still inexpensive by northern standards. Below the restaurant is an international bookstore, an *artesanía* store selling high-quality local crafts and an art gallery with expensive but beautiful paintings.

A staple favorite for sit-down dining is in the **Hotel Ali Shungu**, at the northwest end of Calle Quito, ☎ 6-920-750. Attractively decorated with fine weavings and crafts, the ambiance here is quite pleasant. The food, too, leaves nothing to be desired. Enjoy live music on Friday night, but call ahead for reservations as it is often booked.

Pizza Siciliana, Sucre 10-03, has the best pizzas in town. It's a good group hangout and is relatively popular. Prices are moderate and portions are big, with vegetarian options. Expect a good crowd and live music on weekends. Actually, it seems to be the same folk band that plays everywhere else. They just spend their evenings rotating around between the most crowded restaurants, accepting donations and selling CDs.

Another good Italian option is **Café César**, on Sucre between Morales and Salinas on the second floor. It's open for dinner until late in the evening. The pasta and pizza dishes are pretty good by Ecuadorian standards, and, what a surprise, you can expect live music on the weekends.

Native Food of the Northern Andes

Traditional cuisine throughout Ecuador's Andean region, particularly in the north, includes a variety of interesting combinations. Baked pork is a favorite staple, often served with *llapingachos*, a kind of flattened potato and cheese pancake (absolutely delicious!). **Cuy**, a guinea pig-like animal – usually spit-roasted – offers a tasty meal in the poorer regions when served with potatoes. Be warned, however, that cuy is served in its natural form, and will more than likely be smiling up at you from the plate. After all the effort of peeling back the (now crisp) fur, there isn't much left to enjoy. Soup dishes are also common, and may include a white corn dish called *morocho*, or a barley-rice soup known as *arroz de cebada*. Another favorite is *locro de papa*s – a delightful, thick potato soup, with chunks of salty cheese and avocado in the middle. Traditional drinks include *leche de tigre*, which combines hot milk with brandy; a fermented rice drink known as *chichi de arroz*; and *canelazo*. A hot drink with fruit, liquor and cinnamon, *canelazo* offers a warm and tasty mid-afternoon treat after a day of hiking in the cool highlands.

■ Ibarra

There are numerous restaurants downtown, most of which are centrally located within several square blocks that surround the main plazas from Moreno south to Velasco. The best pizza, served up at **El Horno**, at Rocafuerte and Flores, is super-cheap and fresh oven-roasted. A close second, though, is **La Trattoria Rusticana**, on Sucre and Parque Moncayo, with a nice setting and popular with locals as well as foreigners. **Grán Chifa Kam**, at Olmedo 7-62 and Oviedo, has good, inexpensive Chinese food. For Ecuadorian cuisine, try **Antojitos de mi Tierra**, at Plaza de Ibarreñidad. Very inexpensive and popular, it is open for lunch and dinner. Note that Ibarra is a sleepy town, and none of the restaurants stay open too late. The best option for dining in the area is at **Hostería Chorlaví** (see *Where to Stay*, page 148).

Shopping

This region is filled with artesanía villages and stores. In Otavalo, there are far too many places to detail here. In fact, you will see more wool sweaters than you ever thought possible. The shops farther away from Poncho Plaza tend to be more reasonable, but shop around as quality and prices vary significantly. Also note that prices are typically higher on market day, and you are better off early in the week. Various travel and shipping agents can ship packages of souvenirs overseas from Otavalo – a good idea if you do end up buying a lot. Tour operators can arrange visits to the local communities where the crafts are made, where they can often be purchased more cheaply than in Otavalo or Quito. See pages 133 and 135 for a list of operators.

Nightlife

Otavalo is a relatively sleepy town, but just keep your ears and eyes open for the latest local scene. The traditional Andean music is always a highlight here, and there are usually at least a couple of *peña* bars with live folk music, at least on weekends. **Peña Tucano**, at Morales and Modesto Jaramillo, is quite popular for loud salsa and the occasional folk tune, as is **Peña Bar Chop**, just across the street. Both are loud, especially on weekends, so don't pick a hotel close by. For more traditional folklórica, try the nearby **Peña Amauta**, on Morales and Jaramillo. It's open on weekends. And be sure to catch the live show at **Hotel Ali Shungu**.

In Ibarra, follow the university students on weekends for the best nightlife, including **El Barbudo**, on the Plaza de la Ibarreñidad at Moncayo and Sucre. It's closed at the beginning of the week; otherwise, it's open as late as the locals want to indulge. For more of a dance scene, try the popular **Tequila Rock**, at Oviedo and Sucre, open Thurs-Sat nights until late.

Central Highlands

Ecuador's **Avenue of the Volcanoes** is the backbone of the Central Highlands, a long and beautiful stretch of eternal mountain views. Snow-capped volcanoes peer through layers of mist and each curve of the highway presents a new vision. The highest peaks, several of which are active volcanoes, lie in this stretch of the Andes. Opportunities for adventure include hiking, trekking, mountaineering and horseback riding. Mountain biking and road touring are coming into their own. Birders and photographers will find this region a pleasure. Wildlife viewing abounds, particularly in the higher-elevation *páramo* zones.

Ecuador's highlands span the entire country, as the Andes actually cross several countries in South America. This chapter focuses first on the central area – one of the more visited regions in the country – south of Quito to Riobamba. To the southwest, in the region around the adventure-oriented town of Baños, our travels split toward the Oriente, the upper stretches of the Amazon Basin. This is a transition zone between the highlands of the Andes and the Amazon rainforest, neither here nor there, but definitely somewhere that you will want to visit. As such, it is treated as a separate section of this chapter.

Quito South to Riobamba

■ Flora & Fauna

The Cordillera landscape is, in a word, massive. Intermountain valleys have been primarily converted to farmland. High altitude grassland offers habitat for grazers and flowering plants that attract beautiful hummingbirds such as the **Andean hillstar**. Rising along the slopes of snow-studded volcanoes, the land gives way to the *páramo* life zone, where dwarfed vegetation and only the hearty survive. In places like Cotopaxi National Park and the more distant peaks, the **Andean condor** soars with a 10-foot wingspan, while an orange-faced falcon, the **carunculated caracara**, darts between shrubs hunting small rodents. The **mountain lion** (puma) continues to rule the animal kingdom on the ground, with **white-tailed and dwarf deer**, **rabbits** and the **Andean fox**, or colpeo, roaming the region. There are miles of abundant trout streams, particularly in the more remote areas of this region.

■ Getting Here

 The Andes run north to south, dividing Ecuador almost perfectly in half. The upper Amazon Basin lies to the east, and the Pacific lowlands to the west. The Cordilleras themselves line the sides of a deep valley. Flanked on both sides by this enormous range is the Central Valley and the Pan-American Highway.

The Pan-American Highway is the main road within this region. Buses from Quito and elsewhere travel the Pan-American daily. The Pan-American runs north-south and is the major transportation cord that unites all of Ecuador. From Quito, it is the obvious and only choice for traveling south toward Cotopaxi, Chimborazo, and other regional destinations. Travelers generally go toward the Cotopaxi area, or down to Baños, with plenty of options in-between. The more distant Andean countryside is much more isolated and makes for incredible adventures if you are willing to get off the beaten track a bit. Flights are also available from Quito to Latacunga.

■ Getting Around

 Unless you rent an automobile, the easiest way to travel in this region, as with much of Ecuador, is by public transportation. **Buses** frequent even the most remote villages. Just catch a bus from Quito to the major town nearest your final destination, then transfer to buses for the next largest town or village. Even if you are heading to a fairly remote area, it won't take more than a couple of transfers. If you are driving, bring a guide or be prepared to ask for directions. Most roads are not sign-posted. Fortunately, everything is a turn-off from the Pan-American Highway.

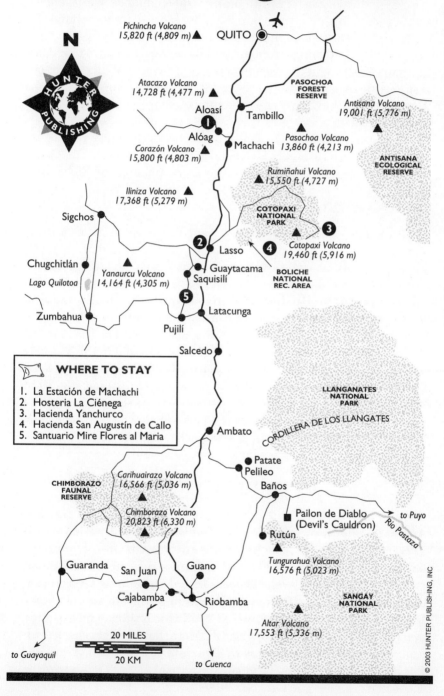

Central Highlands

WHERE TO STAY

1. La Estación de Machachi
2. Hosteria La Ciénega
3. Hacienda Yanchurco
4. Hacienda San Augustín de Callo
5. Santuario Mire Flores al Maria

© 2003 HUNTER PUBLISH-ING, INC

■ Visitor Information

All arrangements for tours, destinations, and accommodations within the Central Highlands are best made in Quito (see pages 94-97 for more details) or Baños for excursions farther south and east (see page 192). Latacunga, Ambato and Riobamba also have tour operators that operate in this region (see pages 174-75). While larger cities provide most modern services, the smaller towns, such as Machachi, may have post and communications options (an Andinatel office). Although telephones are available at mid-level to high-end accommodations, such as Hacienda La Ciénega, the more remote retreats, such as Yanahurco, depend on radio contact with Quito. Modern services are available in Latacunga, Ambato, and Riobamba.

Latacunga

In Latacunga, most services are centrally located near Parque Vicente León and the cathedral, which is at Quito and Maldonado. **Telecommunications** (Andinatel) and the **post office** are located at Quevedo and Maldonado. There are a few Internet cafés nearby. The **Banco de Pichincha** and **Banco Popular** are both located on Parque Vicente León; and **Filanbanco** is on Quito and Guayaquil. Other than small stores, there is a **Saturday market** on the Plaza de San Sebastián and quality *artesanía* (crafts) are sold in the Tuesday market at the Plaza de Santo Domingo (on Calle Guayaquil, between Orellano and Quito). Buses traveling through Latacunga stop right on the Pan-American at 5 de Junio; from there you can walk over the river into downtown or catch a taxi. Plaza El Salto, on Amazonas and Valencia, has taxis and *camionetas* (trucks for hire) nearby.

Ambato

In Ambato, the **post office** is adjacent to Parque Montalvo, at Castillo and Bolívar, and is open from 7:30 am to 7:30 pm. The Andinatel **telephone** office is open Mon-Fri, 8 am-9:30 pm at Castillo 03-31 and Rocafuerte. The new **Café Internet** is open 8 am-8 pm daily at Castillo 06-48 and Cevallos. **Banks** that provide ATM services and/or change travelers checks include **Banco de Guayaqui**l, at Sucre and JL Mera; **Banco del Pacífico**, at Cevallos and Lalama; **Banco del Pichincha**, at Parque Cevallos on Lalama and Cevallos; and **Cambiato**, at Bolívar 694 and JL Mera, for travelers checks/currency exchange. The **Ministry of Tourism** office, at Guayaquil and Rocafuerte (near the Hotel Ambato), is open Mon-Fri. For **shopping**, try Supermaxi, at Centro Comercial Caracol, Av. de los Capulies and Mirabales, in Ficoa; or Supermercado, Centro Comercial Ambato, Parque 12 de Noviembre. Ambato's **hospital** is at Pasteur and Nacional, ☎ 3-821-059. The main **bus terminal** is near the train station about 1½ miles northwest of the central city.

Riobamba

In Riobamba, international **telephone** calls can be made at Andinatel, located at the bus terminal and at Tarquí between Primera Constituyente and Veloz. **Post office** and **fax** service is available at 10 de Agosta and Espejo. **Internet** is available at a number of cafés, including **Cybernet Café**, at Rocafuerte 21-25 and Guayaquil; **Andino Café**, on Av. Daniel L. Borja 35-15 and Diego Ibarra; and **Café Ashoka**, Carabobo and 10 de Agosto, 2nd floor. Rates range from US$1-US$2 per hour. The best (private) **hospital**, Policlínico, is at Olmedo and Cuba, ☎ 3-965-725. The main **bus terminal** is at D L Borja and Prensa. The **train station** is centrally located at D L Borja and Carabobo.

The helpful **Ministry of Tourism** office in Riobamba is located on Av. Daniel L. Borja and Brasil. **Banco de Guayaquil**, on Primera Constituyente 2626 and García Moreno, accepts Visa and American Express. **Banco de Préstamos** at Parque Maldonado, on Primera Constituyente and Espejo, accepts MasterCard; **Banco del Pacífico**, at Av. Miguel A León and Veloz, also accepts MasterCard; and **Banco la Previsora**, at Colón 22-35 and 10 de Agosto, accepts Visa.

■ Touring & Sightseeing

Alóag

The first noteworthy town south of Quito along the Pan-American Highway is Alóag. Although there is nothing of much interest for the curious traveler, this is where the road west to Santo Domingo de los Colorados and the Pacific Lowlands splits off from the Pan-American Highway. Buses and trucks pull off the road here for minor repairs and tire changes.

Machachi & Aloasí

A bit farther south lies **Machachi**, a small town just north of the main turnout for Cotopaxi National Park. Although not a destination itself, Machachi is coming into its own as a departure point for trips into the backcountry, especially Cotopaxi National Park. And foreign travelers can give eternal thanks to Machachi for its mineral spring water and Agua Gutig bottling plant. Safe drinking water never seemed so precious as when traveling through Ecuador.

Aloasí, a village just north and across the highway from Machachi, offers an even nicer rural setting, accommodations and home base for exploring the region, especially around Volcán Corazón and the Ilinizas.

Latacunga

A couple of hours south of Quito is Latacunga, the capital of the province of Cotopaxi. With nearly 40,000 people, it is historically interesting – dating back to the pre-Incan Puruhá Indians – but lacks character or much to see and do. An erupting Cotopaxi Volcano has reduced Latacunga to ashes three times in the last two centuries. Although it was rebuilt each time, the town has lost much of its original architecture and, as a result, is now quite modern, in a developing-country sort of way. It has a nice central plaza, gardens and a few restored colonial structures worth visiting.

Use Latacunga as a stopping point during the magnificent drive through the Avenue of the Volcanoes or as a base for local excursions, including Lake Quilotoa, the native markets of Pujilí and Saquisilí, and surrounding indigenous villages.

Most of the activity, including tourist services, centers around **Parque Vicente León**, at Quito and Maldonado. The main church is here, along with several hotels and restaurants (there are also a few farther northwest toward Río Cutuchi and the railroad tracks). Other points of interest include the **Casa de la Marqueses de Miraflores**, at Orellana and Echeverría, which has a museum in a nicely renovated colonial mansion. The highlight includes a display on the Mama Negra festivities that occur on September 24, paying homage to slaves brought over by the Spanish during the colonial era. **Casa de la Cultura**, at Vela 3-49 and Salcedo, is the best museum in town,

Latacunga

N

Train Station

Salvador

Gen. F. Alfaro

J. Amdrade

V. Torres

5 del Junio

100 YARDS
100 METERS

Panamericana

Río Curuchi

Melchor de Benavides

Río Yanayacu

Pacha

Toa

Cemetery

Calixto Piño

Camionetas

Felix Valencia

Plaza El Salto

Vela

Guayaquil

Amazonas

Juan Echeverria

2 de Mayo

Belisario Quevedo

Sucre

Padre Salcedo

Telephone Office

Post Office

General Maldonado

Tarqui

Hermanas Paez

Quito

Iglesia Santo Domingo

Sanchez de Orellana

Quijado Ordóñez

Parque Vincente Léon

Municipio

1. Estambul
2. Rodelú
3. Tour Operators
4. Museo de la Casa de la Cultura
5. Buses to Saquisili & Chugchilán
6. Buses to Quevado & Zumbahua
7. Buses to Quito
8. Buses South

built upon the foundations of a Jesuit monastery. It also hosts a variety of activities during local celebrations.

Ambato

The first large city south of Latacunga (beyond San Miguel de Salcedo) and the fourth-largest city in the country, is Ambato. The capital of Tungurahua province, Ambato – known as the "City of Flowers and Fruit" – is home to a bustling population of 150,000 and counting. Originally the site of several pre-Incan indigenous groups, Ambato became a permanent rest stop, or *tambo*, for people traveling from Quito to Cuenca during the reign of the Incan Empire. Upon arrival in the first half of the 16th century, the Spanish built (and rebuilt several times) a colonial town here, only to see it destroyed over and over again by earthquakes, the latest in 1949. As a result of this geological bad luck, very little historical architecture or artifacts remain and it lacks the colonial charm of many other places in Ecuador.

Nevertheless, Ambato is surging ahead with a rocketing population and booming economy, based in part on the pharmaceutical industry. It's an interesting city to visit, particularly during the Monday market, which is the largest in Ecuador. Unless you enjoy bumper-to-bumper traffic, however, it is best to park and wander around on foot. You'll be amazed at the fantastic display of colorful sights, sounds, and smells – a true merging of indigenous culture with modern life.

Festival of Fruit & Flowers

 Each year, at the beginning of February, Ambato, known as "The Garden City," is home to the famed Fiesta de las Frutas y de las Flores, a colorful celebration that showcases the best of local talent. Among the festivities are street parades with colorful floats decorated with – you guessed it – flowers and fruit, traditional folk music performances and dancing. The festival is a very popular destination for Ecuadorians, as well as foreign travelers, so be sure to make hotel reservations well in advance.

The culture buff shouldn't have a problem filling a day or two in Ambato, as the city has quite a few interesting sites, including numerous churches and parks, and a natural history museum. It also has museums – once homes – of two of Ecuador's most renowned intellectuals, Juan Montalvo and Juan León Mera, a famous essayist, novelist and playwright, sometimes referred to as the "Cervantes of South America," was born in Ambato in 1832. **Juan Montalvo's house** is now open to the public as a museum on the corner of Bolívar and Montalvo, ☎ 3-821-024. There is no entrance fee. The "**Quinta de Mera**" is the farm where Juan León Mera, another Ambateño writer and poet, was born and raised. Mera is most famous for writing the Ecuadorian national anthem. Also converted into a museum, the house is surrounded by very pleasant, tree-lined gardens. To get there, take a taxi from the city center. The house is in the nearby suburb of Atocha.

Central Highlands

Ambato

E. Alforo

Sevilla
15

E. Espejo

M. Eguez

Lalama
$
7   16

Martinez
5
$
17

JL Mera

6

2

12   14

Montalvo

Cuenca
Rocafuerte
Bolivar
Sucre
Cevallos
JB Vela
12 de Noviembre
Castillo

10
19 9
13
11
3 4

Quito

1 8

Guayaquil
18

Pérez de Anda

Rio Ambato

Olmedo

WHERE TO STAY & EAT

1. Hotel Ambato/Restaurant
2. Gran Hotel
3. La Buena Mesa
4. Parrilladas El Gaucho
5. Chifa Jo Fua
6. La Brasa Roja
7. Pizzería Fornace

200 YARDS

200 METERS

OTHER SITES

8. Tourist Office
9. Casa de Cultura Museum
10. Casa de Montalvo
11. Post Office
12. Museo de Ciencias Naturales
13. Parque Juan Montalvo
14. Parque Cevallos
15. Mercado Colombia
16. Mercado Central
17. Parque 12 de Noviembre
18. Plaza Urbino
19. Andinato Telephone Office

The **Natural History Museum** (Museo de Ciencias Naturales) is located in the city center, on Sucre, near the Parque .Cevallos. It is home to a collection of stuffed birds and bottled animals. It's not bad if you like that kind of thing.

The **Casa de la Cultura**, on Montalvo between Rocofuerte and Bolívar, has a nice little café/art gallery, a great place for a coffee and a slice of chocolate cake, or to meet and chat with local artists and intellectuals, for whom this is a popular haunt. They have exhibitions featuring the work of local artists – some good, some not so good – although it is all a matter of taste. They also have live folk music from time to time, the occasional movie night, and have even been known to throw in a comedy night now and again. Be warned though – as the obvious foreigner, you will be the brunt of every joke.

Ambato is a major junction for roads to many destinations in Ecuador. To the north is Quito and the Central Highlands, to the south is Cuenca, Loja and the Southern Highlands, as well as the route to Guayaquil and the coast. To the east is Baños and the road to the jungles of the Oriente. It is also a home base for finding a guide to climb or explore Volcán Chimborazo to the south, as well as Sangay, Altar and Tungurahua .Volcanos Ambato is about 85 miles and 2½ hours south of Quito via the Pan-American Highway. You can't miss it as it lies directly along the highway.

Riobamba

South of Ambato along the Pan-American Highway is Riobamba, the capital of the Chimborazo province and an important hub for climbers. Offering modern services, outfitters, gear and provisions, it tends to cater to mountain folk more than to the typical "gringo trail" traveler. From Riobamba, you may be able to witness the peaks of up to five volcanoes on a clear day, including the renowned Chimborazo, Altar and Tungurahua.

With nearly 120,000 inhabitants, Riobamba is an important city that links the north with the south and the Pacific Coast. In fact, the spectacular steam engine train ride that once began along the coast in Guayaquil drops travelers here, offering an incredible display of changes in the land and the people along the way.

Located in the Tipi Valley, Riobamba and the surrounding region is known for its cultural heritage and agricultural and commercial activity. It perseveres with a flare of colonial aristocracy and the pace here is slow. As for the adventure traveler, Riobamba's primary attraction is its ideal location for local hiking, trekking, and climbing excursions.

If you are staying here, by now you have figured out that all cities, towns, and even moderately sized villages are arranged in colonial-style grid-like patterns, with at least one central plaza and park. **Parque Maldonado** is the main plaza in Riobamba. As throughout the city, there are several well-preserved colonial structures around the park, including **Santa Bárbara Cathedral**. Other parks include **Parque Sucre** and **Parque 21 de Abril**, which has great views of the valley.

The Devil's Nose!

Once stretching from the Coastal City of Guayaquil to the historic Andean capital of Quito, Ecuador's railway was a true feat. Upon completion around the turn of the 20th century, it unified Ecuador for the first time ever. Now, only remnants of this technological wonder remain, a victim of the elements and road development. Today, this train ride is geared primarily to the foreign traveler and doesn't really fulfil any practical transportation needs. One particular section that remains in operation is the spectacular route between Riobamba and **Alausí** (not to be confused with Aloasí, above) to **Sibambe**. In fact, the railway connected all the way to Guayaquil until the El Niño storms of 1997. From the rooftop of the train it is such a spectacular ride, with views of Chimborazo. An engine on each end of the train is required to make it up and down the "Devil's Nose," which connects a series of steep switchbacks up the mountainside. And the view into native life as you pass indigenous villages is a special treat.

From Riobamba, the train departs at around 7 am on Wednesdays, Fridays and Sundays for Alausí and then down the Nariz del Diablo – the Devil's Nose – to Sibambe and then back up to Alausí, at which point you have to get off. Note that this is a full day's journey. You can purchase tickets at the train station in Riobamba, preferably a day ahead of time. Alternatively, you can hop on the train at Alausí to travel down the nose and back. Or, if you are coming from the coast, get off the bus at **Sibambe** by midday and catch the ride up to Alausí. Inquire locally in Riobamba or with South American Explorers in Quito (☎/fax 2-225-228, explorer@seac.org.ec), as the schedule is irregular and may have changed.

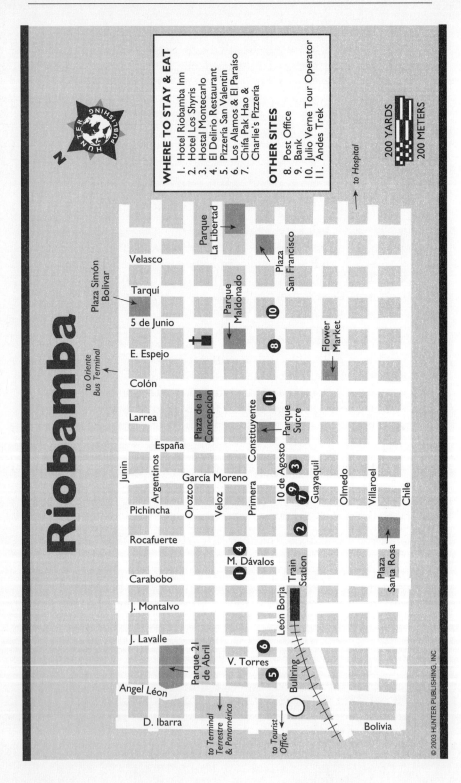

Riobamba

WHERE TO STAY & EAT
1. Hotel Riobamba Inn
2. Hotel Los Shyris
3. Hostal Montecarlo
4. El Delirio Restaurant
5. Pizzería San Valentin
6. Los Alamos & El Paraiso
7. Chifa Pak Hao &
   Charlie's Pizzería

OTHER SITES
8. Post Office
9. Bank
10. Julio Verne Tour Operator
11. Andes Trek

200 YARDS
200 METERS

to Hospital

Velasco
Tarquí
5 de Junio
E. Espejo
Colón
Larrea
España
Argentinos
García Moreno
Pichincha
Rocafuerte
M. Dávalos
Carabobo
J. Montalvo
J. Lavalle
Angel Léon
D. Ibarra

Junin
Orozco
Veloz
Primera
10 de Agosto
Guayaquil
Olmedo
Villaroel
Chile

Plaza Simón Bolívar
to Oriente Bus Terminal

Parque La Libertad
Plaza San Francisco
Parque Maldonado
Flower Market
Plaza de la Concepción
Constituyente
Parque Sucre
Train Station
León Borja
V. Torres
Bullring
Plaza Santa Rosa
Parque 21 de Abril

to Terminal Terrestre & Panamérica
to Tourist Office
Bolivia

© 2003 HUNTER PUBLISHING, INC

The **Convento de la Concepcion**, south of the Plaza de la Concepción (also referred to as the Plaza Roja), at Orozco and España (entrance at Argentinos and J Larrea), open Tuesday-Sunday, is a restored convent that now serves as a religious art museum. The museum is impressive, to say the least, offering displays of priceless 18th-century art.

Market day is Saturday in Riobamba and it's another regional highlight, drawing natives from all over to the city. It is as much a social event and symbol of unity as it is a chance for the indigenous communities to purchase daily necessities. The local **San Alfonso Market** is in the eastern part of the city near the cross streets of Junín and 5 de Junio. Other markets include **La Condamine**, located at Carabobo and Colombia, **San Francisco** (the church), near Parque La Libertad at San Francisco and Velasco, and **La Merced**, near the church on Guayaquil and Aspajo. Of more interest perhaps to the foreign shopper is the market just south of the Convento de la Concepción.

Getting to Riobamba is easy, as it sits along the Pan-American Highway. By bus, it is four hours from Quito in the north, five hours from Cuenca in the south. The central bus station is at Eplicachima and Av. D L Borja, but the station serving Baños and the Oriente is located at Espejo and Córdovez. Taxis between stations and around town are advised.

■ Adventures

 The Central Sierras offer endless miles of scenic exploration. Mountaineering is the obvious regional highlight for the extreme adventurer, as the glistening peaks from Cotopaxi to Chimborazo and everything in-between invite those with technical experience or are willing to learn. Trekking and camping in the backcountry are as beautiful as they are accessible, though you also have to be prepared for adverse weather conditions. The hiking opportunities in the *páramo* countryside are superb, in many cases requiring only a landmark to aim for. Although there are plenty of trails, including sections of the most famous trail in the Americas, the Inca Trail, the *páramo* landscape is wide open. Several guest haciendas also provide horseback riding options in the same areas, an excellent way to experience the Sierras.

Photographers and birders, as well, will be pleasantly surprised. The stark and enormous landscape combined with equatorial lighting and unique wildlife make this a very special place. Where else can you find the Andean wolf, the endangered spectacled bear, and the majestic Andean condor all in one day?

On Foot & With Gear

El Corazón

 A great warm-up hike and introduction to the Central Highlands is on Volcán El Corazón. Just south of Machachi, take the road west to the village of Aloasí and continue toward the extinct volcano (15,657 feet elevation). A great base for exploring the mountain and surrounding countryside is La Estación Machachi (see *Where to Stay*, page 177), which has great views of Corazón from the dining room window. From there, it takes up to five hours to reach the summit. Or just make a day of exploring the surrounding countryside and chatting with the locals.

Ilinizas

The first major reserve south of Quito worth playing in is located along the Western Cordillera around the Ilinizas Volcanoes. This region is filled with endless dirt roads and trails, although pointing to a mountain and heading in that direction is quite a bit easier than finding your way back if you are not familiar with the countryside. Your best bet is traveling with a local or a professional guide. At the least, know how to speak Spanish well enough to ask for directions.

The volcanoes are set within the newly created Ilinizas Ecological Reserve (see *Eco-Travel* section, page 175), a massive protectorate, including such highlights as open *páramo* countryside, the namesake peaks, **Lake Quilotoa** and intact western cloud forest habitat. Although the two main peaks of Illiniza are the sixth- and eighth-highest points in Ecuador, they are a bit overshadowed by the massive royalty of Volcán Cotopaxi across the valley. Nevertheless, they are well worth the effort it takes to ascend them.

If you do not hire a guide from Quito, drive or take a bus from Machachi to El Chaupi, three miles farther south along the Pan-American and then four miles to the west. From El Chaupi, the walk to the *refugio*, located in the saddle between the two peaks, takes about eight hours. Alternatively, you can catch a *camioneta* from El Chaupi, or, more likely, from Machachi (under $14) to the La Vírgen parking lot near the *refugio*. See Hostal Casa Nieves, page 177, for a nice home base to explore Ilinizas.

Camionetas

Though public buses are a great and very cheap way to travel around the Ecuadorian countryside – even in the rural areas – they take a bit more logistical juggling. *Camionetas* are trucks for hire that often hang out around the main plaza in any decent-sized village or town. They charge a bit more than buses, but are still reasonable, especially if you have a few people sharing.

The easier summit to attain is **Illiniza Norte** (16,762 feet). With extreme caution, it can be climbed without technical gear in several hours from the refuge. **Illiniza Sur**, at 17,161 feet, is actually one of the most difficult climbs in the country, requiring technical ice-climbing gear and experience. Between the two peaks is a climber's refuge with cooking facilities that sleeps 12. Be sure to bring a sleeping bag and pad, all of your supplies, and a good topographic map.

The Condor Trek: From Papallacta to Cotopaxi

If you are looking to escape to the backcountry for one of the more spectacular and challenging multi-day treks in Ecuador, the Condor Trek is the hike to do. This journey offers wonderful Andean scenery along the Eastern Cordillera range and perhaps the best opportunity to spot the famed Andean condor. Travel over *páramo* habitat, through river valleys, and among flat lagoons and ancient lava flows. En route, pass the spectacular peaks of **Antisana** and **Sincholagua** and wind up face-to-face with **Cotopaxi Volcano**.

Watchable Wildlife

 Spending time in the backcountry of Ecuador's Central Andes provides one of the best chances you will have to spot the largest flying bird in the world – the endangered Andean condor. The condor is Ecuador's national bird, and aptly nicknamed the "King of the Andes," which says something in such an awe-inspiring place. With a wingspan of up to 11 feet, this member of the vulture family is completely monogamous, living with its chosen partner for life. Often, one of only 100 or so remaining Ecuadorian condors can be seen soaring in the more remote backcountry areas.

Central Highlands

Several outfitters in Quito provide guide services for the Condor Trek. If lugging all of your own gear sounds like hard work, you can sign up for a tour with pack animals, although carrying your own pack provides a greater sense of achievement at the end of the day. If you decide to go it alone, this route requires good navigational skills and topographic maps (IGM 1:50,000 Papallacta, Laguna de Mica, Sincholagua, and Cotopaxi). Also, be sure to talk with someone who has done the trek before. A detailed route description can be found in Rachowiecki, Thurber and Wagenhauser's *Climbing and Hiking in Ecuador* (Bradt Publications, 1997).

Cotopaxi National Park

Hiking and climbing opportunities on Cotopaxi Volcano and throughout the park are superb. From the main entrance, the first major stopping point along the rugged dirt road is **Laguna Limpiopungo**, set among the southeastern flanks of the jagged and scenic **Rumiñahui Volcano**, a haven for Andean bird life. Having lived near the ocean, I was quite surprised when I first heard the old familiar cry of the seagull, at an altitude of 12,426 feet! The call is actually that of an Andean gull that resides near the lake, which is really more of a marsh. A few species of ducks also reside there. The *páramo* habitat in this area is truly unique. You'll see hummingbirds, the Andean lapwing, and an orange-faced falcon known as the carunculated caracara, as well as the characteristic dwarfed vegetation.

At Limpiopungo, you can stroll around the lagoon, enjoy a wonderfully scenic picnic, or set up camp not too far away. Weather permitting, the views of Cotopaxi Volcano looming in the east – at 19,283 feet – are fabulous. There is also a small trail along the east side of Lake Limpiopungo that heads northwest toward the summit of Rumiñahui, at 15,408 feet. Although the summit can be reached without technical gear, it is a rough and rocky scramble and should not be attempted by the casual hiker. Other than that, you can hike just about anywhere without getting lost. Just pick a landmark and head toward it. Remember that everything here is more distant than it appears due to the massive scale of the mountains. Cotopaxi actually looks as if you can throw a rock and hit it. Be sure to bring plenty of water.

From the lagoon, it's a long hike or a breathtaking hop, skip, and jump (by auto) to the parking lot on Cotopaxi. At the parking lot below the climbers' refuge you will immediately notice the high altitude of 15,042 feet. Hiking from here to the refuge, at 15,696 feet, may seem like a stone's throw away, but it is a very exhausting "walk." Spend at least a few days in the highlands before attempting it. The trail leads directly from the parking lot to the refuge and is straight-forward.

From the climbers' refuge the route to the summit of Cotopaxi is not very technical for an experienced climber. It is a classic introduction to climbing in the Andes and a bit of a social event for many people. The hut is always loaded with enthusiastic travelers. However, some technical gear and experience are required. At the least, novice climbers should hire a guide to summit. Top-quality climbing outfitters in Quito charge up to $180 for a guided overnight trip to the summit, including transportation from Quito and all gear. Make sure you have tried a few lower-altitude peaks first, and are well acclimatized before attempting Cotopaxi. December through April are the best months for climbing here.

There are two routes from the Pan-American Highway into Cotopaxi. The north entrance to the park is about 1½ hours south of Quito (and about 10 miles south of the town of Machachi) via the Pan-American Highway. You'll see a sign on the left next to a Clirsen NASA sign, and a road that leads through the Boliche National Recreation Area. This route takes longer, depending on road conditions, but is more scenic. The more obvious and accessible southern entrance is a few miles farther along the Pan-American and is also marked with a sign that heads east into the park. This entrance passes through the park's administration center and also through a large stand of introduced pine forest. The two entrance roads meet up in the center of the park a short distance from Lago Limpiopungo. It takes several hours by car from Quito just to arrive at Lago Limpiopungo, as the backcountry roads are bumpy and dusty (or muddy during the rainy season).

Buses can drop you off at the entrance to the park (be sure the driver knows where you want to be dropped off). From there, it is possible to catch a ride with an incoming tourist vehicle or truck from Latacunga. Mountaineers often find rides with *camionetas* in Latacunga that take them all the way to the parking lot just below the climbers' refuge on Cotopaxi.

You pay the US$10 entrance fee to Cotopaxi National Park at the main entrance. There is also a small, and rather eerie, park museum several miles beyond the main entrance gates, as well as an administration building. A nice trail with posted natural history signs (to practice your Spanish) also begins adjacent to the museum. Typical hours are 8 am-4 pm, though the staff tends to take irregular and generally long lunch breaks somewhere in the middle of the day. Inquire about sleeping arrangements, as there are a couple of primitive shelters and campsites at the administration building and near the entrance to the park. The climber's refuge costs $10 per night per climber, and offers 30 beds, a kitchen and plenty of traffic.

A Nice "Stroll"

A week-long trek around Cotopaxi is a great way to spend some quiet time. The elevation gain is not significant, and the hike is not very strenuous. The route involves a dirt road around half of the mountain. Make sure to bring plenty of food, water, and rain gear. The route is simple to follow. The following maps are useful: IGM 1:50,000 Machachi, Cotopaxi, Sincholagua, and Mulalo. Refer to Rachowiecki, Thurber and Wagenhauser's *Climbing and Hiking in Ecuador* (Bradt Publications, 1997) for a detailed description of the trek.

Quilotoa Lake

Northwest of Latacunga lies the spectacular emerald-colored crater lake, Quilotoa, also within the Ilinizas Ecological Reserve. The lake is brilliant in its intensity of color, with a backdrop that includes several distant snowcapped volcanoes. Exercise extreme caution if you plan on hiking the rim, as many sections are slippery or have been destroyed by earthquakes. Allow six to seven hours to hike around the rim. Just viewing the lake amid the Sierra backdrop is spectacular and well worth a visit.

Buses from Latacunga pass through Pujilí and Zumbahua (about 2½ hours), generally once a day. If the bus is going all the way to Quevedo, get off when the road splits at Zumbahua. Buses from Zumbahua travel by Laguna Quilotoa (30 minutes) to Chugchilán (2½ hours) and Sigchos (another hour). You can also do the reverse from Latacunga. Alternatively, *camionetas* from Latacunga cost up to $50 for the longest stretch to Chugchilán (under $40 to Quilotoa), and less from closer towns. Getting to Lake Quilotoa over the scenic Andean countryside is half the fun.

From Latacunga, head west off the Pan-American on the road to Pujilí (which is paved until there) and Zumbagua. You can catch a bus from Latacunga along this route as well. The first point of interest is **Pujilí**, about six miles west of Latacunga, where there's a large market on Sundays and a smaller one on Wednesdays. About 35 miles west of Pujilí is **Zumbagua**, a tiny indigenous village with a great local market on Saturdays. From the village plaza, cross the bridge and follow the road north to the lake, about nine miles from Zumbagua.

In **Saquisilí**, just south of the town of Guaytacama, a few miles west of the Pan-American Highway, market day is Thursday. It is one of the most incredible local markets in Ecuador, and one of the more important ones. Native people fill the streets, the plazas, and every nook and cranny. Wandering ponchos and narrow-brimmed felt hats, fruits, meats, vegetables and goods of every size, shape, color, smell, and sound overwhelm the senses. In fact, if you are not used to traveling in similar countries, it may take quite a bit to stomach some of what you will witness.

Indian Markets

For a native treat, stop at the villages of **Saquisilí** and **Pujilí** on market day. Visiting them in conjunction with Lake Quilotoa is a great excursion away from the main travelers' route. Located a bit off the beaten Pan-American path, these authentic Amerindian markets are well worth the visit. They cater to locals and are the focal point of village life. Don't expect to find much in the way of tourist-oriented arts and crafts, although even here the renowned Otavaleños from the north now cater a bit to the foreign traveler. For the most part, what you will find is anything related to daily necessities, as well as a beautiful indigenous culture, rich in color and tradition.

Hotels in the Latacunga area fill to capacity on Wednesdays, Thursdays and, to a lesser extent, Saturdays as a result of these markets. Be sure to make reservations in advance.

The entire loop starting on the Pan-American Highway and going through Saquisilí, Toacazo, Sigchos, Chugchilán, Laguna Quilotoa, Zumbahua, Tigua, and Pujilí (or in reverse order) is less than 60 miles, but it takes over six hours of driving time because of rough roads winding through spectacular scenery. In addition to Pujillí and Saquisillí, you can spend literally days exploring this region, complete with beautiful countryside, small indigenous villages and adventures galore. Pick up a good map. There are many ways to connect the dots by bus or car, foot, horseback or bike. Whichever way you go, it will be good. For local excursions, advice and a good place to stay in this region, see the Black Sheep Inn (page 179).

Chimborazo Volcano

Several of Chimborazo's peaks are over 19,600 feet high (20,633 feet being the high point), and all are within the 147,630-acre **Chimborazo Faunal Reserve**. The more modest **Volcán Carihuairazo**, one of the 10 highest peaks in the country, lies just to the northeast and is also visible from the highway. Both Carihuairazo and Chimborazo are dormant and have been for some time. Although there are no formal tourist services in the reserve, visiting Chimborazo is not difficult. Most people go to climb, but there is plenty of excellent hiking and multi-day trekking available within the reserve. The habitat is open *páramo*, so it is convenient to just park and hike. Day-trips are possible from Riobamba, either with a guide or you can arrange transportation with a *camioneta* (near the train station) to the first refuge. A nice hike is to the second refuge, which takes under an hour.

There are two routes into the reserve. The Ambato-Guaranda Road, the less traveled of the two, approaches from the north. An easier entryway is from the south via the village of San Juan, several miles west of Riobamba. A gravel road intersects both routes and leads to a parking lot just below the climbers' refuge at 15,696 feet. From the refuge there are a number of different routes to the summit, but all require solid ice-climbing experience, technical gear, and a guide. Chimborazo is shrouded in clouds most of the year. The best time to try the summit is June through September. Quality guides can be hired in Quito, Ambato, or Riobamba (see pages 94-97, 174-75).

On Wheels

Mountain Biking

One activity that continues to gain popularity in **Cotopaxi National Park** is mountain biking. Miles of dirt roads, wide-open space and an absence of traffic make this area perfect for the avid biker and shuttle-supported novice alike. A favorite ride with travelers and local mountain biking outfitters is to start at the parking lot below the climbers' refuge and ride downhill, away from the summit. Note that, at this altitude, it is not a ride you would want to be doing up toward the refuge. There aren't a lot of single-track options available, but just pedaling through such a surreal lunar landscape, as well as occasionally brushing by a herd of wild horses, is an awesome experience.

Otavalo produce market

Indigenous attire for all ages

Waterfall near Baños, the life force of the Amazon

Traditional attire in the Central Highlands

Native of the Central Highlands

Baños

Above: Indigenous family in the Central Highlands

Below: Volcán Cotopaxi

Baños

Bike Tours & Outfitters

The **Biking Dutchman**, in Quito at Foch 714 and J.L. Mera, ☎ 2-2568-323, fax 2-567-008, www.bikingdutchman. com, pioneered mountain biking in Ecuador. They offer the best equipment with dual suspension bikes and top-of-the-line components. Customized, full-package trips are available.

In Riobamba, **Pro Bici**, Primera Constituyente 23-51 and Larrea, ☎ 3-960-189, offers guided trips into the surrounding region, as well as bike rentals. They have reasonable equipment and quality service.

The area around Lake Quilotoa and its surrounding villages is recommended for biking. Numerous indigenous villages dot the countryside and traffic is far removed, while the scenery is up-close and friendly. Inquire with bike outfitters or South American Explorers (☎/fax 2-225-228, explorer@seac.org.ec) in Quito for options.

By 4x4

Many major tour operators in Quito offer 4x4 day-trips to Cotopaxi National Park. They generally charge from $25 to $50 per person, with vehicle transport, lunch, and services included. If you want to hike on Cotopaxi, make sure your tour includes transportation all the way to the parking lot and not just to Lago Limpiopungo. The park entrance fee is $10 and is usually not included in the price of a tour. You can also make arrangements by *camioneta* in Latacunga for transportation into Cotopaxi National Park and other areas.

Around Quilotoa, the Black Sheep Inn offers vehicle-supported trips in the surrounding countryside (see *Where to Stay*, page 179).

On Horseback

Horseback riding in this region is a special treat because of the scale and beauty of the surrounding countryside. Open space is readily available, to say the least. The best options for quality horseback outfitters are available through lodging, particularly **Casa Nieves** in the Ilinizas region and all of the listed lodges in the Cotopaxi region (see *Where to Stay*, pages 177-79). In fact, **Hacienda Yanahurco**, which includes a massive 64,000-acre private reserve, offers day-long or longer horseback excursions as a part of the package. In one day, on horseback, I had the good fortune of witnessing wild deer, alpaca (belonging to the farm), Andean wolf (fox), trout (fishing) and the prize – an Andean condor! I am not a horseback riding enthusiast, but I can't recommend it enough.

■ Tour Operators & Guides

At haciendas, local guides work at or in conjunction with individual lodges. Though horseback riding is generally available at most accommodations in the region, there are several quality outfitters in Quito and Riobamba that offer climbing, hiking, and mountain-biking excursions in Cotopaxi and throughout the Central Highlands. Because their activities overlap, they are listed together.

Quito

Companía de Guías, J. Washington and 6 de Diciembre, ☎ 2-2504-733, www.companiadeguias.com, guiasmontania@accessinter.net, is a top-quality ASEGUIM-certified (Ecuadorian Association of Mountain Guides) outfit. Guides are very professional and speak several languages. This organization is at the high end of the cost spectrum for climbing, but is worth the price.

Surtrek, Amazonas 897 and Wilson, ☎ 2-2563-857, offers comparable expertise, is ASEGUIM-certified, and is well known for its climbing and trekking trips. They are multi-lingual and also rent gear. Check them out online at www.surtrek.com. Surtrek's office in Ambato, at Los Shyris 210 and Luis Cordero, over a mile south of the city center, ☎ 3-2844-448, offers quality climbing services in the surrounding region and gear rental.

Safari Ecuador, Calama 380 and J.L. Mera, ☎ 2-2552-505, from the US, ☎ 800-434-8182, fax 2-2223-381, admin@safari.com.ec, www.safari.com.ec, is ASEGUIM-certified and specializes in volcano climbs, day-trips to Otavalo and Cotopaxi, and hiking, as well as camping trips. They also rent mountain bikes. This is a friendly, top-notch company.

Latacunga

Expediciones Amazónicas, at Quito 16-67 and Padre Salcedo, ☎ 3-800-375, expedicionesamazonicas@hotmail.com, offers trekking tours, as well as climbing and jungle excursions. Or try **Montaña Expediciones**, Quito 73-99 and Guayaquil, ☎ 3-800-227, for Cotopaxi hiking, trekking and ASEGUIM-certified climbing guides.

Metropolitan Touring, at Bolívar 19-22 and Castillo, ☎ 3-824-084, fax 3-829-213, has an office in the Centro Comercial Caracol, Av. de los Capulies and Mirabeles.

Riobamba

Alta Montaña, Av. Daniel Borja 35-17 and Diego de Ibarra, ☎ 3-942-215, aventurag@laserinter.net – from equipment rental and photography to horseback riding, biking and mountain climbing/trekking, they have it all.

Expediciones Andinas, a couple of miles outside town on the road to Guano, ☎ 3-964-915, offers climbing services.

Well recommended is **Andes Trek**, Colón 22-25 and 10 de Agosto, ☎ 3-940-964, F 3-940-963. In addition to climbing and trekking, they have mountain biking and equipment rental.

Julio Verne Travel, at Calle 5 de Junio 21-46 and 10 de Agosto, ☎ 3-963436, julioverne@andinanet.net, www.julioverne-travel.com, offers adventure travel into the surrounding region, including hiking, trekking and climbing volancoes.

■ Eco-Travel

Ilinizas Ecological Reserve

 A recent addition to the parks and reserves of Ecuador is Reserva Ecológica Los Ilinizas, encompassing a massive 370,500 protected acres. Blanketing high altitude *páramo* grassland and humid subtropical (cloud) forest, the reserve is a welcome addition to protected areas in Ecuador. Highlights include the namesake volcanic peaks and the famous emerald-colored Lake Quilotoa, both of which offer plenty of hiking and climbing adventures. See *Adventures* (page 170) for more. The cloud forest habitat can also be explored from Lake Quilotoa, at 12,426 feet, and down the western Pacific slopes to an elevation of 5,232 feet.

Cotopaxi National Park & Volcano

Ecuador's mainland showpiece is Cotopaxi (meaning "neck of the moon"), a beautifully symmetrical, snowcapped, active volcano. The entire park, at just under 84,000 acres in size, is one of the country's major natural attractions and a tourist destination for both foreigners and nationals. At 19,283 feet, Cotopaxi is the country's second-highest peak and is purported to be the highest active volcano in the world. There are several other peaks within the park as well, including 15,408-foot **Rumiñahui**.

The land itself is what draws people here, punctuated by the photogenic Cotopaxi Volcano. The wide-open, lunar-like landscape, with ancient lava flows, is all encompassing. It is a testament to Cotopaxi's power as an unimaginable natural force, destroying nearby towns and villages several times in the last three centuries. Now, the *páramo* vegetation reflects a tundra life zone, more than one would expect near the equator, with wind-swept grassy vegetation known as *pajonales*. Thicker intermittent bushes and shrubs provide shelter to numerous bird species and mammals. Highlights include the Andean hillstar, lapwing, carunculated caracara, the renowned condor, the puma (or mountain lion), rabbit, deer and Andean wolf (really a fox).

Options for adventure within Cotopaxi National Park are unlimited. The park is ideal for the avid mountaineer and offers countless miles of hiking, trekking, and mountain-biking trails (see *Adventures*, page 168). Whether you take a light stroll through the *páramo* grasslands around **Lago Limpiopungo**, climb to the summit of **Cotopaxi Volcano**, or trek around the volcano for a week or more, Cotopaxi will literally take your breath away. Weekdays are best for avoiding the crowds. February through May is quite cool and wet, although not to the detriment of sightseeing and other short excursions.

Chimborazo Reserve & Volcano

From Ambato, the Pan-American Highway continues south through Riobamba and into the Southern Highlands. To the west of the highway lies the staggering mass of Chimborazo Volcano. Ecuador's highest mountain and one of the taller peaks in all of the Americas, Chimborazo tops out at 20,634 feet.

DID YOU KNOW?

For all of you trivia buffs, the summit of Chimborazo is farther from the center of the earth than any other point of land on the planet, the result of our ever-spinning planet and the resulting equatorial bulge.

It is difficult to comprehend how magnificent this behemoth is until you venture close to it. From Ambato, take Route 50 through Guaranda. After about an hour, turn left at the abandoned white house on a dirt road that leads to the refuge. From Riobamba, head west toward the village of San Juan. Turn north (right) on the road to the refuge and park for a great close-up view of Chimborazo's west face. See *Adventures* (page 172) for ideas on exploring the park.

■ Where to Stay

ACCOMMODATIONS PRICE SCALE	
Unless otherwise noted, prices are per room, up to double occupancy. Some prices are per person, particularly with all-inclusive packages, but these generally include meals, lodging, guide services and other amenities.	
$	Under $25
$$	$26 to $50
$$$	$51 to $100
$$$$	Over $100

Machachi

La Estación de Machachi, ☎ 3-309-246, located next to the old train station in the village of Aloasí, just south and across the highway from Machachi, is less than a mile off the Pan-American. This quaint, family-style hotel is a converted farmhouse with a colonial feel and great views of El Corazón Volcano. In fact, this is a wonderful base from which to explore the mountain and surrounding countryside by foot, beginning right at the front door. The home and grounds are beautiful, and the staff is very friendly. Enjoy the family atmosphere in the common living room, complete with fireplace and welcome cocktails. Decent food is served in the dining room on the second floor, and the broad windows offer great panoramic views on clear days. The rooms are small but clean, with thick wool-blanketed beds for the cool winter nights. This is a great, economical home base for excursions to Cotopaxi, Corazón, the Ilinizas and other locales. $

Nearby is **Hostal Casa Nieves**, ☎ 2-2315-092, two or three miles outside town (look for the sign just after the turnout to Aloasí), to the west of the Pan-American Highway, just before the village of El Chaupi. Casa Nieves has been recommended as a simple, yet comfortable, family-run operation, with hot water and options for meals and horseback riding available. It is the ideal location for exploring Ilinizas. $$

Cotopaxi Region

Relatively close to Cotopaxi, just outside the town of Lasso, is the famous **Hacienda La Ciénega**, ☎ 3-719-052, fax 3-719-093, hcienega@uio.satnet.net. La Ciénega is the oldest and most renowned accommodation in the vicinity. Built in 1580, the property included land that once spanned from Quito all the way to Ambato – as part of a grant from the King of Spain. Typically Spanish in style, the main building boasts an attractive garden courtyard and the grounds include acres of eucalyptus-shaded gardens and lawns. Colonial furnishings adorn the rooms and new additions include a popular restaurant, bar, and lounge area. This historic landmark has offered its services to royalty, heads of state, and diplomats over the last several centuries, as well as quite a few adventure travelers. Horseback riding is available at a nominal cost. If possible, reserve a room in the original hacienda. $$

Cuello de Luna, just off of the Pan-American Highway across from Cotopaxi's southern entrance, ☎ 9-700-330, www.cuellodeluna.com, reservas@cuellodeluna.com, is conveniently located and recommended. It offers a nice hacienda setting with a wonderful view and is reasonably priced. $$

Hostería San Mateo is south of Lasso along the Pan-American at Vía Latacunga, Km 75, ☎ 3-719-015, san_mateo@yahoo.com, www. hosteriasanmateo.com. It offers a quiet escape, despite its proximity to the highway. With peek-a-boo views of Cotopaxi and Ilinizas, this comfortable retreat is close to Cotopaxi without being too far off the beaten path (which can be much appreciated after you've had your share of bumpy dirt or cobblestone roads). With a capacity for up to 15 guests, San Mateo provides six comfortable rooms and one cabin for up to five people, all decorated in traditional style. Amenities include a warm fire-lit lounge and covered patio, good restaurant and bar, horseback riding options and plenty of space to stroll around. $$

Hacienda San Agustin de Callo is located in the southern foothills of Cotopaxi National Park, ☎ /fax 3-719-160, in Quito, ☎ /fax 2-906-157/8, info@incahacienda.com, www.incahacienda.com. This is definitely at the high end of accommodations. Although it is a relative newcomer to the area as a hotel, remnants of Incan royalty still exist in this attractive, early 19th-century hacienda. Built on the site of a ruined palace, the chapel includes part of an Incan building and you can still see the original carved stones in the dining room. The hacienda is a beautiful, remote getaway, and meant to be just that. Rooms are elegantly adorned with antiques, fireplaces, and hot-water baths.

Fishing, hiking, horseback riding, and mountain biking are all available. It's pricey but worth it. All-inclusive. $$$$

Another rural retreat is **Hacienda Yanahurco**, in Quito, Pasaje A #25 and J.M. Agascal, ☎ 2-2241-593, fax 2-2445-016, yanahurco@ impsat.net.ec, www.yanahurco.com.ec. Located three hours from Quito on the southeast side of Cotopaxi, Yanahurco is a place of the past, of *vaqueros* and wild *toros*, of peace and harmony with the land. The enormous 64,220-acre private refuge provides the opportunity to escape amid the backdrop of Cotopaxi, Antisana, Sincholagua, and Quilindaña. It is a working hacienda that encompasses elevations from 11,445 to 13,734 feet and includes 2,000 head of cattle, 100 riding horses, and 200 wild horses. Rustic but comfortable, the rooms offer full baths, hot water, and fireplaces or heaters for warmth. There's even an on-site generator. Although this land is near the equator, it can be quite chilly around Yanahurco.

A professional outfit, the staff has put together a variety of package tours that include hiking, fishing, camping, mountain biking and four-wheel-drive excursions. This sanctuary for Andean wildlife is also a paradise for anglers, with 19 rivers and streams and a small lake. Prices include all meals and package tours. $$$$

☆ **The Black Sheep Inn**. If you are interested in spending some time in the backcountry near Lake Quilotoa, there are accommodations available in each of the small villages, though they are very basic. This is the best home base for exploring the region. The inn is just north of the lake and south of the village of Chugchilán. Contact them directly via e-mail at info@blacksheepinn.com or visit their website at www.blacksheepinn.com. Prices as of publication are $18-$38 per person, including dinner and breakfast, and free tea and coffee and purified water. Lunches, home-baked desserts, cheese from the local Swiss-styled cheese cooperative, and full bar, including Chilean wines, are also available. The Black Sheep Inn provides hiking maps and can arrange transportation, mountain biking and horseback riding excursions. The simple accommodations offer surprising comfort for such a remote location. $$

Ambato

A relatively pricey option is **Hotel Ambato**, at Guayaquil 01-08 and Rocafuerte, ☎ 3-412-005, fax 3-412-003, hambato@hotmail.com. It offers the amenities of a more modern facility, and is still inexpensive. There are comfortable, clean rooms with private baths, telephone/TV, good views, a nice outdoor patio and a recommended restaurant. Breakfast included. $$

The **Gran Hotel,** also downtown at Lalama 05-11 and Rocafuerte, ☎ 3-825-915, fax 3-824-235, is an okay choice in the mid-quality level. Rooms offer private baths with hot water, TV and telephone. There is a good restaurant and on-site parking. $

There are plenty of budget choices in and around the city center, as well as near Parque 12 de Noviembre.

Riobamba

Riobamba, though an attractive colonial town, doesn't offer any great, luxury hotel options in the city center, though there are plenty of good budget to mid-level accommodations. In fact, prices here are very reasonable. One of the best downtown choices is **Hostal Montecarlo**, at 10 de Agosta 25-41, between G Moreno and Espana, ☎ 3-960-557, which incorporates a restored, late colonial house. At under $25, it provides comfortable rooms with private bath, TV and telephones. There is an attractive courtyard and a restaurant. $

The **Hotel Los Shyris**, near the train station at 10 de Agosto and Rocafuerte 21-60, ☎ 3-960-323, fax 3-967-934, is a step down in price and quality, though still a good choice at under $10 per night. Clean rooms offer private or shared baths, friendly management and an overall good value. $

Hotel Riobamba Inn, at Carabobo 23-20 and Coinstituyente, ☎ 3-961-696/941-311, fax 3-940-974, is in between the above two in price and quality, with clean, comfortable rooms and private baths with hot water. Some rooms have TV and telephone. $

The two best options around Riobamba are just outside of town, offering more rural settings.

Albergue Abraspungo, about a mile northeast of town on the road to Guano, ☎ 3-940-820, fax 3-940-819, www.abraspungo.com, info@ abraspungo.com, is built in tasteful hacienda style. This excellent rustic retreat has modern amenities, including private baths, TV and telephone, in this excellent rustic retreat. Rooms vary from $40 to $70 per night. Horses can be rented, and climbing as well as other guide services are available for trips in the surrounding area. $$-$$$

Reportedly, one of the best hotels in the region is the **Hostería La Andaluza**, 4½ miles north of Riobamba on the Pan-American Highway, ☎ 3-904-223, fax 3-904-234, handaluz@ch.pro.ec. In a restored hacienda in a rural setting, it has great views, a nice restaurant and comfortable rooms. $$-$$$

Camping

Camping in **Cotopaxi National Park** is available at officially designated sites. Most of the park is relatively flat and the open terrain offers plenty of camping space. One popular spot is near **Lago Limpiopungo**, though camping is not available right by the lake.

A great way for climbers to acclimatize is to set up camp near Limpiopungo and then backpack for a day up to the climbers' refuge below the summit.

Camping is also available in **El Boliche National Recreation Area** within the exotic pine forest. Inquire ahead in Quito for permits or at the administration building heading into the park. As with the more popular volcanic peaks, there is also a climbers' refuge ($10 per night) on Cotopaxi. In addition, there are a couple of primitive shelters available within the park.

Refugios, the climbers' refuges, exist on Cotopaxi, Ilinizas and Chimborazo. Bring your own gear and food.

■ Where to Eat

Machachi

La Estación de Machachi in Alausí offers tasty meals that can be included in the price of the stay. Otherwise, there are a couple of public cafés in Machachi a few miles down the highway. Try **Restaurante Pedregal**, on the main road into town, just before the park. Expect basic, but tasty meals. **Café de la Vaca**, a couple of miles south of Machachi along the Pan-American, is a good resting spot for coffee, ice cream or a quick meal if you are traveling long-distance along the Pan-American Highway.

Other than public restaurants on the Pan-American Highway or cafés in small towns like Machachi, most of your meals in this region will either be included with lodging (see *Where to Stay*, pages 177-80) or you should bring them with you.

Ambato

The best restaurant in Ambato for the foreign traveler is at the **Hotel Ambato**. Otherwise, the nearby **La Buena Mesa**, at Quito 924 and Bolívar, ☎ 3-824-332 (closed Sundays) is the finest establishment in town. Buena Mesa emphasizes French cuisine and is relatively pricey, but recommended for good food and atmosphere.

Steaks are served up at the popular **Parrilladas El Gaucho**, located at Bolívarand Quito, ☎ 3-282-969 (closed Sundays). For cheap *chifas* (Chinese food), try the popular **Chifa Jao Fua**, Cevallos 756 near JL Mera, for cheap, good value. Or **Chifa Nueva Hong Kong**, located at Bolívar768 and Martinez; dirt cheap, it's also a good option for budget meals. Plenty of inexpensive meals are available in the main city center and especially around the market, with an emphasis on chicken dishes. **La Brasa Roja**, on JL Mera near 12 de Noviembre, is a popular choice.

There are also several pizzeria restaurants in the downtown area, including **La Fornace**, at Cevallos 17-28. The inexpensive Italian dishes, pizza being the specialty, and pleasant, casual atmosphere make La Fornace a good choice, though there are other options in the neighborhood.

Riobamba

The best dining experiences in Riobamba are had at the haciendas outside of town, particularly, **Hosteria la Andaluza** (see *Where to Stay*, above). In downtown Riobamba, try **Pizzeria San Valentín**, at Torres and Borja, or **Charlie's Pizzeria**, at G Moreno between Guayaquil and 10 de Agosto, for the best Italian food in town. Both are popular.

For Chinese food, the **Chifa Pak Hao**, next to Charlie's Pizzeria at G Morena and Guayaquil, ☎ 3-964-270, is okay for a cheap downtown meal, though there are several other Chinese food places in the area. Near the railway station is the inexpensive and good **Chifa Joy Sing**, Guayaquil 29-27 and Carabobo, ☎ 3-961-285.

In the mid-price range, a good option is the restaurant at **Cabana Montecarlo**, in conjunction with the Hostal Montecarlo (see *Where to Stay*, above). The food is decent, with an international selection, but expensive by Riobamba standards. Recommended for breakfast.

Perhaps the best restaurant in Riobamba itself is **Café Concerto El Delirio**, at Primera Constituyente 28-16 and Rocafuerte, ☎ 3-967-

502. Set in the former home of Simon Bolívar, it offers expensive and delicious meat and seafood dishes, a great atmosphere, attractive courtyard and live Andean music. It caters to tour groups.

Baños Area

Just south of Ambato, veer off the Pan-American Highway to the southeast toward Baños. As you pass through Salasaca and then Pelileo, the "blue-jean" capital of Ecuador, the road to Baños quickly loses elevation. The countryside becomes greener and lusher, with magnificent views overlooking the Río Pastaza canyon. Soon enough you'll be scrambling for the camera as the winding road offers glimpses of the impressive Tungurahua Volcano. It is particularly beautiful on a clear afternoon as sunset approaches, when the snow-covered peak reflects a soft peach-colored light. If you are arriving from Quito or a larger urban center, you will find yourself on immediate relax mode upon entering Baños. If you are arriving from some remote section of Ecuador, you will find this the perfect place to readjust to "civilization."

Baños lies on a narrow stretch of land surrounded by the steep lower slopes of Tungurahua to the south and the deep gorge of the Pastaza to the north. It is one of the most popular tourist destinations for both Ecuadorians and foreigners alike, and is a major gateway between the Andes and the Oriente. Famous for its natural hot-spring baths, mild climate, and accessibility to numerous outdoor activities, Baños maintains a characteristically laid-back atmosphere most of the time. Weekends, however, tend to be a bit of a carnival show, complete with loudspeakers, fantasy auto-train rides, and screaming children. Baños is a small town, yet it's filled with shops, tour outfitters, restaurants, and plenty of places to walk around. Relaxing seems to be the main sport here, though there is plenty to do for the active enthusiast. Baños has a bit of something for everyone.

Downtown Baños is arranged in a characteristic colonial pattern, centered around **Parque Central** and **Parque de la Basílica**. The main east-west street in town is Ambato, which hugs both of the parks. Across from the Parque de la Basílica, is the **Basilica** itself. It is the centerpiece of life for visiting Catholic pilgrims and purported to be the site of miraculous cures, as portrayed by paintings on the walls of the church. Personally, I think it is a great excuse for locals to bring the kids to Baños. There is also a small on-site museum, as well as stalls along the street between the church and the park selling religious trinkets, toys and *melcochas* (excruciatingly sweet toffee). Other Baños landmarks include the **Manto de la Vírgen Waterfall**, or Hair of the Virgin, and its associated **Baños de la Vírgen**, or hot baths, at the southeastern part of town. These are the most popular baths, though there are several others. To the southwest, up the mountain a bit and up many flights of stairs, is the rather strange **Statue of the Virgin**, watching over Baños with spectacular views. Unfortunately, she doesn't seem to watch over tourists hiking up to this point, as there have been reports of robbers assaulting people on their way. Don't hike there alone, especially at night.

■ Getting Here & Getting Around

From Ambato, buses depart regularly for the hour-long ride southeast to Baños and some head on to Puyo. If arriving from Quito and the bus is continuing south to Riobamba, make sure to transfer in Ambato.

■ Visitor Information

Modern services, including banks, post and communications, are located along Calle Ambato, the main pedestrian street in Baños. The **post office**, is on Ambato and Halflants just across from Parque Central. Nearby, on Halflants and Rocafuerte, also adjacent to the park, is the **Andinatel** office for telephone calls. Inquire at your hotel about the latest Internet cafés, or try **Banos.net**, on Alfaro, between Ambato and Oriente. There are several laundry facilities within a couple of blocks of downtown, or ask around at the hotels, as some of them offer services.

For money matters, **Banco del Pacífico** is located on Montalvo and Alfaro, open Monday-Friday. They will change travelers checks. MasterCard and ATM services are also available. **Banco del Pichincha**, on Ambato, cashes travelers checks.

Terminal Terrestre, the main **bus station**, is on the main road into town, Ave. Amazonas, between Reyes and Maldonado. From here, you can catch a taxi to a hotel, but most everything is within walking distance.

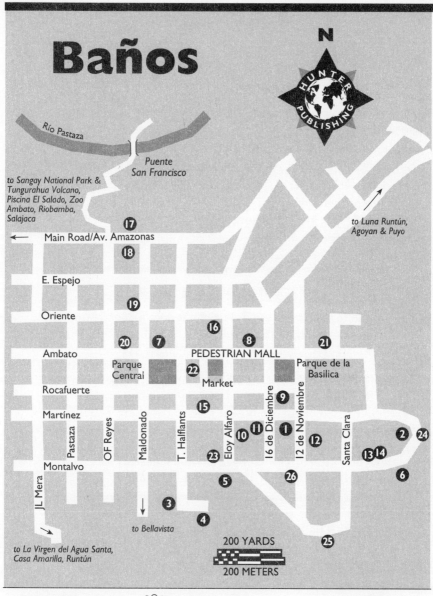

Baños

Río Pastaza

Puente San Francisco

to Sangay National Park & Tungurahua Volcano, Piscina El Salado, Zoo Ambato, Riobamba, Salajaca

to Luna Runtún, Agoyan & Puyo

Main Road/Av. Amazonas

E. Espejo

Oriente

Ambato

Parque Central

PEDESTRIAN MALL

Market

Parque de la Basilica

Rocafuerte

Martínez

Pastaza

OF Reyes

Maldonado

T. Halflants

Eloy Alfaro

16 de Diciembre

12 de Noviembre

Santa Clara

Montalvo

JL Mera

to Bellavista

to La Virgen del Agua Santa, Casa Amarilla, Runtún

200 YARDS

200 METERS

© 2003 HUNTER PUBLISHING, INC

WHERE TO STAY

1. Hostal Plantas y Blanco, Hostal Cordillera
2. Hotel Sangay
3. Hostal Isla del Baños
4. Hostería Monte Selva
5. Villa Gertrudis
6. Hotel Palace

WHERE TO EAT

7. Rico Pan
8. Donde Marcelo
9. El Jardín
10. Le Petit Restaurant
11. Café Hood, Paolo's Pizzería
12. Café Higuerón
13. Café Cultura
14. La Casa Mía
15. Casa Hood
16. Hard Rock Café

OTHER SITES

17. Sugarcane Stalls
18. Terminal Terrestre
19. Tsantsa Tours
20. Rainforestur
21. Basilica, Museum
22. Post Office
23. Bank
24. Hot Baths
25. Swimming Pool
26. Playground

■ Touring & Sightseeing

Salasaca

 On the way to Baños is the small town of Salasaca, a good place to stop and check out high-quality **tapestries**. These tightly woven *tapices*, made of wool that generally comes from local sheep farms, often incorporate impressive animal designs. Although a bit modernized these days, the Salasacas continue to dress in indigenous attire that, for the men, includes black ponchos, white trousers, and handmade, broad-brimmed white hats with the brims often tilted up both in front and in back. The same hats identify the women, who wear colorful shoulder wraps around long, dark dress-like *anakus*.

Victims of the Incas

Unique to this area, the Salasacas reflect a deep history of forced migration by the Incas. Originally from Bolivia, the Salasacas were victims of the Inca plan to uplift and move people they conquered. The Inca strategy was to take their subjugated neighbors out of their element and thereby minimize the chance of a revolt. The Salasacas have since maintained much of their cultural identity, but are now facing other pressures. As Baños becomes increasingly popular among tourists and affluent Ecuadorians, land issues and modern cultural changes threaten to destroy the native way of life. So far, they have held their ground.

You can't miss Salasaca on the way to Baños. Notably, the weavings, the indigenous people and, more recently, the Otavaleño stands selling other goods are visible along the road.

Pelileo

Pelileo is a small town on the highway between Ambato and Baños, famous for the denim goods manufactured there. Look out for (fake) Tommy Hilfigers, Levis and Calvin Kleins. The streets are literally lined with outlets and, if your bus slows down at all, peddlers will undoubtedly hop on and try to give you the hard sell, before moving on to the next unsuspecting busload. I think the classic item is "Nike" jeans, with a patch placed prominently on the apparel for all to see.

Baños

Zoo

Yes, believe it or not, there is a zoo in Baños. The facilities are clean and rather impressive but the cages are relatively small. Unless you're spending quite a bit of time birding in the thick of a tropical forest, this may be your best chance to see a harpy eagle. The harpy, one of the largest eagles in the world, has a seven-foot wingspan and the ability to snatch monkeys and sloths from the branches of trees. As you would expect, the zoo appeals primarily to children, and groups of schoolchildren often visit.

The zoo is less than two miles west of the main road out of Baños. You can walk there in about 45 minutes, rent a bike, or take a taxi. The sign off the main road is obvious. Open 9-5 daily. Admission nominal.

■ Adventures

On Foot

There are numerous hikes in the Baños area. Some of the better ones require getting out of town a bit and into the surrounding countryside. A nice introductory hike is down and across the Río Pastaza, then up any number of trails on the north side. Spectacular views of Tungurahua open up across the valley on clear days, and local tourist maps are available in town that highlight some of these. Head toward the bus station and across the main road, toward the sugarcane stands. A path behind the booths leads down to a suspension bridge and the beginning of the hike.

A favorite hike and a good warm-up is along the side of the mountain that surround Baños. The views of the town below and the countryside around it are magnificent, and the trail itself is not as steep as it may look from the bottom. Tiny homes and farms dot the side of the mountain, with cliff-side gates that open up to spectacular views. It's fascinating to watch the locals working fields on the steep slopes, one leg constantly a step above the other just to maintain balance.

For this hike, head toward the mountain, up Maldonado, until the path begins. The path circles around the town and leads toward **Bellavista** (you'll see a small white building and a cross). From there, if you feel energetic, you can continue for another mile to the community of **Luna Runtún**. Alternatively, head toward the statue of the virgin, *La Vírgen de Agua Santa*, which overlooks Baños. Behind the statue is another footpath and another good hike.

A popular hike nearby is up **Volcán Tungurahua**, the snow-capped peak that watches over Baños. Tungurahua, which means "Little Hell" in Quichua, is still active and is the source of the thermal baths in town (see page 192). In fact, Baños was temporarily evacuated in late 1999 due to an increase in volcanic activity from Tungurahua, which went so far as to lightly blanket the town with ash. Though it has since quieted down, anything is possible, so be sure to inquire before heading there. **Sangay Park** descends to the southeast of Tungurahua deep into the southern Oriente, much of which is inaccessible.

Many of the climbing guides offer hiking excursions as well (see following pages). Or you can inquire with the tour operators and agencies lining the streets of Baños.

Climbing With Gear

Although an easy ascent for experienced technical climbers, the hike to the climbers' *refugio* on Tungurahua is beautiful and a great workout. From the entrance to the park it's a good four- to five-hour hike and a 3,270-foot elevation gain to the climbers' refuge. Much of the ascent is through remnants of cloud forest and above timberline amid beautiful wildflowers. If you want only a day-hike, turn around soon after arriving at the refuge. You don't want to miss your ride back to Baños, as I did. Returning to town in the dark, after several additional hours of walking down the mountain, is not a pleasant ending to a great hike.

If you intend to climb to the summit, spend the night at the refuge ($5) and wake up for the ascent before sunrise. Many tour outfitters provide guiding services and climbing equipment, though be sure to do your research thoroughly if you are using one based out of Baños, as many of them are shoddy.

Take a taxi or the milk truck from Pensión Pattys to the park entrance; entrance fee is $10. Arrange to be picked up at a specific time, or go with an all-inclusive guide service based out of Baños.

Volcanic Activity

 Recent volcanic activity on Tungurahua has forced an official ban on hiking and climbing to the *refugio* and summit. Though this may change at any time if the mountain quiets down, you are literally risking your life by going there if it is active. Inquire locally at a tourist office (not a climbing tour operator) about the latest conditions and warnings.

Be sure to thoroughly investigate the quality of climbing outfitters and guides, including their license and equipment. Many of the warnings with jungle excursion tour operators (below) apply here as well. Note that several operators based in Baños also offer climbing excursions to Cotopaxi and Chimborazo.

Guides

Expediciones Amazónicas, Oriente and Halflants, ☎ 3-740-506, expedicionesamazonicas@hotmail.com, is one of the top companies for leading climbs up Tungurahua. Their guides and equipment are better than those at most other outfitters, and they charge just $50 for the two-day trip. The guides at the budget hostel **Pensión Patty**, Eloy Alfaro 556 and Oriente, ☎ 3-740-202, are another good option if you want to climb the volcano. They have mules that can lug your gear.

Jungle Excursions

Baños is an ideal place to organize a tour into the Oriente and the rainforest of the upper Amazon Basin. Many of the myriad tour operators that line the streets offer a wide range of trips into the jungle. Prices here are generally much less expensive than from Quito, but the quality of the tour and destination is usually lower as well. If you have a limited amount of time or are on a budget, this is the place to start. It's easy to find other travelers with similar interests, form a group, and make an otherwise expensive trip far more economical.

On Horseback

Options for horseback riding are abundant. Most tour operators offer half- to full-day trips, but quality varies from outfitter to outfitter. This is an area where you definitely get what you pay for. A good half-day price is about $20. Many tours loop around Baños along the hiking trails mentioned above. Others travel deeper into the countryside and are a bit more enjoyable. Make sure you know what you are paying for – i.e., a good, healthy horse with a saddle and stirrups that fit properly. If you want to really help the locals, stay away from the higher-priced outfitters and hire a community member who has a good horse and offers horse-back-riding services. They'll be happy to show you around and often can use your business. Be wary, though, of poorly kept animals.

Hostal Isla de Baños, Halflants 1-31 and Montalvo, ☎ 3-740-609, offers high-quality half- and multi-day horseback riding trips suitable for all experience levels. Their horses are in good shape. Alternatively, try **Ángel Aldaz**, Montalvo and J.L. Mera, ☎ 3-740-175. He charges about $10 per half-day ride without a guide, a bit more with one. Otherwise, inquire within the numerous tour agencies and operators that line the streets of Baños. **Geotours** offers a quality horseback riding trip (see *Rafting*, page 192, for more about them).

On Wheels

Mountain Biking (& Hiking) from Baños to Puyo

For years now, the bike ride along the **Río Pastaza Canyon** on the road from Baños to Puyo has been popular with foreign travelers. In fact, this ride, along with Cotopaxi, is what put scenic mountain biking on Ecuador's map. From Baños, the dirt road descends gradually toward Puyo and the upper Amazon Basin. The southern edge of the road drops off immediately, well over 1,000 feet in some places, and provides spectacular views of the Río Pastaza deep within the narrow gorge. On the opposite side of the gorge is a great expanse of beautiful, untouched cloud forest, small patches of steep farmland, and towering waterfalls.

Many bikers take a few moments away from the saddle to hike down to the **Pailón del Diablo**, or the Devil's Cauldron. Park (and lock) your bike at the village of Río Verde near the marked trailhead and enjoy the easy descent to the suspension bridge above the river. From the bridge you'll have a good view of an impressive waterfall. To get closer to the falls, follow a side-trail up and through private property.

You may have to pay a small fee to pass, but your money helps protect the surrounding forest.

From Río Verde, the road continues to drop in elevation as the ecological life zone drifts toward that of the upper Amazon Basin. At the village of **Río Negro** there is another trail down to the Río Pastaza. Shortly thereafter, you'll arrive at the small village of **Mera**, with incredible views of the upper Amazon Basin. Most people call it quits at this point, as the road from here is paved and the best vistas are behind. To return to Baños, hitch a ride with a bus or truck. I think a great way to head into the Oriente from Baños is on a bike until this point and, if you can work it out, send the bikes back with the outfitter and continue on your own toward Puyo.

Traffic can be a bit discouraging along the road, but buses are used to bicyclists so be aware but don't be afraid. Most people find that this minor discomfort is more than compensated for by the beauty of the ride. Weather, too, can affect road conditions. A dry and bumpy dirt road can turn into a mud pit during the frequent summertime rains.

Bike Outfitters

 Bikes rentals in Baños are prolific, but most are in poor condition. Make sure you give your bike a test drive before you rent it, and carry a spare tube and the proper tools. **Taller de Bicicletas Alexander**, at Oriente and Alfaro, ☎ 3-741-151, offers a good selection of roadworthy mountain bikes. They carry a few dual-suspension bikes. If you don't find what you need there, ask around at the better hotels in town for their recommendations. Inquire at the **Hotel Isla de Baños** for biking tours; they have better equipment than most of the bike rental shops in town.

On Water

Whitewater Rafting

 The vicinity around Baños provides Class II and III+ whitewater rafting opportunities. Numerous guides offer trips, but many of these have are not qualified to be on the water. This is also a high population center so the rivers are polluted. It is not an area where you would want to fall out of the raft and swallow a mouthful of water. Check the "Travelers Comment Book" at Café Hood for the latest on the quality of rafting operators and guides. In addition to humorous accounts, you will find good advice and warnings. Better yet, wait to go rafting until you get to the Oriente, where the quality of rivers and guides are generally higher.

Geotours, on Maldonado south of the bus station, ☎ 3-740-703, is the best rafting outfitter in town. They offer half- and full-day trips for $25 to $50 per person, as well as full-day trips along the Río Pastaza for under $60, all-inclusive.

Thermal Baths

There are two sets of thermal baths around Baños. The **Piscina de la Vírgen** is located near the southeastern edge of town, right next to the landmark waterfall, the Manto de la Vírgen. Head toward the falls, which is visible from almost anywhere in town. The entrance to the hot springs is adjacent to the waterfall. Keep in mind that weekends here get a bit crazy, so you may be sharing the baths with many Ecuadorian families. The alternative, **El Salado Hot Springs**, just over a mile outside town, is much less crowded.

The walk to El Salado takes about 45 minutes (or, if you've got a car, a few minutes). Take a left at the bridge (on vía al Salado) and continue until you arrive. Both El Salado and the Piscina de la Vírgen springs are open daily. Admission is about $1.

■ Tour Operators

Baños is full of tour operators; they're everywhere, offering everything. But be wary. Many of these tour operator "pirates" lack integrity and any sense of responsibility to the environment, the Ecuadorian culture, or their clients. Check to make sure they are licensed (ask to see it); if they are, they have at least minimal standards and pay service-industry taxes. Spend some time talking to them and asking questions so that you know exactly what to expect. Request a written contract as well. Some outfitters may focus more on wildlife viewing, while others offer cultural tours. Prices generally range from $25 to $50 per person per day.

Note that many operators will take you into the more developed areas in the Tena region via Puyo, though some offer trips deeper into the jungle as well. In addition, the entire first and last day will usually be a travel day, so a "three-day" jungle trip is more or less a one-day visit. If you are paying at the lower end of the spectrum, you are pretty much guaranteed a bad time with a less than responsible tour operator. There are, of course, some quality outfitters, as follows.

Baños Outfitters

Rainforestur, Ambato near Maldonado, ☎ 3-740-743, rainfor@interactive.net.ec, offers seven-day trips to the Cuyabeno Reserve. The company also provides shorter trips based near Tena, and their guides speak several languages. Costs average around $50 per person per day, with a minimum group size of four people.

Tsantsa Expeditions, Oriente near Eloy Alfaro, ☎ 3-740-957, fax 3-740-717, is native-owned and -operated. They use Shuar Amerindian guides and are very knowledgeable about local culture and natural history. They're also one of the region's few environmentally sensitive outfits.

Geotours (see *Rafting*, page 192, above) also offers jungle excursions, as does **Deep Forest Adventure**, at Rocafuerte and Halflants, ☎ 3-740-403. Their multilingual guides have received positive reviews. For longer excursions deeper into the jungle, inquire with the well-recommended **Vasco Tours**, at Alfaro and Martínez, ☎ 3-741-017, vascotours@andinanet.net – groups only.

Expediciones Amazónicas, Oriente and Halflants, ☎ 3-740-506, expedicionesamazonicas@hotmail.com, is one of the top companies for leading climbs up Tungurahua. Their guides and equipment are better than those at most other outfitters, and they charge just $50 for the two-day trip.

■ Eco-Travel

Sangay National Park

 The 672,000-acre Sangay National Park stretches from near Baños, where hiking and climbing up Tungurahua Volcano is readily available, to an extremely remote region of Ecuador over 43 miles to the southeast. It is large enough to cover portions of Morono Santiago, Chimborazo and Tungurahua provinces and includes elevations of 3,200 feet along the lower eastern foothills all the way up to a 17,400-foot peak, making it one of the most ecologically diverse parks in Latin America. Sangay was listed as a World Heritage Site in 1983 and dubbed a World Heritage Site in Danger in 1992, due to the affects of the illegal Guamote-Macas road. Three volcanoes highlight the park, from north to south – Tungurahua (16,403 feet), El Altar (17,393 feet) and Sangay (17,103 feet), the first and last of which are active.

Due to the variable topography, the weather can vary dramatically. The moisture-laden Amazon Basin provides ample rainfall along the lower eastern slopes (of the Eastern Cordillera), even more rainfall higher along the slopes – where the Andes capture moisture from the airflow – and relatively little in the higher elevations of the western slopes. Thus, ecological life zones transition from alpine and *páramo* habitat near the higher peaks, down to subtropical rainforests in the Amazon Basin. At the higher elevations, lichens and bryophytes characterize the vegetation and fauna such as the puma, mountain tapir, Andean wolf and guinea pig inhabit the region. There are also the jaguar, condor and the endangered spectacled bear, as well as over 500 bird species, some of which are endemic and survive in restricted ranges.

See *Adventures on Foot* section, page 188, for hiking and climbing opportunities in the park. Note that since late 1999 Tungurahua Volcano (near Baños) has been relatively active after 80 years of sleeping and, as of this writing, continues to emit steam, gas and ash intermittently at low levels. Inquire locally about recent developments, as it will most likely continue to affect not only activities, but possibly the town of Baños, which was evacuated recently.

■ Where to Stay

ACCOMMODATIONS PRICE SCALE
Unless otherwise noted, prices are per room, up to double occupancy. Some prices are per person, particularly with all-inclusive packages, but these generally include meals, lodging, guide services and other amenities.

$	Under $25
$$	$26 to $50
$$$	$51 to $100
$$$$	Over $100

 A number of relatively inexpensive hotels line the streets in Baños. Some places cost as little as $2 per night and all are close to the center of town. The more expensive hotels are of much better quality, but, generally, anything above $15 per night is considered mid-plus range.

Hostal Plantas y Blanco, at 12 de Noviembre and Martínez, ☎/fax 3-740-044, offers a nice rooftop patio, adjoining restaurant (great breakfast!) and nice atmosphere. Located a couple of blocks from the town center, it's quiet, relaxed, and a very popular budget choice. The rooms are clean and comfortable with private, hot-water baths. There are laundry, spa and telephone services, and there's even a video-rental room. They tend to fill up before other budget accommodations. $

Next to Plantas y Blanco is another inexpensive, much more tranquil option (though I can't remember the name of it for the life of me). This Ecuadorian-owned hotel is recommended for its quiet but pleasant atmosphere, patio terrace with private parking and clean rooms with private, hot-water baths.

The popular **Residencial Villa Santa Clara**, 12 de Noviembre and Velasco, ☎ 3-740-349, offers very inexpensive rooms in the main house and slightly more expensive ones in newer cabins. Private baths with hot showers are included. Kitchen facilities are also available for guest use. $

Casa Nahuazo, Vía a El Salado, ☎ 3-740-315, is a clean and comfortable retreat just minutes from town, near the El Salado mineral baths. The friendly expatriate owner used to offer great travel information and a nice, quiet atmosphere, though the hotel is now under new management. Cozy double rooms include private, hot-water baths. Continental breakfast is included in the economical price. $

Just a touch more expensive, the **Hostal Isla de Baños**, at Haflants and Alfaro, ☎ 3-740-069, islaba@interactive.net.ec, is definitely one of the better values in town. Priced at the lower end, it nevertheless falls in the mid-range for comfort, amenities and atmosphere. The bar and highly recommended restaurant (great breakfast with delicious baked goods) complement a very pleasant garden. Simple but attractive and comfortable rooms are upstairs above the reception area. The friendly staff is informative, in English, Spanish and German, and can organize top-quality horseback-riding and biking trips into the surrounding countryside. $

Near the waterfall is the **Hotel Palace**, Montalvo 7-03, ☎ 3-740-470, fax 3-740-291, also in the mid-price range. Set back from "downtown," the Palace provides a bit more tranquility when there aren't too many children running around – and a few extra amenities. Between the nice garden, swimming pool, sauna, and spa, there is plenty of opportunity to rest here. An attached restaurant offers good meals, and rooms include telephones, TVs, and private baths. Rooms do, however, vary in quality, so ask to see yours before you agree to it. $$

Nearby, the **Hotel Sangay**, Plaza Isidro Ayora 101, ☎ 3-720-917 fax 740-490, www.sangayspa.com, is just across from the waterfall and baths. Larger in scale, it has 72 rooms and facilities well-suited for Ecuadorian and foreign travelers. Amenities range from a thermal pool, hot tub, and tennis courts to a nice restaurant and bar with a view of the waterfall. Rooms throughout are comfortable and modern, though they tend to be a bit nicer in the newer of the two buildings. $-$$

Villa Gertrudis, at Montalvo and Alfaro, ☎ 3-740-441, offers a family atmosphere in a beautiful converted home. Relax by the garden or go for a swim in an unusually large pool. Tasty meals in their restaurant are included in the price. Quite a popular establishment, it is often full during peak-season weekends, so check before you go. $

A step up, with a jungle feel, is the **Hostería Monte Selva**, Montalvo and Halflants, ☎ 3-740-224, fax 3-854-658, which has 12 attractive cabañas built into the hillside overlooking Baños. The very pleasant gardens include a pool and sauna with a great view. Individual cabins are comfortably perched along the cliff, as are the restaurant and reception area. These cozy cabins offer a nice retreat without ever leaving town. $$

Luna Runtún Resort, Km 6 on the road to Runtún, ☎ 3-740-882, in the US, ☎ 888-217-8254, fax 3-740-376, lunaruntun@ecuadorexplorer. com or info@lunaruntun.com, www.lunaruntun.com. The name means "fortress of the moon," and this colonial-style *hostería* has a magical charm to it – a beautiful, secluded, romantic mountain resort. The Swiss-Ecuadorian couple who built it have invested all of their dreams in this getaway. The attractive buildings are scattered among terraced gardens that overlook Baños and the valley below. The guestrooms range from singles to a presidential suite with a fireplace. Some of the facilities border the edge of the volcano itself and offer spectacular views. All rooms are comfortable and well-decorated and include private, hot-water baths. The restaurant serves delicious food, using organic vegetables grown on the property. Just beyond the botanical garden and cattle farm are trails leading into the surrounding countryside. The friendly staff can also help with travel services. All-inclusive, with dinner and breakfast. Prices are per room for one-four people. $$$$-$$$$+

East of Baños is **El Otro Lado**, a secluded bungalow retreat offering peaceful simplicity along a beautiful river and near a towering waterfall. To get there, go just past Río Verde on the road to Puyo, and hike down the Pailón del Diablo Trail. Reservations can be made through travel agents in Quito or Baños, to make sure they have room for you. It's located deep within the Río Pastaza gorge only a few yards from the screaming Pailón del Diablo waterfall. Pack lightly, as the hike down to the bungalows is fairly vigorous with a full load (but more than worth the effort). Inquire with local agencies in Baños to see if it is still open under the same management, which may have recently changed. Meals are included in the price. $$

■ Where to Eat

 Despite the fact that the town revolves around tourism, Baños does not have many exceptional restaurants. There are, however, a few good choices and numerous inexpensive but mediocre establishments lining the streets in all directions.

The restaurant at **Hostal Isla de Baños**, Haflants and Alfaro, ☎ 3-740-069, islaba@interactive.net.ec, has the best bakery in town and serves delicious American- and European-style breakfasts. Enjoy the morning air in an outdoor dining room set in a very nice flower garden. Prices are reasonable at under $5 and can be included in the price of the accommodations if you are staying there.

Rico Pan, Ambato and Maldonado, offers a good selection of Western-oriented breakfasts and also makes some of the best bread in town. After breakfast, stock up for the afternoon hike.

Café Hood, 16 de Diciembre and Martínez, serves delicious breakfasts and the best vegetarian and international meals in Baños. Complete with a book exchange, travelers' notebook, candles, alternative music, and young gringo travelers, it maintains a real "café" ambiance. The Hood is very popular for all meals, and justly so. The food is delicious. The nearby **Casa Hood** (on Martínez between Halflants and Alfaro), once under the same ownership, offers similar specialties, as well as movies and slide shows at night.

El Jardín, just down the street on the Parque de la Basílica, offers simple dining on a very pleasant garden patio. Inside, there's a small art gallery. The food is not bad and the setting is nice and peaceful. There's even a hammock near one of the tables.

Café Higueron, 16 de Diciembre and Martínez, serves typical Ecuadorian food, mainly tasty meat and vegetarian dishes. Their desserts are delicious.

Le Petit Restaurant, Eloy Alfaro 2-46 and Montalvo, is about as close as you can get to French cuisine in Baños. It is a bit more expensive by Baños standards, but it's popular, thanks to its good food and relaxing atmosphere. They have live music on some weekends.

Donde Marcelo, Ambato near 16 de Diciembre, is a great place to enjoy a *cerveza* while people-watching on the main section of the pedestrian street. I've taken some of my favorite photographs from here. When you're through with your drinks, head inside for good – though relatively pricey – food.

You'll find the best pizza in town at **Paolo's Pizzeria**, next to Café Hood. Some people swear by it, but my guess is that when you've been on the road for a while in a foreign country, anything remotely close to an American pie tends to knock your socks off.

La Casa Mía, Montalvo and Santa Clara, near the waterfall, is about as elegant as restaurants get here. La Casa specializes in Ecuadorian and Italian food, and has efficient service, along with occasional live music.

The best restaurant in the Baños area is at **Luna Runtún Resort**, up the road to Luna Runtún. Spectacular views overlooking Baños add to the good service and even better food. Local dishes include organic vegetables grown on the property, trout from nearby waters, and potatoes grown in the local mountains. The setting is quite romantic.

■ Shopping & Entertainment

 There are about as many shops as there are tour operators in Baños, selling everything from T-shirts to rubber boots, to authentic indigenous handicrafts. They are all centrally located around the main downtown area, especially the side-streets off Ambato. Check around for varying quality and prices. The main bars and dance clubs are centrally located as well. Eloy Alfaro, heading north off of Ambato, has several open-air and indoor bars, including the **Bamboos Bar**, with a jungle décor. It's well-decorated and has a nice atmosphere when there are actually people there. Bamboo is popular for modern and salsa dancing among the younger crowd, both locals and backpackers. And there is the (not) **Hard Rock Café**, just north of Ambato on Alfaro, which is slightly more hit or miss, attracting foreign travelers more than locals. I prefer the open-aired seating at the nearby unnamed patio bars.

Cuenca & the Southern Highlands

Ecuador's topography undergoes a drastic change in the short distance between the coast and Cuenca. Humid tropical lowlands and hazy banana plantations give way to cool mists, jagged peaks and fertile valleys. Travel in the Southern Highlands is slow, as the elements create constant erosion and eternally battle against human efforts to maintain the highways and byways. If you have a strong

stomach for heights, the intermittent openings in the clouds offer breathtaking views.

South of Riobamba are the provinces of Cañar, Loja and Azuay, with Cuenca – the capital of the latter – retaining by far the most colonial charm of any city of its size. Just over an hour north of Cuenca are the ruins of **Ingapirca** – which actually pre-date the arrival of the greatest ancient empire in the Americas – with **Azogues**, the provincial capital of Cañar, in-between. West of Cuenca is the expansive landscape of **El Cajas National Park**. Quite a bit farther south is the remote capital of **Loja**, an even smaller, quainter colonial city, with **Vilcabamba** and the **Valley of Longevity** just beyond. To the southeast is **Podocarpus National Park**, spanning from the tips of the Andes down deep into the Oriente.

The land is truly beautiful in this part of Ecuador, with a pleasant climate and fertile valleys due to lower elevations. Still relatively untouched, it has charming colonial architecture and the people are genuine. You are now in southern Ecuador, one of the least visited and most underrated regions of the country.

Southern Highlands

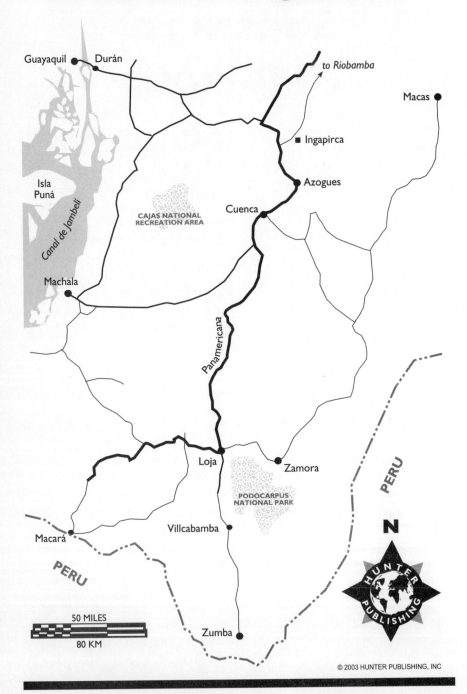

Guayaquil • — Durán

to Ríobamba

Macas •

■ Ingapirca

Isla
Puná

Azogues •

CAJAS NATIONAL
RECREATION AREA

Cuenca •

Canal de Jambeli

Machala •

Panamericana

Loja

Zamora •

PODOCARPUS
NATIONAL PARK

PERU

N

Villcabamba •

Macará •

PERU

50 MILES

80 KM

Zumba •

History

Don't let the colonial architecture fool you into thinking that the Spanish were the main inhabitants here. Cuenca's human history began well before the arrival of the Europeans. In fact, even the remnants and ruins of the Inca Empire provide false testimony as to the first people to set foot in this region. Cuenca's earliest known inhabitants, the **Cañaris**, had developed a very sophisticated culture here by about 500 AD, revolving primarily around agriculture and astronomy. The Cañaris were an industrious people known for their exceptional metalwork, particularly their ability to make jewelry.

Unfortunately for the Cañaris, they were not destined to hold this land forever. After about 1450, the Incas, under the leadership of the mighty Túpac Yupanqui, were determined to expand their empire north from the ancient capital of Cuzco. The Cañari people were just as determined, however, to resist this expansion. They fought Yupanqui's forces successfully for several years before finally giving in. The Incas took over and renamed the area **Tomebamba**, or "River Valley of the Knives," then built an illustrious city to rival Cuzco as the new Inca capital. Perhaps the Cañaris were the fortunate ones, because this was not to last.

Less than half a century later, in the mid-1500s, the **Conquistadors** arrived. The Spanish demolished the magnificent city and rebuilt it in typical colonial fashion. From then on, the city was to be called **Santa Ana de los Cuatro Ríos de Cuenca**, or the "City of Four Rivers." The Spanish, however, were not the last people to leave their mark on Cuenca. An influx of **European Jesuits** in the second half of the 19th century permanently altered the culture, religion, politics, and architecture of the city. Signs of the Jesuit influence remain in churches and other buildings that stand to this day.

Today, Cuenca maintains an air of historical charm, with cobblestone streets, architectural styles that blend together several cultures, and exceptional arts and crafts. Yet it is also a bustling and modern city with more than 350,000 people. In fact, it's the third-largest city in Ecuador. It is truly a place where the magic and mystery of yesterday meets the heartbeat of today.

Cuenca & the Southern Highlands

Flora & Fauna

Páramo grasslands dominate the landscape of the high-altitude southern Sierras – a land of steep slopes, jagged peaks, and variable weather conditions. In addition to the *páramo* typically found in the central Sierras, pockets of the small *quinua* tree can be found in Cajas National Park, just west of Cuenca. More of a shrub than a tree, the *quinua* provides habitat for a variety of unique plants and animals. There are also unusual hummingbirds, unique to this region, living among the hundreds of tiny lakes and lagoons. Other magnificent creatures include condors, mountain toucans, giant conebills, deer, rabbits and pumas.

To the southeast of Cuenca, closer to the city of Loja, lies the massive expanse of **Podocarpus National Park**, with a wide range of ecological life zones that stretch from upper *páramo* down to the limits of the upper Amazon Basin. Varied topography and weather have created evolutionary patterns favorable to numerous endemic species. Here you can find animals typical of the *páramo* merging with the more tropical flora and fauna of the southern Oriente. In addition to being a birder's paradise, the park is also home to large mammals such as the puma, mountain tapir, and the rare spectacled bear.

Getting Here & Getting Around

Many travelers enter the region surrounding Cuenca by continuing south from the Central Highlands via the Pan-American Highway. The other land route is from Guayaquil and the southern coast. The Quito-Guayaquil and Guayaquil-Cuenca roads meet in El Tríunfo. If you're flying in, the **Mariscal Lamar Airport**, located on Av. España, is close to town and offers weekday flights to and from Guayaquil and Quito. If you're heading for the coast, change planes in Guayaquil. For the rest of the country, fly to Quito first. **TAME** airlines has a desk at the airport, ☎ 7-862-193, as well as an office downtown, at Grán Colombia, down the alley between Hotel Presidente and Hotel Conquistador, ☎ 7-827-609. TAME offers two flights daily between Quito and

Cuenca except on Saturday, when there's no afternoon flight, and Sunday, when there's no morning flight. Expect to pay up to $60. Fights to Guayaquil cost slightly less than $30. **SAETA** also has a desk at the airport, ☎ 7-804-033, and downtown at Benigno Malo 7-35 and Córdova, ☎ 7-839-090. To reach Loja, TAME, offers flights between Quito and La Toma airport in Catamayo, which is less than 20 miles west of Loja, ☎ 7-573-030.

The **bus terminal** in Cuenca, on Av. España close to downtown, has numerous daily departures to Quito, Guayaquil, and Loja. Other departures, such as those to the southern Oriente, are a bit less frequent. Inquire at the station information desk. By bus it takes 8½ to 10 hours to travel between Cuenca and Quito, depending on road conditions and weather. The trip to Guayaquil takes four hours, more or less. The bus ride from Guayaquil to Loja takes about nine hours. Buses between Quito and Loja take 12 to 14 hours and stop at all major points in between. If you have your own automobile, the Pan-American Highway offers a fairly simple ride. It takes about eight hours to travel between Quito and Cuenca.

Visitor Information

■ Azogues

 Azogues, the capital of the Cañar province, has a **bank**, **telephone** office and **post office** just off of the central plaza at Bolívar and Serrano. The **church** lies just to the south. A few blocks to the northwest is the bus terminal, on Av. 24 de Mayo and Mayo (where the Pan-American Highway cuts through town).

■ Cuenca

The **Ministerio de Turismo** office, on Córdova and Benigno Malo, ☎ 7-839-337, mituraus@cue.satnet.net, provides helpful information and an artistic map of Cuenca that highlights all of the main churches and provides a nice layout of the city. It's open Monday through Friday from 8-12 and 2-4. The **Associación Hotelera del Azuay**, Córdova and Padre Aguirre, ☎ 7-821-659 or 7-836-925, ☎/fax 7-826-301, offers information on hotels in the area. The **Ministerio del Ambiente** (Ministry of the Environment), at Bolívar 5-33 (third floor), has information on Cajas National Park. The **post office** is on the corner of Calles Borrero and Grán Colombia, and the **Pacífictel phone** office is on Benigno Malo between Córdova and Sucre.

Ask around for **Internet** cafés, as there are a few within close proximity to most of the accommodations mentioned in this chapter, though they mushroomed in numbers for a couple of years and then thinned out. They are usually associated with hotels that cater to international travelers. Keep in mind that Internet connections tend to be expensive here, compared to Quito.

Banco del Pacífico is at Benigno Malo 9-75. It accepts MasterCard, has an ATM and offers good rates for travelers checks. **Banco la Previsora**, at Grán Colombia and Benigno Malo, accepts Visa. **Banco de Guayaquil**, at Sucre between Hermano Miguel and Borrero, and **Banco del Pichincha**, at Bolívar 9-74 and Malo, both exchange travelers checks. **Hospitals** include the Military Hospital, Av. 12 de Abril 7-99, ☎ 7-827-606, and the Hospital Vicente Corral Moscoso, Av. El Paraíso, ☎ 7-822-100. The **bus station** is next to the airport on Av. España.

 A useful website for Cuenca travel information is www.cuencanet.com

■ Loja

The **Minesterio de Turismo** office is at Bernardo Valdivieso 08-22, south of 10 de Agosto ☎ 7-572-964, ☎/fax 7-572-964. Check with them for local guides offering trips into Podocarpus Nacional Park. Also visit the **Minesterio del Ambiente**, on Sucre between Imbabura and Quito, ☎ 7-563-131, which administers the park and has good maps. The **post office** is at the corner of Colón and Sucre, and the **Pacífictel** phone office is on Eguiguren and Valdivieso, a block east of the central park. For bank services, including Visa, MasterCard and ATM, **Banco de Buayaquil** is on J A Eguiguren between Valdivieso and Olmedo.

The **bus station** is 1¼ miles north of downtown on Av. Cuxibamba, paralleling the river. **Taxis** can be found in the city center and in the area around the central park, Parque Central. The **Military Hospital** is at Colón and Bernardo Valdivies, ☎ 7-578-332. There is a **clinic** at Cuxibamba and Latacunga, ☎ 7-581-077.

■ Vilcabamba

In Vilcabamba, most services are located around the central plaza and church. The **tourism office** is at Bolívarand Diego Vaca de la Vega, next to the Pacífictel **telephone** office. Just north, next to the police station is the **post office**, on Agua de Hierro near Bolívar. **Bus** companies park near the market on Juan Montalvo.

Touring & Sightseeing

■ Cañar

 North of Cuenca is the small indigenous town of Cañar, offering a pleasant setting and a peaceful area to relax or to enjoy a country stroll. The best day to visit is on Sunday – market day – when the sleepy town livens up. Cañar should be of particular interest to those visiting the Inca ruins at **Ingapirca**, as it is the nearest major population center. Buses travel frequently between Cuenca and Cañar (at least one an hour) and the journey takes only a couple of hours. From Cañar, it is a quick hop on a bus or *camioneta* to Tambo and the ruins just a few miles away.

■ Biblián

Less than 19 miles south of Cañar is the small village of Biblián, interesting primarily for the **Santuario de la Vírgen del Rocío**, in the hills above the Pan-American Highway. The Sanctuary was built and continues to be worshiped as the site of a miracle that saved locals from a bad drought. Otherwise, keep driving.

■ Azogues

Located between Cañar and Cuenca on the Pan-American Highway, this sleepy town is the capital of the province of Cañar, with a population of around 35,000. There is not much of interest to the traveler, other than perhaps the main plaza and local church. Look around for local *artesanía* shops if you are interested in native design.

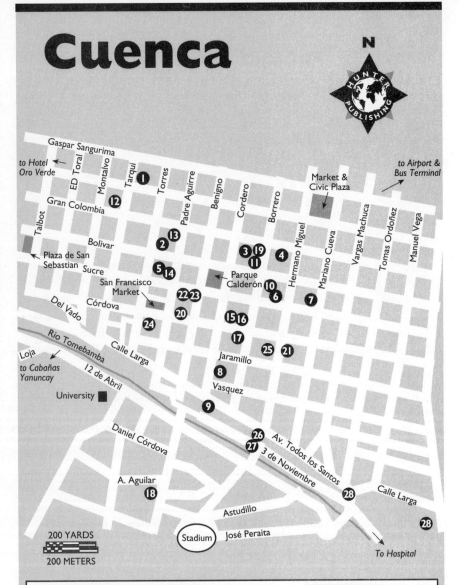

Cuenca

N

HUNTER PUBLISHING

Gaspar Sangurima

to Hotel
Oro Verde

ED Toral

Montalvo

Tarqui

Torres

Padre Aguirre

Benigno

Cordero

Borrero

Market &
Civic Plaza

to Airport &
Bus Terminal

Gran Colombia

Vargas Machuca

Tomas Ordoñez

Manuel Vega

Talbot

Bolivar

Plaza de San
Sebastian Sucre

San Francisco
Market

Córdova

Del Vado

Río Tomebamba

Loja
to Cabañas
Yanuncay

12 de Abril

University

Daniel Córdova

A. Aguilar

Calle Larga

Jaramillo

Vasquez

Hermano Miguel

Mariano Cueva

Parque
Calderón

Av. Todos los Santos

3 de Noviembre

Astudillo

José Peraita

Calle Larga

To Hospital

200 YARDS
200 METERS

Stadium

① ⑫ ② ⑬ ⑤ ⑭ ㉒㉓ ⑳ ㉔ ③ ⑲ ⑪ ④ ⑩ ⑥ ⑦ ⑮⑯ ⑰ ㉕ ㉑ ⑧ ⑨ ㉖ ㉗ ⑱ ㉘ ㉘

WHERE TO STAY & EAT

1. Hostal Macondo
2. Gran Hotel
3. Hotel El Dorado
4. Hotel El Conquistador,
   Hotel Presidente
5. Hotel Inca Real
6. Hotel Paris Internacional
7. Posada del Sol
8. El Cafecito
9. Hotel Crespo

10. Hostal Nusta
11. Hostal La Orquídea
12. Restaurant Villa Rosa
13. El Pedregal Azteca
14. El Huerto
15. Chifa Pak How
16. La Cantina Bar
    & Restaurant
17. Restaurant El Jardín
18. La Napoletana Pizzería

OTHER SITES

19. Post Office
20. Hotel Association
21. Tourist Info
22. Flower Market
23. Casa de Cultura
24. San Francisco Church
25. Museo de las Conceptas
26. Wunderbar
27. Museo de Artes Populares
28. Inca Ruins

■ Cuenca

Cuenca, set below the sprawling mass of Chimborazo and the Avenue of the Volcanoes, is the major urban center in the south. The topography here is harsh and steep, intermixed with deep, lush, and fertile valleys. The difficult terrain has kept Cuenca and the region south of it disassociated from the rest of Ecuador for many years. It is only within the last several decades that transportation and communication have linked this area with the rest of the country. As a result, a distinct colonial charm persists in this provincial capital and the people remain more or less untainted by the effects of tourism. Cuenca also supports a flourishing arts community and is one of the country's cultural centers.

At 7,684 feet in elevation, Cuenca lies within a lush river valley flanked by mountain ridges and divided east-to-west by the Río Tomebamba. Just north of Tomebamba is the original colonial section of town. This area is of most historical interest to the traveler and provides many lodging and restaurant options. To the south is modern Cuenca, which includes the university, stadium, businesses, and suburbs. As with many places in Ecuador, geographic features delineate the city's boundaries. In the north, the city ends with the valley at the Río Machángara, and in the far south two more rivers, the Yanuncay and Tarquí, form the border. Cuenca is thus also known as the City of Four Rivers.

Hot Springs in Baños

Not to be confused with the resort town of Baños, described in the previous chapter, the sulfur springs at this Baños, a few miles southwest of Cuenca, are much hotter. If it's peace and quiet you're after, then you should probably come here during the week, as it is a popular weekend getaway for Cuenca locals seeking relaxation. You can catch a taxi to this Baños from Cuenca for under $3 or take one of the frequent buses.

There are many attractive and charming sites throughout the colonial section of Cuenca. It's a relatively sleepy city, so you might as well relax, enjoy the slow pace and take a stroll while visiting some of these attractions.

City Stroll

No trip to Cuenca is complete without wandering among the cobble-stone streets and enjoying the beauty of the colonial architecture. Cuenca is a small big city, developed in a traditional Spanish square-grid pattern. The long, narrow streets run primarily north-south and east-west, and are closed in by the tall walls of colonial buildings. Wandering around, it's quite easy to become disoriented without a landmark as a point of reference. Relax and continue meandering; you can easily reorient yourself with a map and a cross-street. The architecture is fabulous, the culture is rich, and the churches are impressive to the point of being overwhelming. Grab a seat on a bench at the Parque Calderón, the main plaza downtown, and watch the world go by.

Myriad other churches and cathedrals, architectural and decorative testimonies of splendor, line the streets of Cuenca and many are quite fascinating. Each provides another affirmation of the undying faith of the people.

Parque Calderón

The streets of Simón Bolívar, Sucre, Benigno Malo and Luis Cordero surround Parque Calderón, which is the main plaza. Nestled between the old church and the massive new cathedral, the plaza is where it all seems to come together, both as a landmark and as a focal point for local activity. As community space is important throughout Ecuador and Latin America in general, plazas tend to lie adjacent to the other major facet of local communities – the churches. And the enormous new cathedral, along the western edge of the plaza, resonates with the faith of the locals.

Plaza Civica

A few blocks to the northeast, at Mariano Cueva and Mariscal Lamar, is another plaza and daily market. The Civic Plaza market offers household supplies and daily goods, catering more to the locals but it's worth a glance. There are a couple of hotels near here.

There are 52 churches in Cuenca, one for each Sunday of the year. Most of them are conveniently located within several square blocks of the plaza. If your interest lies in architecture or religious sites, pick up a nicely illustrated map from the Minesterio de Turismo tourist office (Miguel 686 and Córdova) for an artistic idea of where the best ones are located.

Catedral de la Immaculada

Adjacent to Parque Calderón, dominating the entire west side of the square, is the massive new cathedral, la Catedral de la Immaculada, referred to locally as simply La Catedral. If the outside view does not impress you, take a step through the doorway and enter a building intended to hold 10,000 people (don't forget to take off your hat). The extraordinary size of the structure and the many worshipers praying inside are a true testimony to the significance of religion, and particularly the Catholic Church, in Ecuadorian lives. During a recent visit there were women kneeling in front of the altar and chanting. The beauty of their song echoing among silent worshippers in such an enormous space was truly moving.

The cathedral is a fairly recent addition to Cuenca. Construction of the building began in 1885 when the city (or the church) decided it had outgrown the old cathedral, **El Sagrario**, located along the southeastern side of the plaza. The old cathedral grew up over an Inca site with colonial Cuenca itself, beginning in 1557. The recently renovated old church still has a few Inca stones visible, facing the plaza.

The new cathedral is on Cordero, between Bolívar and Sucre, across Parque Calderón from the old cathedral.

El Carmen de la Asunción

Although the church, built in the 17th century, is not always open, this is one of my favorite street corners, particularly for the mystery inside and the spectacular flower market out front. A group of nuns in the attached convent live in seclusion from the rest of the world, devoted entirely to the higher calling of eternal prayer. They do not venture much into the outside world, and visitors provide offerings at the church entrance. Meanwhile, the colorful flower market in the plaza stands in stark contrast to the solemnity within. If you enjoy photography, this is a hot spot, but, due to the narrow streets and high colonial structures, the window of opportunity for proper lighting is pretty narrow. The church is one block west of the old cathedral on Mariscal Sucre.

The Convent of the Immaculate Conception Museum

This, the Museo del Monasterio de las Conceptas, is the best religious museum in Cuenca, offering an interesting display of colonial religious art. The convent's first order in Ecuador, which began in Quito, was founded in Cuenca on July 13, 1599. Construction of the church itself began in 1682 and was completed in 1729, with additions built in the 1800s. Restoration of the building in the mid-1980s allowed the church to "exhibit its cultural heritage." The museum now consists of various rooms on two floors that wrap around an interior garden courtyard. Within are displays of religious art, from paintings and sculptures to statues, crucifixes, and large nativity scenes. Photographs of the early nuns working in the convent complement antique displays of the tools they used, such as the earliest spin "washing machine" and dough-making devices. There is also a simple attached chapel.

The convent is located at Hermano Miguel 6-33, ☎ 7-830-625, open Tue-Fri, 9-4, and Sat, 9-12. Admission is approximately $2.

Río Tomebamba & the Inca Ruins

From the historic center of Cuenca, head south a few blocks to Río Tomebamba, which currently divides the old town from the new. Attractive colonial buildings adorn the north bank of the river and the area makes for quite a nice walk, regardless of the fact that it's within a bustling metropolis. Don't be surprised to find an occasional vendor selling handcrafted jewelry, young artists experimenting with colors, or even the occasional rock climber testing her skills on a bridge built centuries ago. One of the more photogenic scenes is when there is a colorful array of washed laundry laid out to dry along the riverbank with a backdrop of traffic, honking horns and modern buildings. It is not uncommon on a Saturday afternoon in many towns to see small groups of indigenous women standing in the local river with the water about their knees, washing their laundry and catching up on the week's events.

As you walk southeast along 3 de Noviembre and the river, you'll see the Inca ruins at the intersection of Calle Larga and Av. Todos los Santos, near the bridge. Most of the ruins were destroyed and buried beneath colonial architecture, but what remains is worth a visit.

Entrance to the ruins is free. A small museum on the site displays a few interesting artifacts, but open hours vary.

Museo de Artes Populares

Near the junction of Calles Larga and Hermano Miguel, follow the steps leading down to the Río Tomebamba for the entrance to a small but interesting museum operated by the Centro Interamericano de *Artesanías* y Artes Populares (CIDAP). Displays include traditional musical instruments, ceremonial attire, and handicrafts. The museum focuses on local or regional exhibits, but some rotate over time and may include displays from across the globe.

The museum is located on Hermano Miguel 3-23, ☎ 7-829-451. It's open 9:30-5 on weekdays (closed midday for lunch) and 10-1 on Sat. There is no actual entrance free, but they appreciate and depend on donations.

Museo del Banco Central

The best overall museum in Cuenca is the Museo del Banco Central, ☎ 7-831-225, in the southeastern part of town near the mouth of the Río Tomebamba and the ruins. The large, modern building is not very obvious and the last time I was here there was still no sign outside. The entrance is on Calle Larga near Huayna Capac. In addition to religious art, there are traditional musical instruments, archeological artifacts from the Cañaris and Incas, and a display of black and white photographs of colonial Cuenca. Alternating displays cover modern art topics.

The museum is open Mon-Fri from 9-6, except during lunch hours, and Sat 9-1. Nominal entrance fee.

Museo de Arte Moderno

This museum of modern art, on Sucre 15-27 and Coronel Talbot, ☎ 7-831-027, houses a small collection of contemporary art, and periodically exhibits new collections, mostly the work of local artists.

It's open Mon-Fri, 8:30-6, and Sat and Sun, 9-3. Admission is free.

Museo de Las Culturas Aborigenes

This museum has an interesting collection of pre-Columbian artifacts, on Av.10 de Agosto 4-70 and Rafael Torres, ☎ 7-880-010, 7-888-461. It's private collection owned by a Dr. J. Cordero López. The museum is open to the public Mon-Fri, 9-6. The building has a pleasant courtyard, where you can enjoy refreshments.

Cuenca & the Southern Highlands

■ Chordeleg & Gualaceo Cultural Excursions

If you happen to be in Cuenca on a Sunday, treat yourself to a couple of authentic markets in the nearby towns of Gualaceo and Chordeleg. Situated about 1½ hours east of Cuenca, these famous markets are within walking distance of each other. Leave early in the morning, spend the day browsing, and you can make it back to Cuenca by afternoon.

Gualaceo is a colonial town with an upbeat atmosphere. The Sunday market is more than the weekly center of economic activity. It is a social gathering, a colorful display of a deep-rooted culture at its finest. Don't expect the hammocks, sweaters, arts, and crafts of the Otavalo market. Do expect an amazing display of indigenous life. Fruits and vegetables of all shapes, sizes, and colors abound, as do roasted pork, medicinal herbs, and natural remedies. Bartering is intense. From the youngest of the young to the oldest of the old, everyone is involved – it's all a part of life here in the southern Sierras.

The countryside bordering Gualaceo is dotted with villages and people that specialize in various crafts. You'll find everything from Panama hats, jewelry, and weavings to ceramics and guitars. These "craft trails" are very popular, but they're difficult to find without a good guide. If you know what you're looking for, then pick and choose. Otherwise, select your guide and enjoy meeting the local craftspeople in their own homes. Just southeast of Gualaceo along a paved road is Chordeleg, a haven for fine jewelry. With everything from traditional filigree to contemporary items in gold and silver, *joyerías*, or jewelry shops, line the main road and plaza. Chordeleg's Sunday market, quite a bit smaller than the one in Gualaceo, is also worth a visit. This area is also known for woodcarvings, ceramics and Panama hats.

Frequent daily buses run between Cuenca and Gualaceo. If hiring a taxi in Cuenca, make sure to set up a time for a return pickup. **Expediciones Apullacta**, at Grán Columbia 11-02 and General Torres, ☎ 7-837-815, apullacta@cedei.org, offers excursions into local crafts communities, where you can experience first-hand the work of local *artesanías*.

Saraguro Indians

Nearly four hours south of Cuenca toward Loja, and a bit beyond the small town of Ona, is the large indigenous population of Saraguro. Uniquely identified in traditional attire, the proud Amerindians were relocated during the Inca reign from the remote southern stretch of Bolivia's Lake Titicaca. Today, their language (still Quichua, but very distinct), culture and attire persevere and set them apart from any other group in Ecuador. Be sure to visit the market in town on Sunday, when rural natives arrive in splendor to shop, sell and trade. You can't miss the town. Its entrance is marked with a huge sign proclaiming their pride and importance.

■ Loja

Just over five hours south of Quito by bus, Loja is Ecuador's southernmost city, far removed from any other major population center and therefore relatively unaffected by fast-paced transformation that the rest of the country is undergoing. Loja is a good jumping-off point for exploring Podocarpus National Park, to the southeast, and the southern Oriente. Alternatively, many travelers following the gringo trail or heading to Peru, continue farther south toward the village of Vilcabamba. Although the Pan-American continues toward Peru, it is not a well-traveled route. Some travelers heading south to Peru stop here for a relaxing layover.

Founded in 1548, Loja is the oldest colonial city in Ecuador, and its relative isolation down through the years has allowed it to maintain an atmosphere of tradition. Today, Loja boasts more than 120,000 inhabitants. Set at an altitude of 6,867 feet, the city enjoys a climate that is quite pleasant throughout the year. The pace here is slow and the people are friendly. All you really have to do in Loja is relax and enjoy the scenery.

The original section of downtown Loja was developed in a traditional colonial pattern, with compact streets and square blocks that are located around the main plaza at the cross streets of 10 de Agosto and Bolívar. Abutting the plaza is the Catedral, as well as other museums and points of interest. Wandering around by foot is easy; the downtown area is of most interest to the foreign traveler. Once you get the itch to visit Podocarpus or Vilcabamba, it's time to move on.

Cuenca & the Southern Highlands

Loja

N

HUNTER PUBLISHING

Rio Zamora

Rio Malacatus

Rio Malacatus

Juan de Salinas

José Félix Valdivieso

Quito

Av. Iberoamerica

Av. Universitaria

Parque Simón Bolivar

Imbabura

Colón

8

José Antonio Eguiguren

3

R. Pinto

L. Guerrero

1

Diez de Agosto

4

Market

2

Rocafuerte

Miguél Riofrio

Azuay

Parque Central

Telephone Office

B. Valdivieso

6

7

Olmedo

Jl Peña

24 de Mayo

5

Av. Alonso de Mercadillo

MA Aguirre

18 de Noviembre

Lourdes

Sucre

Bolivar

Plaza de la Independecia

L. Palacios

Macara

Sports Complex

Av. Ortega

Av. Orillas del Zamora

to Hostal Aguilera International

1. Acapulco
2. Gran Hotel Loja
3. Libertador
4. Hotel Riviera
5. Don Quijote
6. Museo del Banco Central
7. Tourist Office
8. Casa de Cultura

200 YARDS

200 METERS

© 2003 HUNTER PUBLISHING, INC

Loja has a few decent hotels, and even the best are relatively inexpensive. All are within walking distance of Parque Central. Modern services, including post, communications, and medical, are also in this downtown area (see *Visitor Information*, page 203). It takes about 13 hours from Quito by car, and up to 18 hours by bus (or 10 hours from Guayaquil). From Cuenca, it is only a three- or four-hour drive, longer by bus. TAME offers daily flights from Quito to La Tola, the Loja airport, which is actually about 25 minutes from town in Catamayo. From Catamayo, public transportation is available to Loja by taxi or bus.

■ Vilcabamba

Vilcabamba and its mystic reputation as the "Valley of Longevity" is a quiet southern retreat set within a scenic, rolling countryside. Locals here are reputed to live unusually long, healthy lives, to the extent that scientists from the US, Europe and Japan, have actually come to the "enchanted valley" to investigate the phenomenon. Personally, I think their longevity probably is due to the lack of stress in such a pleasant climate and environment, as well as the quality of the air and water in the area.

So, what is there to do here? Most visitors just relax and soak up the healthy atmosphere, with options for luxurious spa treatments at a couple of the local resorts. Vilcabamba is also a popular point of departure for trips to Podocarpus National Park, and its surrounding countryside is great for hiking and horseback riding.

Cultural Sensitivity

Some travelers come to Vilcabamba to find and purchase the mind-altering San Pedro plant. Natives once used this plant during a very lengthy and spiritual ceremony. Note that anyone selling the plant to foreigners as a finished product has no respect for his or her own culture and is severely frowned upon by natives. Please be respectful.

The town is very small and laid-back, with a population of about 2,000 and a very heavy foreigner influence. The climate is very pleasant, and socializing consists of relaxing with newfound friends and chatting the nights away. The area has attracted alternative folks who offer pleasant accommodations, organic gardens, massage therapy,

Cuenca & the Southern Highlands

and a generally healthy lifestyle. In fact, immigrating utopia seekers have resulted in quality accommodations and amenities at cutthroat rates. With regard to climate, the end of May through September is the best time to visit Vilcabamba, with the weather getting progressively chilly and rainy thereafter (though it is never too bad).

By taxi ($10) or car, the trip usually takes less than an hour from Loja to Vilcacamba, a bit longer by bus. A useful website for travel information is www.vilcabamba.org.

Adventures

As with the central Sierras, the Southern Highlands offer infinite miles of scenic landscapes to explore either on foot or on horseback. For backcountry excursions you can't do much better than El Cajas and Podocarpus National Parks, and the latter is ideal for the avid birder who is willing to rough it. Although organized mountain biking has not yet been popularized in this region, the countryside beckons. Riding horseback through the picturesque landscape around Vilcacabamba is popular with locals and travelers alike.

 In addition to those listed below, and because things change over time, remember that the Ministry of Tourism in Cuenca and Loja will always have the latest list of private guides and tour operators for any activity you are interested in.

■ On Foot

Inca Trail to Ingapirca

 For a true journey into the past, hike a section of the famed Inca Trail. Once spanning the entire length of the empire, the Inca Trail stretched from Quito in the north all the way south to Santiago, Chile. The road, a massive transportation and communication network, continues to provide views into a world hardly changed in hundreds of years. Within Ecuador, the best section of this trail involves a three-day trek that begins in the central Sierras and ends at the Inca ruins of Ingapirca.

Experience native life as it has remained in the rural highlands since the 16th century. Admire scenic vistas. Climb steep switchbacks. Scramble through tight rock formations. Hop across narrow rivers and hike through muddy marshlands. Follow forgotten footpaths and camp among ancient ruins. And end at the best-preserved Inca temple in Ecuador. If you have a few days and enjoy camping and backpacking, then this is the trip for you.

Outfitters in Quito, Riobamba, and Cuenca offer complete tour packages. It's also possible to hire a local guide for logistical support. The nearest major town for an overnight before beginning the hike is Alausí, between Riobamba and Cuenca. From Alausí, head to Achupallas, about 15 miles away, where the trek begins. Ask around for a local *camioneta*, which should cost no more than $10. Carry all camping equipment and enough food and water for up to four days (you won't find much in Achupallas). The route is difficult to follow in some places, and good topographic maps (IGM 1:50,000 Juncal) are required if you plan to go without a guide.

El Cajas National Park

To the west of Cuenca, El Cajas is one of the better places to visit if you are looking for time away from "civilization." It is a stark and stunning place. While breathtaking, El Cajas is not a place for the casual naturalist, and is far from a "walk in the park." At over 13,080 feet, the *páramo* countryside is exposed to harsh weather. Rain and persistent winds are common. Camping requires quality gear and a sense of stoicism, while trails are steep and difficult to follow. Bring a guide or a good map and a keen sense of direction. Of use are the IGM 1:50,000 maps of Cuenca, Chaucha and Chinquintad.

A hike around **Laguna Toreadora**, near the visitors' center, makes for a nice day-long excursion from Cuenca. Arrive early in the morning to give yourself a chance of good weather. A full day is required to summit **Cerro San Luis**, on the opposite side of the lake from the park refuge. Other multi-day hikes beyond the refuge are equally worthwhile, but, unless you're an experienced camper and backcountry navigator, they require a guide. El Cajas offers some great overnight trekking opportunities and wonderful vistas.

To get to the main entrance and visitors' center of El Cajas, take the road from Cuenca to Miguir. Buses depart from Cuenca to Miguir early in the morning – the ride takes about 1½ hours to Lake Toreadora, where you will find local visitors on the weekends. The entrance station is before the visitors' center and lake.

Cuenca & the Southern Highlands

Tour Operators

For exploring the Cuenca region, including Ingapirca and El Cajas, the following tour operators are recommended. **Ecotrek**, in Cuenca at Larga and Luis Cordero, ☎ 7-842-531, fax 7-835-387, offers trips into Cajas and Kapawi, in Ecuador's southern Oriente (see pages 217 and 378). They are very knowledgeable and are a top-quality organization. **Expediciones Apullacta**, at Grán Columbia 11-02 and General Torres, ☎ 7-837-815, apullacta@cedei.org, has been recommended for day-trips to El Cajas, with transport and meals included. Or try **Río Arriba Expeditions**, at Hermano Miguel 7-14, ☎ 7-830-116, negro@az.pro.ec – bilingual guide included.

Also for day tours to Cajas and Ingapirca, try **Santa Ana Tours**, Córdova and Borrero, ☎ 7-832-340. Independent guide **Eduardo Quito**, ☎ 7-823-018, is also highly recommended. He is reportedly very knowledgeable about the region and speaks English. **Metropolitan Touring**, on Sucre and Hermano Miguel, ☎ 7-831-463, www.metropolitan-touring.com, is always top notch. Although they are the largest touring company in the country, they do a good job, utilizing local experts.

Podocarpus National Park

The area to the southeast is even less explored than El Cajas and even more exceptional in its varied topography. The highlands of this park offer hiking opportunities, while its eastern stretches meet the upper Amazon and provide some of the best birding for the determined birder. For hiking, get information at the ranger station and/or maps in town (see *Eco-Travel* section, below). Inquire at the Ministry of Toursim offices in Loja and Cuenca for local tour operators and individual guides. In Vilcabamba, contact **Refugio Solomaco**, at Sucre and Toledo, ☎ 7-673-183, solomaco@hotmail.com, for details on all-inclusive trips into the park.

Around Vilcabamba

Vilcabamba and the Río Yambala area offer opportunities for pleasant countryside hikes as far as the eye can see, or longer overnight backpacking and camping as well. A nice hike is along the Río Vilcabamba toward El Chaupi. For longer excursions and supported multi-day trips into Podocarpus National Park, inquire with **Llama Walking Tours**, ☎ 7-580-061, anneli@llamandina.com, or ask around at the local hostels for suggestions and route information. There is also a tourist office along the main plaza in town that can point you in the right direction.

Birders will be amply rewarded with a wonderful array of opportunities, including the region east of Vilcabamba in the headwaters of the upper Yamburara Valley. For more on this and a complete bird list, visit Vilcabamba's website at www.vilcabamba.org.

■ With a Fishing Pole

Both El Cajas and Podocarpus National Parks have numerous high-altitude lakes and streams. Bring along a pole; many of these offer excellent trout fishing, though the fish aren't the biggest you've seen.

■ On Horseback

As in most other regions of the Andes, there are grand opportunities to ride horseback around Cuenca, with trips that last from one to several days. The hard part isn't where to go, it's where to find a decent outfitter. The area around Vilcabamba is ideal for horseback riding at a leisurely pace – with a consistently pleasant climate and a wide-open, scenic countryside. In fact, this area is known for its horses, which are one of the main attractions during festivals, such as Carnival in February.

In Cuenca, **MontaRuna**, at Grán Colombia 10-29 and General Torres, ☎ /fax 7-846-395, montarun@az.pro.ec, offers excursions of varying length. Destinations include Ingapirga and the Inca Trail, as well as Cajas National Park and other areas in this region. They also offer trekking and top-notch jungle tours. They have multilingual guides.

Several hostels can arrange horseback rides, either with or without guides. The **Hostal Madre Tierra,** ☎ 7-580-269, 7-580-687, www.madretierra1.org, hmtierra@ecua.net.ec, and **Hostería Las Ruinas de Quinara,** ☎ 7-580-301, www.lasruinasdequinara.com, ruinasqui@hotmail.com, can make arrangements. Actually, pretty much any hostel you are staying at will help to set up a trip, even if they cannot do it directly themselves. For horseback riding trips to Podocarpus, **Roger Toledo** is based in Vilcacamba, on Agua de Hierro near Bolívar. He offers multi-day trips into other areas as well.

■ On Wheels

By Bicycle

In and around Cuenca, try **Eco Rutas**, near Hotel Crespo along the river, ☎ 7-842-571, for bicycle equipment and information about trips in the surrounding countryside. There's also **Tecno Cycle**, at Tamariz 3-15 ☎ 7-839-659; **Ciclismo Total**, at Solano and Av. del Estado, ☎ /fax 7-451-390, offers guided biking excursions around El Cajas and the countryside surrounding Cuenca.

A couple of hostels in Vilcabamba rent bicycles and provide information for the local countryside. Don't expect high-end bicycle gear, but their bikes are fine for touring the area, which offers wonderful sightseeing opportunities. Try **Hostería Las Ruinas de Quinara**, ☎ 7-580-301, www.lasruinasdequinara.com, ruinasqui@hotmail.com, or ask at the local tourist office. Even with a guide, be sure you, or they, have all of the necessary tools to fix flat tires and other problems.

Eco-Travel

■ Around Cuenca

Ingapirca Ruins

Approximately 35 miles north of Cuenca are the best-preserved remnants of the Inca civilization in Ecuador. Ingapirca is actually a Cañari word meaning "Walls of the Incas." Before the Incas conquered them and modified the site for their own needs, around 1450, it was used by the Cañaris and was referred to as *cashaloma*, which roughly (at best) translates into "where stars are pouring from the heavens" and suggests its astronomical significance. Strangely enough, though, notice that the current name is based on the language of the first inhabitants, yet describes the place within the context of their conquerors.

Located just west of Cañar off the Pan-American Highway, Ingapirca sits low upon a hill overlooking picturesque valleys to the west. Beyond the village of Ingapirca is the entrance to the ruins, where you can visit a small but very interesting museum and local handicraft booths. Walk ahead and step back in time to explore the **Temple of**

the Sun. This former observatory and temple is an elliptical, low-lying stone building, and is believed to have served ceremonial and religious purposes. While the Cañaris worshiped the night skies and used the facility as an observatory, the Incas were sun-worshipers and modified it accordingly. This parallels other sites in Ecuador, including Cuicocha (north of Quito), where excavation has revealed remnants of both moon and sun calendars.

Ingapirca's true purpose during the short period of Inca residence depends on whom you are speaking with. In addition to a ceremonial site, it most likely also served as a *tambo*, or resting place along the royal Inca route to Quito, as well as a granary and military base for watching over the rebellious locals. Although not as magnificent as the lost Inca ruins of Macchu Picchu in Peru, Ingapirca is nevertheless intriguing and well worth a visit.

The site is open from 8-5 daily, but the museum is closed on Sundays. The entrance fee is about $4 and hiring a quality guide from Cuenca or at Ingapirca itself is highly recommended. Several tour operators in Cuenca offer complete packages for less than $50. You can hire a taxi, but it will probably cost as much as a guide with transportation. The budget route would be to catch a bus from Cuenca (less than $2, 1½ hours) and have the driver drop you off at the entrance on the right side, about a mile before Cañar. From there, hitch a ride with a passing vehicle for the remaining nine miles to the site.

For guided trips to Ingapirca, try **Santa Ana Tours**, on Córdova and Borrero in Cuenca, ☎ 7-832-340. Independent guide **Eduardo Quito**, ☎ 7-823-018, is also highly recommended. He knows a great deal about the region and speaks English.

El Cajas National Park

Picture an incredibly harsh and mountainous landscape, barren and sparse, yet hauntingly beautiful, with countless emerald lakes and ponds dotting the countryside. You have just entered the Parque Nacional de Cajas, a 69,000-acre reserve with plenty of potential for the active outdoor enthusiast. If you're lucky enough to visit Cajas on a clear day (or minute), you'll be rewarded with incredible views of picturesque lakes, distant mountains, and a unique ecosystem that is home to a variety of flora and fauna. Wildlife includes mountain toucans, hummingbirds, Andean gulls, black frogs, and the occasional Andean condor. Camping is permitted within the park, as is trout fishing. (See *Adventures On Foot*, page 217, for specifics.)

A few buses run daily between Cuenca and the park; most depart early in the morning. Check with the Ministerio de Turismo office, on Córdova and Benigno Malo in Cuenca, ☎ 7-839-337. Taxis are expensive, even with hard bargaining. You might as well hire a guide, with everything included. When scouting outfitters from Cuenca, ask if their prices include lunch and the $10 park entrance fee (usually, they do not). Maps are available at the ranger station just past the park entrance. More accurate topographic maps are available at the IGM office in Quito.

> *The Instituto Geografico Militar, on Jimenez, near Parque El Ejido, sells the best topographic maps of Ecuador. They are open from 8 am to 4 pm, Mon-Fri. To get there from 12 de Octubre, climb the hill on Jiménez, cross Colombia to Paz y Mino, go behind the military hospital and turn right.*

The best time to visit Cajas is during the dry season, from August to January, which is cooler but with less precipitation. The ranger station/refuge offers four bunks and primitive cooking facilities for a nominal fee. Alternatively, check with **Ecotrek** in Cuenca, Calle Larga 7-108 and Luis Cordero, ☎ 7-842-531, about the **Huagrahue Páramo Lodge** at the boundary of the park. It comes highly recommended by previous guests. Or try **Cabanas Yanuncay** (see *Where to Stay*, page 225) for guide services into the park.

■ Near Loja & Vilcabamba

Podocarpus National Park

Parque Nacional Podocarpus, all 361,312 acres of it, is a brilliant display of numerous ecological life zones merging to form a variety of unique habitats. Quite a few visits are required to even scratch the surface of this special place. Fortunately, the initial entrance fee buys a pass that is good for a week.

Located southeast of Loja, Podocarpus spans from mountainous *páramo* habitat at over 11,772 feet elevation down to the southern Oriente at 3,270 feet. The major life zones include upper premontane, with excellent hiking routes available, tropical cloud forest, which is highlighted with incredible birding opportunities, and finally, the lower subtropical elevations, with virgin rainforest and endemic species abounding. Because of its inaccessibility and varied topography, Podocarpus is less visited than other national parks in the country. Created to protect the region's biological diversity, endemic species, and the only large expanse of undisturbed forest in southern Ecuador, Podocarpus is, ironically, one of the more threatened areas in the country. Illegal colonization, hunting, and mineral concessions are serious concerns in an area that lacks appropriate funding for protection. Your visit and dollars are desperately needed and will be amply rewarded with an incredible experience.

The park's entrance and administrative center is the **Cajanuma entrance**, located south of Loja on the road to Vilcabamba. Enter via the marked dirt road on the left, heading east into the park. At the visitor's center, lodging is available and various trails provide easy access into the park. Some trails are short loops that take only a couple of hours, while others may require an overnight expedition through various ecological life zones.

Unique to this area are the **podocarpus trees**, for which the park is named. Three species of these coniferous trees can be found here. As the park spreads east, misty, thick cloud forests quickly engulf the landscape and provide habitat for incredible species like the **spectacled bear**. This shy, endangered animal is the only bear found in South America. Other creatures within the park include the solitary puma, mountain tapirs, and the Andean fox. As the elevation drops, the ecology merges with that of the upper Amazon life zones and wildlife typical of the Oriente.

Podocarpus is also a birder's paradise. Incredibly, some estimates place up to 800 species of birds within the park's boundaries. In addition to an abundance of birds and other animals, Podocarpus boasts several thousand vascular plant species, many of which have not yet been catalogued. The number of unique species here, found nowhere else in the world, is extraordinary in Podocarpus. The combination of topography and unique weather patterns has created habitats found nowhere else on earth.

To get there, head south toward Vilcabamba and take a left at the sign for Cajanuma, about nine miles south of Loja. About five miles later is the Cajanuma ranger station, which you can hike to. Or you can catch a taxi from Loja. Bunk beds and camping are available from the ranger station and trails lead up to the lakes and *páramo* habitat. Bring all camping gear and food. The park entrance fee is $10. Maps of the area, including main entry points, are available at the Ministerio del Ambiente in Loja, located on Sucre between Quito and Imbabura, ☎ 7-571-534.

Cuenca & the Southern Highlands

Several ecological organizations provide useful information, including **Fundación Ecológica Podocarpus**, at 18 de Noviembre and Eguiguren in Loja, ☎ 7-572-926. In Zamora, check with **Arco Iris**, Segundo Cueva Celi and Clodoveo Carrión, ☎ 7-572-926, or **Programa Podocarpus**, Clodoveo Carrión and Pasaje M. de J. Lozano, ☎ 7-585-924.

The other major access point into the park is from the southern Oriente side via Zamora.

Where to Stay

ACCOMMODATIONS PRICE SCALE	
Unless otherwise noted, prices are per room, up to double occupancy. Some prices are per person, particularly with all-inclusive packages, but these generally include meals, lodging, guide services and other amenities.	
$ . . . . Under $25	
$$ . . . . $26 to $50	
$$$ . . . . $51 to $100	
$$$$ . . . . Over $100	

■ Ingapirca

 Posada Ingapirca, with sweeping views, is 1,500 feet from the ruins. For reservations, ☎ 7-290-670, or in Cuenca, ☎ 7-838-508, 831-120, ☎/fax 832-340. Reasonably priced, Posada Ingapirca offers country comforts and a great restaurant in a setting well away from the urban outlets.

The classic budget traveler's hostel is **El Cafecito**, at Honorato Vasquez 7-36 and Luis Cordero, ☎ 7-832-337, www.cafecito.net. It's complete with modern art, modern music, and young backpackers. The rooms, all of which are clean and comfortable for the price (which is next to nothing), surround a courtyard area for hanging out. There's also a good café perfect for relaxing with a *cerveza* or cappuccino. They have happy hour cocktails, and overall a great atmosphere. $

The comparably priced **Grán Hotel**, at General Torres 9-70 and Bolívar, ☎ 7-831-934, ☎/fax 7-833-819, is one of the most popular budget choices in Cuenca, as popular as El Cafecito. A relaxing patio complements good food. They also offer laundry services, color TV, and private baths with hot water guaranteed. Very inexpensive for the quality. $

Hostal Macondo, at Tarquí 11-64 and Mariscal Lamar, ☎ 7-840-697, ☎/fax 7-833-593, macando@cedei.org, is one of the better budget choices in Cuenca. A restored and converted colonial home, the Macondo has basic, comfortable rooms with shared hot-water baths and nice gardens. The staff is friendly and provides great service. They offer day-trips in and around the city, although I haven't tried one, so can't comment on quality. They are also affiliated with a language and cultural exchange program, if you want to study Spanish during your visit. $

Hostal Nusta, on Borrero near Sucre, is a quaint and simple hotel designed in traditional colonial style. Although falling well within the budget category, it is quite peaceful and charming in its simplicity. The rooms, all of which are enormous, are very clean (but very bare) and surround a brick courtyard with small, corner gardens. Request a room on the front side of the hotel for a double-door balcony that overlooks the activity in the street below. If your interest lies more in peace and quiet, however, move toward the rear of the building. Water is hot most of the time, bathrooms are clean, and laundry service is available upon request. $

Just down the street from Hostal Nusta is the modern **Hostal La Orquídea**, at Borrero 9-31 and Bolívar, ☎ 7-824-511, ☎/fax 7-835-844. It's surprisingly clean and quite bright on the inside, with painted hues of sunshine yellow. Although the Hostal's basic cafeteria-style restaurant, **La Casa del Sol**, is lacking in character, the rooms are nice and the staff is quite friendly. Amenities include money-exchange and fax services, laundry facilities, and more. Singles, triples, and suites are available. $

Cabañas Yanuncay, at Canton Gualaceo 2-148, between Av. Loja and Las Americas, ☎ 7-883-716, ☎/fax 7-819-681, provides rustic charm, comfort, and benefits that surpass the other accommodations in its price range. Located about 10 minutes from the colonial center of town, this is your best choice if you're looking for tranquility off the beaten path. The cabañas include shared or private baths, a hot tub and sauna, and great patio views from comfortable hammocks overlooking the grounds below. Stroll through the organic farm, learn about the natural herbs grown here, and check out the llamas, horses, and a cow. Yanuncay also provides larger, family-style accommodations ideal for longer stays. $

Posada del Sol, at Bolívar and Mariano Cueva, ☎ 7-838-695, ☎/fax 838-995, pdelsol@impsat.net.ec, is a nice option, still on the lower end, but a step up from the budget hotels. It has decent rooms with private baths and balconies, along with breakfast and laundry services. Internet access, as well as horse and bike rides into Cajas National Park, are added bonuses here. $$

Nuestra Residencia has been recommended as an enjoyable mid-range – though inexpensive by North American standards – hotel, located at Los Pinos 1-100 and Lazo, ☎ 7-831-702, ☎/fax 835-576. A friendly home with a central lounging area, bar and television are available and full breakfast is included in a night's comfortable stay. $-$$

A step up is a consistent favorite, the **Hotel Inca Real**, located at Torres 8-40 and Sucre, ☎ 7-831-066, ☎/fax 7-840-699, incareal@cue. satnet.net. This colonial mansion-turned-hotel is centrally located two blocks east of Parque Calderón. Rooms, each decorated differently, surround three attractive courtyards blanketed with flower and fern gardens. The main courtyard of this renovated building is ideal for lounging or dining. The restaurant, serving breakfast, lunch and dinner, provides a large menu and indoor or outdoor dining on the patio courtyard. Rooms are small but well adorned and comfortable, and the staff is very friendly. $$

The **Hotel Presidente**, at Grán Colombia 6-59, between Hermano Miguel and Presidente Borrero, ☎ 7-831-066 or 7-831-341, ☎/fax 7-831-979, htlpres@etapa.com.ec, is centrally located and modern. The view of Cuenca and the neighboring countryside from the eighth-floor restaurant and bar is grand. Spacious rooms are attractively decorated with wood furniture. All the modern amenities are available, including laundry, valet parking, and business/banquet services. Group rates are available for 15 or more people. $$

Next door to the Hotel Presidente, and of similar price and quality, is the **Hotel El Conquistador**, ☎ 7-841-703 or 7-831-788, ☎/fax 7-831-291, hconquise@etapa.com.ec. It's clean and interestingly, if not strangely, decorated with conquistador memorabilia. A stay here includes continental breakfast and comfortable accommodations. Many of the rooms have balconies with views. Room service, a convention hall, and a business center are available, along with a restaurant, bar, and, on weekends, a discotheque. $$

Overlooking the Río Tomebamba and bordering the north section of town, the elegant **Hotel Crespo**, at Calle Larga 7-93 and Cordera, ☎ 7-827-857, ☎/fax 7-839-473, wins first place within its price category. Ideally located along the river and away from most of the downtown hustle and bustle, the Crespo is a charming building with a mix of colonial and modern architecture. Some of the spacious and well-decorated rooms have riverside views, as does the highly recommended restaurant. It's worth spending a few dollars more for a room along the river. $$$

A good choice within the "modern" category is the **El Dorado Hotel**, at Grán Colombia 7-87 and Luis Cordero, ☎ 7-831-390, ☎/fax 7-847-390, eldorado@cue.satnet.net. It's located in the historic center of town just west of the El Conquistador and Presidente Hotels. A small step up from the others in price range, the El Dorado also has a bigger feel, with over 90 rooms ranging from singles to presidential suites. The views from the sixth-floor restaurant are superb, as are those from the piano bar. Although the staff is friendly and helpful, the atmosphere is a bit formal, and business attire is common. There's a gym and spa. $$$

Categories of Lodging

In Cuenca, as in Quito, lodging can be broken down into three main categories. The first is **low-end** hostels and hotels. Next is **mid-range** lodging, which usually involves converted colonial homes or other buildings. The last category is the **higher-end** modern hotels. Although Cuenca is small for a city, its "downtown" area spreads out a bit. The hotels recommended below are more-or-less centrally located.

■ Cuenca

The most expensive hotel in Cuenca is the **Hotel Oro Verde**, a couple of miles away from the historic downtown on the road to Cajas, at Ordonez Lazo, ☎ 7-831-200, ☎/fax 7-832-849, www.oroverdehotels. com, ov_cue@oroverdehotels.com. Completely refurbished, the Oro Verde is a part of the international Oro Verde luxury hotel chain. It sits near a small lake and is surrounded by eucalyptus trees, with pleasant, peaceful grounds. Gardens stretch from the lake to the banks of the Río Tomebamba. Families can enjoy the playground and small pool for children, and adults can use the weight room, sauna, bar, and the nice restaurant. The helpful staff can arrange guide services into Cajas and other surrounding areas. This is an extremely professional and high-quality establishment and, accordingly, the highest priced. $$$$

Just outside Cuenca, serving the hot springs at Baños, is the **Hostería Durán**, at Km 8 Vía Baños from Cuenca, ☎ 7-892-485. It offers higher quality accommodations and access to the hot springs and steam baths. The general public may also use the springs for a nominal fee. $$

■ Loja

Loja's hotels seem to be a step up in quality for what you pay, compared to many other places in Ecuador. At the bottom end, the **Hotel Acapulco**, at Sucre 07-49, ☎ 7-570-651, is simple and basic, yet comfortable for the budget traveler. Rooms include TVs and private baths with hot water. There's also a small restaurant on the premises, breakfast included. $

The **Hostal La Riviera**, situated at Universitaria and 10 de Agosto, ☎ 7-572-863, has the best rooms among the low-end choices. Clean and comfortable accommodations include TVs and phones.

Just south of town in a quieter neighborhood is the **Hostal Aguilera International**, at Sucre and Emiliano Ortega, ☎ 7-563-189 or 7-572-461, ☎/fax 7-572-894. While smaller and more tranquil than the other hotels in the area, it also offers more of the mid-range amenities, such as color TV, gym and sauna. Admittedly, though, it is a bit characterless. $

The most modern establishment in the area is the **Grand Hotel Loja**, on the corner of Av. Iberoamerica and Rocafuerte, ☎ 7-575-200 or 7-575-201, ☎/fax 7-575-202. It is relatively new and popular with businesspeople, with nice rooms and a good restaurant. It also has spa services, including sauna, Jacuzzi and Turkish baths. Overall, this is good value. $-$$

La Libertador, at Colón 14-30 and Bolívar, ☎ 7-560-779 or 7-570-344, ☎/fax 7-572-119, is one of the better options in town, with comfortable rooms on three floors. (Ask for one of the newer rooms.) Amenities include a swimming pool, sauna and a relatively nice restaurant. Feel free to ask the friendly and informative management about local excursions. $$

■ Vilcabamba

At the plaza in Vilcabamba is **Hotel Valle Sagrado**, ☎ 7-673-179. Very basic, clean, and quiet, this hotel is popular among travelers looking to economize. The good vegetarian restaurant is a big draw. $

The simple but pleasant **Parador Turístico Vilcabamba**, ☎/fax 7-580-272 or 673-122, is just outside of town, about half a mile from the plaza. Overlooking the Río Vilcabamba, the Parador has clean rooms, private and shared hot-water baths, and a good, inexpensive restaurant. The Parador is operated by the same family as the Hostería de Vilcabamba, below. $

For a very pleasant stay, try the **Hostería Las Ruinas de Quinara**, ☎ 7-580-301, www.lasruinasdequinara.com, ruinasqui@hotmail.com. The "Ruins of Quinara," a renovated tropical fruit farm, now offers plenty of comforts and a panoramic view of the Sacred Valley of Longevity. Exotic plants, a tasty restaurant with homegrown organic food and a central poolside garden compliment cozy rooms (private and shared), game room with billiards, sauna, Turkish bath, Jacuzzi, and other amenities you would never expect at this price. Great value. $

The popular **Hostal Madre Tierra** is just over a mile north of town, before Vilcabamba if you are arriving from Loja, ☎ 7-580-269, 7-580-687, www.madretierra1.com, hmtierra@ecua.net.ec. It's a nice setting for young travelers. Cabañas come with shared baths and breakfast and dinner are included. A book exchange, videos, and a pool and steam bath are added bonuses. They also offer massage therapy, for an additional charge. The restaurant serves delicious vegetarian dishes. $-$$

The Ecuadorian-run and flower-happy **Hostería Vilcabamba** is at the north entrance of town, ☎ 7-673-131 or 7-580-273, ☎/fax 7-580-272. It has clean and spacious rooms with private, hot-water baths. It's also home to the finest restaurant in town and is considered by many to be the best place to stay. Its pool and spa, which are open to the public, are great for relaxing after a workout in the exercise room. Spanish lessons are also available. Rooms at the Vilcabamba run $20/night. $

■ Camping

Camping is available in **Podocarpus National Park** and **El Cajas National Park**. Inquire at the Ministerio de Turismo or Minesterio del Ambiente offices in Cuenca or Loja, where you can also pay the park entrance fee. The visitor's center at **El Cajas** has a simple lodge that can accommodate up to 20 people, as well as provide information on where to camp within the park. On the edge of Podocarpus, the nature reserve **Las Palmas**, ☎ 7-637-186, offers camping.

A limited amount of **camping gear** is sold in Cuenca at **LRM**, at Torres 7-98 and Sucre. You can rent equipment at **Acción Sports**, at Bolívar 12-70, ☎ 7-833-526.

Where to Eat

■ Cuenca

Real Mexican food can be sampled at **El Pedregal Azteca**, at Grán Colombia 10-33 and Padre Aguirre, ☎ 7-823-652. Enjoy the ambiance and live music on weekends. The food is not bad either, though it is slightly overpriced.

One of my favorite places to eat, for value and atmosphere is **Raymipampa**, on Benigno Malo 8-59, on a corner of Plaza Calderón, ☎ 7-834-159. Among other typical Ecuadorian dishes, they have one of the best *locro de papas* (thick potato soup, with chunks of salty cheese and avocado) in the country. They also serve good ceviches, tasty chicken dishes and a chocolate milkshake that takes first prize. They have two other locations in town, one on Sucre 9-13 and Benigno Malo, and the other on Remigio Crespo 1-20 and Av. del Estadio.

El Jardín, at Córdova 7-23 and Borrero, ☎ 7-831-120, is one of the more reputable restaurants in town not associated with a hotel. With mood lighting, fine dining, and friendly service, this is the perfect place for entertaining out-of-town guests. El Jardín falls in the mid-price range, although it is expensive by local standards.

The **Villa Rosa Restaurante**, in a converted colonial home at Calle Grán Colombia 12-22 and Tarquí, is reputed to be as good as, if not better than, El Jardín. Price, quality and atmosphere are comparable to El Jardín and are a bit more on the fine dining side than other restaurants mentioned below.

Opposite El Jardín is **La Cantina**, popular as a restaurant and meeting place and a great place to enjoy a drink. Music on weekends and a nice setting make it an ideal gathering place. The food is pretty good, but drinks are expensive.

El Huerto, Aguirre 8-15, formerly a Hare Krishna-operated restaurant under a different name, is one of the better options for good vegetarian food. The lunch of the day is a great value at just over $1. The restaurant may be closed during non-peak hours.

Wunderbar, on Hermano Miguel and Calle Larga, halfway down the steps, also has nice food and pretty big servings. It's popular with hip young Cuencanos, as well as travelers, and has a great atmosphere. Try their pasta dishes.

The restaurant/café and lounge at **El Cafecito** (see *Where to Stay*, above) offers a small, but good menu with a few tasty vegetarian options. It is often full of backpackers sipping capuccinos and listening to American music. Try the quesadilla if you're looking for a light meal. Prices here are very reasonable.

The **Chifa Pack How**, Córdova 772 and Cordero, has a comfortably bright setting, decent portions, and reasonable prices, making it one of the better *chifas* in town. If you understand Spanish, you can catch up with the evening news on their communal TV that seems never to shut down. One friend's compliment was that the food here was better than any Chinese food he could find at home in the Netherlands!

Popular among the locals for Italian food and great pizza is **La Napoletana Pizzeria**, at Federico Proano 4-20. You can dine in or have it delivered.

For good Ecuadorian cuisine, try **Los Capulies**, at Córdova and Borrero, ☎ 7-832-339. Los Capulies offers perhaps the best combination of atmosphere – including Andean music on many nights – great food and reasonable prices. Another favorite is **Molinos de Batan**, near the river at 12 de Abril and El Vadom, ☎ 7-811-531, though the prices are increased by its location. Overall, however, it's a nice option for local cuisine.

The best restaurants in Cuenca are often associated with the top-end hotels. Included in this category is **La Casona**, in the Hotel Crespo, where the specialty is French and international food. Situated along the river, the restaurant's view alone is worth the trip. **La Cabala Suiza**, in the Oro Verde Hotel, is another restaurant renowned for its international dishes. The pizza will definitely keep you coming back.

■ Loja

The best high-end restaurants here are in **La Libertador** and the **Grand Hotel Loja**. **Don Quijote**, at Rocafuerte and Macará, has been recommended as having the best pizza in town, though I haven't scaled Loja's streets looking for a better one. For steaks and meat dishes, try **Parillada Uruguaya**, at Iberoamérica and Salinas. International options include **Chalet Francia**, at Valdivieso and Eguiguren, which is well recommended, and **México**, at Eguiguren 1585 and Sucre.

For an afternoon snack or a nice dessert at the end of a long day, stop by **El Holandés,** on Benigno Malo 9-51. They have great ice cream, pastries and fruit salads.

■ Vilcabamba

Perhaps not surprisingly, due its emphasis on health, relaxation and longevity, Vilcabamba offers some of the best in organic vegetarian (and non-vegetarian) cuisine in the country. Several of the hostels provide delicious, healthy meals and a few will serve non-guests as well, including **Hostería Vilcabamba**, ☎ 7-673-131 or 7-580-273, **Parador Turistico**, ☎/fax 7-580-272 or ☎ 673-122, and **Cabañas Río Yambala**.

Entertainment & Shopping

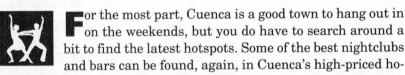

For the most part, Cuenca is a good town to hang out in on the weekends, but you do have to search around a bit to find the latest hotspots. Some of the best nightclubs and bars can be found, again, in Cuenca's high-priced hotels, particularly at **Oro Verde** and **El Crespo**. A few hotels have discos, but I can't personally vouch for the trendy dance scene. If you're looking for live music and dancing, expect to find it only during the weekends. Better yet, get to know some locals and join in their festivities.

El Cafecito, on Honorato Vásquez and Luis Cordero, is usually a fun place to hang out early in the night. Locals and travelers tend to gather there by around 6 pm for the beginning of happy hour. It picks up from thereafter, particularly on the weekends, with music and a lively atmosphere.

As mentioned above, **La Cantina** (Las Capulies) is a popular place to meet with friends, as is the **Picadilly Bar**, just across the street. Both are fun places to relax in a somewhat fancy atmosphere, and they're a little pricey. For more of a local scene, try **Santu**, at Larga and Mariano Cueva. The **Wunderbar**, near Río Tomebamba (halfway down the steps at the end of Hermano Miguel), is a lively establishment. It has several rooms indoors, as well as seating outdoors by the garden when the weather is warm. It attracts a younger crowd and serves up live music on occasion. The staff was super-friendly, and it's the only place in Cuenca, if not all of Ecuador, where you can get a Grolsch Amber Ale. Highly recommended.

For a great night of salsa dancing, or just checking out the scene, go to **La Mesa**, on Grán Colombia between Machuca and Ordoñez. This is a small club, but has a great atmosphere and reasonably priced cocktails. It runs late into the night.

For a change of pace there are also a few movie theaters in Cuenca, including one at the **Casa de la Cultura** and another across the way, with regularly scheduled afternoon and evening shows. The **Teatro Cuenca**, at Padre Aguirre 10-50, is another option.

If you are interested in local *artesanías*, you can do no better than in and around Cuenca – renowned for its jewelry since pre-Inca times – unless you knock on the doors of the experts themselves. Other quality local crafts include weaving, basketry, Panama hats and woodcarvings, to name a few. The **Centro Cultural Jorge Moscoso**, at Córdova and Hermano Miguel, ☎ 7-821-114, offers quality *artesanía*, museum displays and working exhibitions. **El Barranco**, at Hermano Miguel 3-23 and Av. 3 de Noviembre, offers a co-operative with a wide variety of handicrafts. For Panama hats and other goods, check along Grán Colombia and Benigno Malo. For jewelry and other handicrafts, try **Arte Artesanías**, at Borrero and Córdova, or **Joyeria Turismo**, Grán Colombia 9-31.

If you need groceries, there is a **Supermaxi** in Cuenca at Grán Colombia and Avenida de las Americas.

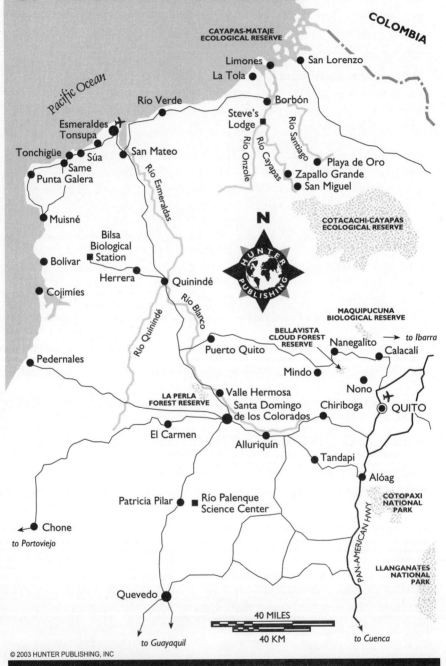

Western Slopes & North Coast

COLOMBIA

Pacific Ocean

CAYAPAS-MATAJE
ECOLOGICAL RESERVE

Limones
La Tola

San Lorenzo

Río Verde

Borbón

Steve's
Lodge

Esmeraldes
Tonsupa

Río Onzole
Río Cayapas
Río Santiago

Tonchigüe   Súa
Same
Punta Galera

San Mateo

Playa de Oro
Zapallo Grande
San Miguel

Río Esmeraldas

Muisné

N

COTACACHI-CAYAPAS
ECOLOGICAL RESERVE

Bilsa
Biological
Station

Bolívar

Herrera

Quinindé

HUNTER
PUBLISHING

Cojimíes

Río Blanco

Río Quinindé

MAQUIPUCUNA
BIOLOGICAL RESERVE

BELLAVISTA
CLOUD FOREST
RESERVE

Puerto Quito

Nanegalito

to Ibarra

Calacalí

Pedernales

Mindo

Nono

LA PERLA
FOREST RESERVE

Valle Hermosa
Santa Domingo
de los Colorados

Chiriboga

QUITO

El Carmen

Alluriquín

Tandapi

Alóag

COTOPAXI
NATIONAL
PARK

Patricia Pilar

Río Palenque
Science Center

PAN-AMERICAN HWY

LLANGANATES
NATIONAL
PARK

Chone

to Portoviejo

Quevedo

40 MILES

40 KM

to Cuenca

to Guayaquil

Western Slopes to the Pacific Coast

A trip through the western slopes of the Andes toward the Pacific Coast offers a dramatic change in scenery and culture. With the Pacific mist, the barren ruggedness of the highlands transforms almost immediately into lush vegetation and large agricultural plantations. As descendants of the former slave society from the coastal region mix with the natives of the highlands, a unique mix of Afro-Ecuadorians, Amerindians, and mestizo Ecuadorians populates this region. Most native and foreign tourists pass through these western slopes only en route to the beaches along the coast. A few travelers, though, especially birders, have come to experience a secret that they would just as well keep to themselves – that there is more than meets the eye behind the curtain of traveled highways.

Ecuador's Pacific lowlands and coast lie west of the Andes. From some of the tallest peaks in South America, it is only a short distance and a quick drop in elevation to the greatest body of water in the world. In between, driving west from Quito, a couple of routes descend through steep mountain slopes, among thick cloud forests and a land of rich plantations. The rugged topography of the higher-elevation mountains has several intact cloud forests. Although only in small, protected pockets, these are remnants of life zones that once prospered along Ecuador's western Andean slopes. The coast, however, abounds with miles of white-sand beaches, pounding surf and lowland rainforest habitats. This chapter covers both.

The Western Slopes

■ History – A Banana Republic

 The forests that once covered the western slopes of the Andes in this region of Ecuador were unlike any on earth. The region's fertile soils, however, eventually attracted massive agricultural development, and soon there were banana plantations, African oil palm farms, and cacao farms. As with the coastal region around Guayaquil, bananas and similar crops offered a new source of income and caused a shift in political power. Road development and the colonization that followed also led to farming smaller subsistence crops throughout the area.

By the 1970s bananas had become Ecuador's leading export and that remains true today. Now, enormous plantations cover the land, and only a few small remnant cloud forests exist in private reserves.

The African oil palm farms continue to produce crops and desecrate the land, leaving behind the barren remnants of a booming industry. Fortunately, the steep slopes, tourism revenue, and the insight of individuals interested in conservation have protected the few remaining natural areas in this region.

■ Flora & Fauna

 Tropical wet forest dominates the steeper western slopes of the Andes. Although much of this area has been deforested and converted into agricultural land, a few remaining stands of cloud forest provide habitat for unique species that are usually found in higher elevations. These include the jaguar, the giant anteater, and the mantled howler monkey, which still exist at places such as Bilsa Reserve. Endemic plants and birds are also prolific in these reserves.

■ Getting Here & Getting Around

 The paved **Puerto-Quito Highway**, which passes through the Mitad del Mundo (Equatorial Monument) north of Quito, is the fastest way through the western lowlands and to the coast. It provides access to destinations such as Mindo, Maquipucuna, and Bellavista reserves. Another highway joins it and also connects the Northern Highlands with the coast.

This route breaks from the Pan-American Highway south of Quito at Alóag and heads through the main city of Santo Domingo de los Colorados. Buses from Quito's bus terminal cover these routes between Quito and the coast on a daily basis.

The gateway city to the north coast is **Esmeraldas**, from which frequent buses head into the highlands. There is also a regional airport with flights to and from various destinations, including Quito (see *The North Coast*, page 253).

■ Visitor Information

Most tour operators and travel services for this region are based in Quito. See *Quito and Vicinity*, pages 94-97, for details. Rates for money exchange are also favorable in Quito. **Santo Domingo de los Colorados**, about halfway between Quito and the coast, is a rapidly expanding city. Modern services are available there, including banking, post, communications and medical facilities. There are also accommodations for travelers who want to make it a home base for exploring the region. Most people, however, will choose to stay at lodges within specific reserves.

Banks in Santo Domingo include Filanbanco, at Avenida de los Tsáchilas and Quito, and Banco Internacional, at Avenida Quito and Río Blanco. The **post office** is at Avenida de los Tsáchilas and Río Baba. The **Andinatel telephone** office is on Avenida Quito between Río Blanco and Río Toachi in the San Francisco building. The **bus terminal** is about a mile north of downtown on Av. de los Tsáchilas. **Taxis** are available from here to the city center and vice-versa.

■ Touring & Sightseeing

Santo Domingo de los Colorados

The primary transportation route from Quito to the coast is along the main "highway" through the city of Santo Domingo de los Colorados. From Quito, head south along the Pan-American Highway to the town of Alóag and turn right, to the west, on the obvious road to Santo Domingo de los Colorados ("Vía a Santo Domingo de los Colorados"). The road meets up with the Puerto-Quito Highway, about halfway to Esmeraldas on the coast. Points of interest along this southern route include the **Tinalandia Ecolodge**, the **Río Palenque Science Center**, **La Perla Forest Reserve**, and the **Bilsa Biological Station**.

Western Slopes to Pacific Coast

The largest city between Quito and the coast, Santo Domingo de los Colorados is a good place to begin explorations of the region's natural attractions. Most travelers stay in Santo Domingo if they are not lodging at one of the facilities mentioned below.

As a destination in itself, Santo Domingo is not on my hotlist. In fact, it was not much of a city until after the road to the coast was built, though now it has close to 200,000 inhabitants. It is named after the original regional natives, **Los Indios Colorados**, who were once known for their red, earthen-dyed, bowl-cut hair and native dress. There is a reserve for these natives nearby, although the **Tsáchila** people, as they prefer to be called, don't wear their traditional attire.

Now the city is a busy economic center, especially as it relates to the surrounding plantation activity. Most people detour around the city center and continue on. It may, however, be a good base if you are interested in exploring the surrounding region.

> *As in any busy city, practice caution late at night and watch your belongings in busy market areas.*

■ Adventures

For many visitors, the primary attraction of the western slopes are the ecological reserves close to Quito, within an abundance of species, particularly birds. They provide excellent nature retreats that are comfortable, yet only a short distance from "civilization." In addition to birding, general wildlife viewing, and just relaxing, there are ample opportunities to hike among ecological life zones completely different from those within the Avenue of the Volcanoes. The difference here, though, is that you may want to bring along your rubber boots. Once you reach the coast, of course, there are plenty of surf- and sand-related activities, as well as lowland coastal rainforest communities to visit. But we'll save that for the next section.

On Foot

Birding & Hiking

The closest nature retreats – all of which offer spectacular cloud forest adventures – are **Bellavista**, **Maquipucuna Reserve** and the **Mindo-Nambillo Protected Forest**. These are special places that not only provide habitat for unique and prolific bird life, but also plenty of exploratory trails for the avid hiker.

Bellavista, one of the highest cloud forest reserves on the western slopes, is set atop a magnificent ridge that overlooks a breathtaking expanse of steeply ridged and often misty forest. From the lodge, nearly a dozen trails provide self-guided and locally guided access into the steep hillsides that make up the reserve. Catch a dawn or dusk hike and you will be amply rewarded, sighting many of the 320 bird species known to live here. And back at the ranch, the views are spectacular when the clouds lift.

Maquipucuna Reserve is even larger than Bellavista and includes a broader elevation range, from 9,156 feet at its high point down to 3,924 feet above sea level. As one would expect, there is even more species diversity and change in ecological life zones here. In fact, Maquipucuna and its adjacent protected lands are home to the endangered spectacled bear, in addition to offering miles of self- and locally-guided trails. Upon pre-arranged arrival, you can obtain self-guide maps to the reserve, catering not only to butterfly-chasing children and those wanting a relaxing stroll, but also to the avid hiker looking for a good workout.

Adjacent to Maquipucuna is the **Mindo-Nambillo Protected Forest**, the largest of the reserves in this area. Unlike Maquipucuna, however, it is a patchwork of private land and government-held parcels, with the village of Mindo as gateway. MindoNambillo is more of a lodge-based destination. Trails lead into Mindo-Nambillo from the nearby village of Mindo, but if you intend to really explore the wilderness, it's best to hire a guide. In the reserve and on the trails, birds (like the brilliant cock-of-the-rock) and butterflies steal the show, although howler monkeys also call this area home and can be heard – if not seen – at dawn. Bosque Protector Mindo-Nambillo, which protects over 49,000 acres of forest, is one of the best examples of an intact contiguous ecosystem along Ecuador's western slopes. The region is renowned for birding opportunities.

See *Eco-Travel*, page 240-42, for directions and details on these reserves, as well as the *Where to Stay* section for a description of the accommodations. Other reserves provide opportunities for the hiker, birder, and general nature enthusiast, but they cater more toward environmental education, science and research. They are described in full in the *Eco-Travel* section, below.

On Water

There are hundreds of miles in Ecuador for world class whitewater rafting and kayaking. The two most popular rivers on the western slopes, particularly due to their proximity to Quito, are **Ríos Toachi** and **Blanco**. The closest to Quito and therefore the most rafted is the Toachi, offering solid class III-III+ during the high water season of January to May. Keep in mind that development in the region has made this river less than pristine (don't swallow the water!). It's at least a 2½-hour drive from Quito each way to the put-in and take-out. Paralleling the Toachi is the Upper Río Blanco, offering solid class III rapids from January to May. It takes a bit longer for this trip, but the scenery is spectacular and it is a great overnighter before or after the ride. The two rivers join farther west to form the Río Blanco.

Several rafting outfitters based in Quito offer rafting trips along the western slopes. Check around and make sure they are well qualified before choosing one. One of the best Quito-based outfitters is **Yacu Amu** ("Water Spirit" in Quechua), located at Baquedano E5-27 and Juan León Mera, ☎ 2-2236 844, fax 2-2226 038, info@yacuamu.com, www.yacuamu.com. Also recommended is **Explorandes**, at Presidente Wilson 537 and Diego de Almagro, ☎ 2-2222-669, fax 2-2556-938, explorandes@ecuadorexplorer.com, www.ecuadorexplorer.com/explorandes. American-operated **ROW Expediciones**, PO Box 579, Coeur d'Alene, ID 83816, ☎ 800-451-6034, fax 208-667-6506, rowinc@aol.com, www.rowinc.com, offers high quality and North American standards. Their office in Quito is at Robles 653 and Amazonas, 3rd floor, ☎ 2-2239-224, fax 2-2522-977, row@uio.satnet.net. **Eco-Adventur** has also been recommended, at Calama 339 between Juan León Mera and Reina Victoria, ☎ 2-2520-647, fax 2-2223-720, info@adventur.com.

■ Eco-Travel

The Puerto-Quito Highway

El Pahuma Orchid Reserve

With a grand opening in January of 2002, El Pahuma Orchid Reserve offers a model for future cloud forest conservation in Ecuador. Working with the **Ceiba Foundation for Tropical Conservation** (Eugenio de Santillán N34-248 and Maurián, Quito, ☎ 2-2432-240/246, fax 2-2453-583, www.ceiba.org/, mail@ceiba.org), this is a great project to support. In addition to orchid gardens and various nature trails – one leads to the majestic 295-foot-high **Shunguyacu Waterfall** – the reserve offers a nice visitor's center with a restaurant and private accommodations. There is habitat for rare birds and there have even been sightings of the endangered spectacled bear. Simple overnight bunks are also available at the "Bear's Den" cabin and the reserve itself is becoming an attractive day excursion from Quito, especially for school groups.

Bellavista Reserve

I think that Bellavista is the best close escape from Quito. The reserve offers a unique and beautiful nature retreat, including a cozy and picturesque ecolodge set atop a ridge, overlooking forested valleys in all directions. The reserve itself is in a high-altitude cloud forest that encompasses several hundred acres of primary and secondary forest. Much of this area was previously logged, but efforts to reforest it have been underway for several years now. The owners are constantly working to conserve and expand the reserve, promoting scientific research and local environmental education. They also work with university groups and international students abroad. See *Where to Stay* (pages 246-48) for specifics about the ecolodge.

You can reserve through Quito tour agents or contact Richard Parsons, ☎/fax 2-2232-313 or 2-2901-536, ☎ 9-490-891, www.ecuadorexplorer. com/bellavista, bellavista@ecuadorexplorer.com. While in Quito, call for directions to the lodge, as the best route depends on road conditions. Driving on the Puerto-Quito Highway north of the city, past Mitad del Mundo and toward the coast, turn left at the bridge (Km 52) just before the small town of Nanegalito. Head up the gravel road to Tandayapa and drive on through the village until you see the signs at the top of the ridge. Or take the old road to Mindo via Tandayapa.

Maquipucuna Biological Reserve

This reserve is approximately 45 miles northwest of Quito. Operated by Fundación Maquipucuna and originally purchased by the Nature Conservancy, the reserve serves to further conservation, scientific research, environmental education, and community development based on ecotourism. The successful preservation of this 9,880-acre reserve (and its 24,700-acre buffer zone) can be attributed in part to its rugged topography of steep slopes and deep valleys.

Maquipucuna is in the headwaters region of the Río Guayallabamba. The reserve includes intact and biologically rich premontane and montane cloud forests and a variety of life zones at elevations from just over 3,270 to 9,800 feet. Some 80-90% of the area is primary forest; the rest is secondary forest and overgrown pastures. The reserve boasts an incredible diversity of bird life, with well over 300 species, as well as sheltering the endangered spectacled bear. There are numerous trails, both self-guided with maps and with local guides. For more on the open-air ecolodge that is operated in conjunction with the reserve, see the *Where to Stay* below, page 248.

Contact the foundation at Baquerizo 238 and Tamayo, La Floresta, Quito, ☎ 2-2507-200/201, fax 2-2507-201, roberto@maquipucuna.org. In the USA, c/o Institute of Ecology, The University of Georgia, Athens, GA 30602-2202 USA, ☎ 706-542-2968, fax 706-542-6040, usa@maquipucuna.org, www.arches.uga.edu/~maqui.

Driving from Quito, travel along the Puerto-Quito Highway through Mitad del Mundo and Calacalí (northwest) for a couple of hours. Turn at Nanegalito on the right for the rough and bumpy ride down the dirt or mud road through Nanegal, until you come to the signpost for the reserve. Check at the bus station in Quito for the daily departure to Nanegalito and Nanegal.

Volunteering at Maquipicuna

To learn more about the endangered spectacled bear, including World Wildlife Fund reintroduction efforts, visit their site at www.panda.org. Then, in the search box, type "spectacled bear."

For volunteer opportunities with Fundación Maquipicuna and other Ecuadorian conservation-oriented foundations, visit www.thebestofecuador.com/volunt.htm.

Mindo-Nambillo Protected Forest

This beautiful premontane cloud forest – a veritable birder's paradise – lies just a few hours west of Quito at elevations of 4,250 to over 14,700 feet. Officially protected as the Bosque Protector Mindo-Nambillo, it is administered by a private local organization, the Friends of Mindo-Nambillo Forest (Amigos de Naturaleza de Mindo-Nambillo), located in the nearby village of Mindo. They can provide directions and guides, as well as accept the entry fee into the park. Mindo, in short, serves as a great example of what was once typical forestland along Ecuador's western slopes. The reserve, combined with the adjacent Maquipucuna Biological Reserve to the north, protects thousands of acres of primary forest. It's a hotspot of biological diversity and ongoing scientific research.

Entrance to the reserve is $2. The fastest way to Mindo from Quito is via the Puerto-Quito Highway through the Mitad del Mundo (Equatorial Monument) and Calacalí. The village of Santa Rosa is only a couple of hours from Quito. Just beyond it is the turnoff for Mindo, which you'll reach after a few miles on this rough road. Be sure to check road conditions before heading out. The best birding guide is **Vinicio Pérez** (Correo Central de Mindo, ☎ 2-2612-995). Make arrangements with **Friends of Mindo**, on the main road into town, or in Quito at ☎ 2-2455-907, prior to visiting the reserve. Or contact **Safari Ecuador**, Calama 380 and Juan León Mera, Quito, ☎ 2-2552-505, fax 2-2223-381, admin@safari.com.ec, www.safari.com.ec, in the US, ☎ 800/434-8182. Safari offers general and birding tours that include trips to Mindo and Bilsa.

On the Road through Santo Domingo de los Colorados

Bilsa Biological Reserve

The 7,770-acre **Bilsa Biological Station** is a nature reserve and center for field research and environmental education. It was created with a grant from the Jatun Sacha Foundation in 1994 and preserves a critical piece of Ecuador's remaining coastal premontane forest.

Located in the Mache Mountains, Bilsa has a unique blend of flora and fauna. Although physically isolated from the Andes, the reserve protects species previously thought to be endemic to the western Andean highland forests 62 miles to the southwest, as well as species endemic to the Choco, a pluvial forest of southern coastal Colombia. The region's rugged topography (981 to 2,616 feet in elevation) and the coastal climate keep Bilsa's ridges shrouded in fog. These ridges sustain cloud-forest species usually restricted to much higher elevations. Rare animals found at the reserve include the jaguar, several species of small cats, the long-wattled umbrella bird, the giant anteater, and abundant populations of the threatened mantled howler monkey. In addition, more than 30 new plant species have been discovered at Bilsa.

In 1996 the Jatun Sacha Foundation established the reserve's **Center for the Conservation of Western Forest Plants**. The center serves as a base for community extension and outreach programs emphasizing agroforestry, health, environmental education, and the development of community management plans. Each year it produces approximately 100,000 tree saplings for use in reforestation projects, including 90 species of tropical fruit and nut trees and 60 local woody species. The center is also planting ornamental gardens in the cabin areas at Bilsa. Scientists, volunteers, ecotourists, and leaders of educational groups are all encouraged to work at Bilsa. Visitors to the reserve are always welcome, but keep in mind that most people involved with the station are working. Travelers must make reservations. See lodging section below (page 249) for a description of available accommodations.

To get there, take a bus to Quininde (to the northwest of Santo Domingo). From Quininde, small trucks at the gas station at Cinco Esquinas provide transportation to Bilsa. Getting to Bilsa during the wet season (January-June) can be difficult. You'll have to disembark at the last stop the truck makes – usually La Y de La Laguna – and hike the remaining seven miles to the reserve on a muddy road. You must notify reserve personnel by radio from Jatun Sacha's Quito office prior to arrival. The clean and safe **Hotel Sans** is a good place to spend the night in Quininde. Reservations should be made through the Jatun Sacha Foundation office in Quito: Pasaje Eugenio de Santillán N34-248 and Maurián, Urb. Rumipamba, ☎ 2-2432-240, 2-2432-173, 2-2432-246, fax 2-2453-583, www.jatunsacha.org, jatunsacha@ecuadorexplorer.com. For volunteer projects, e-mail volunteer@jatunsacha.org. Researchers should provide two months advance notice. Jatun Sacha must approve research activities.

During the dry season (July through December) it is a bit chilly at night and usually foggy. The wet season (January through June) is warmer and is marked by clear skies alternating with heavy rains. Note that roads to some of these destinations can become impassible at any time with heavy rains, and may require hours of mud-slugging in rubber boots.

La Perla Forest Reserve

Twenty-five miles northwest of Santo Domingo toward the coast, this is a solitary survivor in a region of overwhelming agricultural development. La Perla Forest is the only stretch of uncut forest along this road to the coast. Its owner, Suzanne Sheppard, fought for years to finally obtain official protected status for the land. She now offers tours of the reserve and runs environmental education programs for local youth and school groups.

Spend at least a few hours exploring this small but beautiful lowland forest. It is home to numerous species of unique flora and fauna that were once common along Ecuador's lower elevation western slopes. It is well worth the $5 entrance fee, which pays for the services of a Spanish-speaking guide. Your dollars go a long way in showing support for a battle to protect the region's biodiversity. Camping on the reserve is permitted, but you must bring your own equipment and supplies.

Suzanne Sheppard, Bosque Protectora La Perla, Casilla 17-24-128, Santa Domingo de los Colorados, ☎ 2-2725-344 or 2-2759-115. From Santo Domingo, head south toward Quevedo on the Santo Domingo-Quevedo Road.

☆ Río Palenque Science Center

A forested island in a sea of banana, palm, and cacao plantations, the Río Palenque Science Center is a research facility on one of the last stretches of intact primary western lowland forests in the country. Situated along the Río Palenque about an hour south of Santo Domingo, the station was established nearly 30 years ago to allow researchers to study the region's flora and fauna. Although relatively small (about 247 acres), the private reserve is a haven for threatened plants and animals. More than 1,000 species of plants, many of which were not previously known, have been catalogued in the area, as have hundreds of bird, butterfly and other insect species.

Contact Calaway Dodson, Centro Cientifico Río Palenque, Casilla 95, Santo Domingo de los Colorados, ☎ 2-2232-248. Head south from Santo Domingo on the road toward Quevedo and turn left into the entrance road at Km 48. Follow the sign and head north for another 35 miles to the station entrance.

■ Where to Stay

ACCOMMODATIONS PRICE SCALE

Unless otherwise noted, prices are per room, up to double occupancy. Some prices are per person, particularly with all-inclusive packages, but these generally include meals, lodging, guide services and other amenities.

$	Under $25
$$	$26 to $50
$$$	$51 to $100
$$$$	Over $100

Western Slopes to Pacific Coast

In & Around Santo Domingo de los Colorados

 In Santo Domingo de Los Colorados, you can find several hotels along busy (and noisy) Av. 29 de Mayo, but none is really worth recommending. They are all about the same, so check around to find a decent room away from the noise.

You have better options outside of town, at the relatively new **Hotel Don Kleber**, a mile north of Santo Domingo on the Quininde-Esmeraldas Highway, ☎ 2-2761-956, fax 2-2761-243, which offers comfort and style at a good price. Away from the downtown hustle and bustle, the Don Kleber has a tranquil setting and modern facilities. Enjoy a relaxing lounge session at the bar above the poolside patio. Thirty choice rooms have private baths and hot water. Located halfway between the Central Andean Valley and the coast, the hotel includes an upper-level restaurant serving tasty meals from both regions. $

The popular **Hotel Zaracay**, Av. Quito 1639 on the main highway east of town, ☎ 2-2750-316 or 2-2750-429, fax 2-2754-535, is reputedly the nicest accommodation in the area. With a pleasant atmosphere and all the amenities, rooms are spacious, air-conditioned and have balconies that overlook a large interior garden patio. There is a part-time casino and disco, along with a relaxing pool area, a restaurant, and a bar. $$

Across from the Zaracay is the more modest **Hotel Tropical Inn**, Av. Quito on the main highway east of town, ☎ 2-2761-771 or 2-2761-772, fax 2-2761-775. Reasonably priced modern rooms, include three- and four-person suites, have private baths, hot water, TVs, and phones, and most come with air-conditioning. There's also a pool. $$

☆ **Bellavista**, c/o Richard Parsons, ☎/fax 2-2232-313 or 2-2901-536, ☎ 9-490-891, www.ecuadorexplorer.com/bellavista, bellavista@ecuadorexplorer.com, is a favorite nature retreat. It has comfortable facilities, excellent birding opportunities, wonderful views and relative proximity to Quito. I particularly enjoyed this modest but cozy lodge. British-owned, the main building is a three-story dome-shaped structure with a bar and restaurant on the first level. The 360-degree views are optimal no matter which way you are facing, offering bright, airy and intimate surroundings for chatting with newfound traveler friends.

Upstairs are five adjacent triple rooms with balconies and private baths. The upper level consists of a circular dorm-style room, with a shared bath and hot water. There are also separate cabin-style accommodations with multiple rooms that can be rented out to larger groups or as individual rooms. Delicious meals are cooked using organically grown vegetables. Camping facilities are available at a lower price, and several miles of trails provide ample opportunity to explore the surrounding forest. The lodge is near the Mindo-Nambillo Forest Reserve.

Reservations can be made through tour operators in Quito or direct. Call for the best directions to the lodge, as the best route depends on road conditions at the time. Driving on the Puerto-Quito Highway north of the city, past Mitad del Mundo and toward the coast, turn left at the bridge – Km 32 – just before the small town of Nanegalito. Head up the gravel road to Tandayapa and drive on through the village until you see the signs at the top of the ridge. Alternately, take the old road to Mindo via Tandayapa. $$$-$$$$.

The visitor's center at **El Pahuma Orchid Reserve** offers a wonderful retreat near Quito (see *Eco-Travel* page 40).

☆ **Tinalandia Hotel** is at Casilla 8, Santo Domingo de los Colorados, ☎ 2-2449-028, fax 2-2442-638, www.tinalandia.net, tinaland@ramy. com. Heading west on the road to Santo Domingo a few miles before the city, turn left at the stone sign for Tinalandia – the stone is on the right side of the road. This accommodation is one of the oldest reputable ecolodges in Ecuador. The lodge abuts the Río Toachi and an ancient nine-hole golf course and pocket of forest that is known for its birding opportunities. Situated at around 2,000 feet above sea level, the comfortable accommodations are near several hundred acres of relatively undisturbed premontane wet forest. The original owner of the modern facility, Tina Garzon, transformed the grounds to accommodate nature lovers when she first arrived many years ago. Her son now operates the hotel and has continued to upgrade the facilities and promote local research and environmental education. Activities include hiking, horseback riding, swimming, rafting (through a local outfitter) and less-than-world-class golf, with world-class birding on the side.

Cabins and private rooms are spread across the grounds and all include electricity, private baths, and hot showers. The staff is friendly and helpful, offering a real extended-family atmosphere. Many guests, especially birders, return often to enjoy the solace and the

Western Slopes to Pacific Coast

prime access to other reserves in the area (including those mentioned above). $$, meals included.

☆ **Maquipucuna Biological Reserve Lodge** is at Baquerizo 238 and Tamayo, La Floresta, Quito, ☎ 2-2507-200/201, fax 2-2507-201, roberto@maquipucuna.org. In the USA, c/o Institute of Ecology, University of Georgia, Athens, GA 30602-2202, ☎ 706-542-2968, fax 706-542-6040, usa@maquipucuna.org, www.arches.uga.edu/~maqui. It is situated at the low end of a river valley, combining rustic beauty with all the necessary amenities, including cold *cervezas*. Thatched-roofs and bamboo buildings blend into the natural environment, while the open sides of the common room provide views of the adjacent forest and its colorful hummingbirds and butterflies. Indeed, the experience here is one of pure relaxation. The kitchen serves a variety of scrumptious dishes using food grown by the local community. There are maps and several self-guided trails into the surrounding wilderness, and local guides are available upon request. Make arrangements before you arrive if you require English-speaking guides.

To get there, from Quito travel along the Puerto-Quito Highway through Mitad del Mundo and Calacalí (northwest) for a couple of hours. Turn right at Nanegalito onto the rough and bumpy dirt or mud road through Nanegal, until you come to the signpost for the reserve. Continue on until you arrive. Check at the bus station in Quito for the daily departure to Nanegalito and Nanegal. $$ (meals included in price).

☆ **The Hostería El Carmelo de Mindo**, Valle de Mindo, ☎ 2-2224-713, ☎/fax 2-2546-013, www.mindo.com.ec, is about half a mile outside the village of Mindo. The cabañas are a good choice for birders and nature travelers. There are inexpensive camping or dormitory options, as well as more expensive private rooms. All accommodations are on attractive grounds adorned with fruit trees and gardens. The family that owns and operates the Hostería is very friendly and happy to lead guided trips into the forest. $$ for private cabins, $ dorm-style rooms.

For a more modest place with a family-feeling about it, try **El Monte**. Contact them directly in Mindo at ☎ 2-2765-472, www.ecuadorcloudforest.com/index.html or elmonte@ecuadorexplorer.com. Alternatively, you can make a reservation through the Cultura Reservation Center at Café Cultura, Robles and Reina Victoria in Quito. The Ecuadorian-American couple who run El Monte have done a wonderful job of creating a pleasant atmosphere, with ecotourism and sustainable development in mind. The facilities consist of three hand-made cabins built of renewable materials, plus a central lodge for socializing. Double-story A-frame cabins house one to four people and feature an open-air common room, a bedroom and a bathroom upstairs. The food comes from local organic gardens, with a vegetarian emphasis. Though there is no electricity, staying at El Monte is a comfortable and pleasant experience. $$+ per person, which includes lodge, meals and guide services.

The new **Mindo Garden Lodge**, ☎ 2-2252-488/9 in Quito, or 800-538-2149 in the US, casablan@uio.satnet.net, is said to be the nicest ecolodge in the Mindo area, although I have not visited. Situated along the Río Mindo, private cabañas offer seclusion and comfort. Let me know what you think. $$$

☆ Reservations for the **Bilsa Biological Reserve** should be made through the Jatun Sacha Foundation in Quito, ☎ 2-2451-626, fax 2-2250-976, jatunsacha@ecuadorexplorer.com. The three field cabins, which come with dining, conference, and work areas, can accommodate up to 45 visitors at a time. Ten private rooms in a new building include shared showers and outhouses. Mattresses, sheets, blankets, mosquito nets, and candles are provided. Solar panels offer some electricity (but flashlights are recommended). All meals are eaten in a common dining area below the rooms. Visitors to the reserve are always welcome, but keep in mind that most people involved with the station are working. Travelers must make reservations. $

☆ **Río Palenque Science Center** has accommodations available for tourists, but the center is geared more toward research than visitors' needs. Rooms with bunk beds are in the main building, and two include private baths and cold-water showers. The rest of the rooms come with communal bathrooms. Electricity is available most of the time and there are kitchen facilities, but bring your own supplies. See page 245 for more details. $-$$

Camping

Camping is allowed in several of the private reserves listed in this chapter. **Bellavista Reserve** (page 241) offers camping facilities near the ecolodge. **La Perla Forest Reserve** (page 244) offers camping as well, and is actually the only way to visit the forest on an overnight stay.

■ Where to Eat

The best restaurants in Santo Domingo are associated with the better hotels in town, particularly Hotel Tropical Inn and Hotel Don Kleber. Most meals are organized in conjunction with accommodations or a set tour itinerary. The lodges at Bellavista, Maquipicuna, and Tinalandia, for example, serve food to their guests. Meals must be prearranged at places like the Río Palenque Science Center and Friends of the Mindo-Nambillo Forest Riverside Shelter.

Hotel Tropical Inn, Av. Quito on the main highway east of town, ☎ 2-2761-771 or 2-2761-772, fax 2-2761-775, houses a good restaurant catering to foreign travelers. Prices are fair and the food is tasty. The menu selection is good, although it's mostly seafood.

The modern, clean, and comfortable restaurant at **Hotel Don Kleber**, a mile north of Santo Domingo on the Quininde-Esmeraldas Highway, ☎ 2-2761-956, offers various Ecuadorian dishes, including tasty coastal cuisine.

For Chinese food, there are plenty of *chifas* in town, but most are of poor quality. One exception is the **Chifa Tay Happy** near Parque Zaracay. It's nothing spectacular, but it's not bad by Ecuadorian standards.

The **Elite Restaurant**, on Av. Quito and Sachila, is the place to go for a quick and inexpensive meal.

The North Coast

When I first thought about going to the coast from Quito, I didn't know what to expect. My only other experience with the Pacific Ocean was in the Galápagos, so you can imagine how my pre-conceived notions were blown away. Upon descent from the Andes (at nearly 10,000 feet), several short hours produced a massive land and climate transformation. Immediately, we were whisked along steep mountain ridges and through thick clouds blanketing lush tropical forest. Strangely enough, the land changed again with the blink of an eye. I found myself staring at an endless expanse of African oil-palm plantations. Perhaps even more noticeable was the transformation in the people, the communities by the wayside becoming predominantly Afro-

Ecuadorian. Here was yet another incredibly beautiful culture staring back at us as we passed.

Finally, we came around a bend and there it was – the coast, with thin, sandy beaches and rough, choppy waves. Far from the tropical Caribbean beaches I had expected, this is indeed the Pacific Ocean, where the sand connects thick vegetation with pounding surf. Our journey was far from over, however, and we headed north. At one point, where the poorly maintained road actually turned onto the beach, we had to wait an hour for the tide to recede. It was a wonderful social gathering, with women capitalizing on the event by selling fresh-cooked seafood dishes, and the men taking the opportunity to break from the day's work. Finally, our bus driver could wait no longer, and as our guide had guessed, he was the first to make a go through the wet sand and waves. Soon enough we were all on our way across the beach. We have just arrived at our ocean-side lodge and now it's time to relax. Tomorrow's journey will carry us far upriver into the coastal lowland tropical forest. We will stay near a mixed black-Indian community. The people here are so friendly, with many warm smiles. I can't wait to absorb myself in their culture and explore the magic of their land. (Traveler's account)

Esmeraldas is the main city along the north coast and is located about a half-day's drive northwest from Quito. Most international travelers that come to Esmeraldas are just passing through, heading northwest to explore the lowland rainforests or southeast to play on the beaches. Pockets of Afro-Ecuadorian communities line the shore, while long thin beaches approach coastal inlets, shrimp farms, and a few remaining mangrove swamps. To the north the land is less accessible and the roads are less reliable. The climate is hot and wet, and canoes are the main means of transportation. Although the majority of coastal and western lowland Ecuador has been deforested, this region has not been quick to accept the idea of a paved society. It is still one of the wildest, remotest, and most biologically diverse places in the entire world.

■ History

 The northern coastal provinces of Esmeraldas and Manabí have a rich and varied history that is unique within the country. Evidence of early inhabitants is found along the central coast in the form of earthenware figurines from the **Valdivia** culture, dating back to before 1500 BC. This culture eventually became absorbed into other groups that united un-

Western Slopes to Pacific Coast

der the coastal **Caras** and, eventually, the people of the highlands. By the time the **Spanish** arrived in the early 1500s, the **Atacames** people in the area surrounding Esmeraldas had a fairly well-developed and settled society in the **La Tolita** culture. They were particularly adept at jewelry making – especially when it came to green emeralds set in silver and gold. As a result, the Spanish named the area Esmeraldas.

Soon after their arrival, the Spanish began to import African slaves to replace the natives, who were already dying off. Some of these slaves were sent to mine gold. A system of slavery, followed by debt tenancy, continued until the end of the 19th century, and today the people here are the most poverty-stricken and suppressed group in all of Ecuador. The black communities now make up over 75% of the region's population (10% of the country's population).

Today, although racism throughout Ecuador remains significant and severe, the coastal black, white, and Indian communities do live next to each other harmoniously in some areas. A unique mix of African and Latin cultures is obvious in the music and dance of this beautiful people, and they are truly some of the friendliest Ecuadorians you will encounter.

■ Flora & Fauna

 Weather patterns, including rainfall that in some places exceeds even the levels of the Ecuadorian Amazon, combine with a varied topography to create unique ecological life zones. Flora and fauna in some areas are more typical of Colombia and Central America. Endemic animal species abound and tropical forests meet the crashing waves of the Pacific Ocean. This contrasts with the dry coastal communities to the south, which result from the cooler Peruvian ocean currents.

Mangrove forests and estuaries were once common along the coast. However, as is true in the south, many of these areas have been converted to shrimp farms. The region inland from Borbón, along the Río Cayapas and within the Cotacachi-Cayapas Reserve, protects the least-disturbed tropical lowland rainforest in western Ecuador, which is home to species that exist only here. Heading south, the land along the coast is much drier, although pockets of the less-developed lowlands, just a bit inland, are covered with lush cloud forests, the result of thick coastal fog that inundates the land for many months each year. Here, magnificent birds, many of them endemic, prosper along with howler monkeys and the nocturnal kinkajou.

■ Getting Here & Getting Around

TAME offers daily flights between Quito and Esmeraldas (except on Sundays). Their office in Esmeraldas is on Bolívar, just off the central plaza, ☎ 6-712-663.

By road, the two main routes to Esmeraldas are:

- The Puerto-Quito Highway, north of Quito and passing through the Mitad del Mundo monument;

- The highway to Santo Domingo de los Colorados, which turns west off the Pan-American Highway south of Quito near the town of Alóag.

These two roads join northwest of Santo Domingo de los Colorados and continue to Esmeraldas. Frequent buses to and from Quito's bus terminal take less than six hours. The bus trip between Esmeraldas and Guayaquil takes eight hours.

■ Visitor Information

Esmeraldas is the major city along the north coast and offers modern necessities such as mail service, communications, banking, and medical facilities. There are also a few outfitters who can provide guiding services into the surrounding region. Most tours and travel services, however, are based in Quito. Often, a tour will begin in Quito or you will fly into Esmeraldas, meet with your prearranged transportation, and head off to a particular destination.

Modern services in Esmeraldas are all centrally located between Salinas and Rocafuerte (running east-west) and Bolívar and Olmeda (north-south), including the half-dozen or so **bus stations**. There are a couple of **banks** on Bolívar, including Filanbanco, between Piedrahita and Cañizares, and Banco Central, between Juan Montalvo and Rocafuerte though rates and services are better in Quito. **Post and communications offices** are in the same building at the corner of Juan Montalvo and Malecón Maldonado. The **tourist office** is on Bolívar and Mejía, ☎ 6-714-528. The **TAME airline** office is at Bolívar and 9 de Octubre, ☎ 6-726-863. The **hospital** is on Av. Libertad heading north toward the Las Palmas suburb.

In **San Lorenzo**, near the Colombian border, the **Ministerio del Ambiente**, on the main plaza, has useful information for visiting local reserves. The **Andinatel phone office** is on Av. Camilo Ponce across from the Hotel San Carlos. **Buses** depart daily from the main square for Esmeraldas and Ibarra in the Andes.

■ Touring & Sightseeing

Esmeraldas & North Coast

Four to six hours from Quito, depending on road conditions and how "loco" your driver is, the ocean port capital of Esmeraldas rises up above the coast. The view is attractive from a distance, especially as the city lights begin to sparkle against the backdrop of the sun setting over the Pacific. Upon closer inspection, though, this bustling port and booming oil-refinery town is not a place you will want to spend much time. Now the largest port in the north, with a population approaching 150,000 people, Esmeraldas is growing rapidly. It is a popular travel destination for vacationing Colombian and Ecuadorian highlanders. The country's trans-Andean oil pipeline from the Oriente ends here, and a new oil refinery has boosted employment and the economy. Unfortunately, it has also resulted in Esmeraldas being less pleasant and more dangerous than it once was, with rapid urban growth and crime. Nevertheless, it is a jumping-off point for some of the regional attractions.

Esmeraldas has the most modern facilities in the region. The better hotels and beaches – though "better" is a relative term – are found in **Las Palmas**, the suburb to the northwest of Esmeraldas. Mail service, communications, banking, and medical facilities are available, although they are better in Quito. The major access to Esmeraldas from Quito is via Santa Domingo or by plane to the nearby airport, about 20 minutes away. Taxis are available at the airport.

Unfortunately, Esmeraldas is very unsafe in virtually all parts of town. Always take a taxi at night and avoid the city center and downtown Malecón or waterfront area after dark. Even Las Palmas is not safe, so always be aware of your surroundings.

Río Verde

A couple of hours northeast along the coast from Esmeraldas is the small community of Río Verde, noted here primarily as the home of **Cabañas Pura Vida** (see *Where to Stay* below), which is a very peaceful beachside cabaña-style resort. About all there is to do here is relax or take a break en route to or from somewhere else.

Borbón

Heading north along the coast from Esmeraldas, the "highway" winds along the coast for a pleasant drive, although road conditions can be quite rough. Borbón is a small port town on the way to the coastal rainforest from Esmeraldas and into the Cotopachi-Cayapas region. With fewer than 10,000 inhabitants, most of whom are Afro-Ecuadorian, Borbón is basically a disheveled Colombian immigrant and logging town thrown together with lumber industry leftovers and scrap metal. It's also a common meeting place and jumping-off point for organized tours into the lowland rainforest communities farther inland. You probably won't want to spend much time here. Farther northwest is the town of San Lorenzo (below).

Depending on road conditions, it takes up to four hours to reach Borbón from Esmeraldas. If you're arriving at the Esmeraldas airport, you can hire a taxi there and go all the way to Borbón for well under $50.

San Lorenzo

The northernmost town along the Ecuadorian coast is San Lorenzo, near the Colombian border and therefore home to a mix of nationalities. It lies in a marshy area near the lowland coastal tropical forests, though it also connects with a roadway to Ibarra in the highlands. Though quaint, it is also very hot and humid and is primarily a point of disembarkation into local lowland rainforest reserves and communities, noted in the *Eco-Travel* section, page 240, as well as the nearby coastal estuaries within the **Cayapas Mataje Ecological Reserve**. From San Lorenzo, it is possible to cross over to Colombia by boat launch.

South of Esmeraldas: Vamos a la Playa

To head southwest from Esmeraldas is to go to the beach, relax, and play. Fortunately – or unfortunately, depending on how you look at it – tourism's peak season and Ecuadorian/Colombian vacation times do not coincide. During the hot, wet season from December to April, beachside resorts and hotels often fill up, particularly around holidays and weekends. The beaches are loaded with sunbathing vacationers from Quito and Colombia, and the clubs are hopping at night. Western vacation time, which centers between the months of May and September, occurs at a cooler, foggier time of the year. Many tourist accommodations close down at times, particularly during weekdays. The atmosphere is much more tranquil, consisting of small pockets of gringo travelers looking for places to relax, commune, and party. Look around and see what works for you.

Atacames/Tonsupa

Southwest of Esmeraldas along the coast is the beach-resort town of Atacames, where vacationing Quiteños and Colombian families flock for holidays and wet-season weekends. Numerous resort hotels line the beaches and the noisy nightlife seems endless at times. There are plenty of opportunities to find good mid-priced accommodations with amenities and coastal access. In fact, that's why people come here: to go to the beach, party and relax. Outside of Playas and Montañita in the south, Atacames is the most popular destination along the coast for international travelers. Hang out long enough and chances are you'll bump into someone you know.

Buses heading from Esmeraldas to Muisne pass by often and stop at the central bus stop, just outside of town. To get to the center, walk on the diagonal road behind the bus stop and cross over the pedestrian bridge. Turn right on 21 de Noviembre, which will take you to the Malecón (the main waterfront street). Alternatively, hire a bicycle taxi from the many that hang out around the bus stop.

While at the beach, keep in mind that the ocean currents and undertow can be very strong here, as with anywhere along Ecuador's coast. Also, thieves and armed robberies are reportedly on the rise along the beach to the southwest. It's best to leave valuables at the cabana and stroll along the beach with friends.

Most tourist facilities in the area are comparable in style and quality to those elsewhere on the coast. The only problem you might have is in finding a room. Fortunately, there are plenty to choose from and usually all you need to do is poke around until you find something appealing. If you prefer a more tranquil setting, head to the smaller town of Tonsupa, located just a few miles north of Atacames.

You can catch a taxi in Esmeraldas or at the airport directly to the Atacames/Tonsupa area. Buses also leave regularly from Esmeraldas heading southwest down the coast. The ride from Esmeraldas takes about 45 minutes and costs less than $1. Most buses stop near the road to the footbridge, but check with your driver to make sure. Many of the nicer hotels in the area can arrange for an airport pickup from Esmeraldas. By car, the turnoff for the highway west to Atacames, "Vía a Atacames," is at the major traffic circle a few miles south of Esmeraldas on the main highway from Santo Domingo.

Súa-Same Area

Just a few miles down the coast from Atacames is the fishing village of Súa. Here you'll find a transformation in the land, a return to the natural, with low mountains and patches of wet and dry tropical forests. Súa is great as a day trip from Atacames or as a destination in itself if you're interested in the culture of a fishing community. Expect to find better rates but fewer choices for beachside accommodations.

Just a few miles southwest of Súa lies the isolated resort getaway of Same, lined with a nice stretch of gray-sand beach. A popular retreat for the affluent, Same is the last of the resort areas below Esmeraldas along the north coast. From here, the main road stretches inland and upward before returning to the coast and ending at the port and island town of Muisne.

By bus or car, the Súa-Same area is a couple of miles beyond Atacames on the Vía a Atacames Highway from Esmeraldas.

Muisne & Mangrove Forests

For a complete change of pace, head to the small port town of Muisne, where shrimp farming and shipping dominate the economy and mangrove estuaries line the shore. Muisne, on an island across the bay, is one of the last places along Ecuador's coast where undisturbed mangrove forests remain intact. Primarily because of its distant location and active support from a foundation known as FUNDECOL, Muisne's mangrove forests have successfully resisted coastal development and conversion to shrimp-rearing ponds. Motorized boats can be hired in town to visit the extensive estuary and mangrove forests. Alternatively, FUNDECOL, located a block off the plaza, ☎ 5-480-167, offers guided tours into mangrove estuaries, lowland rainforest, and a bird sanctuary.

Take the Vía a Atacames Highway from Esmeraldas all the way to the end of the road at **El Relleno**, across the estuary from Muisne. From Esmeraldas, get on a bus heading all the way to Muisne, a few hours away. Or catch a bus from Atacames, Súa, or Same. At the end of the highway in El Relleno, hop into a motorized water taxi for the 10-minute ride across the Río Muisne to the village of Muisne. At Muisne, follow the main "road" into the village center and on to the ocean.

Western Slopes to Pacific Coast

■ Adventures

Culture & Nature, on Foot & by Water

In addition to a few lodge-based packages described below, community-based ecotourism at places such as Playa de Oro and San Miguel offer great multi-day excursions. In fact, getting to these places is half the adventure, especially when one considers bad roads, rough weather, not necessarily friendly villages and long dugout canoe rides. Activities include hiking, birding and water-based travel upriver, as well as more culturally focused events, depending on where you are visiting. Heading farther into the reserve will provide the opportunity for better birding and wildlife viewing, in areas that monkeys and even jaguars still call home. Keep in mind, though, that this is relatively undeveloped territory for tourism and there are few tour operators. The best approach is to go through outfitters or non-profit organizations that have contacts with these communities and can help to make arrangements, and then visit them directly, using local guides to explore the region. See *Eco-Travel* section below for more details.

On the Beach & in the Surf

Just southwest of Esmeraldas, in Atacamas and surrounding communities, are beachside resorts, complete with all the adventurous amenities. During peak Ecuadorian and Colombian holiday season, expect crowds, kids, parties and beach-going nightlife. During other times of the year, strolling along the beach, swimming and just plain old hanging out is common. Note that during the busy season the beaches aren't as clean or safe for walking, especially at night. Head farther southwest of Atacames for the more tranquil communities of Súa and Same. Northwest of Esmeraldas, the beaches are generally safer, cleaner, more quiet and less crowded than around Atacames, as there is less resort build-up here.

Whale-Watching

From June to September, whale-watching excursions near shore are popular in the resort areas southeast of Esmeraldas. The main sighting destination is **Punta Galera**, between Atacames and Muisne. In Atacames, on the Malecón (the waterfront street), inquire at **Cabañas Caida del Sol** (☎ 6-731-246) for whale-watching trips. In the smaller bay and resort village of Súa, inquire at your hotel about arranging an excursion. And in the eco-reserve of Playa Escondida, which is closer to Punta Galera, arrangements are easily made to search for whales.

Sea Kayaking

The infrastructure for sea kayaking isn't very well developed in this part of the country, but the sport is an excellent way to see the coast, offering opportunities to visit places that you can't get to on land. A multi-day trip from Esmeraldas to Muisne, for example, incorporates visiting remote beaches, sea cliffs, ancient fishing villages, estuaries, mangroves, coastal rainforest, as well as viewing whales and an abundance of unique coastal bird life.

Another wonderful option, incorporating the adventure of kayaking with a cultural and nature journey, is a multi-day trip inland around the Cotacachi-Cayapas region. Kayaking from village to village and into the reserve, staying with local communities and hiking in lowland rainforest are highlights of such an experience.

For trips that include all of this, contact the US-based **Amazon Adventures**, 2711 Market Garden, Austin, TX 78745, ☎ 512-443-5393, fax 512-442-8515, jmc12@amazonadventures.com, www.amazonadventures.com, for set itineraries and to make arrangements. Or go directly to their outfitter in Quito: **Eco-Adventur**, a recommended rafting and kayaking company, at Calama 339 between Juan León Mera and Reina Victoria, ☎ 2-2520-647, fax 2-2223-720, info@adventur.com.

■ Eco-Travel

 Most travelers in this region, particularly young backpackers and Colombian vacationers, head to the coast for a little R&R on the beaches. More recently, however, people are discovering that the riches of this land go far beyond that. Ecotourism, with an emphasis on local culture, is picking up speed as more communities adjust to the tourism industry, particularly in the region around the Cotacachi-Cayapas Reserve. Trips include local coastal rainforest excursions via dugout canoe and hiking on nature trails. The birding is exceptional here as well, and photographic opportunities are excellent.

North of Esmeraldas

Cotacachi-Cayapas Ecological Reserve

From 600 feet above sea level to the summit of Cotacachi Volcano at 16,150 feet, Cotacachi-Cayapas protects the largest expanse of ecological habitat in Ecuador, along the western slopes of the Andes. Thanks to its extremely varied topography, the 504,917-acre reserve spans numerous ecological life zones and harbors many species unique to the region. From tropical lowland rainforest to premontane and montane cloud forest, the prolific birdlife is ideal for the avid birder. Hiking in the region offers an exceptional array of flora and fauna for the nature enthusiast. Just as intriguing, however, is the opportunity to experience local cultures that are unique to this region.

Entrance into the lower elevations of Cotacachi-Cayapas proper is best via Playa de Oro along Río Santiago or from the community of San Miguel and the Río Cayapas. Officially, the park entrance fee is $20, payable at the ranger station in San Miguel. The "rangers" also act as guides for about $10 per day. Camping is available wherever there is space. Be sure to pack out everything that you pack in. The higher-elevation portion of the reserve is accessible only from the area around Lago Cuicocha, northwest of Otavalo in the highlands (see *Northern Highlands*, page 127, 135).

The rainy season, from December through May, is better for transportation along the waterways, although there are more mosquitoes – especially at dawn and dusk. The cooler, drier season from August to December offers a more pleasant climate and better wildlife viewing, but the lower river levels make navigation more difficult. June through August is generally nice.

The best way to see this region is by staying in the community of Playa de Oro along the Río Santiago or the community of San Miguel along the Río Cayapas. From Borbón, make arrangements for the two-hour boat ride to either village. The Cotacachi-Cayapas Reserve itself can be reached via San Miguel and the Río Cayapas.

The People of Cotacachi-Cayapas

Two distinct cultures, the Afro-Ecuadorians and the native Chachi people, dominate the area in and around Cotacachi-Cayapas. As early as the 1500s, the Spanish began transporting African slaves into the Esmeraldas province to work in gold mines and on plantations. Today's Afro-Ecuadorians are descendants of these slaves. Historically one of the most suppressed people in all of Ecuador, their culture nevertheless flourishes with a particular rhythm and tradition of dance and music. Colorful songs and celebrations echo with Pacific rhythms from instruments such as the *bombo*, *cunno*, and *maraca*, and music of the rain-forest from the bamboo *marimba*, *chonta*, and *caucho*. To witness the beauty of their dance or a brief smile from a friendly welcomer is to feel the magic of this enchanting culture.

The indigenous Chachi (Cayapas) people have resided in the Cotacachi-Cayapas region for 4,000 years. Today, only about 5,000 remain, but they continue to preserve their myths and traditions. Many speak only their native tongue, Cha'palaachi. They live in traditional thatched-roof huts along the banks of the Río Cayapas. The women are experts at weaving baskets of natural fiber with beautiful designs, a practice that is several thousand years old. You can purchase these famous crafts in Quito or directly from the women.

These two ethnic groups have separate and unique cultures. Both know the land intimately but in different ways, and have shared the rainforest for over 400 years. Now, in their efforts to survive with the forest, they are opening their doors and experimenting with ecotourism. These people are fully aware of what is at stake here, and it is important as travelers that we are as well.

Playa de Oro

Situated along the Río Santiago is the community of Playa de Oro, or "Gold Beach." Named perhaps in reference to the region's history as a gold-mining mecca, or more likely because of the golden sparkle of grains on its sandy beaches, Playa de Oro is one of those special places you won't forget.

The village is currently experimenting with ecotourism. This began with the help of an organization named **Ecocienca** (Ecuadorian Foundation for Ecological Studies), a non-governmental organization dedicated to conservation and, by necessity, to promoting community development in ways that are benign to the natural environment.

The forests around Playa de Oro are more pristine than other areas along the Río Cayapas. You can spend time with a bilingual guide exploring the trails and you may spot the impressive umbrella bird. It's also possible to hike the trails alone, as there are signs along the way. See *Where to Stay*, page 268, for a description of the facilities.

Contact **Ecociencia** in Quito, at Isla San Cristóbal N44 and Isla Seymour, Casilla 17-12-257, ☎ 2-2451-338 or 2-2451-339, fax 2-2249-

334, www.ecociencia.com. Ecocienca works in conjunction with a local organization, **SUBIR**, which now makes the arrangements for trips in and around these communities and in the Cotacachi-Cayapas Reserve. SUBIR is based in Borbón, up the hill at the end of the main street, or in Quito ay Apartado 17-21-190, ☎ 2-2528-696, fax 2-2565-990, subir@care.org.ec.

Inquire with **Angermeyer's Enchanted Expeditions**, at Foch 726 and Av. Amazonas in Quito, ☎ 2-2569-960/2-2221-305, fax 2-2569-956, info@enchantedexpeditions.com, www.enchantedexpeditions.com. This responsible tour operator recently offered trips to Playa de Oro and San Miguel.

San Miguel

San Miguel, on the Río Cayapas, is the site of another wonderful community-based ecocultural tourism project and of the ranger fee station for entry into Cotacachi-Cayapas Ecological Reserve. Ecocienca, the Ecuadorian Foundation for Ecological Studies, is working in conjunction with San Miguel and the community of Playa de Oro along the Río Santiago (see above) to combine tourism and other economic alternatives with scientific research and conservation.

Located just before the northwest boundary of the Cotacachi-Cayapas Reserve, San Miguel is a community of blacks living adjacent to indigenous Chachi families along the shoreline of the Río Cayapas. Many of the Chachi here speak only their native language of Cha'palaachi, and even fluent Spanish speakers will find it difficult to understand the stuttered and fragmented speech of these Afro-Ecuadorians. Fortunately, body language, smiles, and other facial expressions are universally understood.

A several-day organized tour that blends a mix of canoeing, hiking through primary forest, and spending time with both cultures can be arranged through Ecociencia. Music, dancing, and special celebrations top off the trip and really make you feel like a part of the community. The tourism facilities are well developed and comfortable, yet they're also quite rustic. Beds include mosquito netting, while private baths with flush toilets and rainwater showers are surprisingly clean. You can enjoy downtime after each day's activities, relaxing on porches or in the common rooms.

The community of San Miguel is a few hours from Borbón via motorized canoe on the Río Cayapas. Water taxis take a couple of hours longer, but are less expensive. Contact **Ecociencia**, Isla San Cristóbal

N44 and Isla Seymour, Casilla 17-12-257, Quito, ☎/fax 2-2451-338 or 2-2242-417, fax 2-2249-334, www.ecociencia.org.

Comparable eco-travel opportunities exist with the privately owned **Steve's Lodge** and FUNDEAL's **Verdes Tropicos Choco Lodge** (See *Where to Stay*, pages 268-69).

Cayapas-Mataje Ecological Reserve

From San Lorenzo near the Colombian border, excursions into the ecologically rich mangrove forests of the Cayapas-Mataje are a great way to explore the coastal marine environment. Included in most tours are boating, swimming, visiting a couple of archeological sites from the pre-Columbian La Tolita culture and just hanging out on the beach. In San Lorenzo, contact **Jaime Burgos Echegaray** at the restaurant La Estancia, for trips into the reserve and visits to indigenous communities farther into the Cotacachi-Cayapas region. **Coopseturi**, ☎/fax 6-780-161, office on the boat dock, also offers day-long excursions to the reserve.

South of Esmeraldas

Playa Escondida

About 1½ hours southwest of Esmeraldas is Playa Escondida, a remote stretch of isolated beach that is well off the beaten path. Formed by the Río Malpelo, this "hidden beach" and half-moon bay offers a getaway that is far removed from the normal resort-style development along the coast. Now operated as a 24-acre private ecological refuge, Playa Escondida offers hiking, camping and swimming in a very relaxing environment. Rustic but comfortable accommodations abut the beach, an area of secondary forest and a small, tranquil bay. Its Canadian owner has created a model of ecological tourism, complete with native-style accommodations and composting latrines. Permaculture and reintroduced turtle release efforts complement the comforts of an open-air restaurant, with fresh seafood caught daily and a wide variety of dishes with fresh organic veggies from their garden. The facilities can accommodate up to 30 people. Overall, it is a wonderful setting. For information, ☎ 9-733-368 or 9-551-128, judithbarett@hotmail.com, www.intergate.ca/playaescondida.

From Esmeraldas, travel southeast along the main coastal road to the small fishing village of Tonchingue. The turnoff to Playa Escondida is a mile beyond Tonchigue at Km 10 via Tonchigue-Punta Galera. Take a bus from Esmeraldas (or Muisne in the south) to Tonchingue and catch a truck (local *ranchera*) toward Punta Galera for about $8-10. Camping is available for $5.

Western Slopes to Pacific Coast

Around Muisne

Trips by boat to the local estuary and mangrove forests are available through local hotels and the conservation organization FUNDECOL. Efforts support preservation of the last remaining mangroves in the area, most of which have been devastated by the shrimp farming industry, resulting in near ecological collapse for the local marine ecosystem and subsistence lives for the people. These excursions are a great way to view the local marine environment, while supporting a worthwhile cause. See Muisne in *Touring and Sightseeing*, page 257, for contact information and directions.

■ Where to Stay

ACCOMMODATIONS PRICE SCALE
Unless otherwise noted, prices are per room, up to double occupancy. Some prices are per person, particularly with all-inclusive packages, but these generally include meals, lodging, guide services and other amenities.

$	Under $25
$$	$26 to $50
$$$	$51 to $100
$$$$	Over $100

Esmeraldas & Las Palmas

 In downtown Esmeraldas at Libertad 407 and Ramón Tello, the **Hotel Apart Casino**, ☎ 6-728-700, fax 6-728-704, is the best hotel in the city, though that isn't saying much in this relatively downtrodden town. It is modestly priced, with modern rooms and amenities, decent service and a good restaurant. $

 One of the good things about this region is the great seafood and many tasty dishes prepared with coconut milk.

At the budget end downtown, try the **El Cisne**, centrally located near the plaza, at 10 de Agosto and Olmedo, ☎ 6-723-411. $

The best hotel in the area is the **Costa Verde**, Luis Tello 809 and Hilda Padilla, ☎ 6-728-714 or 6-728-715, fax 6-728-716, just a stone's throw from the beach in Las Palmas, the suburb just north of Esmeraldas. In fact, Las Palmas is the only area worth staying or walking around. The comfortable units include balconies, kitchenettes, air-conditioning, and private baths. There is a Jacuzzi and sauna, as well as a small pool. Guests can enjoy tasty meals served up at the restaurant. $-$$

A less-expensive alternative a bit closer to downtown is the **Hotel Cayapas**, located on Av. Kennedy and Valdez, ☎ 6-711-022, fax 6-721-320. In addition to a garden setting with a nice atmosphere, the hotel's comfortable rooms include hot-water baths and air-conditioning. Its excellent seafood restaurant is also worth checking out, even if you're not staying here. For some, this is a prime location – close enough to downtown without being amid all the madness of the city center. $

The only other decent option in the city is the **Hotel del Mar**, at the beach end of Av. Kennedy, ☎ 6-723-708 or 6-713-910. The quality of the rooms varies, but some have ocean views and air-conditioning. $

North of Esmeraldas

To the north along the coast and less than 10 miles from Esmeraldas in the tiny village of Camarones is **Hostería La Fragata**, ☎ 6-701-038, 6-729-001, or 6-584-601. This is the place to stay if you need an overnight near Esmeraldas, but prefer coastal solitude to the city. Relax and enjoy comfortable cabañas and a delicious seafood dinner on a bluff overlooking the ocean. Half of the village is usually down on the beach, bargaining over the fresh catch of the day. The sunset views from the restaurant are wonderful, and Lucho, the friendly and enthusiastic owner, will be happy to sit down and chat with you. La Fragata, which can accommodate up to 30 people, has shared rooms with bunk beds, private rooms, and a suite complete with a living area and kitchen suitable for a family or several people. It also offers tours on the adjacent land that include swimming, hiking, fishing, and learning about the local agricultural efforts. $ per person.

Continuing northeast to the small town of Río Verde, the Swiss-owned **Cabañas Pura Vida** (on the main road just before town) offer another tranquil setting, with an ocean view and often a wonderful breeze. Amenities range from simple double rooms to cabañas on the beach, a TV/game room and a Jacuzzi. The laid-back and friendly staff is often floating about the comfortable open-air dining area and will be more than happy to point you toward the local weekend dancing festivities. The cabañas are recommended, though they are a bit more expensive than the rooms, up to $30 per night. Some organized tours beginning in Quito now use Pura Vida as an overnight stop before continuing on to the Cotacachi-Cayapas Reserve in the morning. From Río Verde, it's another hour of driving along a mostly paved road to the jumping-off point at Borbón. $-$$

South of Esmeraldas

While the province of Esmeraldas has no shortage of ocean water, it does lack good fresh water for urban use. Many of the hotels, therefore, use brackish water for showers. Fresh water is trucked in and shortages can sometimes occur before a new delivery. If you don't mind a little salt in the water, save money and stay at the more modest accommodations. Also, keep in mind that hotel suites in resort towns are often set up to accommodate families. Economizing with groups is very convenient. Again, the prices here are based on double-occupancy. Single travelers should expect to pay more.

 Bring a mosquito net when traveling in this region, and a lot of insect repellent, as malaria is rampant here.

Tonsupa

Hotel Club de Pacífico, in Tonsupa at Km 20 on the "Vía a Atacames" road, ☎ 6-731-056 or 6-731-053, fax 6-731-368, is pleasantly located along the beach a few miles northwest of Atacames. Relax poolside or on your own private beach for as long as it takes to get a tan or finish your novel. Rooms include cable TVs, ceiling fans, private baths, and hot water. Good eats are also available from the restaurant's appetizing menu. $

Atacames

In Atacames itself, the main drag between the Ocean and the Río Atacames is where you'll find most of the hotels, bars and restaurants. One of the best higher-end values in town is The **Villas Arco Iris**, or "rainbow bungalows," ☎ 6-731-069, fax 6-731-437, arcoiris@andinanet.net, www.villasarcoiris.com. They offer comfort, seclusion, and a nice ambiance. The individual cabañas come complete with hammocks on open-air porches. Each air-conditioned cabin also has a private bath with hot water. Tucked away neatly behind the main section of town at the north end of the beach, the hotel can be difficult to find. Ask for directions. $$

The largest of the hotels is **Hotel Casa Blanca**, ☎ 6-731-031, 6-731-389, or 6-731-390, fax 6-731-096, built more to accommodate sheer numbers than to provide a quality atmosphere. The list of amenities here is extensive, however, and there's an outdoor restaurant and bar. Quality rooms or individual cabins for large groups are clean and comfortable, with air-conditioning, cable TV, private baths, and hot water. The beach is adjacent to and directly accessible from the hotel grounds. $$-$$$

The **Hotel Castel Nuevo**, ☎ 2-3223-608 (or 2-2223-262 in Quito), fax 2-3223-452, boasts three swimming pools, including the largest in town. Set near the beach, comfortable rooms include private baths, hot water, and fans. There's plenty of opportunity here to lounge about in the shade or chat with new friends at the bar. $$-$$$

One of the better choices for low-end accommodations along the beach is **Galerias Atacames**, ☎ 6-731-149. Just to the right of the foot-bridge to the beach and adjacent to many other hotels, this is where budget travelers who have drifted to the coast end up staying. The English-speaking owners are friendly. The restaurant's food is delicious food and the prices are reasonable. $

The American-owned **Hostal Chavalito**, along the same beachfront area as Galerias Atacames, ☎ 6-731-113, also does a good job of catering to international budget travelers. It offers rooms with private baths and, in a couple of cases, balconies with views of the ocean. The owner here can be quite entertaining. $

Stepping up a notch in quality and price, but still economical for two to four people, is the German-owned **Cabañas Caida del Sol**, ☎ 6-731-479. Enjoy a nice atmosphere in the individual cabins, with private baths and ceiling fans. The mini-fridge is perfect for keeping those *cervezas* cool until it's time to watch the sunset over the Pacific. $$

Súa

In Súa, try **Hotel Súa**, ☎ 6-731-004, for a room with a view. Their restaurant serves delicious local seafood and French cuisine. All rooms have private baths and hot water. $-$$

Hotel Chadra Ramos, ☎ 6-731-006 or 6-731-070, offers a bit more character and is probably the best value in town. There are good views and a tasty restaurant, as well as a small beach adjacent to the property. $

Western Slopes to Pacific Coast

Same

In Same, the best value within the budget category is **La Terraza**, ☎ 6-544-507. It's near the beach, has a good, inexpensive restaurant and bar, and is a popular place to hang out. $

Hotel Club Casablanca, ☎ 6-252-077, fax 6-253-452, www.ccasablanca.com, casablan@uio.satnet.net, is a true resort. Located just outside of town along the beach, Casablanca has nice rooms with private baths and a full set of upper-class facilities. Without leaving the premises, you can enjoy swimming, dining, a discotheque, and even tennis. The Club Casablanca also offers airport transfer from Esmeraldas at an additional cost. $$$$

Muisne

The town of Muisne is not a major tourist destination, so options for accommodations are limited. Check rooms for security before making a decision. The best choice on the island is **Hostal Mapara** (on the beach), with a restaurant ($) or the even cheaper **Hotel Galápagos**, ☎ 6-480-158. It is very inexpensive, but secure, and also has a restaurant and private baths. $

Cotacachi-Cayapas Region

Playa de Oro offers a full eco-cultural tourism experience in a unique, albeit remote and relatively untouched, community (see *Eco-Travel*, page 261). The tourist facilities consist of thatched-roof structures built on stilts. Guest rooms open onto a common porch, complete with a bench, table, and comfortable chairs. The rooms are spacious, with plenty of shelves, mosquito net-covered beds, and clean private baths with running water and flush toilets. A three-tiered septic system handles waste, and lighting is available via photovoltaic solar electricity or candlelight. $$$ per night, meals and services included. Advance notice and minimum stay required.

☆ **San Miguel** is a community with comparable facilities, as both of these ecotourism projects were developed together. $$$ per night, meals and services included. Advance notice and minimum stay required.

☆ **Steve's Lodge** (less than an hour from Borbón at the junction of the Río Cayapas and Río Onzole), is the longest-standing reputable ecolodge in the region. This is a good starting point for exploring Cotacachi-Cayapas. The lodge offers three-day package tours ($300 per person) that include trips up the Cayapas to visit native Chachi and Afro-Ecuadorian communities, to experience their culture, cere-

Inca ruins in Cuenca

Above: Volcán Chimborazo

Below: Panning for gold along the Río Napo

Sacha Lodge, lower Río Napo

Along the Río Napo

Above: Typical jungle lodge accommodations, Río Napo region

Below: Cabañas Alinahui, Río Napo region

Above: Home on the Central Coast

Below: When the tide comes in, the nets go out in Manglaralto

Above: Drying out paja toquila, used to make Panama hats

Below: Mud baths near the Central Coast

Catch of the day in Puerto López

monies, and way of life. They also lead excursions into the reserve, enabling you to see the prolific wildlife.

Steve's Lodge lies on a fairly developed, cattle-grazed plot of land, but it is quite popular and maintains a good reputation. Perhaps it's the family atmosphere. Simple and rustic, the lodge has a good view of the river and comfortable double rooms with shared baths and electricity. $$$

Steve and Laura Tarjanyi are the owners. Contact them at Casilla 187, Esmeraldas, nagy@pi.cro.ec.

From Borbón, catch a motorized canoe for about $20 (bargain hard) or a regular passenger canoe for about $2. Arriving without notice at Steve's Lodge is usually not a problem, or you can make prior arrangements with the Tarjanyis to be picked up in Borbón. Ask for a discount if you're traveling with a group.

☆ **Verdes Tropicos (Green Tropics) Choco Lodge** is a bit farther up the Río Cayapas from Steve's Lodge. Contact FUNDEAL, Verdes Tropicos Choco Lodge, 1227 Reina Victoria and Calama, Quito, ☎ 2-2507-245 or 2-2507-208, fax 2-2238-801 or 2-2507-284, fundeal@pi. pro.ec. This community-based ecocultural tourism project operates in conjunction with FUNDEAL, the Foundation for Alternative Development, in and around their own reserve.

FUNDEAL actively supports community initiatives to conserve nature, preserve culture, and promote community development with ecotourism as an alternative to forest exploitation.

Set back in a small clearing, the Choco Lodge is next to the river and surrounded by forest near the community of Santa María. Cabañas, built in the traditional Chachi style, have thatched roofs and are raised on stilts. Visitors enjoy relaxing views as they swing from hammocks and watch the tropical world float by. Although the comfortable facilities often make it seem difficult to leave, there are places to go, people to visit, and things to see. Four- or five-day tours (about $100 per person per day) take in everything from Chachi shamanism to Afro-Ecuadorian *marimba* music. $$$

Camping

Camping is available within the Cotacachi-Cayapas Reserve and requires a knowledgeable guide to get around. Inquire at the Ranger Station in San Miguel. Along the coast there are few designated camping sites associated with cabañas. If you decide to camp on the beach, be cautious about leaving your belongings unattended. Camping is also available at **Playa Escondida** for $5 per night.

■ Where to Eat

Restaurants along the coast offer a great selection of seafood. In fact, seafood is a staple here (what a surprise), and the cuisine is good enough to warrant its availability throughout the highlands, at least in the major cities. *Ceviches* – mixed raw fish and vegetables marinated with lime juice (almost like a cold soup and absolutely delicious) – are a local favorite. Be careful, though, to order a dish like this only in a restaurant that is used to serving travelers. The last thing you want to deal with this far from proper medical treatment is bad fish or shellfish. Other common meals include mixed *camarones* (shrimp, rice, and vegetable dishes), the catch of the day with rice and fried plantains, and *cocado*, seafood cooked with coconut, resulting in a distinct, sweet flavor. This is not to be confused with *cocadas*, another specialty of the coast, which are sweets made from grated coconut and enough sugar to rot all your teeth before you know it. Of course, it's delicious.

Esmeraldas & Las Palmas

A simple but fantastic selection of entrées is served up in a truly local establishment at **La Sultana del Valle**, Av. Libertad and Parada, on the way to Las Palmas, ☎ 6-712-988. It's open until 10 pm. Ceviches, the catch of the day, and an unpretentious atmosphere are the specialties here. This place offers the town's best bang for your buck.

Another good and inexpensive seafood restaurant is **Los Redes**, open until at least 10 pm. It's located at the Central Plaza downtown, along Bolívar. This is just one of the many casual and popular local establishments.

 Watch for thieves in this downtown neighborhood after dark.

For the best Chinese food in town, try the **Chifa Asiático** (on Cañizares near Sucre). It stays open as long as the customers keep coming and is an ever-loyal backup for those times when you've simply had enough of the coastal cuisine.

The **Restaurant Tiffany**, at the east end of Av. Kennedy in Las Palmas, ☎ 6-710-263, is open until midnight and is the best restaurant in Esmeraldas. Satisfy your palate with international and Ecuadorian cuisine. The portions are generous and the prices won't crush your budget. The Las Palmas location is a quiet beachfront area.

The best hotel restaurants include **La Fragata** in the **Costa Verde Suites** and the **Fenix Restaurant** in the **Hotel del Mar**. Both specialize in seafood, good service, and tasty meals. Downtown, at Libertad 407 and Ramón Tello, ☎ 6-728-700, fax 6-728-704, the **Apart Hotel Casino** also has a great restaurant.

Atacames

There are more beachside restaurants and bars here than you can shake a stick at. The best ones will be obvious as they are more popular. Wander along the beachfront street until you find one that appeals to you. Toward the western edge of town are the better *cevicherías*.

In areas outside of Esmeraldes, your overnight stay will typically be part of an all-inclusive package. Be sure to check ahead of time, though, as sometimes you will need to bring meals with you. And you may need to pick up a supply of snacks or lunch options before departing from "civilization." Waiting interminably for the local taxi boat may leave you with no option but the local "store" (hut), which means crackers and an ancient can of sardines. Not a bad meal when you're stuck in the middle of nowhere!

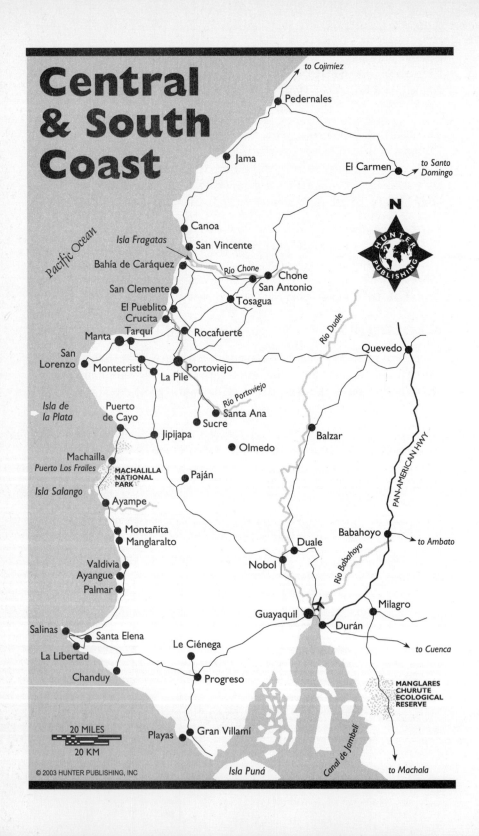

Central & South Coast

to Cojimíez

Pedernales

Jama

El Carmen

to Santo Domingo

Pacific Ocean

Canoa

Isla Fragatas

San Vincente

Bahía de Caráquez

Río Chone

Chone

San Antonio

San Clemente

Tosagua

El Pueblito

Crucita

Tarquí

Rocafuerte

Río Duale

Quevedo

Manta

San Lorenzo

Montecristi

Portoviejo

La Pile

Río Portoviejo

Santa Ana

Isla de la Plata

Puerto de Cayo

Sucre

Jipijapa

Olmedo

Balzar

Machailla

Puerto Los Frailes

MACHALILLA NATIONAL PARK

Pajón

Isla Salango

Ayampe

Montañita

Manglaralto

Babahoyo

to Ambato

Duale

Río Babahoyo

Valdivia

Ayangue

Palmar

Nobol

Milagro

Guayaquil

Durán

Salinas

Santa Elena

Le Ciénega

to Cuenca

La Libertad

Chanduy

Progreso

MANGLARES CHURUTE ECOLOGICAL RESERVE

PAN-AMERICAN HWY

N

20 MILES

20 KM

Playas

Gran Villamí

Isla Puná

Canal de Jambeli

to Machala

© 2003 HUNTER PUBLISHING, INC

■ Getting Here & Getting Around

Most people fly to Ecuador via Quito or Guayaquil, which are both international hubs. **TAME** offers daily flights between Quito and Guayaquil, as well as between Quito and Manta, the second-largest coastal port in Ecuador.

From Quito by land, the central and southern coast is accessible via Santo Domingo, and from Guayaquil via La Libertad near Salinas. The towns and sites in this region are separated along the main coastal highway, called La Ruta del Sol (Road of the Sun). Just pick a place and catch the bus from the bus terminal heading in the right direction. They generally stop at each town.

■ Visitor Information

Outside of Guayaquil, the main towns in this region are Bahía de Caráquez, Manta, Puerto López, and Salinas, from north to south. Each town offers at least basic modern facilities, including post and communications, in the form of a Pacífictel telephone office.

In **Bahía de Caráquez** there is a Banco de Guayaquil on Av. Bolívar and Riofrío. Check around at the hotels for Internet access. The post office is located at Bolívar and Aguilera. The Pacífictel telephone office is at Alberto Santos and Arenas. Taxis are available along the Malecón or waterfront, and *pangas* (small boat taxis) for San Vicente can be found at the city docks.

In **Manta**, Banco del Pacífico is on C 13 and Av. 2. The post office is near the Malecón, or waterfront street, on Calle 8 and the Pacífictel telephone office on the Malecón and Calle 11. The bus station is behind the fishing harbor, near Calle 7 and Av. 8, and the local tourism office is on Calle 9 and Av. 4, ☎ 5-2611-471, or at the Ministry of Tourism, on Paseo JM Egas between Calles 10 and 11, ☎ 5-2622-944.

In **Portoviejo**, the Ministry of Tourism office is at P Gaul and J Montalvo. The post office is on Ave. Ricaurte and the central park and the police station is just to the south near Ave. Chile. To the west of the city center and Río Portoviejo is the bus terminal. There is a small regional airport just outside of town.

In **Puerto López**, facilities are minimal. If you need a bank or modern communications, head south to La Libertad or Salinas on the

Santa Elena Peninsula. In **Salinas**, there is a centrally located Pacífictel, as well as Internet access at Café Planet (Av. 10 and Calle 25) and a couple of banks, including Banco del Pacífico (Enriquez between Calles 18 and 19) and Banco de Guayaquil (travelers checks, Visa and Amex), on the Malecón. The post office is on Calle 17 and Av. 2.

■ Touring & Sightseeing

The Central Coast – from North to South

☆ Bahía de Caráquez & Vicinity

 Better known as Bahía, this is an attractive coastal resort town that claims to be the entrance to Ecuador. Legend states that a tribe named the "Caras" arrived in Bahía de Caráquez aboard balsa wood sailing vessels, having come "from where the sun sets." This was recounted by Ecuador's earliest historian, the Jesuit priest Juan de Velasco, in *The History of the Kingdom of Quito* (1789). The Spanish founded Bahía de Caráquez in 1624 as the second major port for Spanish exports. Now it doubles as a small port city and shrimp-farming community. The new hotels are a good indicator that tourism dominates its economy at this point. It's just a hop north via ferry, across the mouth of the Río Chone, to endless miles of sandy beaches.

Bahía remains a small and clean town of under 20,000 people, worth a visit if only to admire the setting (though there is plenty to do for a short stay). In fact, Bahía has become something of a model for sustainable development. As a result, the people here are much more conscious of environmental and community development issues than in other places throughout the country. Ecotourism has emerged in an effort to create sustainable jobs, while educating both locals and foreign travelers about preserving the region's precious biological diversity and a healthy urban community.

A nice day excursion is the short boat ride to **Isla de Fragatas**, where mangroves, nesting frigate birds and other wildlife live (see *Eco-Travel*, page 291).

Better beaches and family-style hotels and bungalows are across the bay in the smaller coastal town of **San Vicente**, along the main street near the beach. The setting here is a bit more relaxed than in Bahía, and you can save money with larger groups in the family-oriented

Bahía de Caráquez

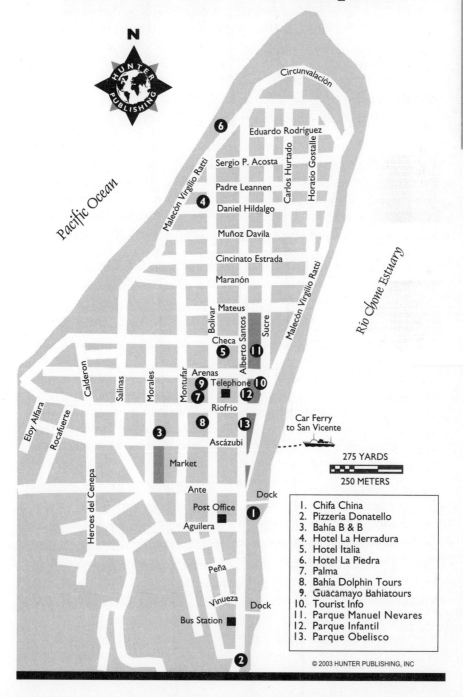

N

Circunvalación

Pacific Ocean

Río Chone Estuary

Malecón Virgilio Ratti

Eduardo Rodríguez

Carlos Hurtado

Horatio Gostalle

Sergio P. Acosta

Padre Leannen

Daniel Hildalgo

Muñoz Davila

Cincinato Estrada

Maranón

Bolivar

Mateus

Alberto Santos

Sucre

Checa

Malecón Virgilio Ratti

Calderon

Salinas

Morales

Montufar

Arenas

Telephone

Riofrio

Ascázubi

Market

Ante

Post Office

Aguilera

Peña

Vinueza

Bus Station

Eloy Alfara

Rocafuerte

Heroes del Cenepa

Car Ferry
to San Vicente

Dock

Dock

275 YARDS

250 METERS

1. Chifa China
2. Pizzería Donatello
3. Bahía B & B
4. Hotel La Herradura
5. Hotel Italia
6. Hotel La Piedra
7. Palma
8. Bahía Dolphin Tours
9. Guacamayo Bahiatours
10. Tourist Info
11. Parque Manuel Nevares
12. Parque Infantil
13. Parque Obelisco

cabañas. San Vicente can be reached via Río Chone by road, or on a ferry from Bahía.

Heading north from San Vicente, there are a few stretches of isolated beaches, fishing villages, and basic accommodations. One of the best of these is in the village of **Canoa**, less than 10 miles north of San Vicente. Quite a bit farther north, between Cojimíes and Pedernales, stop and relax at many isolated stretches of sandy coast. Camping is available anywhere, but it is best to find accommodations that offer camping on the premises.

Manta

Manta, the next major port town to the south and the largest along the central coast, is a thriving city based on fishing and tourism. With over 150,000 people, though, it does not top my list of places to spend time. But the town is lively, has a waterfront location, and is the second largest Ecuadorian port after Guayaquil. Nights, especially, are active along the Malecón, or waterfront, and you can absorb the local culture, bar-hop and people-watch. The beaches are not great, but some of the surrounding areas, particularly to the northwest, are better.

To the north of downtown is **Murciélago Beach** and the area known as **Bahía de Manta** (Manta Bay), with nice beaches and cabañas to stay in. This area attracts holidaying Ecuadorians more than foreign travelers.You'll probably have it all to yourself if it's during their off-season. To the southeast of the main port is the fishing harbor, and across the Río Manta is the suburb of **Tarquí**, which gets very lively, crowded, loud and a bit dirty during the peak season. Keep an eye on your belongings here. Although there are numerous hotels in this area, you are better off staying at one on the Malecón near the northwestern side of Manta.

Regular bus service is available in and out of Manta to most of the main coastal destinations. From Bahía, the trip is under two hours, four hours to Guayaquil, and five hours to Santo Domingo de los Colorados (you can continue to Quito from there).

Farther northeast is the small resort/beach town of **Crucita**, with more tranquil beaches and adventures that include surfing, windsurfing and paragliding.

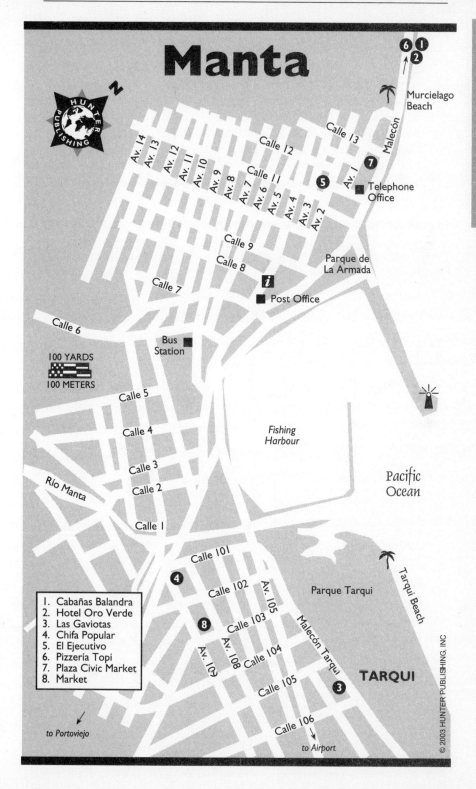

Manta

6 1 2

Murcielago Beach

Calle 13

Calle 12

Malecón

Calle 11

7

5

Av. 14
Av. 13
Av. 12
Av. 11
Av. 10
Av. 9
Av. 8
Av. 7
Av. 6
Av. 5
Av. 4
Av. 3
Av. 2
Av. 1

Telephone Office

Calle 9

Calle 8

Parque de La Armada

Calle 7

i

Post Office

Calle 6

Bus Station

100 YARDS

100 METERS

Calle 5

Calle 4

Fishing Harbour

Calle 3

Calle 2

Pacific Ocean

Río Manta

Calle 1

Calle 101

4

Calle 102

Av. 105

Parque Tarqui

Tarqui Beach

1. Cabañas Balandra
2. Hotel Oro Verde
3. Las Gaviotas
4. Chifa Popular
5. El Ejecutivo
6. Pizzería Topi
7. Plaza Civic Market
8. Market

8

Calle 103

Av. 108

Calle 104

Malecón Tarqui

Av. 109

Calle 105

3

TARQUI

Calle 106

to Portoviejo

to Airport

© 2003 HUNTER PUBLISHING, INC

Montecristi & Panama Hats

If you are traveling between Manta and other coastal destinations to the south, the main road splits at the small town of Montecristi. This is where you will see the best Panama hat makers in the country. The hats are made from a palm-leaf plant known as *paja toquilla*, which is grown along the region's western slopes. You can visit the shops and homes of Panama hat makers in Montecristi.

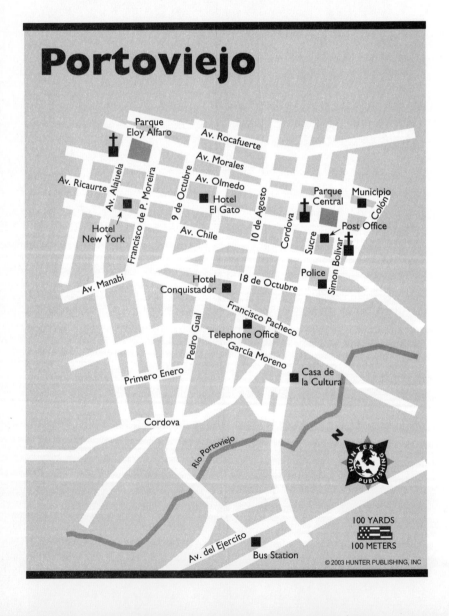

Portoviejo

Parque Eloy Alfaro
Av. Rocafuerte
Av. Morales
Av. Ricaurte
Av. Alajuela
Francisco de P. Moreira
9 de Octubre
Av. Olmedo
Hotel El Gato
Av. Chile
10 de Agosto
Cordova
Parque Central
Municipio
Colón
Sucre
Simón Bolívar
Post Office
Hotel New York
Av. Manabi
Hotel Conquistador
18 de Octubre
Police
Francisco Pacheco
Pedro Gual
Telephone Office
García Moreno
Primero Enero
Casa de la Cultura
Cordova
Río Portoviejo
100 YARDS
100 METERS
Av. del Ejercito
Bus Station

© 2003 HUNTER PUBLISHING, INC

Portoviejo

Accessible from Quito in the Andes and Guayaquil to the south, the provincial capital of Portoviejo, with over 150,000 inhabitants, is one of the larger commercial cities in Ecuador. It does not offer much for the traveler – unless dodging traffic and breathing polluted air is your idea of fun – although it may be a stopping point between coastal destinations or the Andes and the coast.

The South Coast: Puerto López to the Santa Elena Peninsula

Puerto López

The next major coastal town south of Manta and joining the highway is Puerto López. This once-sleepy fishing town is becoming popular as a home base for local nature excursions along the coast and into Machalilla National Park, as well as for whale-watching and island excursions. It's also a great place to soak up the local fishing culture as you stroll along the shore. Every morning the beach buzzes with activity as men return with the catch of the day. If you hang out long enough, you're sure to be invited to join in a game of beach soccer. There are also a few open-air restaurants, basic accommodations, and tour operators near the main road from the coastal highway to the beach and along the Malecón, or waterfront street, itself.

Montañita

Montañita is a small coastal fishing village that has become increasingly popular with the beach-going crowd. It has a reputation as the best surfing spot in the country and hosts competitions throughout the year, especially from January through May. Indeed, the surf can be pretty good, but the strong currents and undertow can be a hazard, as can the stingrays close to shore. Despite these apparent drawbacks, Montañita is a destination for surf bums and beach parties.

Just a few years ago there was a long and sandy beach in front of the village, but the last El Niño wiped it out, at least for the time being.

Montañita is less than 35 miles south of Puerto López, and is also accessible along the coastal highway from La Libertad in the south. In Montañita, ask at the gringo hotels where to rent a surfboard and take surf lessons. Randy Hood, a California surfer gone local, is a good contact through the Casa del Sol (see page 297). Baja Montañita is the area just north of the main village along the cliffs, offering the best surf and the most recent development.

For quieter beachside attractions, **Olón**, a few miles north, has a long stretch of white sand and surf, though there aren't any recommended hotels here. **Ayampe**, several miles farther north and near the provincial boundary at the Río Ayampe, is an exceptionally nice resort on the cliffs overlooking the ocean (see Hotel Atamari, page 296).

Manglaralto

South of Machalilla National Park and Puerto López, and near the beach resort of Montañita, is the small fishing community of Manglaralto. Walking along the beach between the two villages (when there is a beach) is a great way to explore the coast. From Manglaralto, it takes an hour to half a day, depending on how much time you spend swimming, bodysurfing, or just chasing after washed-up shells and sand crabs. In Manglaralto, you won't see sunbathing Westerners, but you will find local Ecuadorians fishing or swimming.

Accommodations in Manglaralto include **Hostería MaraKaya**, with simple but very clean double rooms, including mosquito nets over the beds, private baths, and heated showers (don't hit your head on the electrical device). This hotel is the home base for Earthwatch projects heading into the Loma Alta Cloud Forest (see *Trekking the Loma Alta Cloud Forest*, page 285). You can also inquire with **Pro Pueblo**, a local community development organization, about local ecotourism efforts, including Loma Alta. Along the beach, the open-aired **Las Tangas** restaurant offers delicious seafood and a pleasant atmosphere. If it looks deserted, just wait or ask around. They always seem to open just as people arrive.

Manglaralto can be reached by bus or car from La Libertad in the south or Puerto López in the north via the only major road along the coast. It's just a couple of miles south of Montañita.

Salinas & the Santa Elena Peninsula

About 1½ hours south of Manglaralto and a couple of hours west of Guayaquil (95 miles) is the popular resort town of Salinas, located on the Santa Elena Peninsula. With under 25,000 permanent residents, this coastal resort city – referred to as the Miami of Ecuador – booms with affluent Guayaquileños from January to April, especially during weekends and holidays. The rest of the time, Salinas feels like a high-rise ghost town.

Oil development, which stimulated the city's original growth in the 1930s, now cowers quietly in the shadow of tourism. Many middle- and upper-class city dwellers that regularly flock to Salinas rent out their own apartments, hotel suites, or family homes. The beaches

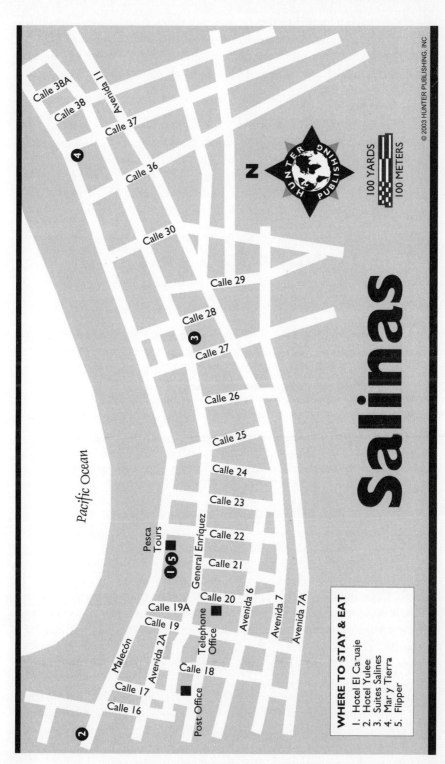

© 2003 HUNTER PUBLISHING, INC

Salinas

N

HUNTER PUBLISHING

100 YARDS
100 METERS

Pacific Ocean

Calle 38A
Calle 38
Avenida 11
Calle 37
Calle 36
Calle 30
Calle 29
Calle 28
Calle 27
Calle 26
Calle 25
Calle 24
Calle 23
Calle 22
Calle 21
Calle 20
General Enríquez
Pesca Tours
Avenida 6
Avenida 7
Avenida 7A
Calle 19A
Calle 19
Avenida 2A
Malecón
Telephone Office
Calle 18
Calle 17
Calle 16
Post Office

WHERE TO STAY & EAT
1. Hotel El Caruaje
2. Hotel Yulee
3. Suites Salines
4. Mar y Tierra
5. Flipper

here are average, but they can be somewhat dreary between June and August. Hotels line the waterfront street, and you can swim in the bay, though it is not as sanitary during peak months. Salinas has a lively night scene.

Buses from Guayaquil to Salinas take about three hours. You may need to transfer in La Libertad onto a bus heading toward Salinas.

Just east of Salinas and the highway's turning point toward Guayaquil is **La Libertad**, a bustling fishing town of more than 50,000 people that serves as the region's transportation hub. Although there's not much there for the eco-adventurer, it's interesting enough to warrant a stroll in between bus transfers and does have a few decent hotels.

■ Adventures

On Foot

The Chongón Colonche Mountains

 Among the lesser-known gems in Ecuador are hidden cloud-forest communities that are accessible only through your own efforts, places that are remote and sometimes hard to reach. But the rewards of hiking into these lush forests are genuine, as noted by a recent traveler:

 "I awoke to the soft patting of rain drops mixed with roaring echoes that shook me out of my dreams. It was as if the forest herself was speaking to us and was enough for me to ask our guide what was going on. Well, the roars were from a troop of howler monkeys and I later learned that the rain wasn't rain at all! Wow, this is going to be a great trip, I thought. And indeed, the longer we stayed the less I wanted to leave."

Cloud forests along the slopes of southwestern Ecuador may appear to be a bit of an anomaly when you consider that this region receives enough rainfall to support only a desert environment. Yet it is as rich in thick vegetation and biological diversity as the Amazon. From around June through December, the coastal fog, known locally as *la garua*, engulfs the land and is captured by vegetation along the lowland slopes. As a result, water constantly drips, breathing life into the forest. In fact, this "capture" phenomenon provides the foundation for the entire watershed and brings fresh water to local communities. In most of these areas, however, cattle ranching, farming and woodcutting seriously threaten the remaining forests.

Trekking the Loma Alta Cloud Forest

In 1993, a small group of renowned scientists and local conservationists was surveying local forest cover when their airplane crashed in the cloud forest above the community of Loma Alta. Two of the world's leading tropical scientists were killed, though a couple of people survived the crash and made it to Loma Alta. When the biologist that survived returned with an **Earthwatch** project leader, the community knew that it was destined to support a major undertaking to try and save one of the last remaining coastal lowland cloud forests. Since then, Earthwatch returns each year to help promote community development, scientific research and conservation of the cloud forest.

Earthwatch, in conjunction with the New York-based not-for-profit organization, **People Allied for Nature**, met with considerable resistance while trying to create a bioreserve. Conservation efforts meant not clearing the forest, which, in the eyes of the community, meant not putting food on the table. As a result, conservation and scientific research efforts evolved into a community development program.

As a part of the project, they researched and compared water volume capture between untouched forest and converted pasture and agricultural land. Environmental education efforts made it clear to the community why their watershed was drying up. The problem, though clear, had no obvious answers. What forms of "sustainable" alternatives to deforestation could they hope to employ? Local income during Earthwatch projects helps a bit, but what happens when, inevitably, these organizations pull out?

Among other efforts, People Allied for Nature and the community of Loma Alta now offer ecotours into the local cloud forest. Although support for these trips is currently very unstructured, any effort to visit will be amply rewarded. The cloud forest, located four to six hours by foot and horseback from the village of El Suspiro, within the community of Loma Alta, is a jewel for birders and nature enthusiasts. Its remote location, rugged terrain (the last hour-long, mud-caked scramble up to the forest shelter is called "heartbreak hill"), and variable weather patterns make this destination rarely visited. In fact, it is a mix of wet and dry throughout much of the year. The forest, however, is incredible! Troops of howler monkey shake the early dawn, nocturnal kinkajous drop fruit from the treetops during the evenings, and the bird life here is spectacular.

The cabaña in the forest offers primitive facilities and can comfortably accommodate up to 10 people (bring a sleeping bag and pad). Groups are encouraged to visit and, with enough notice, arrangements can be made through People Allied for Nature to provide guides and cooking equipment. If you have a special interest, such as birding or botany, give them plenty of time so they can find the appropriate person. If you speak Spanish, however, or don't mind a little communication barrier, hiring the knowledgeable community members as guides is recommended (PAN can also arrange this).

In the US, contact Claude Nathan, People Allied for Nature, ☎ 212-279-7813. If you are already in Ecuador, contact Marlene at the Hostería Mara Caya in Manglaralto, ☎ 4-2901-294, to make arrangements. Pro Pueblo, in Manglaralto, just north of Calle Constutución, ☎ 4-2901-208, propueblo.org.ec, is working with another organization, PMRC, across from the church, ☎ 4-2901-343, on local sustainable development programs. They can also make arrangements for these and other ecotourism excursions. Contact Earthwatch in the US at ☎ 800-776-0188, info@earthwatch.org, www.earthwatch.org.

Strolling on the Beach

Beaches are a highlight in this part of Ecuador. With miles and miles of white sand shores and pounding Pacific surf, the beaches offer everything from casual day strolls to multi-day camping treks from north to south (or vice versa). There are so many endless expanses, it is easy to find a secluded stretch along the coast once you move away from the resort towns. For those wanting to explore a large section of the coast, a decent map with the location of periodic towns and villages should suffice, as the coastline straddles the main highway. North of Bahía and San Vicente, for example, there is plenty of beach exploring to be had, with minimal development, but enough small towns and villages to keep you going. Farther south near Puerto López and toward the Santa Elena Peninsula, there is much of the same, but note that even outside of the resort towns, the closer you get to Guayaquil, especially during the holiday season, the more crowded the beaches become.

Machalilla National Park

This park offers great exploratory hiking options, including hiking through tropical dry forest that directly accesses beautiful and relatively remote beaches around Los Frailes. Other options include hiking up toward higher elevation habitats and a local cloud forest while visiting the community of **San Sebastián**. Arrangements can be made at Alandaluz Ecolodge (see pages 293, 296), Puerto López or inquire at the national park headquarters. See *Eco-Travel* section, page 292, for more details. **Bosque Marino,** in Puerto López near the main bus terminal, has good bilingual guides for hiking and birding trips through the park. Also in town, on Córdova, is **Sercapez,** ☎ 5-604-173, offering great camping and hiking excursions through the park, to archeological sites, as well as to San Sebastián. They also offer water-based excursions similar to those described below.

On Horseback

 In Puerto López, **Machalilla Tours,** ☎ 5-604-154, Malecón and Julio Zuleta, offers day excursions by horseback in Machalilla National Park. Farther north, in Bahía de Caráquez, horseback riding treks that support community ecotourism efforts can be taken with **Guayacamayo-Bahía Tours**, Av. Bolívar 902 and Arenas, ☎ 5-691-107/412, ☎/fax 5-691-280, ecopapel@impsat.net.ec or ecopapel@ecuadorexplorer.com.

On Water

Surfing

 Just south of Puerto López and Machalilla National Park is one of the best-known surf spots in Ecuador. **Montañita** has itself become a destination in a part of the country not typically on the gringo route. Montañita is frequented by locals during the hot vacation months of late December to April, as well as being the backpacker's beach of choice throughout much of the year. This is an area that caters well to the foreign traveler, with a relaxed atmosphere, good waves and a nice stretch of beach. You can rent surfboards and take surfing lessons through Randy Hood and Casa del Sol (see page 297), among others.

About 10 miles north of Bahía de Caráquez and San Vicente is the small fishing village of **Canoa**. Here you can find less-crowded beaches and great surf from around December through April. After May, the fog rolls in, with cooler temperatures, stronger breezes and a rougher ocean. There are fewer gringos than in Montañita, so you may find yourself sharing this secluded beachfront escape with locals or vacationing Ecuadorians. In Canoa, just ask around for the latest in surfboard rentals and lessons, as well as horseback riding options. Your hotel is always the best place to start.

Whale-Watching, Diving & Island Excursions

 Don't let the weather dissuade you, as it is pleasant along the coast even if a bit overcast. And from June through September, whale-watching has gained in popularity along Ecuador's central coast. One major attraction includes whale-watching excursions into the waters near **Puerto López** and **Machalilla National Park**. Here, the journey can produce sightings of protected humpback whales on their migration north from Antarctica. The humpback is a truly graceful species and one that is not shy about being near boats, though you should avoid tour operators that actually chase the whales up close. Many outfitters based in Puerto López offer whale-watching excursions as well as trips to the park's Isla de la Plata for coastal wildlife viewing and snorkeling. Prices for all of these water-based adventures are around US$30 for a full-day excursion. Make sure you check ahead as to what is included, as the national park fee is generally not. A few of these companies also offer diving excursions.

Machalilla Tours, ☎ 5-604-154, Malecón and Julio Zuleta, leads whale-watching and island trips, as well as excursions within the mainland portion of the park. Inquire about their horseback riding as well. **Ecuador Amazing**, also in Puerto López on Córdova, offers the same. Call them in Quito, ☎ 2-2542-888, info@ecuadoramazing.com, www.ecuadoramazing.com. **Manta Ray**, in Puerto López along the Malecón, or waterfront, ☎ 5-604-233, is recommended for whale-watching and island trips, as well as having one of the more comfortable diving vessels in Puerto López (though this isn't saying much). Also for diving, PADI-certified guides will accompany you from **Exploratur**, located in town along the Central Malecón, ☎ 5-604-123. Expect to pay up to $100 for a full day's dive package and be sure to inquire ahead of time.

Other recommended outfitters in the area include **Salangome Travel**, ☎ 5-604-120, in Puerto López, on the main road from the "highway" to the beachfront, for boat trips to Isla de la Plata and Machililla National Park. They charge about $40 per person, including the park entrance fee; or try **Pacarina Travel**, in Puerto López or at Alandaluz, ☎ 5-604-173.

Though not as well developed as in Puerto Lopex, there are also opportunities for whale-watching in **Bahía**, offered through **Guayacamayo-Bahía Tours,** Av. Bolívar 902 and Arenas, ☎ 5-691-107/412, ☎/fax 5-691-280, ecopapel@impsat.net.ec or ecopapel@ecuadorexplorer.com.

Deep-Sea Fishing

Deep-sea fishing trips based in **Salinas** are very popular and highly recommended. Try **Pesca Tours,** ☎ 4-2772-391; or, in Guayaquil ☎ 4-2443-365. They charter boats (gear included) for six to 10 people. The day-long trips cost about $60 per person if you fill the boat. Whale-watching opportunities also exist in Salinas, and during the peak months of December to early May, Salinas is a lively town with plenty of other water-based adventures, including skiing and Jet Skiing. Inquire at the nicer hotels for these activities.

On Wheels

In Bahía, **bicycle** rentals and suggested routes are available through **Guayacamayo-Bahía Tours,** Av. Bolívar 902 and Arenas, ☎ 5-691-107/412, ☎/fax 5-691-280, ecopapel@impsat.net.ec or ecopapel@ecuadorexplorer.com. Biking north from San Vicente toward Canoa is a beautiful way to see the coastline and leave the crowds behind.

In the Air

Paragliding

The small coastal resort of **Crucita** – between Manta and Bahía – offers hang-gliding and paragliding opportunities along the renowned sea cliffs. This area can get crowded, especially during weekends and holidays, but there are plenty of nicer beaches to the north. The sea cliffs, which are a habitat for an abundance of local seabirds, offer wonderful wind-powered activities. Though it is high on my list of things to do, however, I have to admit I have yet to try paragliding myself. North of Bahía, the smaller fishing village of Canoa is also known for paragliding from sea cliffs.

El Niño & Ecuador

El Niño, a term coined by fishermen along Latin America's west coast, means "the little boy," though over the years this force of nature has done far more damage than the name suggests. In fact, it is named after the Christ Child because its intensity tends to peak around Christmas. Rains pick up and persist as waning trade winds and a reversal of surface ocean currents causes the eastern Pacific to warm up well beyond normal. Fishing drops off for reasons other than the rough seas. The cold Humboldt Current that supplies rich nutrients fails to support the normal abundance of marine life, which dies off en masse. Winds and violent tropical storms force everyone inside for days and even weeks on end. Mountainsides wash away, sometimes taking entire villages with them.

This is a reality in Ecuador and Peru, where the last El Niño caused billions of dollars in damage, tossed national economies into turmoil and killed hundreds of people. Force of nature? Yes. Enhanced by human hand? Absolutely!

Research from the National Center for Atmospheric Research supports the fact that this phenomenon is increasing in intensity and duration, while increasing in frequency – now occurring every two to seven years. They suggest global warming is a contributor. Compound this with regional deforestation, which eliminates the earth's natural ability to absorb water, and it becomes all too apparent what the future holds for the coast of Ecuador. The question is, what can we do about it? The obvious answer includes lifestyle choices and supporting moves away from a carbon-based economy. In addition, we can contribute toward re-vegetation and ecotourism like those occurring in Bahía.

■ Eco-Travel

Bahía & the Río Chone Estuary

 Although Bahía has similarities with other urban centers, it has managed to develop in a way that is more benign to the environment. It still has a long way to go, but it is a step ahead of many cities. They are operating with the help of **Planet Drum Foundation**, a San Francisco-based organization dedicated to bio-regionalism, described as "a grassroots approach to ecology that emphasizes sustainability, community self-determination and regional self-reliance." One of the major town projects includes re-vegetating the surrounding land to prevent mudslides, a phenomenon that devastated parts of the town – and indeed entire villages in Ecuador – during the El Niño floods of 1997-98. Other projects include developing alternative energy sources, treating sewage biologically, clean water preservation, and incorporating community and household ecology into the lives of local inhabitants. This is all new, having only begun in 1999, so it will take time before success can be measured. In the meantime, though, you can help by donating time or money, or simply start by visiting their website at www.planetdrum.org.

There are many other destinations around Bahía that are also nature-oriented and/or operated in conjunction with these "sustainable" efforts. The **Río Chone estuary** offers one example of a delicate balance between ecotourism and the community's traditional shrimp farming. Ecotourism provides local income while maintaining ecological integrity. Shrimp farming, on the other hand, benefits mainly foreigners, while desecrating the local environment. You can visit the Río Chone estuary by boat and experience the mangrove forests and marine life. Nearby islands include **Isla de Fragatas**, where the magnificent frigate bird resides, and **Isla Corazón**, which has a newly built boardwalk for visitors.

Bahía Tour Operators

For local excursions, inquire with **Bahía Dolphin Tours,** Av. Bolívar 1004 and Riofrío, ☎ 5-692-097, ☎/fax 5-692-088), for trips to **Chirije**, a unique and historically important archeological site in the vicinity. They also offer trips to native villages farther inland. Another option is **Guayacamayo-Bahía Tours**, Av. Bolívar 902 and Arenas, ☎ 5-691-107/412, ☎/fax 5-691-280, ecopapel@impsat.net.ec or ecopapel@ecuadorexplorer.com. They offer local programs and donate proceeds to support community efforts. Ask about their island trips to see nesting seabird colonies, the organic shrimp farm, as well as whale-watching and horseback trekking. Bikes are also available. Another Bahía-based tour operator is **El Ceibos**, at Av. Bolívar 200 and Calle Checa, ☎/fax 5-690-801, mobile 9-714-7340, ceibos@hotmail.com, www.geocities.com/etours_ecuador. Although I am not familiar with them, their code of ethics is to support local efforts.

South of Bahía less than an hour is **Chirije** (chee-ree-hey), one of the newest and nicer eco-archeological parks along the coast. In addition to miles of untouched beaches, there are 588 acres of tropical dry forest with trails for hiking, birding and horseback riding, as well as archeological excavations of pre-Incan culture and an on-site museum. East along the Río Chone is the city of **Chone** and the nearby wetland known as **Ciénega de la Segua**, with prolific birdlife. Heading north, across the Río Chone from Bahía, just over 10 miles from San Vicente along pristine beach, is **Canoa**. In addition to great surfing, there are other community efforts worth visiting in the area. In fact, you could easily spend weeks around Bahía having a blast.

Machalilla National Park

Heading south from Manta or Portoviejo, the main road through the small city of Jipijapa continues on to Guayaquil or west back to the coast near Machalilla National Park and Puerto López. The park is unique in Ecuador because it is the only coastal national park and because of the habitats it protects, including rocky coastline, sandy beaches, scrub vegetation, and tropical dry forest, as well as cloud forest habitat, archeological remains, and an area off the coast that encompasses Isla de la Plata. Overall, the park covers about 138,000 acres on land and water.

Primary access into the park is from the south on the coastal road, or via the road from Jipijapa to the northeast. Most foreign travelers enter from the south, from the eco-resort, Alandaluz, or one of the beachfront communities farther south. The park entrance fee is $20, which provides a pass to reenter for several days. This is ideal – and necessary – if you want to explore the mainland and participate in offshore activities such as whale-watching or visiting Isla de la Plata. You can pay the entrance fee at the entrance station a few miles north of town or at the park headquarters in Puerto López, where there is also a small but informative museum.

One park highlight is at the **Los Frailes** beach area. To reach it takes a good hike through tropical dry scrubland, which keeps many people away, but those who make the trek have one of the nicest beaches around all to themselves. From the main road through the park, inquire about the pullout or ask the bus driver to drop you off at the trailhead. It may not look like much more than a coastal desert at first (bring plenty of water), but the trail soon meets coastal cliffs, nesting seabirds and lovely sandy beaches. Intermittent rocky areas provide tidal pools and good snorkeling opportunities.

Tours of **Isla de la Plata** are arranged in Puerto López or Alandaluz. The island is home to a unique combination of life zones. Flora and fauna similar to those found in the Galápagos are mixed with plants and animals from the mainland. Nesting seabird colonies, including those of the giant waved albatross, blue- and red-footed boobies, gulls, pelicans, and terns, are major attractions. An added bonus is the presence of several species of whales and dolphins from mid-June to October. Snorkeling is also available along a few coral reefs. See *Adventures* section, page 288, for tour operators or inquire at Alandaluz Ecocultural Center, below.

Agua Blanca & San Sebastián

Within the Machalilla National Park is the small town of Agua Blanca and the starting point for trips to San Sebastián. Agua Blanca offers a small but intriguing museum that showcases local pre-Columbian culture. About six miles farther inland and up in elevation is the cloud forest community of San Sebastián, with a community-based ecotourism project added in recent years. A few miles north of Puerto López on the road to Machalilla is a signpost marking the turnout east to Agua Blanca. Inquire at the tourist office in Puerto López or Machalilla Park entrance, or at Alandaluz Ecocultural Center for arrangements.

☆ Alandaluz Ecocultural Tourist Center

Hostería Alandaluz offers a world-class ecolodge right on the beach (see *Where to Stay*, page 296) and provides ecological and nature-oriented ventures into the region. Here, swimming, hiking and local tours into Machalilla and Isla de La Plata are popular. Alandaluz has worked to promote local environmental education, recycling, and community-based ecotourism efforts. Tour packages can now be arranged for visitors to local natural destinations and communities.

Alandaluz is between Puerto López and Montanito, just south of the village of Puerto Rico, ☎ 5-604-173. Arrangements can be made in Quito, ☎ 2-2543-042, ☎/fax 2-2525-671, travel@amingay.ecx.ec.

Loma Alta Cloud Forest Reserve

The Loma Alta Cloud Forest Reserve is one of Ecuador's only community-created, legally protected bioreserves. See page 285 for a full description of the project.

Valdivia

South of Puerto López, about half-way to Salinas, is Valdivia, named after the country's earliest known pre-Columbian inhabitants. There is a small museum here with remains and interpretive displays of the Valdivian culture, as well as an ecolodge. Othewise, this is a relatively uneventful place to visit.

■ Where to Stay

ACCOMMODATIONS PRICE SCALE	
Unless otherwise noted, prices are per room, up to double occupancy. Some prices are per person, particularly with all-inclusive packages, but these generally include meals, lodging, guide services and other amenities.	
$	Under $25
$$	$26 to $50
$$$	$51 to $100
$$$$	Over $100

Bahía

 Vacationing highlanders flood Bahía on holidays and during their "summer" weekends. The influx of people creates distinct peak-season accommodations prices. Finding the right place – at the right price – is usually just a matter of wandering around a bit.

Hotel Palma, Av. Bolívar 914 and Riofrío, ☎ 5-690-467, is the budget travelers' choice. Aside from its inexpensive and popular restaurant, however, the hotel is bare. Rooms vary in quality; some include shared or private baths and fans. $

A better alternative is the comfortable, friendly, and affordable **Bahía Bed and Breakfast**, Ascázubi 322 and Morales, ☎ 5-690-146. Rooms with private baths and hot water are more than adequate for budget travelers. Breakfast is included and the family and dining rooms are cozy. $

Hotel Italia, Av. Bolívar and Calle Choca, ☎ 5-691-446/137, ☎/fax 5-691-092, close to the center of town and across from the children's park, is modern and relatively fancy. It's also one of the best accommodations available downtown. The small but pleasant rooms are clean and comfortable, and the restaurant serves up a great selection of affordable food. $

For a big step up, head north of downtown along the beach to **Hotel La Herradura**, Av. Bolívar and Hidalgo, ☎ 5-690-446, ☎/fax 5-690-265. The owner and staff are friendly and the rooms are clean and interestingly decorated. The hotel's location is more appealing than that of hotels in the city center, and the restaurant is fantastic. $$$

Even more upscale is the **Hotel La Piedra**, north along the beach at the end of Av. Bolívar, ☎ 5-690-446/780, ☎/fax 5-690-154. Located right on the water, the hotel enjoys a Pacific view and direct access to the beach. Large, modern rooms are comfortable, spacious, air-conditioned, and include private hot-water baths. A poolside patio, bars, and an international restaurant help make La Piedra feel like an upscale resort. $$$

North along the coast, in Canoa, where the beaches and sea sports are plentiful, try **Bambu**, on the beach, ☎ 9-753-696, for one of the better budget choices. $. Or **Hostería Canoa**, just south of town, with private baths, nice atmosphere and a popular restaurant. $.

Manta

Hotel Oro Verde, beachside, along the Malecón and Calle 23, ☎ 5-629-200, ☎/fax 5-629-210, is part of the luxury chain and is the best in Manta. For a full description of modern amenities, visit their website at www.oroverdehotels.com and search for Manta. $$$

For comfortable, modern cabañas, visit **Cabañas Balandra**, northwest of town on Av. 8 and C20, ☎ 5-620-316, ☎/fax 5-620-545. This is a nice, safe retreat away from the busy nightlife of the Malecón. All modern amenities make this a great choice for groups. $$$

In the southeastern suburb of Tarquí, your best bet is **Hotel Las Gaviotas**, on the Malecón and C106, ☎ 5-620-140. It is adequate, but you are better off in the northern suburb of Manta near Murciélago Beach. $$

Portoviejo

If you're staying in Portoviejo, the best value is the **Hotel Conquistador**, at 18 de Octubre and 10 de Agosto, ☎ 5-631-678. Rooms with private hot-water baths, TV, telephone and air-conditioning. $-$+

Other reportedly good choices in the budget category include **El Gato**, Pedro Gual and 9 de Octubre, ☎ 3-3636-906, and **New York**, at Olmedo and Moreira, ☎ 3-3632-044. $

At the high end is **El Ejecutivo**, across the street at 18 de Octubre and 10 de Agosto, ☎ 3-3632-105, fax 3-3630-876. It's nice and modern. $$$

Puerto López

Puerto López is pleasant town, but there aren't a lot of good lodging choices. One of the best is the inexpensive but nice **La Terraza**, just north of the downtown part of the Malecón, and up on the hill overlooking the port, ☎ 5-604-235. There are rewarding views, peaceful comfort and great meals. $

In the next-to-nothing price range, and very popular among budget travelers, is **Los Islotes**, at Malecón and Córdova, ☎ 5-604-108. Choose from private or shared baths in a relatively nice hotel for the price. Call ahead. $

There are other decent places to stay in Puerto López. Check around in the main downtown area near the Malecón.

Just south of the village of Ayampe is **Hotel Atamari**, Ayampe, ☎ 4-2780-430, or in Quito at ☎ 2-2228-470, fax 2-2234-075, atamari@goecuador.com. Here you will find all the comforts of a luxury hotel, complete with spectacular views of the ocean and Ayampe Bay. There is also an acclaimed restaurant and a nice bar, pool and all of the extras. If you are traveling here from Puerto López by bus, keep in mind that Ayampe is a 15-minute walk from the main highway. Highly recommended. $$$

☆ **Alandaluz Ecocultural Tourist Center** and its Hostería Alandaluz, located between Puerto López and Montañita (just south of the village of Puerto Rico), ☎ 5-604-173, is a world-class ecolodge right on the beach. Arrangements can be be made in Quito, ☎ 2-2543-042, ☎/fax 2-2525-671, travel@amingay.ecx.ec, or through various local travel agencies. Alandaluz, which translates as "winged city of light," is built with traditional architecture and sustainable natural materials to provide a relaxing atmosphere and plenty of comfort. Rooms and cabins vary in style, size, and amenities, depending on your interest. Some have ocean views from under a thatched roof on the second floor and others offer intimate cabaña-style accommodations. All are rustic and simple, but comfortable. The open-air common room and bar is conducive to meeting people and making new friends, and the cozy restaurant offers great seafood, vegetarian, and other cuisines. Some of the lodging includes shared bathrooms with biodigesting toilets. A unique setup, Alandaluz was the first of its kind to offer a relatively self-sustaining and sustainable ecolodge. $$

Alandaluz is only a stone's throw from the beach, where lounging is often a major part of any day's itinerary. Swimming in the Pacific and hiking or signing up for a local tour of Isla de la Plata are also popular. Note that the current here can be very strong, so be careful. Alandaluz has worked to promote local environmental education, recycling, and community-based ecotourism efforts. Tour packages can now be arranged to local attractions through an on-site travel agency. A new program based in Quito through the Green Life Spanish Center also offers a Spanish Study program that combines staying at Alandaluz with local excursions into Machalilla National Park. You can view the program at www.vidaverde.com/coast.asp.

Montañita/Manglaralto

Nearby, the town of Montañita has become popular with young foreign travelers searching for *la playa*. To accommodate their needs, a number of cabañas and beachside accommodations have sprung up in recent years. Several informal bungalows are easy to find adjacent to the beach. Check around for one with an ambiance that appeals to you.

El Centro del Mundo, a very popular budget hostel in Quito, added an enormous lodge right here on the south coast. You can't miss it, situated as it is right on the waterfront. If you're looking for a relaxing place to hang out, party, and meet people, this is it. Rooms vary from dorms with shared baths to private doubles. Inquire at El Centro del Mundo in Quito, Lizardo García 569 and Reina Victorian, ☎ 2-2229-050 $.

Just north of the village on the beach is **Hotel Montañita**, ☎ 4-2901-296, ☎/fax 4-2901-299, hmontani@telconet.net, offering budget comforts, including Internet service, laundry, and a beachside restaurant. $.

For the ultimate surfer's party cabaña, check out **La Casa del Sol**, casasol@ecua.net.ec or rjhood21@hotmail.com, www.casasol.com. Randy Hood, a California surfer who landed here in 1990, now helps to provide surfing support from Casa del Sol and offers one of the coast's self-proclaimed best beach parties. His goal was to create "an integrated travelers' (surfers') hostel – clean, cool and inexpensive enough for the budget traveler," now complete with restaurant, bar, evening entertainment and an Internet connection. Local surfing and whale-watching excursions are also available. $

A complete jump up in quality and price is **Hotel Baja Montañita**, ☎ 4-2901-218, ☎/fax 4-2901-227, in Baja Montañita, along the northern bluffs. Amenities abound in this breezy cliffside resort, including a poolside bar, hot tub, restaurant, and a bar on the beach. $-$$

A mile south of Montañita near the beach, in Manglaralto, is **Hostería MaraKaya**, just off the plaza across from the fire station, ☎ 4-2901-294. This simple but very clean and comfortable hotel has private baths, hot water, mosquito netting and a/c or fans. It has been the home base for Earthwatch Expeditions, which offers trips into the Loma Alta Cloud Forest (see page 285). Speak with Marlene here; she can help organize trips into the forest. Rooms are under $5 per person. $

Salinas

Rooms in Salinas are generally overpriced, even during the off-season. There are no budget accommodations in the town worth recommending; the better places are generally west of Salinas along the peninsula and adjacent to La Libertad (to the east). The **Hotel El Curruaje** (Malecón 517, ☎ 4-2774-282) has a great restaurant and comfortable rooms with views of the ocean. It's very easy to relax here. The hotel's small size, modern rooms, and nice atmosphere make it a popular high-season choice. Check ahead for availability. $$-$$$

On the east end of town, **Hotel Miramar**, Malecón at Calle 39, ☎ 4-2772-115, is a modern, full-service establishment with all the extras. The swimming pool, bars, restaurant, and casino are perfect for the out-of-town location, and rooms come with private baths and air-conditioning. $$$$

Valdivia

The **Valdivia Ecolodge** is in Valdivia along the highway Vía Sta. Elena – Manglaralto, Km 40, ☎ 4-2687-046, valdiviaecolodge@ hotmail.com. It offers beachside cabañas that I can't personally vouch for, but they seem to be the only decent lodging. If you are here, you are probably visiting the archeological museum, with artifacts of this pre-Columbian culture. $$

Salinas/La Libertad

Just west of La Libertad is the modern **Hotel Valdivia**, Urbanización Costa de Oro Fase III, Av. Este, ☎/fax 4-2775-144. Rooms include mini-fridges and balconies that overlook the swimming pool patio. Family apartments are great for larger groups. $$

Nearby is the **Hotel Samarina**, Av. 9 de Octubre and Malecón, ☎ 4-2735-167, ☎/fax 4-2784-1000. Pricey but nice, the Samarina is located on the waterfront (rarely a beach here). Clean and pleasant rooms overlook the ocean or pool area and include mini-bars, TVs, telephones, private hot-water baths, and, in a few cases, air-conditioning. Separate family-style bungalows are the best deals. $$

At the high end in Salinas is **Hotel Casino Calypso**, located on the Malecón next to Capitanía del Puerto, ☎ 4-2773-605, ☎/fax 4-2773-583, calypso@goecuador.com, www.goecuador.com/calypsso/html/hotel.html. It offers full service and standard hotel amenities. This is a 13-floor high-rise luxury hotel, with spacious and comfortable rooms, kitchenettes, private baths and picturesque views of the bay. There is a small outdoor swimming pool, casino and the pleasant **Alta Mar restaurant**, which serves fresh seafood daily. $$$

At a more modest level is **El Carruaje**, Malecón 517, ☎ 4-2774-282, ☎/fax 4-2774-282. Prices here are a bit lower. Rooms have TV and air-conditioning. $$-$$$

In the mid-range, but still modern, is **Suites Salinas**, at Calle 27 and Gen. Enriques Gallo, ☎ 4-2772-759, ☎/fax 4-2772-993, hotelsalinas@porta.net. They have air-conditioning, cable TV, pool, restaurant and a disco. $$

If you're on a budget, the **Yulee**, on Gen. Enriquez Gallo and C 14, near the beach, ☎ 4-2772-028, has been recommended as a good value. They have comfortable rooms in the colorful renovated home, with a pleasant courtyard. $

Punta Carnero

This is just south of La Libertad, with a beach and a hotel of the same name. Although this area is popular with locals during the high season, you can find vacant beaches and excellent whale-watching opportunities during Western summer months. The hotel, on the beach about five miles south of La Libertad, offers seaside comfort with a view. ☎ 4-2775-450, www.hotelpuntacarnero.com. $$-$$$

Camping

Camping is available in **Machalilla National Park**. When you enter the park, ask at the administrative office about designated areas. For tour-operator supported camping and guided excursions into the park, contact **Sercapez**, ☎ 5-604-173, in Puerto López on Córdova. The **Alandaluz Ecolodge** also offers camping spaces at lower rates than the cabañas. If you are camping, but like the amenities of a comfortable eco-resort, including fabulous meals, a nice bar, a common lounge area, and access to a tranquil beach, then this is by far the best place to camp.

■ Where to Eat

Bahía

The best restaurants in Bahía are located in **La Herradura** and **La Piedra Hotels** (see page 295). Both offer a delicious selection of seafood and international cuisine. While they're a bit expensive by Ecuadorian standards, the food is worth every penny.

Another option is to explore along the edge of the Río Chone near the ferry docks, where you'll find several good and inexpensive seafood establishments. These breezy, open-air restaurants always include world-class views and are great places to participate in the nation's coastal pastime – that is, relaxing and watching the world float by.

If seafood isn't your style, you can always succumb to Chinese food at the cheap and cheerful **Chifa China**, midtown on Bolívar. Or, try Italian food at the popular pizzeria **Donatella's**, on Calle Alberto Santos in the southern part of town. It's open every day for lunch and dinner. The pasta and pizzas here vary from good to delicious, depending on how long you've been on a seafood diet.

Tarquí & Murcielago

There are several open-air seafood options along the waterfront in Tarquí, south of the fishing harbor. To the north, closer to Playa Marcielago, quick, cheap and inexpensive seafood cafés also line the Malecón. Otherwise, try **Chifa Popular**, on Av. 109 and 4 de Noviembre in Tarquí, for a quick Chinese food fix. **Pizzeria Topi**, north toward Playa Murcielago at Calle 15 and the Malecón, is a popular pizza and Italian food place. **El Ejecutivo**, Av. 2 and Calle 12, top floor, is probably the best restaurant in town. Excellent international dishes – including non-seafood choices – as well as a great view and reasonable prices make this a top choice.

Puerto López

There are a couple of obvious beachfront options for snacking and full meals throughout the day.

Salinas

Salinas also has easy-to-find seaside eateries, with the nicer restaurants being in the higher-end hotels. On the waterfront, try **Mar y Tierra** for some of the best seafood around. Cheaper and just about as good is **Flipper**, a couple of blocks away. The local market will also have good, fresh and cheap seafood options.

Guayaquil & Vicinity

Guayaquil is a fun-loving, money-making land of coastal plantations and international trade. The climate here is hot and humid, almost unbearably so at times of the year, which would lead you to believe that everyone moves at a slower pace. On the contrary, this is the business capital of the country and home to nearly 3½ million citizens. The people are great, but they are either incredibly rich or extremely poor, and the latter group is growing rapidly. Spend a day or two here, check out the sites, and chat with the locals. It's worth the effort.

The city of Guayaquil does not make my top-10 list of best places to visit in Ecuador (or top 50 for that matter), but I'm not a fan of large urban areas. And proponents of this coastal capital swear by the friendliness of its inhabitants. The city serves as a major international gateway into the country and to the region's natural attractions. Guayaquil is the living force behind half of Ecuador. Located at the convergence of the Ríos Daule and Babahoyo, just 41 miles from the Pacific Ocean, it is so different from Quito and the Sierras as to seem part of an entirely different country.

The surrounding region offers plenty of underrated natural destinations and adventures for the avid travelers, especially along the coast and into the western slopes.

Guayaquil & Vicinity

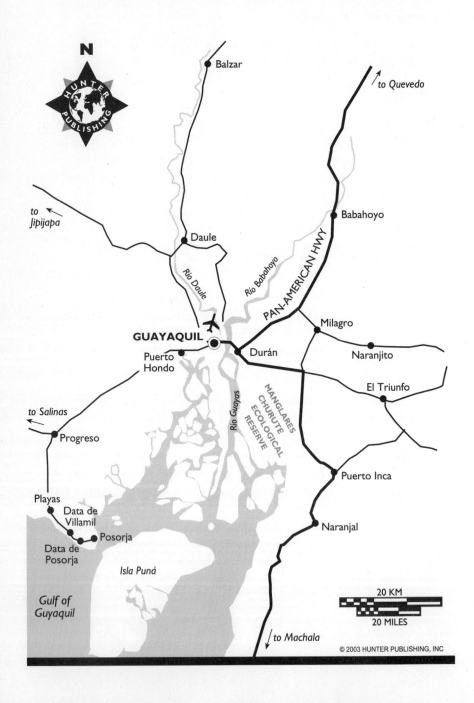

N
HUNTER PUBLISHING

Balzar

to Quevedo

to Jipijapa

Babahoyo

Daule

Río Daule

Río Babahoyo

PAN-AMERICAN HWY

Milagro

GUAYAQUIL

Puerto Hondo

Durán

Naranjito

El Triunfo

MANGLARES CHURUTE ECOLOGICAL RESERVE

Río Guayas

to Salinas

Progreso

Puerto Inca

Playas

Data de Villamil

Naranjal

Posorja

Data de Posorja

Isla Puná

Gulf of Guayaquil

20 KM

20 MILES

to Machala

© 2003 HUNTER PUBLISHING, INC

Central & South Coast

South of Guayaquil is **Machalá**, the capital of El Oro province and home to a half-million people. This isn't a particularly attractive destination itself, though there are possible coastal excursions from here. The main activity in this region is agricultural, primarily banana plantations, as well as shrimp farming and export. For the most part, Machalá is stopping point on the way to Peru.

■ History

Though coastal natives fought well and resisted the earliest **Spaniards**, they fell to Francisco Orellana and Guayaquil was founded in 1547. In fact, the city was named after the last Indian chief, Guayas, and his wife, Quil, who committed suicide rather than submit to the Spanish, which was an assured death anyway. Developed as a port city and built around cocoa, bananas, and other exports, Guayaquil – even during the colonial era – maintained more contact with the outside world than other cities. Since the mid-19th century it has been the liberal political and economic powerhouse behind coastal Ecuador. As the colonial bureaucrats in Quito lost power, Guayaquil was already coming into its own as a major international export and trade center. Leaders from Guayaquil were the voices of liberation for the country and joined forces with freedom fighters from neighboring countries. Ever since, opposing socio-economic and political perspectives have forced Quito and Guayaquil into conflict. Today, Guayaquil boasts the largest urban population in the country and, arguably, the greatest economic power.

■ Flora & Fauna

Although Guayaquil is very much an urban center, a few small reserves around the city offer examples of native vegetation common to this area. Just south around Machalá is the region's largest intact mangrove forest, while a short distance away in the opposite direction is Cerro Blanco with a reserve of tropical dryland forest. Continuing north along the coast and inland, in the Chongón Colonche Mountains, are some of the country's healthiest cloud forests, complete with a mind-blowing array of birds, as well as howler monkeys and predatory cats (see pages 284-85).

■ Getting Here

By Air

Guayaquil offers the only major international airport outside of Quito. The **Simon Bolívar Airport** is a few miles north of downtown along Avenida de las Américas. International flights into Guayaquil are actually less expensive than those into Quito, making it a good place to enter the country if you plan to visit the south coast. The domestic airport is adjacent to the international terminal. Numerous daily flights arrive from and depart to all major destinations within Ecuador, including the Galápagos Islands. In fact, flights to the Galápagos are generally cheaper from here than from in Quito. (All Galápagos flights originating in the capital fly through Guayaquil first.) **TAME** has an office on 9 de Octubre 424, ☎ 4-2560-728. Other airlines have offices at the airport. **American Airlines** is also at Gral Córdova and 9 de Octubre on the 20th floors of Edificio San Francisco, ☎ 4-2564-111. **Continental** is on the Malecón at 9 de Octubre, ☎ 4-2567-241, as is **Iberia**, ☎ 4-2320-664. **KLM** is at the airport and **AeroPeru** is on the 8th floor at Chile 329 and Aguirre, ☎ 4-2513-691.

By Bus

The modern bus terminal is just north of the airport. Bus services are quite efficient, with constant departures and hordes of buses heading in all directions. Just look around and you'll find the bus you need.

■ Getting Around

Downtown Guayaquil lies along the west bank of the Río Guayas and is organized in a grid pattern, with streets running north-south and east-west. The Malecón along the waterfront is a long walkway and a good point from which to get oriented, while Avenida 9 de Octubre is the major east-west thoroughfare. The main downtown area is straightforward and easy to get around. The airport is a few miles north of downtown, and the bus terminal is another mile or so beyond that. Across the river on the east bank, in the suburb of Durán, is the railway station.

Central & South Coast

Taxis

Taxis from the airport into downtown usually cost less than $4. From downtown, it should cost no more than a couple of dollars to go anywhere in the town, other than perhaps to the more affluent suburbs where the better restaurants and nightlife are located. If you consider traffic, it's just as easy to walk to most places in and around the downtown area as it is to drive, although taxis are recommended at night, for safety.

Car Rental

As in Quito, most major international car-rental agencies and a few local ones are available. The easiest place to find a rental car is at the airport, where there are numerous agencies. Prices range from $25 to over $100 per day, depending on the vehicle and duration of rental. Better rates are given for weekly and monthly rentals. If you'll be heading into the backcountry, be sure to rent a four-wheel-drive vehicle. Also, make sure that insurance and mileage are included in the rental fee. Do a complete vehicle inspection ahead of time and note any problems. Check the spare and jack, as flats are common.

Car-Rental Agencies

There are competitive rental agencies at the airport, in addition to those listed here.

Arrancar, Av. de Las Américas, ☎ 4-2283-473; airport, ☎ 4-2288-179 or 4-2286-279.

Avis, Av. de Las Américas, ☎ 4-2285-498; airport, ☎ 4-2287-906.

Budget, Av. de las Américas 900 and Calle Norte, ☎ 4-2394-314 or 4-2284-559; airport, ☎ 4-2288-510.

Ecuacar, airport, ☎ 4-2283-247.

Hertz, Hotel Oro Verde, 9 de Octubre and Moreno, ☎ 4-2327-895 or 4-2327-999 and at the airport.

Central Guayaquil

N

HUNTER PUBLISHING

to Las Peñas

✝ Cemetery

Coronel

Artisans' Market

J. Montalvo

Rocafuerte

Loja

Panamá

to airport,
bus terminal,
Urdessa & Durán

V. Piedrahita

Padre Aguirre

Ferry
to Durán

Galecio

Martinez

Lascano

Mendiburo

Imbabura

Padre Solano

Orellana

Cordova

Urdaneta

Pier 4

Quisquis

Roca

Pier 5

Junín

VM Rendón

Río Guayas

Parque
Central

Paula de Icaza

Plaza de
La Merced

⑲
①
⑱

9 de Octubre

③

②

⑩

Vélez

④

⑳

La Rotunda

P. Moncayo

⑪

Garaicoa

Rumichaca

Avilés

Luque

Boyacá

⑬
⑫

Escobedo

Chimborazo

Chile

Plaza de
San Francisco

P. Carbo

Pichincha

Malecón Simón Bolívar

6 de Mayo

Aguirre

㉑

Montúfar

Ballén

Parque
Bolívar

⑨ ㉒

⑰ Port Captain

⑤

⑥

⑧

㉓

10 de Agosto

⑦

㉔

Clock Tower

Sucre

㉕

⑭

Colón

⑮⑯

to La Bahía Mercado &
Mercado Sur

200 YARDS

200 METERS

© 2003 HUNTER PUBLISHING, INC

⊠ WHERE TO STAY

1. Hotel Oro Verde
2. Hotel Metropolitana
3. Hotel Boulevard
4. Hotel Palace
5. Hotel Delicia
6. Grand Hotel Guayaquil
7. Hotel Continental
8. Hotel Rizzo
9. The Plaza

👨‍🍳 WHERE TO EAT

10. El Pirata Restaurant
11. Restaurant Vegetariano
    Salud Solar
12. La Palma Café
13. Cyrano Café
14. Chifa Mayflower
15. Chifa Himalaya
16. Gran Chifa
17. Yacht Club

● OTHER SITES

18. US Embassy,
    Museo de Arqueología
19. Casa de Cultura
20. Banco del Pacifico & Museum
21. Tourist Office
22. Post Office/Telephone Office
23. Palacio de Gobierno
24. Palacio Municipal
25. Museo Municipal & Library

■ Visitor Information

Guayaquil

The **Ministerio de Turismo** office is located on Ycaza 203 and Pichincha, ☎ 4-2568-764; and at the airport. Travel agents in town offer useful information as well.

The **Pacífictel communications** office, ☎ 4-2560-200, is located on P. Carbo and Aguirre. The **post office**, ☎ 4-2531-713 or 4-2514-710, is in the same building. **Internet services** are available in the better hotels and some shopping malls.

There is a tourism website for Guayaquil at www.turismoguayas.com.

The **US Embassy** is on 9 de Octubre and García Moreno, ☎ 4-2323-570, ☎/fax 4-2325-286. (See the *Appendix* for locations of other foreign embassies.) The **Ministerio del Ambiente** (Ministry of the Environment) office, where you can obtain permission to visit the **Manglares Churute Ecological Reserve**, is on Av. Quito 402 and P. Solano, 10th floor, ☎ 4-2397-730.

A few of the major banks have **ATMs** that accept credit cards. All are conveniently visible in the downtown waterfront area and keep regular hours. The high-end hotels offer money services, such as accepting credit cards and changing travelers checks. They also often provide business/communication services after hours.

Unfortunately, Guayaquil is not the safest city for the foreign traveler. Pickpockets and thieves abound, particularly in the poorer suburbs. Avoid wandering around at night and always leave valuables at the hotel or keep them well hidden.

Machalá

The **Pacífictel communications** office is on Av. Las Palmeras near the stadium and the **post office** is at Bolívar and Montalvo. There is an **Internet café** on Pichincha and 9 de Mayo. The **Banco de Guayaquil** at Rocafuerte and Guayas accepts Visa. **Banco del Pacífico** is at Rocafuerte and Junín, for MasterCard and changing travelers checks.

■ Touring & Sightseeing

Guayaquil City

 Once relatively dilapidated and neglected by Quito bureaucrats that ran the country, much of downtown Guyaquil has been renovated to reflect the cosmopolitan city that it has become, including an urban renewal project along the Malecón in 2000. As such, a walk through the downtown and waterfront areas can be a pleasant way to spend some time in the city. It can take anywhere from a couple of hours to all day, depending on your interests. There are plenty of sights and places to visit, or just to get out and walk around. The best time to go is early in the morning and during weekends, although museums are closed on Sundays. From January to April is the hot, humid and rainy "summer" here (when locals escape to the coast in the north on weekends and holidays). June through December is the cooler, foggier but drier time of the year. May is a transition month.

Most visitors stay at one of the hotels in the downtown area near the centrally located **Parque Bolívar** (officially Parque Seminario), at Calles 10 de Agosto and Chile. You can't miss the park, banked on the west side by a cathedral and surrounded by an enormous iron fence. The attractive gardens, giant shady trees, and seemingly out-of-place land iguanas make it a great place to relax, people-watch, and absorb the surroundings.

Facing the west side of Parque Bolívar is the city **cathedral**. It's on a site that dates back to 1547, but the building itself is barely 50 years old. The original wooden structure burned down and has been rebuilt. The church is quite pleasant, built in a simple but modern fashion with white interior walls and high stained-glass windows.

Just south of the park, on Sucre and Pedro Carbo, is the **Museo Municipal** (Mon-Fri, 9-5, ☎ 4-2516-391, weekends, 10-1), home of the city's library and museum. Displays include archeological, anthropological, and colonial exhibits, as well as changing modern-art shows.

Heading east on 10 de Agosto, turn right at Calle Chile and go south about four blocks until you reach Olmedo. A left on Olmedo provides the opportunity to explore the **market district** of Mercado Bahía and Mercado Sur. Take your time and enjoy the sights, but watch your belongings in these thief-infested market areas.

Continuing toward the waterfront, Olmedo meets the south end of the Malecón Simon Bolívar and a giant statue of **José Joaquin Olmedo Maruri**, a famous Guayaquil politician and poet. From here, enjoy a walk along the waterfront on the Malecón, which offers shady trees, park benches, and views of all the activity along the river.

Heading north, the next landmark is the Moorish-style **clock tower** (you are now back at the crossroad of Calle 10 de Agosto). The **Palacio Municipal** is the gaudy gray building across the street, filled with government offices. Next to it, adjacent to the **Palacio de Gobierno** (Governor's Palace), is a small plaza with a statue. A few blocks beyond the Governor's Palace along the Malecón is the famous *La Rotunda* statue. The scene commemorates the meeting in 1822 of two great Latin American liberators, Simon Bolívar and José San Martín.

Bolívar was the Venezuelan general who liberated Ecuador, Colombia, and Venezuela from Spanish rule, while Martín freed Argentina and defeated the Spanish as far north as Peru. With different political ideologies, Bolívar continued his efforts in Bolivia and Martín returned to Argentina, later to be exiled to France.

North of *La Rotunda* is a **waterfront area** where several docked barges serve as bars and restaurants. They are great places to relax and have a drink. Try **El Pirata**, just a few blocks north of *La Rotunda*; it has inside seating or the shaded upper deck.

Additional barges are moored along the piers to the north, and beyond the pier for the Durán ferry is the colonial district of **Las Peñas**. Well worth a visit, this part of town is also the stomping grounds of many pickpockets and thieves. At the end of the Malecón are the **Plaza Colón** and the historic **Calleñuma Pompillo Llona**.

From here, the energetic can head southwest along Calle Julian Coronel to the **Church of Santo Domingo**, the oldest church in Ecuador. Farther along is the entrance to the magnificent **General Cemetery**, worth a separate trip by taxi if you're too tired for the long walk. Southwest of Las Peñas, surrounded by Calles Loja, J. Montalva, and Avenidas Baquerizo and Córdova, is the famous **Artisan Market**. You could spend hours here browsing and shopping at the various arts and crafts shops.

From Las Peñas, head back south down Calle Rocafuerte toward the hub of downtown. After passing the **Church of La Merced** and its attractive plaza (Rocafuerte and Rendon), you'll arrive at the **Museo Arqueologico del Banco del Pacífico** (P. de Icaza 113, ☎ 4-2328-333, Mon-Fri, 10-6, and odd hours on weekends). Stop in at this enormous bank and head upstairs to the first-rate museum. Powerful displays include archeological remains from throughout the human history of Ecuador. Modern-art displays change regularly. Free.

Back outside, take a right on Av. 9 de Octubre and continue several blocks to the **Parque Centenario**, a plaza that encompasses four square blocks and includes numerous monuments. (Alternatively, after you pass Av. 9 de Octubre, come to the **Church of San Francisco** and its adjoining plaza, then continue south down Calle Chile and back to the beginning of the walk at Parque Bolívar.) **Casa de Cultura** (at the west juncture of the park and 9 de Octubre, Tue-Fri, 10-5, Sat, 10-3), offers a small archeological museum and cultural events such as foreign films at the cinema, lectures, classes, and art shows. The museum is the best in the region, with modern-art displays as well as a collection of interesting ceremonial masks and artifacts. Three blocks west on 9 de Octubre is the **Banco Central's Anthropological Museum** (José de Anteparra 900, ☎ 4-2320-576, Mon-Fri, 10-6, Sat, 9-2). From here, retrace your steps back down 9 de Octubre to Rocofuerte, or make your way southwest until you reach 10 de Agosto. Turn left and walk back toward the waterfront area until you get to Parque Bolívar. You made it!

If you just want to sightsee in the city, one of your best options is simply to hire a taxi and ask the driver to show you around. General travel agents can also provide these services with English-speaking guides, who can offer more insight into what you are experiencing. Try **Ecuadorian Tours**, ☎ 4-2287-111, ☎/fax 4-2280-851, at 9 de Octubre 1900, or **Delgado Travel**, ☎ 4-2560-680, at 9 de Octubre and Córdova, for general services. **Viajes Horizontez** is another recommended guide service, located at P Solano 1502 and Mascote, ☎ 4-2281-260. For day-trips just out of Guayaquil, it is easy to catch a bus to many destinations.

Metropolitan Tours, ☎ 4-2330-300, fax 4-323-050, at 9 de Octubre and Antepara, www.metropolitan-touring.com, offers excursions from the city, as well as trips to the Galápagos Islands in the middle-to luxury-class range. For more economic boats, try **Economic Galápagos Tours**, ☎ 4-2312-447, ☎/fax 4-2313-351, at 9 de Octubre and Córdova.

Whale Tours, at Vélez 911 and 6 de Marzo, 5th floor, ☎ 4-2524-608, offers recommended whale-watching tours, though you're just as well arranging it in Puerto López (see *Puerto López*, page 281).

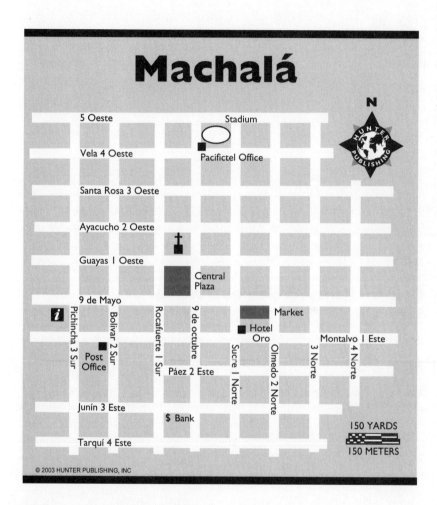

Peru via Machalá

Heading south from Guayaquil is the provincial and banana capital of Machalá, with over half a million residents. It is not particularly wonderful as a destination itself, but can be a good stopover point en route to Peru. There are a couple of routes to the border from Machalá, either through Haquillas or farther south via Macará, the latter of which is the main crossing from Loja in the Andes.

Central & South Coast

■ Eco-Travel

Guayaquil Botanical Gardens

 The *jardín botánico* is the closest nature retreat to downtown Guayaquil. With 12½ acres abutting a privately owned forested area, the botanical gardens are a great place to get away, relax, and learn about Ecuador's rich plant life. The gardens were created by the Ecuadorian Orchid Society and now include a large portion of the country's orchid species, in addition to numerous other plants and trees. Also on the grounds are a spectacular butterfly garden, an auditorium, a restaurant, and a bookstore.

The gardens are about 30 minutes by car north of downtown near the Ciudadela de Las Orquídeas, on Avenida Orellana, ☎ 4-416-975/417-004, open daily 8:30-4, admission $4. Call a day in advance to make arrangements or to have a guide meet you at your hotel. It's also possible to take a taxi to the gardens. Call for specific directions and bring mosquito repellent during the rainy season.

Cerro Blanco Forest Reserve

Less than 30 minutes northwest of downtown Guayaquil is the Bosque Protector Cerro Blanco, encompassing 8,645 acres of tropical dry forest in the Chongón Hills. The property is owned by the Cemento Nacional company and administered by Fundación Pro-Bosque. This small, private reserve offers several trails through dry coastal hillsides among giant ceiba trees. More than 200 species of birds have been identified here, including the endangered giant green macaw. A connection to the moist forests in the north has allowed numerous other animals to survive here as well, including two monkey species, wild pigs, and predatory cats.

The reserve, originally created by Cemento Nacional to discourage people from visiting the limestone hills that they mined, also served to protect the forest from poachers. Cemento Nacional has since added to the size of the protected area and funded the Fundación Pro-Bosque to administer research and manage tourism in the area.

The reserve (open daily, 8-4, entrance $5, camping $7) is at Km 15 on the coastal highway (Vía la Costa) northwest of Guayaquil. The entrance sign and white walls of the cement factory are on the north side of the highway. It takes about 15 minutes to walk to the information center from the highway. Call Fundación Pro-Bosque's downtown office for guides or special arrangements: Edificio Multicomercio, Calles Cuenca and Eloy Alfaro, Local 16, ☎ 4-2416-975 or 4-2417-004, evonhorst@gu.pro.ec.

Playas

A small but important fishing village, Playas is the closest beach-resort area to Guayaquil. It is ideal for a day-trip away from the city and along the beach. During hot-season weekends and holidays, Playas is jam-packed with Guayaquileños looking to cool off. During this time the beaches away from the main town area are best. Things slow down during the off-season and weekdays, when fishing, wildlife viewing, and squawking seabirds become the main attractions. Surfing is also popular here. Look and ask around for the best surfing spots and you're sure to find suitable waves.

Playas is about 19 miles due south of Progresso, which is 40 miles west of Guayaquil. From Guayaquil, catch a bus to Salinas, but get off in Progresso and then take the local bus from there to Playas. By car, take the main coastal highway, Vía a Salinas, toward Salinas, and then turn south (left) in Progresso to Playas.

Machalá: Manglares Churute Ecological Reserve

This reserve protects one of the last remaining mangrove forests in the country. With over 86,450 acres of protected land, the reserve consists of mangroves, tall grass swamps, and tropical dry forest in the hills. This area is typical of what used to line the shores of coastal Ecuador before the shrimp industry and urban development devastated this crucial ecological life zone. This is a great day-long excursion from Guayaquil.

The coastal highway south toward Machalá passes through the reserve to the administration and information center, where maps and guides are available. There are many trails, but it's best to go with a guide or someone familiar with the reserve. Beyond the visitors center is the village of Churute and the road into the mangrove forest. Dolphins are commonly sighted here, as are various species of fish, crabs, and seabirds. The elevated dry tropical forest provides habitat to a variety of unique plants and animals, including two species of monkeys. The only practical way to visit the reserve is via motorized canoe.

In Guayaquil, the Ministerio del Ambiente, Av. Quito 402 and Solano, 10th floor, ☎ 4-2397-730, can arrange canoe trips in the reserve. To get there from Guayaquil, take a bus toward the city of Machalá and ask to be let off at the Churute Information Center. By car, travel southeast out of town toward the suburb of Durán, then head east toward the town of El Tríunfo. Turn south at Km 26, well before El Tríunfo, and drive toward Machalá. The sign for the reserve entrance is on the right side of the road about 10 minutes after the turn. Inquire at the Ministry of Tourism office (Visitor Information section) in Guayaquil for visiting the mangrove estuaries.

In case you need to ask, all roads are described as "Vía a" and then the name of the major town in the direction you are heading.

Chasquitur, ☎ 4-2281-085/084, at Urdaneta 1418 and Av. del Ejercito, offers trips to Manglares Churute Ecological Reserve. Other local excursions include visits to mangrove forests, beaches and coastal islands. In Machalá, try **La Mondea Tours** at Rocafuerte 518 between Junín and Tarqui, ☎ 7-562-230. They also have offices in Guayaquil.

■ Where to Stay

ACCOMMODATIONS PRICE SCALE
Unless otherwise noted, prices are per room, up to double occupancy. Some prices are per person, particularly with all-inclusive packages, but these generally include meals, lodging, guide services and other amenities.

$	Under $25
$$	$26 to $50
$$$	$51 to $100
$$$$	Over $100

Guayaquil

Other than the luxury chains, hotels in Guayaquil generally maintain lower standards and higher prices than elsewhere in the region. Fortunately, it's the rare occasion that an outdoor enthusiast has to spend more than a day or two in Guayaquil.

Hostal Ecuahogar is at Isidro Ayora, in front of the Banco Ecuatoriana de Viviendo in the suburb of Sauces, ☎ 4-2248-357, 4-2248-341, youthost@telconet.net. This is the best inexpensive (youth) hostel in the area. Near the airport and bus terminal, it is suitable for the traveler who is just passing through. A children's skateboard park is, or at least was, just down the street, and there is a good *chifa* around the corner. Clean and well-maintained rooms offer private or shared baths and hot water, in most cases. Amenities include kitchen facilities, a downstairs café, and a nice lounge room on the third floor. Discounts are offered for International Youth Hostel members. Unfortunately, a friend recently reported that the security guard there "arranged" a taxi for her and her friend. The driver took them to an empty field and threatened their lives. They are fine, but, as a warning, be sure you are present when the hotel receptionist calls a tax for you. $

The **Tangara Guest House** is in the Bolívariana suburb north of downtown at M. Sáenz and O'Leary, Block F, Casa 1, ☎ 4-2284-445, ☎/fax 2-2284-039. This is a nice residential area near the airport. A friendly, family-run establishment, it offers the best alternative to downtown. The guest-house is adjacent to the family home. Breakfast is served for an extra $4, and kitchen facilities are available for other meals. Light, airy, and immaculate rooms offer a pleasant change from the regular rifraff in Guayaquil. $$$

Hotel Delicia, Ballen 1105 and Montúfar, ☎ 4-2524-925, is the best ultra-budget hotel in the downtown area, although none of the budget hotels here are very nice. Despite the low price, it is quite clean and safe, an important asset in the area. If it's full here, the hotel across the street is worth looking into (Residencial Baños). $

Hotel Metropolitana, Calles V.M. Randon 120 and Panama, ☎ 4-2565-251 or 4-565-250, is a step up from Delicia but is still reasonably priced. Just one block off the waterfront, the Metropolitana is in a great spot for a morning stroll. Clean fourth-floor rooms have air-conditioning, telephones, and private baths. Hallway balconies overlook the city below. $

Centrally located **Hotel Rizzo**, Ballen 319 and Chile near Parque Bolívar, ☎ 4-2325-210, ☎/fax 4-2326-209, has clean, if antiquated, rooms with private baths, air-conditioning, TVs, and telephones. Windows look out over the street. There is a restaurant/café near the reception area and breakfast is included in the room rate. $$

Nearby is the comparable **Hotel Plaza**, Chile 414 and Ballen, ☎ 4-2324-006/741, ☎/fax 4-2324-195, jplamas@impsat.net.ec. Simple rooms offer the same amenities as the Rizzo, although some have ceiling fans rather than air-conditioning. $$

At the high end of the price scale is **Hotel Palace**, in the commercial heart of the city at Chile 214-216 and Luque, ☎ 4-2321-080, ☎/fax 4-2322-887, hotpalsa@impsat.net.ec, www.hotelpalaceguayaquil.com. ec. This is a good choice if you want modern amenities, priced just below the luxury hotels. Rooms include 24-hour room service, air-conditioning, private baths, cable TV and refrigerators. A travel agency, coffee shop, fax and laundry services are also available. $$$

Hotel Continental is on the corner of 10 de Agosto and Chile, ☎ 4-2329-270, ☎/fax 4-2325-454, informe@hotelcontinental.com.ec, www. hotelcontinental.com.ec. This is an impressive five-star modern treat in the middle of historic and commercial Guayaquil. It is a step up from the Palace, but still priced below some of the luxury hotels. The 90 rooms are all equipped with the standard amenities and attractively decorated with Ecuadorian art. In addition, there are "E-rooms," complete with multi-media computers, as well as several "virtual offices," equipped with the latest technology and Internet connections. In addition to a cocktail lounge and cafeteria, you can enjoy fine dining at the hotel's **El Fortin** restaurant – or just call your order in (they have 24-hour room service). $$$

Most luxury hotels are in the downtown area and offer nice restaurants, cafés, room service, pools, exercise rooms, and more. The least-expensive luxury hotel is the **Boulevard**, Av. 9 de Octubre 432, ☎ 4-2566-700, ☎/fax 4-2560-076. While the rooms and service are comfortable, the restaurant could use some work. Look elsewhere when it comes time to eat. Still, it is a good value for accommodations. $$$

Grand Hotel Guayaquil, Boyaca 1600 and 10 de Agosto, ☎ 4-2329-690, in the US 800/223-9868, ☎/fax 4-2327-251, www. grandhotelguayaquil.com, offers the best overall quality for the price. It shares an entire city block with the largest cathedral in Guayaquil. From the hotel's inner garden, you can see the impressive spires and stained-glass windows. The pool, saunas, gym, squash courts, and massage facilities are an added bonus at the 7,000-square-foot rooftop sports complex! The 175 rooms are spacious, clean, and elegant. The service is excellent. Enjoy quality dining at the hotel's fine restaurant, or stop at the cafeteria, open 24 hours a day. $$$-$$$$

The **Oro Verde** is at Av. 9 de Octubre and García Moreno, ☎ 4-2327-999, ☎/fax 4-2329-350, reservas_gye@oroverdehotels.com, www. oroverdehotels.com. This is one of the largest luxury hotels in the area, with 242 luxurious rooms. It comes with just about everything, including plenty of suites. Its convenient location is closer to the airport than other hotels and the restaurant serves delicious meals. In addition to multiple restaurants, a bar and nightlife in the disco, there is a fitness center, a pool and various business services. Very pricey, but worth it. $$$$

Of comparable quality and price is **Hotel Hilton Colón**, Av. Orellana near the airport, ☎ 4-2689-000, ☎/fax 4-2689-149, meeting@ hiltonguayaquil.com. This is one of the newest and most extravagant of the luxury hotels. $$$$

Playas

In Playas, the nearby beachside resort town, you will quickly be able to discern where you want to stay with a short walk around town. Head south from the bus station toward the Malecón (oceanside street) and east on the Data Highway a few blocks to **Hostería La Gaviota**, ☎ 4-2760-133. This decent beachside establishment has air-conditioning and a nice restaurant. $

Closer in on the Malecón is **Las Playas**, ☎ 4-2760-121, a bit cheaper, but also a good choice with a central location. $

Another 1¼ miles out on the highway, and priced a bit higher, is the Swiss-run **Hostería Bellavista**, ☎ 4-2760-600. Bungalows on the beach are comfortable and recommended; they have a slightly higher price tag than the above-mentioned accommodations. Camping is also available. $$

Machalá

To the south, in Machalá, is another **Oro Verde** hotel. It is located at Circunvalacion Norte, Urbanización Unioro, ☎ 7- 933-140, ☎/fax 7-933-1509, ov_mch@oroverdehotels.com, www.oroverdehotels.com. This hotel features adobe-style architecture and is surrounded by tropical gardens. The 70 modern rooms come equipped with all of the amenities of a luxury hotel. $$$

Much less expensive is the highly recommended **Oro**, at Olmedo and Juan Montalvo, ☎ 7-930-032. Not to be confused with the Oro Verde above, it is nevertheless clean and offers most of the amenities you might require. The restaurant serves good local and international cuisine. $$

Camping

The closest natural retreat with camping is the **Bosque Protector Cerro Blanco** (Cerro Blanco Forest Reserve), west of downtown Guayaquil on the coastal highway. The charge is under $10. (See *Eco-Travel*, page 312). Other than that, the beaches heading northwest away from the city are your best options. In Playas, **Hostería Bellavista** (page 317) offers one of the better nearby beach options.

■ Where to Eat

As is the case in most major international cities, Guayaquil offers a wide range of cuisine from Ecuador and abroad and far too many restaurants to sample in any one lifetime. A few establishments, however, do stand out. Downtown, try **Cyrano** or **La Palma**, located next to each other on Escobedo and Vélez. Both are good choices for light breakfasts and snacks, and they're great places to relax, people-watch, or enjoy a good cup of java.

Most of the best international and traditional Ecuadorian restaurants are in the finest hotels, particularly in the Oro Verde, the Grán Hotel Guayaquil, and the Hotel Continental's internationally acclaimed **Restaurante El Fortín**. Breakfasts, especially, are tasty at the better hotels. They're also reasonably priced (unlike the dinners, which, while outstanding, tend to be quite expensive).

The **Paradero Rustico**, Av. Luis Plaza Danin, is extremely popular with Guayaquileños. Typical Ecuadorian dishes are served to hordes of people crammed into a very small space. Try to arrive by 8 pm to beat the late-night crowds. If it's packed, head next door to **La Casa del Cangrejo**. Also recommended is **Pique y Pase** (Laascano and Carchi), which is a popular hang-out for the younger crowd and has a really good buzz. In the suburbs of Urdesa, several miles northwest of downtown, is **Lo Nuestro**, on Estrada and Higueras. This is the best inexpensive Ecuadorian restaurant in the area.

If you're craving Chinese food, try **The Mayflower**, a popular *chifa* on Colón near Chimborazo. **The Grán Chifa**, P. Carbo 1016 and Sucre, ☎ 4-2530-784, is the best *chifa* in the downtown area. Don't be fooled by the décor and ambiance – the delicious food is actually not that expensive. The nearby **Chifa Himalaya**, Sucre 308 and P. Carbo, ☎ 4-2329-593, is popular with locals and less expensive. **Tsuji**, on Estrada 813 and Guayacanes in the Urdesa District, ☎ 4-2881-183, is the best (and maybe the only) Japanese restaurant in town. Authentic atmosphere and décor complement the delicious food.

Vegetarians don't have many options. The **Restaurante Vegetariano Salud Solar**, Luque and P. Moncayo, offers good, inexpensive meals. Wherever there is a **Hare Krishna**, as at 6 de Marzo 2-26 and 1 de Mayo, you will usually find good, healthy vegetarian food.

Italian food and pizzerias are here as well. Try **Trattoria de Enrico**, Bálsamos 504, ☎ 4-2387-079. The atmosphere here matches the high quality of the food. Prices are mid-range. In Urdesa, **La Carbonara**, Bálsamos 206 and La Unica, ☎ 4-2382-714, is popular with travelers.

Meat lovers will find what they're looking for at **La Parrillada del Nato**, Estrada 1219 and Lureles, where there's a real South American atmosphere, enormous portions, and prices to match. Grilled and barbecued steaks are the specialty here. **Parrillada La Selvita**, Av. Olmos and Las Brisas, is another Argentinean-style restaurant with a nice atmosphere and good steaks. Both of these places are in the Urdesa district. **Donde el Che**, Boloña S21A, comes recommended and has a lively atmosphere.

There aren't as many good seafood restaurants in Guayaquil as one would expect, considering the size and location. Outside of the luxury hotel restaurants, **El Cangrejo Criollo**, at Av. Principal, Villa 9 in La Garzota, is recommended.

■ Nightlife & Shopping

 Some of the best nightclubs and discos that cater to well-off foreign travelers and Guayaquilleños are in the luxury hotels. The disco in Oro Verde is worth a visit. The most popular area for nightlife is **The Kennedy Mall**, which has numerous dance clubs and bars. It caters to the upscale clientele; expect to pay a lot for your cocktails, at least by Ecuadorian standards.

A popular way to spend an evening in Guayaquil, and one that I would recommend if you have the opportunity, is to try one of the infamous *chiva* buses that tour the city after dark. These party buses go on excursions of several hours, hitting all the main hotspots in the city, taking in all the sights and sounds. More often than not, the bus will have a live salsa band on the roof and be serving cocktails there –

which is where you'll be too, by the way. If you have a large enough group of friends, you can actually rent one of these *chivas* privately. Try Viajes Horizontez, ☎ 4-2281-260.

Ecuador's biggest mall is **Mall del Sol**, near the airport at Av. Constitucion and Marengo. A recent addition near downtown is **Centro Comercial Malecón 2000**, near the southern end of Malecón Simon Bolívar. There are plenty of others around the city. Just ask the concierge or taxi driver for the nearest major shopping mall (better the concierge, as the taxi driver may be looking for a longer fare). For daily necessities and an interesting overall experience, the huge **Bahía market** area has it all, but pay close attention to the quality of what you are purchasing. It is near the southern end of the Malecón around Av. Olmedo and extends as far west as Chile.

For handicrafts, the largest open market is **Mercado Artesanal**, in the downtown area between Loja and Montalvo, and Córdova and Chimborazo. Prices are good for the quality, but be sure to shop around and bargain if you feel something is overpriced. There are also good *artesanía* stores along the Malecón, including some at the Centro Comercial Malecón 2000, along the southern stretches of the waterfront street.

The Upper Amazon Basin

~ Northern Oriente ~

Welcome to the wildest place on earth! Ecuador's upper Amazon Basin, referred to locally as the Oriente, awaits you. Spanning most of the Sucumbíos Province, this region is unquestionably one of the most biologically diverse regions on the planet. Here, you can experience incredible wildlife viewing and bird-watching, nature photography, jungle hikes, dugout-canoe

excursions, and a unique mix of native people adapted to life in the heart of the tropics. From bird-size butterflies to butterfly-size birds, from piranhas to vampire bats, from poison-arrow frogs to monster anacondas, and from spider monkeys to howler monkeys, the sky is the limit for the spirited soul.

Go now, while the jungle is still there. Make your voice heard and help to make it last. Don't forget your insect repellent and rubber boots. Be prepared for adverse weather conditions: hot, humid, and wet, and wet, humid and even chilly. And if you can't handle a few bugs, stay in the highlands. Scared yet? Don't be. Most of the time, the climate is actually bearable and often quite pleasant in the Oriente throughout much of the year, and it's more than worth any of the minor discomforts that come with traveling through a tropical rainforest. Whatever you want in accommodations, Ecuador's upper Amazon Basin has it all, from traditional primitive facilities with indigenous communities to world-class ecolodges with plenty of amenities.

Keep in mind, though, that exotic animals are far from common here, primarily thanks to heavy damage to the land by humans, and larger mammals are secretive and often nocturnal. Hidden wonders are here, but they require exploration, patience, and quiet contemplation.

This chapter focuses on the Eastern slopes of the northern Ecuadorian Andes, as well as two gateway towns into the upper Amazon and their respective regional highlights. One such attraction is **Lago Agrio** on the Río Aguarico, which offers access to the Cuyabeno region. The other is **Coca** on the Lower Río Napo, providing access to Limoncocha Biological Reserve, Yasuní National Park and indigenous lands along the Ríos Napo, Tiputini, Shiripuno and Yasuní.

Tena and the Upper Río Napo is the third gateway jungle town and an extension of what is available via Coca, but it is treated in the next chapter with the central and southern Oriente.

History

Though there are a couple of archeological sites that have survived the tropical environment, little is known about the pre-Columbian settlement of the Amazonian region. With the arrival of the Incas and Spanish shortly after, Quichua Amerindians migrated east into the jungle and mixed with previous inhabitants. The earliest recorded travelers to Ecuador's upper Amazon were the Spanish conquistadors and missionaries in the mid-1500s. The first expedition was led by Francisco de Orellana and included a couple of hundred conquistadors, thousands of Indian slaves, dogs, horses and pigs, traveling through a land that became referred to as "Green Hell." Though all but a few conquistadors perished, it was the first recorded expedition to traverse the entire length of the Amazon to the Atlantic. From then on, the Spanish left a lasting legacy in the Oriente, primarily through their missionary influence.

Until **oil** was discovered here in the second half of the 20th century, the region remained relatively undeveloped. Nueva Loja, the official name for Lago Agrio, was first developed as a base of operations for US oil giant, Texaco. This was also the beginning of mass migration from the highlands (from towns such as Loja) and coastal regions of Ecuador, into the Oriente. Once the roads were built, pipelines laid, Indians sedated (or dead) and oil flowing, people streamed in.

In 1979 the **Cuyabeno Wildlife Reserve** was created to protect the rainforest and native communities who were trying to maintain traditional lifestyles. The original 635,000 acres lay southeast of Lago Agrio and incorporated the territories of the Secoya, Cofan, and Siona communities. Oil expansion in the 1980s, however, blazed a trail from

Lago Agrio east to Tarapoa and led to several oil spills and massive forest clearing. As a result, the Ecuadorian government changed the borders of the reserve and increased its size to 1,499,000 acres, moving its boundaries east and southeast from Tarapoa to the Peruvian border. Recent government administrations have all vowed to protect the reserve as it stands today. We'll see.

In addition to the Quichua ethnic group, traditional inhabitants of this the Sucumbíos Province also include the Shuar, Secoya, Siona and Cofan. For the most part, however, they are now confined to small reserves and are quickly becoming assimilated into the Quichua, Latin and Western cultures.

Flora & Fauna

From the eastern slopes of the Andes, the Amazon Basin is born – a massive tropical blanket that covers the entire eastern half of Ecuador. This region is all about water. The upper Amazon Basin itself receives from 60 to 160 inches of rain every year. Volcanic lakes and *páramo* ponds thousands of feet above sea level seep into streams, drain into rivers, and create deep gorges and massive cascades. This water, the lifeblood of the Amazon, flows eastward, slithers through Brazil, and winds nearly 1,900 miles to the Atlantic Ocean.

The vegetation of the Amazon rainforest is straight out of a fairy tale. Thick vines hang low and lush; giant strangler figs, flooded palm forests, bromeliads cupped upward on larger trees, and baby ferns and orchids carpet the forest floor. In fact, the vegetation is so dense, so impenetrable, that it's unlikely you'll see many of the exotic animals hidden within it. Such fabulous creatures as the puma, jaguar, and ocelot are extremely solitary and secretive, preferring to prowl and hunt at night. Further, they make their livings at the top of the food chain, and therefore require large expanses of contiguous forest. As a result, they're the first animals to disappear when human development occurs.

A visit to the rainforest will likely provide sightings of monkeys, sloths, bats, colorful butterflies and other insects. As for birds, rely on your ears. Better yet, rely on your guide's ears. You may spend an hour without a single sighting (unlikely) and then come across an entire flock of mixed species. Among types of birds living here are toucans, parrots, and macaws, predatory hawks and eagles, and various ground-dwelling birds. A rainbow of hummingbirds, almost overwhelming in their diversity and range, completes the list.

Ayahuasca

Ayahuasca is the base ingredient for a powerful hallucinogenic brew, made from the vine of the same name, that has been used for centuries in religious and healing ceremonies, by the people of the Amazon, and in particular the tribal shamans. It is said that the consumption of this brew gives the shamans special powers, such as the ability to commune with spirits, animals and nature, to diagnose illness, treat disease, and even see into the future. The term *ayahuasca* comes from the words *aya*, meaning spirit or ancestor, and *huasca*, meaning vine or rope.

 Ecuador is such a hotspot for birds (and birders!) that you would need an entire book on the subject. Luckily there is one, *The Birds of Ecuador*, by Robert S. Ridgely & Paul J. Greenfield (2001).

Getting Here & Getting Around

The northern Oriente includes the land west of Quito and two major points of access to the upper Amazon Basin: **Coca** on the Lower Río Napo, and **Lago Agrio** on the Río Aguarico. Lago Agrio offers access to the Cuyabeno region, while Coca is the jumping-off point to Limoncocha Biological Reserve, Yasuní National Park and surrounding indigenous areas. These and other waterways, as you'll see, are the primary paths of travel through the Amazon jungle.

■ By Car

 There are two access roadways from the highlands to these destinations, both with frequent bus service, though the rainy season often results in road damage, mudslides and travel delays. One is from **Quito via Baeza** and the other is from **Ambato via Baños and Puyo**. Farther south are two more access roads from the highlands **via Cuenca** and **via Loja**. There is also a developed road connecting Coca and Lago Agrio, to the northeast.

■ By Air

The airport, located a few miles southeast of Lago Agrio, has daily flights to and from Quito (except for Sundays). **TAME**, the national airline and carrier for this route, has an office in Lago Agrio on Orellano near the plaza, ☎ 6-830-113 (or in Quito, ☎ 2-2502-706 or 2-2564-969). Currently, they have cancelled all flights to Coca and do not know when service will be resumed. **AEROGAL** flies to Coca every day except Sunday. They have an office at the airport.

■ By Bus

Buses (less than $10) between Quito and Lago Agrio take about eight hours; those between Quito and Coca take nine hours. Many of the buses from Quito to Lago Agrio run overnight, which is great if you need the rest, but doing this trip during the day is well worth it for the spectacular views as you drop down from the highlands to the tropical rainforest. Keep in mind that the roads, which are poor under normal conditions, may become impassible at times during the rainy season. Between Coca and Lago Agria, the ride takes about three hours. There are also buses to Tena, on the Upper Río Napo (see page 355).

When to Go

During the wet(ter) months of March through September, water levels are higher in the Oriente and travel, i.e., navigation, through the more remote regions, is easier. Temperatures during this time are generally cooler, which is important in an area where humidity is typically 90-100%! The drier season is accompanied by more heat and insects near major waterways, but also allows for more hiking in areas otherwise navigable only by dugout canoe. Either way, expect an unforgettable experience!

Upper Amazon Basin

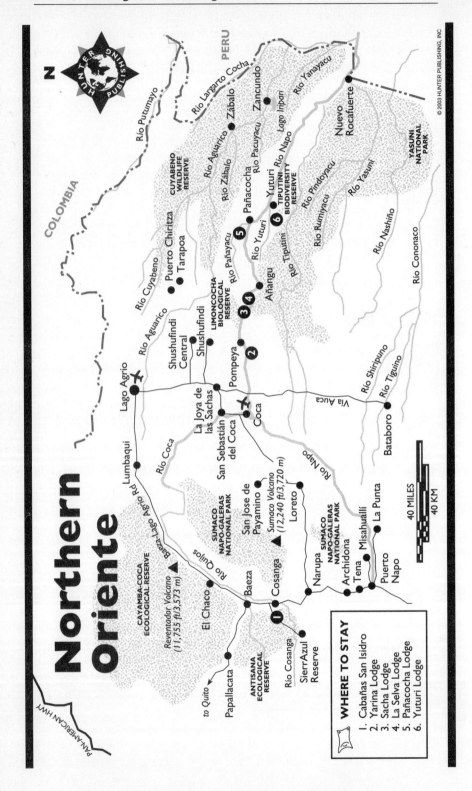

Northern Oriente

N

PERU

COLOMBIA

© 2003 HUNTER PUBLISHING, INC

Rio Putumayo

Rio Largarto Cocha

Rio Yanayacu

Nuevo Rocafuerte

Rio Aguarico

Zábalo

Zancundo

Lago Iripari

Rio Napo

YASUNI NATIONAL PARK

CUYABENO WILDLIFE RESERVE

Rio Zábalo

Pañacocha

Rio Pacuyacu

Yuturi

6 TIPUTINI BIODIVERSITY RESERVE

Rio Pindoyacu

Rio Cuyabeno

Puerto Chiritza

Tarapoa

Rio Pañayacu

5

Rio Yuturi

Rio Tiputini

Añangu

Rio Rumiyacu

Rio Yasuni

Rio Nashiño

Rio Aguarico

Shushufindi Central

Shushufindi

LIMONCOCHA BIOLOGICAL RESERVE

3 **4**

Rio Cononaco

Pompeya

2

Rio Shiripuno

Rio Tiguino

Lago Agrio

La Joya de las Sachas

San Sebastián del Coca

Coca

Vía Auca

Bataboro

Lumbaqui

Rio Coca

Rio Napo

Baeza-Lago Agrio Rd

CAYAMBA-COCA ECOLOGICAL RESERVE

Reventador Volcano (11,755 ft/3,573 m)

SUMACO NAPO-GALERAS NATIONAL PARK

San Jose de Payamino

Sumaco Volcano (12,240 ft/3,720 m)

Loreto

La Punta

Narupa

SUMACO NAPO-GALERAS NATIONAL PARK

Misahuallí

Puerto Napo

40 MILES

40 KM

El Chaco

Rio Quijos

Baeza

Cosanga

Archidona

Tena

Papallacta

ANTISANA ECOLOGICAL RESERVE

Rio Cosanga

1

SierrAzul Reserve

PAN-AMERICAN HWY

to Quito

WHERE TO STAY

1. Cabañas San Isidro
2. Yarina Lodge
3. Sacha Lodge
4. La Selva Lodge
5. Pañacocha Lodge
6. Yuturi Lodge

Visitor Information

The most convenient and best outfitters for this region, particularly with regard to organized tours, are available in Quito. Community-based ecotourism projects, on the other hand, may require additional planning and patience once you arrive, but are worth it if your interest is in a more genuine experience and supporting these efforts.

The main points of departure into the region are the frontier towns of Coca on the Lower Río Napo, and Lago Agrio on the Río Aguarico. These are also the only towns along the tourist path with modern facilities, such as mail and other communications.

■ Coca

In Coca, the **Andinatel telephone office** is at Eloy Alfaro and 6 de Diciembre, and just south on 9 de Octubre is the **post office**. Inquire at your hotel about possible Internet connections, but don't depend on these as phone lines are often down. Bring your money with you, as there are no places to change travelers checks and no ATMs. The **Ministry of Interior Environment** (Ministerio de Medio Ambiente) can help out with national park and interior travel. They are on Amazonas and Bolívar, ☎ 6-880-171. **Buses** congregate on Napo, between Bolívar and Cuenca.

■ Lago Agrio

Along the southeastern edge of town is the main road, Avenida Quito. Almost all tourist services are on this road, which is now paved (but not well). As in Coca, bring your dollars with you. The **Andinatel telephone office** is near the plaza on 18 de Noviembre and Orellana. To the south, across from the market on Av. Quito, is the **police station**. Farther east along Av. Quito and Vicente Narvaez is the **hospital**. The post office is on Rocafuerte and 12 de Febrero. There are no ATMs in Lago Agrio, though you might be able to exchange travelers checks at a higher-end hotel.

Upper Amazon Basin

Touring & Sightseing

■ Baeza

Heading into the Oriente from Quito, the main road passes just north of Volcán Antisana and the thermal hot springs at Papallacta (see page 99 for more on Papallacta). Continuing through the eastern slopes of the Andes and within relatively close proximity to ecological reserves, Baeza offers a potential home base for exploring this majestic transition zone between the higher altitude *páramo* habitats and the lower tropical rainforests. It is a relatively unexplored area, and you will most likely have the countryside all to yourself.

■ Lago Agrio

Lago Agrio, the capital of the Sucumbíos Province, serves as the jumping-off point for jungle excursions into the Cuyabeno Wildlife Reserve. An important oil town of over 20,000 people, its official name is Nueva Loja. The majority of tourists spend very little time here. In fact, most people arrive at the airport and continue straight into the jungle with their tour group. Regular flights are available from Quito to Lago Agrio. Buses from Quito take at least eight hours and cost less than $10. Driving from Quito, take the main road to Baeza and then head northeast on the Baeza-Lago Agrio Road.

The main road in town offers services and supplies for the jungle traveler. Note that this area has seen an increase in problems associated with its close proximity to Colombia. Inquire at the South American Explorers Club in Quito (☎/fax 2-225-228, explorer@seac.org.ec) about current safety concerns before traveling here and into the surrounding, more remote parts of the Oriente, including Cuyabeno.

The name "Lago Agrio" means Sour Lake, which is what the town, Nueva Loja, is commonly called. It received this high honor after becoming the home base of Texaco. No prizes for guessing why. For more insight into the name and the effects of the growing oil industry on this part of the Oriente, read **Amazon Crude** by Judith Kimmerling.

■ Coca

Puerto Francisco de Orellana is well described by Joe Kane in *Savages* (Vintage Books, 1996), an epic first-hand account of his travels through Huaorani territory and their life-and-death struggle against American Oil Companies:

"The port of Coca sits on the north bank of the broad, brown Napo River, in the very heart of the Oriente, which may well be the richest biotic zone on the planet. But as I entered town for the first time, bouncing on the back of a flatbed pickup, what I smelled most strongly was raw petroleum. Coca is ringed by oil wells, and every few days its dirt streets are hosed down with waste crude. Oily mud splashed across my clothes and pack. Down along the roadside, oil had spattered chickens, mules, pigs, barefoot school children, and peasants slip-sliding along on rickety bicycles. It even slopped up onto the spanking-new four-wheel-drive trucks that now and then came blasting down the road at breakneck speed."

Although it has been several years since this publication, the capital of the Orellana Province remains a less-than-wonderful place. It is a small step up from its northern counterpart of Lago Agrio, both in terms of tourism infrastructure and safety. Still, it's a messy place. Nevertheless, Coca's location now allows for access and travel into the remote stretches of the Lower Río Napo region.

Adventures

■ On Water

 On water is how you can expect to spend most of your time exploring the Oriente, especially once you travel beyond civilization and into the deeper parts of the rainforest. Springing into the jungle from either Coca or Lago Agrio, in fact, mandates travel by motorized dugout canoe, the primary mode of transportation for everyone. Trips to the Cuyabeno Wildlife Reserve and the Lower Río Napo region, including Yasuní National Park and other indigenous lands, all require travel by water. If you are going to the more remote locations, be sure you are prepared. Depending on the season and the rains, the rivers can be mellow with a consistent blazing equatorial sun, or they can swell after a cool tropical downpour. Nevertheless, these are your roadways and they are a wonderful way to experience the best of the Oriente. They are also great places to swim, and any jungle trip will include plenty of time to splash in the water.

Fishing

Trout fishing is readily available throughout the higher elevations of the Eastern Cordillera slopes, especially in places like **Antisana Ecological Reserve**. **Laguna Mica** is especially well known by anglers. The area around **Baeza** offers endless trout streams.

■ On Foot

Baeza Area Hikes

Driving from Quito, the main highway passes down the eastern slopes via Baeza. If you are not arriving with a guide from Quito, ask for local guides and trail information, as this is a great area for everything from a scenic stroll around the San Rafael Falls to climbing Antisana Volcano and a multi-day trek up Raventedor Volcano. Perched between the high elevation of the Andes and the Oriente, this cool misty region offers steep mountainous features, but the landscape is much greener, with flowing streams, lakes and waterfalls in the surrounding land. There is some dairy and even trout farming in the surrounding communities.

Antisana Ecological Reserve (page 334) offers 296,400 acres of wide-open country and numerous ecological life zones to play in, as it spans the Eastern Cordillera and changes significantly in elevation. If you don't have your own guide, try Quito-based tour operators. In Beaza, check in at the pleasant, family-feel restaurant **Gina**, which serves great trout and is an excellent lunch stop when heading into the Oriente.

Antisana Volcano

Gear and a lot of experience are required for the 18,829-foot-high Volcán Antisana, Ecuador's fourth-highest peak and arguably one of its most difficult for hikers. Highlighting the well-protected Antisana Ecological Reserve, the namesake volcano is well off the beaten path. That, combined with a lack of easy access and technical difficulty, makes Antisana one of the less-climbed peaks. Nevertheless, for the hearty and determined, the glaciated crater rim offers four peaks and serious adrenaline challenges for the experienced climber.

You must be completely self-sufficient to climb Antisana, with all-season camping gear and several days worth of food and water (or a purification system). The small town of **Píntag** offers access to the mountain. There are several routes between the different peaks and a guide is recommended (see pages 94-97). Otherwise, refer to *Climbing and Hiking in Ecuador* by Rachowiecki et al (Bradt Publications) for specific routes and directions. For general hiking in the reserve, use these maps: IGM 1:50,000 of Píntag, Papallacta, Laguna Micacocha and Sincholagua; and IGM 1:100,000 Píntag map for climbing Antisana.

San Rafael Falls

A small private reserve adjacent to the massive Cayambe-Coca Ecological Reserve, San Rafael offers a relatively easy trail through mid-elevation cloud forest. The hike is primarily of interest to birders and those looking to stretch out on the long drive between the Andes and the Amazon. Picturesque falls and river crossings make this a refreshing hike. See page 333 for directions.

Reventador Volcano

Reventador surprised scientists and locals alike in November of 2002 with an eruption that spewed gas and ash nearly 10 miles into the sky. Be sure to check locally or in Quito about recent activity.

Near the San Rafael Falls and skirting the edge of the Cayambe-Coca Ecological Reserve to the west and the Oriente to the east is Reventador, which peaks out at 11,641 feet. This is a difficult multi-day "hike" up an active volcano that involves wet rainforest bush-whacking (though there is a trail), steep slopes, lava flow and a bit of loose scrambling. Bring quality gear, a knowledgeable guide from

Quito or Baeza, and a good map (IGM 1:50,000 Volcán El Reventador). Though difficult to climb and often cloudy, the peak can provide breathtaking views of the Oriente and surrounding peaks.

The Oriente

The Cuyabeno Wildlife Reserve and Lower Río Napo region offers deep jungle hikes in conjunction with organized tours and visits to all-inclusive ecolodges (*Eco-Travel* and *Where to Stay*, below). Bring rubber boots, though, as many of these areas exist as flooded forests during a good part of the year. In fact, you may find yourself spending more time in a dugout canoe than on dry land.

If it rains while you are spending time in the Oriente, do whatever you had scheduled for the day anyway. After all, this is the rainforest!

Eco-Travel

 You're in the jungle now, so expect hiking through dense foliage and dugout-canoe rides in virgin rainforest. The main attraction here is the incredible birding and wildlife-viewing opportunities. Visiting indigenous communities and learning about natural lifestyles are just as intriguing to foreign travelers who are looking for a bit of cultural adventure.

Official Travel into the Jungle

If you are heading into remote sections of the Oriente, specifically from Coca or Lago Agrio, there are a few legal requirements. They can be arranged with the better tour operators and all-inclusive ecolodges if you are signing up for a tour. Otherwise, you must first obtain permission from the Ministry of Defense in Quito, as well as register with police in Coca or Lago Agrio. This is as much for your own safety as anything else, though it is also no doubt to make sure that travelers aren't poking around where they shouldn't be. Environmental activists continue to be arrested and deported even now.

The ongoing US War on Drugs in Colombia has also resulted in a ripple of guerilla activity that has made certain parts of the jungle, such as the Cuyabeno region, less safe, particularly for American travelers. Check with the South American Explorers in Quito (☎/fax 2-225-228, explorer@seac.org.ec) for the latest safety report. Don't rely on the advice of tour operators, who are trying to sell trips.

■ From Quito to Baeza

Cayambe-Coca Ecological Reserve

The Quito-Baeza Road into the Oriente cuts along the southern edge of the massive Cayambe-Coca Ecological Reserve. At one extreme, Cayambe-Coca encompasses alpine life zones and summits that reach over 19,000 feet, with opportunities for mountaineering, hiking, rock climbing, and ice climbing (discussed in *Northern Highlands*, page 132). At the other extreme, the altitude drops to 2,600 feet and the reserve borders the road from Baeza to Lago Agrio. In between are *páramo* grasslands, numerous high-altitude lakes, and low-lying cloud forests.

The reserve was not created with tourism in mind, and much of its 10 million acres remains undisturbed and rugged. Only guides and skilled explorers will find it easy to venture into and around the reserve. If you want peace and quiet in the massive wilds of the Andes, then this is definitely the place to go.

There are no formal entry points or facilities within Cayambe, so camping and hiring a guide who knows the area well are the only practical options, unless you are a skilled backcountry navigator and map-reader. Inquire with trekking and mountaineering outfitters in Quito.

San Rafael Falls

From Baeza, the Quito-Baeza Road splits toward Lago Agrio to the north (Baeza-Lago Agrio Road) and Tena to the south. Heading northeast through the Río Quijos valley toward Lago Agrio, the first major natural attraction you'll come to is San Rafael Falls. Also known as Coca Falls, this awesome 425-foot cascade is Ecuador's tallest.

Upper Amazon Basin

Although this area is officially a part of the Cayambe-Coca Reserve, there is a small private reserve that surrounds the falls. This is a great place for bird-watching, with possible close-up views of the renowned black and red cock-of-the-rock. Males of this species flock together in a brilliant communal effort to attract females. Various other beautiful bird species, as well as monkeys and the rare spectacled bear, coexist in this habitat.

The turnout to the small reserve is on the south side of the Baeza-Lago Agrio Road, 30 miles past El Chaco at a small concrete building. If you come to the bridge at the Río Reventador, you've gone too far. Follow the entrance road up and around, across a bridge, and to the gated entry point. If you wish to explore the reserve, stay at **San Rafael Lodge** (see page 342).

Antisana Ecological Reserve

Farther (southeast) from Quito is the Antisana Ecological Reserve, 296,000 acres of wide-open countryside. Stretching along the Eastern Cordillera, Antisana is another special place, offering numerous ecological life zones, the result of dramatic elevation changes from high elevation *páramo* to lowland rainforest, where it connects with the Sumaco Napo-Galleras National Park in the Oriente. Though there are plenty of open miles to hike throughout the reserve, as well as lakes and streams for trout fishing, a major attraction is the 18,829-foot-high glacier-capped Volcán Antisana and what it offers for experienced climbers (see *Adventures*, page 331).

■ Cuyabeno Wildlife Reserve

The Cuyabeno Wildlife Reserve has the largest concentration of lakes, lagoons and flooded rainforest in the Oriente. A large portion of its 1½-million-acres remains pristine and intact, yet still accessible to travelers. It is a prime example of where the conflicting worlds of indigenous life, conservation, and tourism meet oil expansion, colonization, and development. Ecuador balances on a tightrope, striving to develop without crossing over into disaster.

The Cuyabeno Reserve is massive and much of it remains inaccessible. Access and transportation are via waterways, primarily the Río Aguarico, Río Cuyabeno and their tributaries. Lago Agrio is the main town in this region and the jumping-off point for visiting the jungle.

Organized tours are the only real way to visit Cuyabeno unless you know the region well, are willing to camp, and can afford to spend exorbitant sums of money. It is not like the Upper Río Napo (next chapter), where you can drive down the road from Misahuallí to a lodge that incorporates ecotourism as part of a package. In Cuyabeno, tour operators, based primarily out of Quito, offer packages that include their own accommodations within and around the reserve. Excursions into the reserve can be arranged through the tour operators listed under *Tours & Tour Operators* (see page 340), and specific ecolodges (listed below). Within and abutting the reserve, some indigenous groups hold rights to certain territories, offering the responsible traveler a wonderful opportunity to experience more local community-based ecotourism projects. Entry into Cuyabeno is $20.

Community-Based Ecotourism

There are several responsible community-based ecotourism programs to choose from in this region, including groups from the Siona, Siecoya (often referred to jointly as Siona-Siecoya because of their related dialects) and Cofan ethnic groups. The Siona *indígenas*, with only about 200 inhabitants remaining, offer trips to three communities in a reserve around Cuyabeno and the Río Aguarico. SIONATOUR, a division of the Siona organization ONISE, is now the community agency in charge of administering ecotourism in the local villages, which vary from complete community involvement to private enterprise with community support. Highlights include hiking, birding, river excursions, learning about traditional culture and architecture, history, fishing, shamanic encounters and, overall, a wonderfully genuine experience. Trips are typically recommended for at least three to four days, and cost around $50 per person per day; smaller groups and shorter stays will be priced at a higher rate. Keep in mind that most of these programs are very flexible and can be tailored to various interests. Arrangements must be made in advance through **SIONATOUR** in Lago Agrio, at 12 de Febrero and 10 de Agosto, ☎ 6-831-875, ☎/fax 6-830-232.

The Secoyas, a related ethnic group of about 300 remaining inhabitants that lives along the Río Aguarico, offers trips to their land through the privately operated Piraña Tours, based in Lago Agrio. For about the same price as most community-based efforts, you have the added benefit of an experienced operator handling all of the logistics and transportation (from Lago Agrio), into the Secoya community. Although I haven't experienced it myself, this program is reputed to provide wonderful guides, food, comfort and incredible experiences with the local shaman. There are two basic programs, which vary in rigor with the trip length. One is generally operated as a four-day trip and the longer, more active program is eight days. Contact **Piraña Tours**, Manuel Silva, Casa de la Cultura, Colombia and 18 de Noviembre, Lago Agrio, ☎ 6-830-624, or in Quito at **Tropic Ecological Adventures**, Av. República 307 and Almagro, Edificio Taurus, Dept. 1-A, ☎ 2-2225-907/2234-594, fax 02-2560-756, tropic@uio.satnet.net, www.tropiceco.com.

The Cofan, whose territory once ranged all the way to the foothills of the Andes, have spent years retreating farther and farther east from the oil industry expansion in order to maintain their lifestyle of subsistence hunting and rotational agriculture. A brave people, in recent years they have gone so far as to march on illegal oil wells in protest and actually stop production activity, but their success has been mixed. They are now reduced to 500 inhabitants in a reserve along the Río Aguarico and another small cluster west of Lago Agrio in the foothills of the Andes. Nevertheless, their "leader," Randy Borman – an American who married a Cofan – has implemented a solid community-based ecotourism (CBE) program, if not an expensive one. As with everything else, though, you get what you pay for. For $60-$120 per day per person, you will visit the most remote stretches of Ecuador's Oriente and the Cofan community of Zábalo. Typical programs last six days, with all of the standard activities offered by other programs, as well as a couple of surprises and extended, more challenging treks available. Contact **Randy Borman** in Quito, ☎/fax 2-2437-844, randyborman@earthlink.net, or **Tropic Ecological Adventures** in Quito, ☎ 2-2234-594/2225-907, ☎/fax 2-2560-756, tropic@uio.satnet.net, www.tropiceco.com. Other responsible outfitters that work with this group include **Transturi** (transturi@uio.satnet.net), **Harpia Tours** and **Wilderness Travel** (1102 Ninth Street, Berkeley, CA 94710, ☎ 800-368-2794, 510-558-2488, fax 510-558-2489, www.wildernesstravel.com. Transturi also officially works with a Quichua CBE project in the heart of the Cuyabeno Reserve at Playas de Cuyabeno.

For full descriptions of the programs and communities involved in these and other CBE projects, including those in Yasuní National Park and the Lower Río Napo region (below), read Rolf Wesche and Andy Drumm's *Defending our Rainforest: A Guide to Community-Based Ecotourism in the Ecuadorian Amazon*. This is a joint venture between the University of Ottowa, the British Embassy in Quito, Abya Yala, The Ecotourism Society, PROBANA and The Nature Conservancy.

■ Coca & the Lower Río Napo Region

As with Cuyabeno, the region surrounding the Lower Río Napo offers deep-jungle excursions into relatively untouched rainforest. Coca is the main "town" in the region and the departure point through the lower Napo. In addition to the land immediately surrounding the Napo and its tributaries, access to places like Yasuní National Park is also available from here. Various organized tours are offered, many of which can be prearranged in Quito, in conjunction with ecolodges described below and CBE projects, covered above.

The two main cultural groups in this region are the Quichua and the Huaorani, with the eastern stretches of the Oriente still relatively undeveloped. Although a fragile arrangement, these areas are protected by Ecuador's largest national park, Yasuní, as well as Quichua and Huaorani protected territories and the very small Limoncocha Biological Reserve. South and west of Yasuní National Park lies the Huaorani Reserve, and to the north – stretching from west to the southeast along the Río Napo – lies a large Quichua reserve. Both of these offer the best chances of maintaining protection for the park with buffer zones, as well as establishing and maintaining responsible CBE projects in this region of the Oriente.

Limoncocha Biological Reserve

The Limoncocha Biological Reserve, northeast of the Río Napo/Río Jivino junction, is a couple of hours downriver from Coca by motorized canoe. Declared a reserve in 1985 and surrounding its namesake lagoon, Limoncocha is only a remnant of the area's once-beautiful scenery and rich biology that, over the years, has been devastated by seismic exploration and drilling, road development and immigration.

Upper Amazon Basin

This 69,000-acre reserve includes flooded forest and oxbow lakes. It also harbors archeological remains from the Napo culture of the 12th century. Ceramic shards and graves provide testimony to a large population and a well-developed culture that flourished in the region prior to contact with the Europeans. Today, the local Quichua community administers rustic cabañas in the area and can provide guiding services into the reserve.

Contact **CONFENIAE** (the Indigenous Association of Limoncocha), Av. 6 de Diciembre 159, Quito, ☎ 2-2220-326, ☎/fax 2-2543-973. It is also possible to hire a guide in Coca and canoe to the reserve.

Yasuní National Park

Yasuní National Park is the current reigning champion when it comes to preserving biological wealth in the Ecuadorian Amazon. Originally created in 1979 to protect the rainforest, Yasuní's current borders incorporate more than 2½ million acres, as well as a reserve for the indigenous Huaorani people. In fact, UNESCO (the United Nations Education, Scientific and Cultural Organization) declared Yasuní an International Biosphere Reserve. The size of the park, however, has changed as often as political interests have, and usually reflects the ever-expanding appetite of the oil industry – rarely with any input from the Huaorani themselves.

There are only a couple of practical ways to visit Yasuní and stay at an ecolodge. Two hours from Coca down the Río Napo is the village of Pompeya, where guests heading into the park register with the Maxus oil company. From the south side of the river, a southbound drive along the oil road ends at the Río Tiputini. From here, another couple of hours via motorized canoe through rainforest will bring you to Tiputini Biodiversity Station. The other way to visit Yasuní is via trails near the military outpost at Anangu, which is near the Sacha and La Selva Lodges. From here, day hikes can be made into the park.

Combine the numerous lakes, rivers, swamps, and forests in Yasuní with minimal development, human habitation, or hunting, and the end result is an unimaginable wealth of biodiversity in large, contiguous expanses of primary forest. This is one of the few places where large predatory cats roam undisturbed, troops of monkeys rule the canopy, dolphins play and caimans float, and where hundreds of bird species sing their melodies.

Contact Tiputini Biodiversity Station or Sacha or La Selva Lodges (see pages 345-46 and 348) to arrange visits to the reserve. Camping is available throughout the park but requires a heavy investment and arrangements with local guides.

Oil Development & Conservation

Oil exploration itself is not always what harms places like Yasuní National Park. Although dozens of oil spills in Ecuador's Oriente have poisoned enough rainforest and indigenous communities to make the Exxon Valdez spill look like a drop in the bucket, there are other forces at work. Most often, it is the deluge of colonization accompanying oil industry roads that hurts most. Where there is colonization, the rainforest and native communities suffer.

Yasuní, fortunately, has managed to avoid this seemingly inevitable end (though several international oil companies are now exploiting the reserve). The reason? The roads have not been built – yet. Although petroleum exploration and extraction are occurring in Yasuní, alternative forms of development that minimize the use of roads are in progress as well. This is largely the result of hard work and pressure from international science, conservation and cultural organizations, as well as native resistence.

The lack of roads makes it much more difficult for travelers to visit the park. Yasuní is one of the most natural areas in the world. Whether it remains this way depends on the actions of energetic special-interest groups and perhaps a bit on you. To find out more about visiting and how to help, contact representatives from the **Tiputini Biodiversity Research Station**, tbs@mail.usfq.edu.ec or tiputini@aol.com.

Supporting international organizations from home, such as Rainforest Action Network or The Nature Conservancy, can help as well. These groups voice your opinion and can pressure oil companies and governments to act responsibly.

The other way to exert a positive influence is by being conscientious consumers. As automobile drivers, we encourage the force that has destroyed the rainforest and many lives. We need to realize the effects of our actions. Simple options may be to drive a more fuel-efficient car, support responsible transportation policies and infrastructure, or to use public transport where possible. All of these are very small steps. By changing our habits and creating an example, as well as researching the companies affecting these areas, and voicing our opinion, we can have a positive impact.

Upper Amazon Basin

■ Tours & Tour Operators

Many tour operators and community-based ecotourism organizations offer the same services. Jungle excursions involve hiking, birding, wildlife viewing, medicinal botany, eco-cultural interactions, boating, fishing, and swimming. You will find descriptions in the sections on those activities. Most tours are associated with all-inclusive packages through ecolodges and they are listed in the *Where to Stay*, page 343.

Outfitters of varying quality operate in and around Cuyabeno and the Río Napo region. Those listed below are reputable, though they are only some of the many tour operators available. Ask plenty of questions before choosing one.

Based in Quito, **Native Life Tours**, Foch E4-167 and Amazonas, ☎ 2-2505-158, 2-2550-836, or 2-2236-320, ☎/fax 2-2229-077, natlife1@natlife.com.ec, offers excursions on Río Aguarico and Río Cuyabeno. Ecuadorian-owned and -operated, the company is one of those "family feel" operations that are always a pleasure to recommend. They have three main, all-inclusive trips ranging in length from three to seven nights, with highlights such as a night walk through the jungle, and their very own lodge, Nativo Lodge, on the edge of the Cuyabeno Reserve. Itineraries are varied to suit individual needs, and guides are professional and very knowledgeable. This is one of the best bets for budget-oriented, deep-jungle enthusiasts.

Of the highest quality, though quite a bit more expensive, is **Ecuador Amazon Expeditions**, Av. República de El Salvador 970, Quito, ☎ 2-2464-780 (in the US, 800-527-2500), ☎/fax 2-2464-702, a branch of Metropolitan Touring. They operate the Flotel Orellana and Aguarico and Iripari camps and are among the best and most responsible ecotour operators in the Oriente.

One of the most ecologically and conservation-oriented is **Tropic Ecological Adventures**, Av. República E7-320 and Almagro, Edificio Taurus in Quito, ☎ 2-2234-594 or 2-2225-907, ☎/fax 2-2560-756, tropic@uio.satnet.net, www.tropiceco.com. Working with local groups, this professional outfit is about as responsible as they come. They offer top quality trips into the jungle, work closely with local indigenous communities and are a good contact for community-based ecotourism projects in the Cuyabeno region. They are a great option for visiting natives, while maintaining a high degree of cultural sensivity.

Another option is the Ecuadorian-owned **Nuevo Mundo Travel and Tours**, Av. Coruña N26-207 and Orellana in Quito, ☎ 2-2564-448/2-2553-826/2-2509-431, ☎/fax 2-2565-261, www.nuevomundotravel.com, nmundo@interactive.net.ec, info@nuevomundotravel.com. They operate the Cuyabeno River Lodge. This organization is very professional and conservation-oriented. Their guides are exceptional and they are priced at the high end of the market, but you get what you pay for.

Neotropic Turis, ☎ 2-2521-212, ☎/fax 2-2554-902, neotropi@uio.satnet.net, offers reasonably priced trips to their own lodge, the Grand Cuyabeno Lake Lodge, in the Cuyabeno Reserve, including guide services and meals.

Kempery Tours, at Pinto 539 and Amazonas in Quito, ☎ 2-2226-583, ☎/fax 2-2226-715, www.kempery.com, kempery@kempery.com offers solid jungle trips in conjunction with the Huaorani around the Cuyabeno Reserve. They also arrange Andes and Galápagos excursions.

For Coca and the Río Napo, **Emerald Forest Tours**, Jaoquin Pinto E4-244, and **Amazonas**, in Quito, ☎ 2-2541-278, ☎/fax 2-2541-543, www.emeraldexpeditions.com, are recommended for trips into Yasuní National Park and the Napo region, including Panacocha. In Coca, they are located near the intersection of Napo and Espejo. ☎ 6-881-155.

In Quito, **Safari Ecuador** is at Calama 380 and J.L. Mera, ☎ 2-2552-505, ☎/fax 2-2223-381; or Roca Pasaje 630 and Amazonas, ☎ 2-2234-799, ☎/fax 2-2220-426, admin@safari.com.ec, www.safari.com.ec. It offers more "down to earth" camping trips into the Oriente's Río Napo region (along the Río Siripuno) and Yasuní, with local guides. They can be reached from the US by calling ☎ 800-434-8182. Safari, which also guides climbing expeditions in the Andes, is a top-quality outfit without the high-end price tag.

In Coca, **Expediciones Jarrín** is at Napo and Moreno, ☎ 6-880-251. Also in Coca is **Paushi Tours**; inquire at Hotel El Auca in Coca (see *Where to Stay*, page 343).

Where to Stay

ACCOMMODATIONS PRICE SCALE	
Unless otherwise noted, prices are per room, up to double occupancy. Some prices are per person, particularly with all-inclusive packages, but these generally include meals, lodging, guide services and other amenities.	
$	Under $25
$$	$26 to $50
$$$	$51 to $100
$$$$	Over $100

■ Baeza Area

 San Rafael Lodge, contact through Hotel Quito, in Quito, Av. Gonzalez Suarez 25-00, or Casilla, 17-01-2201, ☎ 2-2544-600 or 2-2544-514, ☎ /fax 2-2567-284, is a destination for birders and those visiting San Rafael Falls, along the eastern Cordillera and near the town of Baeza. It's particularly popular with birding groups. Simple, but comfortable, it is a nice place to rest between the highlands and the Oriente.

In the northern Oriente, accommodations and camping are offered in conjunction with organized tours and typically include guide services, meals, transportation from Coca or Lago Agrio, etc. The only towns you might spend any time in are Lago Agrio or Coca, and, if you're lucky, that won't be for very long.

■ Lago Agrio

This offers plenty of budget accommodations. Poke around for the latest developments (which are occurring rapidly), as places in this region tend to vary in quality over time. There really aren't any great options in the town itself. Try the clean and modern, but somewhat noisy, **Hostal El Cofán**, Av. Quito and 12 de Febrero, ☎ 6-830-009. Rooms include private baths, fans or air-conditioning, and, in some cases, TVs. Remember, you are not staying here for the ambiance. $

Just outside of town, about a mile west on the main road from Quito, is **Hostal Grán Lago**, ☎ 6-830-015, a bit nicer as a retreat from downtown. It costs more, but is well worth it for better quality, atmosphere and solace. $-$$

The newest, and reportedly best hotel in town, is **Arazá**, Quito and Narvaéz, ☎ 6-830-223, though I haven't been there. $$

■ Coca

In Coca, **Hostería La Misión**, on the Napo riverfront, ☎ 6-880-260, allows an escape from the boomtown's bustle in the only good hotel in town. Air-conditioned rooms complement a quiet and clean atmosphere, a decent restaurant, and a bar. $

The only other acceptable places in town are the budget-oriented **Hotel Oasis**, also on the riverfront near La Misión, ☎ 6-880-127, and **Hotel El Auca**, in the center of town, ☎ 6-880-127. The Auca is popular with budget travelers and recommended as being comfortable. It has cabins with private hot-water baths, a patio garden and knowledgeable and friendly owners. $

"Auca" is the Quichua word for "savages," and is used by the Quichua to refer to the Huaorani ethnic group. Needless to say, this is a direct insult to the Huaorani. In their language, Huaorani means "the people," a name they obviously prefer.

■ Cuyabeno Region: Ecolodges, Riverboats & Camps

☆ **Cuyabeno River Lodge**, operated by Nuevo Mundo Travel and Tours, is a top-quality ecolodge along the Río Cuyabeno. From Lago Agrio, a short journey to the lodge provides quick access to the western stretches of the reserve. Here, most of the exploring is done in canoes around the shallow lakes that surround the ecolodge. This unique habitat is well removed from the other projects on Río Aguarico. It provides opportunities for spectacular wildlife viewing, as well as the chance to venture farther out with a tent-based camp on the shoreline of one of the lakes. Back at the lodge, relax in complete comfort in native-style cabins. Natural materials, cozy rooms, with private baths and water at nature's temperature – overall, this is a very professional outfit, with an emphasis on natural history and environmental sensitivity. $$$$, all-inclusive.

Upper Amazon Basin

Nuevo Mundo Travel and Tours is at Av. Coruña N26-207 and Orellana in Quito, ☎ 2-2564-448/2-2553-826/2-2509-431, ☎/fax 2-2565-261, www.nuevomundotravel.com, nmundo@interactive.net. ec, info@nuevomundotravel.com. This is a professional, Ecuadorian-owned outfitter. Their guides are exceptional. They are priced at the high end of the market, but you get good value. Their president, Oswaldo Muñoz, is a founding member of the Ecuadorian Ecotourism Association. They specialize in cultural and natural history tours to the Cuyabeno Reserve.

☆ **Flotel Francisco de Orellana** is a world-renowned 140-foot riverboat that cruises along the Río Aguarico and some of the most pristine sections of the Cuyabeno Reserve. The Flotel is a wonderful alternative means of exploring the largest rainforest on earth. During a three- or four-night tour you can experience a variety of rainforest excursions with planned activities. Birding, wildlife viewing, and photography are not only spectacular, but almost as accessible from onboard as on the trails. You'll see everything from prolific bird life to freshwater dolphins to floating, moonlit caimans. If you're lucky, you will have the opportunity to swim with the dolphins.

From the spacious sun deck on top of the boat enjoy the world of the Amazon without lifting a finger. If the weather changes, enjoy a good book in the upper deck's bar and lounge room. The comfortable dining room serves delicious food and is a great place to mingle with other travelers. Rooms are simple, yet adequate, with bunk beds, dresser, closets, and private baths with hot water. The boat can accommodate up to 48 passengers.

Planned excursions occur primarily in the mornings and afternoons, while the Flotel cruises along the Río Aguarico during the midday meal, siesta and at night. Jungle excursions include raised platform walks with local indigenous guides, which seems to be a relatively functional relationship between the company and natives. Each evening the guides give a preview of the following day, and the crew are all well-equipped with pressed-white uniforms – just picture *The Love Boat*. In addition, there is a full-time medical doctor onboard. The guides are always available, friendly, and extremely knowledgeable about the region's flora and fauna, as well as cultural and environmental issues. They're also more than willing to give salsa lessons on the deck at night, if you buy them a cocktail or two! Although this is primarily a luxury jungle cruise, they do support conservation, scientific research, environmental education, and indigenous community development. Overall, the Flotel serves as a fine example of how tourist excursions can be conducted in a relatively benign manner. $$$$

Ecuador Amazon Expeditions, Av. República de El Salvador 970, Quito, ☎ 2-2464-780 (in the US 800-527-2500), ☎/fax 2-2464-702, a branch of Metropolitan Touring, operates Flotel Orellana and is one of the best and most responsible ecotour operators in the Oriente.

☆ **La Selva Jungle Lodge**, surpassing even Ecuadorian standards of first-class ecotourism, is praised worldwide as one of the best projects of its kind. Years of experience and a good deal of integrity are the deciding factors here. You would be hard-pressed to find a better ecotourism project than this.

Less than three hours down the Río Napo from Coca, La Selva is next to a pretty lake, Lago de Garzacocha. The lodge uses kerosene lamps and natural showers, relying very little on generators and fossil fuels. Individual cabins use indigenous designs and local materials, and they include mosquito netting and private baths. The common facilities, including the reception area, bar, and adjacent dining room, are simple and rustic, but very comfortable. The cuisine, like the architecture, incorporates local recipes into international-style meals.

Owners Eric and Magdalena Schwartz, who opened La Selva in 1985, work with the local Quichua people to hire professional, high-quality guides. For many years, the Schwartzes have operated a commercial butterfly farm, the first in the region to sell to botanical gardens in the United States. In 1992 they created the Neotropical Field Biology Institute, which invites scientists from around the world to carry out research. If you're interested, inquire ahead about their more primitive camping facilities and overnight stays deeper in the jungle.

Dugout-canoe rides are a part of daily activity, and nature hikes are varied. The observation tower in the forest canopy is remarkable – even if you're afraid of heights. Bird-watchers love the lodge – more than 500 species of birds have been sighted in the area. It's no wonder La Selva Jungle Lodge won the World Congress on Tourism and the Environment Award in 1992.

La Selva Jungle Lodge, 6 de Diciembre 2816, Quito, ☎ 2-2550-995 or 2-2554-686, ☎/fax 2-2567-297, laselva@uio.satnet.net, www. laselvajunglelodge.com. $$$-$$$$

Continuing down the Río Napo and away from Coca, the Oriente changes in character. "Civilization" retreats as nature advances. Eventually, after crossing the tiny black-water paradise of Lago de Pilchicocha, you arrive at your destination. **Sacha Lodge**, tucked beneath a blanket of rainforest on a 3,200-acre private reserve, is truly a special treat in a unique paradise. It is also one of the better examples

Upper Amazon Basin

of ecotourism in Ecuador. Traditional yet cozy accommodations, delicious meals, and professional integrity combine with outstanding opportunities for wildlife viewing and community involvement to create an incomparable experience. Here you can witness the upper Amazon Basin at its finest.

Activities at Sacha are varied and numerous. One major attraction is a 135-foot observation tower. To get there, you have two choices – a wonderful hike through thick forest, or an adventurous paddle down Orchid Creek, a black-water stream that meanders through flooded palm forest, seranaded by a chorus of tropical music. At the tower you climb through, and ultimately above, the rainforest canopy to experience magnificent views. Birding guides have reported seeing more than 80 species from the platform in one morning alone! In addition to a rainbow of birds, other common sightings from the tower include the three-toed sloth and howler and squirrel monkeys.

Other activities at Sacha include nature walks, canoe rides, swimming, and fishing for piranha. Wildlife viewing and bird-watching are popular, as is hiking with a guide, who identifies medicinal plants. The more adventurous can explore the forest at night in search of the elusive puma, the tiny marmoset, the floating caiman, and millions of insects. You can also visit the Butterfly House, one of Ecuador's largest butterfly farms, with more than 40 local species. Or head for the border of Yasuní National Park to check out a parrot lick, where thousands of parrots gather on sunny days to frolic on a clay salt bank. The clay, a sort of antacid for the parrots, draws out toxins from the fruit they consume. The show of squawking colors is spectacular. $$$$

Julio Zaldumbide 375 and Toledo, Quito, ☎ 2-2566-090, 2-2509-504, or 2-2509-115, ☎/fax 2-2236-521, sachalod@pi.pro.ec.

Piranha Encounter!

Traveler's account: "On one of my first trips to the Amazon region of Ecuador, while spending the morning swimming in a quiet little lagoon off the Río Aguarico, I was excited to learn from our guide that we would be fishing for piranha that afternoon. Imagine my surprise as I hopped into the motorized canoe ready to head off to piranha-infested waters, only to be told we would be fishing right where we had just been swimming!"

Don't be put off by this account – the truth is that Ecuadorian piranhas simply don't like the taste of gringo flesh.

☆ **Cabañas Panacocha** is four hours down the Río Napo by private launch (seven hours by motorized water taxi). The accommodations are set on an oxbow lake formed by the Río Panayacu, a tributary of the Napo, which is now under protected status. While in the past the facilities had the reputation of being a bit worn out, its newly renovated and constructed cabins are now much nicer, with natural construction, private baths and water at nature's temperature.

An English-speaking guide will accompany you on various nature trails and canoe rides across the lake. Much of the forest is primary, so the wildlife in this area is prolific. A small observation tower abuts the lodge and provides great dawn and dusk birding opportunities. Swimming and fishing are also available (no need to worry about piranhas). Panacocha is a great place to stay if you don't mind rustic conditions and are on a bit of a budget.

As with other ecolodges in this region, the only way to arrive is with prearranged reservations and a boat ride up the Río Napo (from Coca). Contact Luis García of **Emerald Forest**, Amazonas 1023 and Pinto, Quito, ☎ 2-2526-403, fax 2-2568-664.

If you're a budget traveler looking for a deep-jungle experience, then **Cabañas Jarrin** is the place to go. Don't expect top-quality naturalist guides, magnificent observation towers, parrot licks, or incredible accommodations. Do expect simple but more-than-adequate comfort, shared baths, swimming parties, and young gringo travelers. Jarrin is near Panacocha and offers hiking trails and canoe excursions. Guides are available, but not all of them speak English. Rooms are decent and the atmosphere, while still mellow, is a bit livelier than at the more expensive lodges.

In Coca contact **Expediciones Jarrín**, Napo and García Moreno, ☎ 6-880-251. From Coca, the boat ride takes four hours. Or you can take the seven- to nine-hour boat ride from Tena. $$

☆ **Yuturi Lodge** falls in the high-priced ecolodge category, along with Sacha and La Selva, although it is less expensive than its competitors. By private launch, Yuturi is about five hours down the Río Napo from Coca, offering a more remote location. It is set along the Río Yuturi, a southern tributary of the Napo, on land leased by the local Quichua community. In addition to participating in the normal ecotourism activities associated with this region, you can visit the indigenous community for a taste of native life.

Cabins are very rustic and mosquito netting is draped over all the beds. The common room provides a nice setting above the river. Enjoy delicious meals in a tranquil environment with a nice riverfront view. Electricity comes on in the evening. Climb the canopy tower for the best views and opportunities to witness monkeys and rare birds. Inquire about their new addition, **Yarina Lodge**, located much closer to Coca and reportedly a top-quality ecolodge at a very affordable price.

In Quito, Av. Amazonas 1324 and Colón, ☎ 2-2503-225, ☎/fax 2-2504-037; or, in Coca, ☎ 6-880-172; www.yuturilodge.com, yuturilodge@yahoo.com. $$$

■ Yasuní Area

Tiputini Biodiversity Station

Carol Walton and Kathy Swing helped create the Tiputini Biodiversity Station in an effort to preserve Yasuní National Park, support scientific research and educate the people that visit it. In fact, the only real way to visit Tiputini is through an educational or scientific program. The project is the result of the combined efforts of the Universidad de San Francisco in Quito and Boston University in Massachusetts. Years of work have resulted in one of the best research and ecotourism projects around.

The station is located along the Río Tiputini on 1,482 acres of land adjacent to the park boundary. The sleeping facilities include eight rooms with screened interiors, bunk beds, and clean private bathrooms. Larger rooms have single beds and private baths. All told, the station can handle more than 40 guests. Tranquil views of the river and forest abound from the vista porches, dining, lounge and bar areas, as well as other buildings. Additional facilities include a library and laboratory, which provide opportunities to learn about the region's biology and ongoing research. Rainwater showers flow at nature's temperature, electricity is turned on for a bit in the evening, and the floor fans provide a refreshing breeze in the sleeping quarters. And you won't be disappointed with the quality of the meals.

Scientists here have now documented the presence of 12 species of primates, several of which are common around the facilities, and more than 520 species of birds. The area has more than 1,500 species of trees, and animals such as jaguars, tapirs, capybaras, caimans, otters, and dolphins have been observed along the river. Well-developed trails cover 19 miles of primary forest in the area immediately surrounding the station. A 124-foot tower in the canopy permits fantastic opportunities for viewing wildlife. The only downside to the entire project is the high cost (due to expenses associated with its remote location). Tiputini does offer reduced rates for research and educational groups. $$$-$$$$

Carol Walton, Universidad San Francisco de Quito, Campo Alegre, Casilla 17-12-841, Quito (this is a post office box, not a physical addresss), ☎ 2-2895-723, ext. 243, ☎/fax 2-2890-070, tbs@mail.usfq. edu.ec or tiputini@aol.com.

Community-Based Programs

For the **Cabañas Bataburo**, in Yasuní National Park, contact Kempery Tours, at Pinto 539 and Amazonas in Quito, ☎ 2-2226-583, ☎/fax 2-2226-715, www.kempery.com, kempery@kempery.com. $$$

Añangucocha Lagoon. The Añangu community, across the Napo from La Selva, charges $30/day, which stays in the community. Contact Chris Canaday in Quito for detailed information, ☎ 2-2447-463, canaday@accessinter.net. $$

Sani Isla is also near La Selva. All proceeds go to the Sani Isla Community. Contact them by email at elmontelodge@hotmail.com. $$$

■ Camping

 Camping is available throughout the Oriente, including at the Cuyabeno Reserve and Yasuní National Park. Unless you are a skilled navigator who happens to be native to this region, however, you must make arrangements for an organized tour with one of the operators listed above or with guides from Lago Agrio or Coca.

In the higher altitude and *páramo* habitat of the Cayambe-Coca Ecological Reserve, there are ample opportunities for camping in conjunction with backcountry trekking (see page 333 for more details).

Upper Amazon Basin

Where to Eat

As with accommodations, meals are included with jungle-lodge excursions. There are only a couple of places to find food if you're in Coca or Lago Agrio.

■ Coca

Hostería La Misión, ☎ 6-880-260, on the Napo riverfront, is a bit pricey, but is one of the few eateries in town that caters to tourists. The food, which includes American-style breakfasts, is not bad. If you're looking for something a little cheaper, the restaurant in **Hotel El Auca**, Napo, between Rocafuerte and Moreno, ☎ 6-880-600, is better geared for the budget traveler and is a good place to meet others looking to organize a group jungle tour. Elsewhere, the American-owned **Pappa Dans**, by the river on Napo and Chimborazo, is a good place to hang out in the evenings and meet fellow tourists. It serves good, clean, and safe American food.

■ Lago Agrio

Hotel El Cofán's restaurant, 12 de Febrero and Av. Quito, ☎ 6-830-009, offers the best and safest food in town, although it is a bit pricey. It's nothing to brag about, but then again, this is just a stop on the way to the jungle. Alternatively, try one of the *chifas* in town along Avenida Quito.

When in doubt, or rather when in a small town in Ecuador that seems to have only the sketchiest of options for eating, always head for the local Chinese restaurant – or chifa, as they are known. The food at the ever-popular chifas tends to be a good, safe bet, especially when your other options are limited. Most chifas offer decent vegetarian, noodle, and rice dishes and prices tend to be low.

Central & Southern Oriente

The area surrounding **Tena** and **Misahuallí** is the most-visited rainforest destination in the country. One of the more developed regions of the upper Amazon, it is also the most accessible. Jungle excursions abound and there are still small patches of primary forest, mostly in the form of private reserves. Outstanding rafting, kayaking, swimming, tubing and hiking opportunities are available, as well

as birding, botany, medicinal study, cultural and general nature travel. Farther down the Río Napo, the land becomes more pristine.

In the south, especially along the eastern slopes of the Andes and around **Macas**, the rugged topography and lack of access have preserved some of the best wildlife-viewing opportunities and intact indigenous cultures in Ecuador. In this region, virgin rainforest and the communities of the unique **Achuar** and **Shuar Nations** await the true adventure seeker.

Puyo via Baños is the overland gateway city to both of these regions, and offers its own share of opportunities for eco-cultural excursions, though the area is a bit more developed. It is also the administrative center for indigenous groups and community-based programs in the southern Oriente's Río Pastaza region.

History

The Napo Province, with **Tena** as its capital, is where native Amazonian people and the Spanish first clashed. Tena, founded in 1560, was the main colonial missionary town in the Oriente. Conflict with the indigenous Quijos Quichua people led to uprisings, although the Spanish were able to maintain control. In more recent times the ensuing colonization converted most of the land in this area to agriculture and cattle grazing. Previous conflicts and border disputes with Peru had an impact on travel here, especially farther south. Now that things have settled down a bit, foreigners can once again visit freely, although a military presence is still apparent.

The entire Upper Río Napo region is primarily Quichua territory, and this is most likely the group you will be interacting with. Tena is the economic and administrative center of the region, and the surrounding area is a developed patchwork of agriculture, pastures and secondary rainforest. As Tena is not (yet) an oil town like its jungle counterparts, it remains relatively safe, clean and almost pleasant. Farther south, near Macas, the Shuar and Achuar indigenous people maintain traditional ways of life and continue to survive in largely untouched forest.

Flora & Fauna

 As the Andes descend dramatically eastward into the Napo region, the true tropical lowland rainforest begins with the headwaters of the **Río Napo**. The Central Oriente offers ecological life zones similar to those in the northern region (see *The Upper Amazon Basin*, page 321), with many species that live here and nowhere else on earth. This is due primarily to the mixture of different microclimates created by drastic elevation changes between the Andes and the Amazon, resulting in small pockets of life that evolved separately from their close neighbors. Thus, biologically, the Oriente – with up to 5% of the earth's plant species – is arguably the richest place on the planet.

The area around Puyo, Tena, Misahuallí and the Upper Río Napo is significantly more developed (deforested), although once you head into the jungle, you'll discover the flora and fauna, including monkeys, tapirs, sloths, a few large predatory cats, and a plethora of birds. Though large stands of primary forest exist, recent estimates give the entire Ecuadorian Amazon as little as 10 to 15 remaining years of ecological integrity if current rates of deforestation continue.

The time to go, to learn and to make a difference, is now.

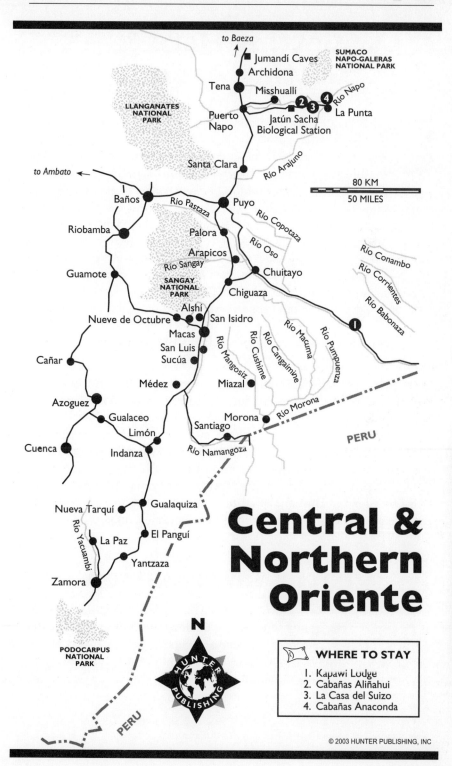

to Baeza

Jumandí Caves
Archidona
Tena
Misshuallí
SUMACO
NAPO-GALERAS
NATIONAL PARK
Río Napo
La Punta
Puerto Napo
Jatún Sacha
Biological Station

LLANGANATES
NATIONAL
PARK

Santa Clara

Río Arajuno

to Ambato

80 KM
50 MILES

Baños
Río Pastaza
Puyo
Río Copotaza

Riobamba
Palora
Río Oso
Río Conambo
Río Corrientes

Arapicos
Río Sangay
Guamote
SANGAY
NATIONAL
PARK
Chuitayo
Chiguaza
Río Babonaza

Alshí
San Isidro
Nueve de Octubre
Macas
Río Macuma
Río Pumpuenza

Cañar
San Luis
Sucúa
Río Mangosiz
Río Cushime
Río Cangaimine

Azoguez
Médez
Miazal

Gualaceo
Morona
Río Morona
Limón
Santiago
Cuenca
Indanza
Río Namangoza
PERU

Nueva Tarquí
Gualaquiza

La Paz
El Panguí
Río Yacuambi
Yantzaza

Zamora

PODOCARPUS
NATIONAL
PARK

N

HUNTER PUBLISHING

PERU

Central & Northern Oriente

WHERE TO STAY
1. Kapawi Lodge
2. Cabañas Aliñahui
3. La Casa del Suizo
4. Cabañas Anaconda

Central & Southern Oriente

© 2003 HUNTER PUBLISHING, INC

Getting Here & Getting Around

Ecuador's Oriente stretches toward the Amazon along the entire eastern slope of the Andes. This chapter focuses on the central and southern Oriente, particularly the region around **Tena/Misahuallí** as the major jumping-off point into the jungle and farther south around Macas. Tena is most accessible by automobile from the Andes via Quito or Baños. The upper route, a road from Quito through Baeza, continues south to Tena, and then east at Puerto Napo to Misahuallí. From Baños, the other (southern) route to Tena offers access to the Oriente via Puyo – which is about halfway between the two – on the Baños-Puyo Road and then the Puyo-Tena Road. The Tena/Misahuallí area offers numerous opportunities exist for everything from short jungle excursions in the immediate vicinity to multi-day trips farther east, where vast expanses of relatively undisturbed rainforest await.

Puyo, the provincial capital of Pastaza, is served by a small airport in the nearby town of **Shell**, which may also serve as a starting point for trips into the Río Pastaza region. The jumping-off point for deep-jungle excursions into the southern Oriente is the much less-visited town of **Macas**. You can get there either by road from Puyo via Chultayo or, more often on arranged tours, by air directly to Macas. Inquire at travel agents in Quito, or contact TAME in Quito for one of several flights per week to Macas (**TAME**, Amazonas 1354 and Colón, 2nd floor; for international flights, ☎ 2-2221-494/495; for domestic flights, ☎ 2-2509-382/83/84/86/87/88; www.tame.com.ec).

Visitor Information

Many tours and travel agents that operate in the central Oriente (Upper Napo) advertise in Baños and Quito, although there are some in Tena and Misahuallí as well.

■ Tena

In Tena, the **tourist office** is in the northern part of town, at Bolívar and Amazonas, and there is an **Internet café** nearby. The pedestrian bridge connects the two halves of town and continues down Av. 15 de Noviembre south to the bus station. Another Internet café, **Piraña Net**, is just southeast of the bridge on 9 de Octubre and Tarqui (expect to wait awhile and pay a lot). The **Andinatel communications office** is on Olmedo and Juan Montalvo. There's a **Banco del Austro** on 15 de Noviembre and Dias de Pineda (Visa and travellers checks). If you're in Misahuallí, you'll need to go back to Tena for these services.

■ Puyo

In Puyo, the capital of the Pastaza Province, the **Andinatel communications office** is located at Villamil and Orellana, and the **post office** is a block to the east, at 27 de Febrero, between Orellana and Atahualpa. There is an **Internet café** nearby, on Calle Atahualpa. The **Casa de Cambio** was on Atahualpa and 9 de Octubre, ☎ 3-883-064 ☎/fax 3-883-064, but this may or may not still be there, so you might want to call in advance. The **Ministerio de Turismo** is on the fifth floor of the Centro Shopping Carmelita, on Ceslao Marín and 9 de Octubre.

■ Macas

In Macas, the **Andinatel telephone office** is at 24 de Mayo and Sucre, and the **post office** is at 9 de Octubre and Comín, near the main plaza, the church, and the Shuar Travel office. There is a **Banco del Austro** at 24 de Mayo and 10 de Agosto (travelers checks and Visa). The bus terminal is also centrally located on Amazonas and 10 de Agosto. There is a small regional airport at Amazonas and Cuenca.

Touring & Sightseeing

■ Tena & Misahuallí

 Tena, the easternmost colonial city in Ecuador and capital of Napo Province, evolved from a missionary town and trade outpost to today's ranching, agricultural, and tourism community. Recently, the oil industry has made its

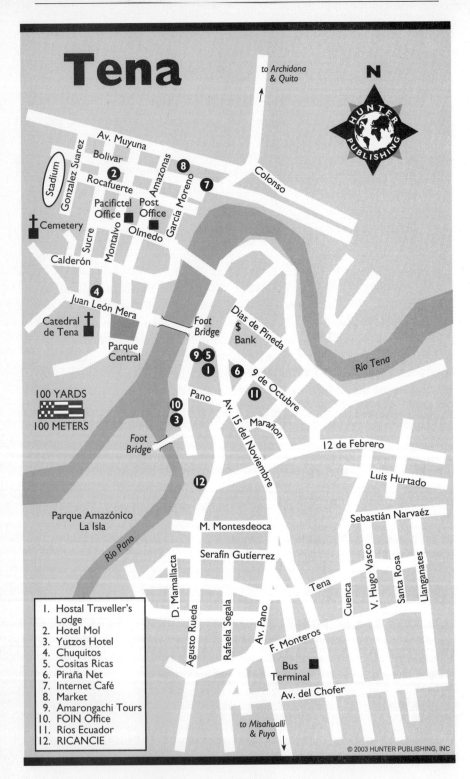

Tena

N

to Archidona & Quito

HUNTER PUBLISHING

Av. Muyuna

Gonzalez Suarez

Bolivar

② Rocafuerte

Amazonas

García Moreno

⑧

⑦

Colonso

Stadium

Pacifictel Office

Post Office

Sucre

Montalvo

Olmedo

✝ Cemetery

Calderón

④

Juan León Mera

Catedral de Tena ✝

Parque Central

Foot Bridge

Días de Pineda

$ Bank

Río Tena

⑨ ⑤
① ⑥

9 de Octubre

100 YARDS

100 METERS

⑩
③

Pano

Av. 15 del Noviembre

Marañon

⑪

Foot Bridge

⑫

12 de Febrero

Luis Hurtado

Parque Amazónico
La Isla

Río Pano

M. Montesdeoca

Serafín Gutíerrez

Sebastián Narvaéz

Tena

Cuenca

V. Hugo Vasco

Santa Rosa

Llanganates

D. Mamallacta

Agusto Rueda

Rafaela Segala

Av. Pano

F. Monteros

1. Hostal Traveller's Lodge
2. Hotel Mol
3. Yutzos Hotel
4. Chuquitos
5. Cositas Ricas
6. Piraña Net
7. Internet Café
8. Market
9. Amarongachi Tours
10. FOIN Office
11. Ríos Ecuador
12. RICANCIE

Bus Terminal

Av. del Chofer

to Misahuallí & Puyo

© 2003 HUNTER PUBLISHING, INC

presence known in this area. Unlike Coca and Lago Agrío, however, Tena remains a tranquil and pleasant town, relatively unspoiled by the nasty side-effects of the oil industry. The Upper Río Napo region, accessed from Tena via Puerto Napo and Misahuallí, is the most accessible and therefore most commonly sought-after destination in the country for jungle trips and world-class whitewater rafting and kayaking. It also has comfortable ecolodges.

From Tena it is just a hop, skip, and jump to Misahuallí and into the rainforest. Keep in mind that the area is fairly well developed, with agriculture, banana plantations, and cattle ranching. There are, however, several ideal places for excursions into *la selva* (the jungle), most of which offer lodging, meals, and all-inclusive guided tours.

Nowadays, Tena and Misahuallí cater to the jungle-seeking tourist, particularly budget travelers. Primarily, they offer places to meet or organize a tour group, eat, sleep, and pick up a few supplies before heading into the rainforest. There are a few fairly good beaches and a nice walkway along the river in and around Tena. Tena is reached from Quito in the north via the road through Baeza, or from Baños on the road through Puyo. Modern facilities, including banks, post, and communications, as well as basic accommodations and restaurants are available here (see *Visitor Information*, page 355).

Just south of Tena on the main road to Puyo is **Puerto Napo**, where a traffic bridge crosses the Río Napo. On the northern bank is the road heading east to Misahuallí, about 10 miles away. This small port town at the confluence of the Ríos Napo and Misahuallí now services jungle tourism as its major focus. Outfitter offices may well be located in Tena, but the outfitters and guides themselves are often courting travelers here, as it is the main jumping-off point into the (less than virgin) rainforest. Other than that, there is not much else to Misahuallí.

■ Puyo

Puyo, the capital of the Pastaza Province, is the jungle's biggest "city," though it only has about 20,000 inhabitants. Although relatively friendly and pleasant compared to many Ecuadorian towns, Puyo doesn't offer too much for the jungle-seeking traveler, other than a resting and supply pick-up point between Baños and Tena, or for those heading south to Macas. An Ecuadorian guide friend claims Puyo is one of his favorite towns for its laid-back, friendly atmosphere, but that may be primarily because he has a girlfriend there! Either way, it is a long bumpy road to the jungle, and Puyo may well

Central & Southern Oriente

provide a needed lunch stop en route. Puyo is often overlooked as a destination, though it does offer options for visiting secondary forest and nearby community-based tourism efforts, as well as trips deep into the Río Pastaza region. See *Tours & Tour Operators*, page 368.

◼ Macas

Travel into the far southern expanses of the Oriente requires heading down toward Macas by plane or by road from Puyo. Macas is the main population and commercial center in the southern Oriente, though it was founded initially as a missionary outpost. The least-explored region in the upper Amazon Basin lies to the east of Macas and offers a rich mix of colonial history and indigenous rainforest life. It takes almost a day to reach Macas by road from Puyo. But beautiful scenery,

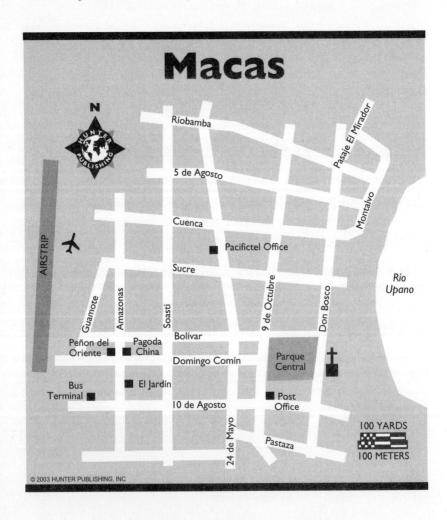

suspension bridges over deep river gorges, undisturbed rainforest, and the people of the Achuar and Shuar cultures make the trip worthwhile.

Situated above the Río Upano Valley, Macas is the provincial capital of Morona-Santiago, with close to 10,000 inhabitants. The town itself offers a laid-back and pleasant atmosphere. Dating back several hundred years, this colonial jungle town remains clean and relatively untainted by the spoils of modern development. Lacking much of a tourism infrastructure (though this is changing), Macas maintains its "lost in time" appeal. It is also the closest population base with an airfield nearby. Unfortunately, the discovery of oil in the vicinity is changing Macas rapidly, though its historical foundation helps to maintain the colonial atmosphere.

From Puyo, along mostly dirt roads, the better part of a day is required to reach Macas on the vía a Macas. TAME offers a few weekly flights to Macas from Quito. From Macas, opportunities to explore the southern Oriente include the Río Pastaza area and Kapawi Lodge (page 378), as well as the lower eastern side of the isolated Sangay National Park.

Adventures

■ On Water

Rafting & Kayaking

From the headwaters of the Amazon River, the eastern slopes of the Andean mountain range provide year-round, world-class white-water rafting and kayaking opportunities through spectacular gorges and breathtaking rainforest. The many rivers and seasonal variations in rainfall provide prime choices for any level of difficulty and intensity, all within close proximity to Tena.

The **Upper Río Napo**, known locally as Jatunyacu (Quichua for "Big Water"), is one of the most popular trips in the region. The Napo offers classic, big-wave, Class III fun with a great jungle backdrop. On one of the two main tributaries of the Amazon River, enjoy a perfect combination of exciting rapids and calm pools. For the timid, the river is also big enough so you can avoid the largest waves and take an easier route. Ideal for families and children is the slower-paced, Class II-III **Río Anzu**. The Anzu, a beautiful tropical river, offers soft adventure at its finest, with small rapids and relaxing pools. Don't forget to ask for the sit-on-top kayak during this trip. For thrill-seekers and expert rafters, the Class VI+ trip down the **Río Misahuallí** is not to be missed. Considered one of South America's ultimate rafting trips, it travels through a deep gorge surrounded by virgin rainforest and crystal waterfalls.

Ecuador has also earned a reputation as a world-class whitewater kayaking destination. Within an hour of Tena you can experience everything from Class II beginner floats to Class V craziness for experts only. For the beginner, it is an ideal place to learn in warm, clean, tropical rivers. As your skill level increases, you can move up the water ladder.

In the far stretches of Ecuador's southern Oriente, near Macas, is the **Río Upano** and the **Namangosa Gorge**, probably the most remote commercially run river in the country. The river itself cuts through the absolutely spectacular Namangosa Gorge, where 300-foot waterfalls shower the rainforest and canyon from all sides. From October to around February, expect Class IV waves and an experience not to be missed if you are traveling through Macas.

For the best water-based activity, **Ríos Ecuador** (info@Ríosecuador. com, www.RiosEcuador.com) is the country's whitewater leader. Contact them in Tena, on the second floor of the Camba Huasi Hotel, across the street from the bus terminal, 15 de Noviembre and 9 de Octubre, ☎ 6-886-727. Or, in Quito, they are at Juan Rodriguez E7 75 and Diego de Almagro, ☎ 2-2569-252 or 2-2906-174. Ecuadorian owner Gynner Coronel Paris is an expert kayaker who spent many years paddling the waters of the US Pacific Northwest. The company offers high-quality rafting trips for $50 to $65 per person per day, including transportation to and from Tena and a tasty riverside lunch. They can also customize multi-day rafting trips that include jungle excursions and stays in traditional Quichua cabañas or first-class ecolodges. Their one-day kayak trips cost $60 per person; an excellent four-day kayaking school for beginners is $250 per person.

DUGOUT CANOES

With most jungle trips, especially the more remote ones, dugout canoes are a staple part of the journey and the adventure. A great way to see the sky – when you're trekking on the forest floor you won't even be able to see the sky, for the dense canopy – canoes are the primary mode of transportation here. The Napo and its tributaries are among the widest rivers in Ecuador.

■ On Foot

Hiking & Birding

For hiking and nature-based travel (birding, jungle excursions, canoeing, learning about medicinal plants), this is the region to visit. Plenty of outfitters and ecolodges operate in the upper Napo region based out of Quito and Baños, as well as the gateway jungle towns of Tena and Misahuallí. Private reserves in this area offer the best chance at birding and wildlife viewing without heading too deep into the jungle.

Spelunking

The area near Tena has excellent limestone caves, the most popular of which are the Cuevas de Jumandí or **Jumandí Caves** (page 364). There are other, more remote options, but the native Quichua culture is very sensitive about entering these sites. For the more adventurous traveler interested in some serious caving in conjunction with visiting local Quichua communities, see *Ecotourism with RICANCIE*, page 363.

Trekking & Backpacking

One wouldn't normally associate volcanoes and the high country with the Amazon Basin, the largest intact rainforest in the world. But the Andes created this sea of green, which actually was once part of the Pacific Ocean millions of years ago. And some of these peaks poke up as islands in the sky along the western fringes of the Oriente, offering great opportunities for the serious trekker.

From Tena, a reportedly arduous but rewarding climb is up **Sumaco Volcano**, at 12,200-feet, in the Sumaco-Galeras National Park. Jutting up from jungle terrain, you will encounter steep slopes with almost impassible, thick vegetation. This area has not been developed, is rarely visited, and trekking is not recommended for casual hikers. The trek begins in tropical lowland rainforest, steadily ascends through misty cloud forest with varying levels of endemic species, and ends in *páramo* habitat. Local guides in the Tena area provide services for the multi-day trek up to the top, where hard-to-match views over the Amazon blanket await the intrepid adventurer. Inquire in Tena with RICANCIE (the Network of Indigenous Communities of the Upper Napo for Intercultural Exchange and Ecotourism) for community-based ecotourism that may involve trips into the park, ☎ 6-887-074. Recent trail developments may have made the trek more accessible. Some climbing guides and tour operators in Quito may offer support. Use the map 1:50,000 *Volcán Sumaco and Pavayacu*.

The lowlands of **Sangay National Park**, closer to Macas, offer rainforest hikes and difficult treks up into the highlands of the currently active **Sangay Volcano** (17,102 feet), but it is much more accessible from Riobamba in the Andes. Inquire with climbing guides and tour operators in Quito or Riobamba.

Eco-Travel

■ The Upper Río Napo – Excursions from Tena & Misahuallí

Sumaco-Galeras National Park

One of the least-explored and least-developed treasures of the Upper Río Napo region is Sumaco-Galeras National Park. The centerpiece of the park is **Sumaco Volcano**, at 12,204 feet, which has been visited on rare occasions and is not recommended without a guide. This is one of the least developed areas in the region, where you will find undisturbed lowland rainforest up to *páramo* vegetation, with breathtaking views. Inquire with climbing tour operators in Quito or local guides in Tena.

Ecotourism with RICANCIE

Based in Tena, the Network of Indigenous Communities of the Upper Napo for Intercultural Exchange and Ecotourism, or **RICANCIE**, is a community-based ecotourism (CBE) program offered by an umbrella organization that represents a network of Quichua communities. As with many other groups in the Oriente, it was oil exploration, and the road development that came with it, followed by colonization and unregulated tourism, that spawned local efforts to create community-based programs. Fortunately, the Quichua people not only have the ability to organize well and adapt to new influences, but they seem to do so while maintaining their cultural integrity. As a result, there are now many opportunities to visit local communities on tours. RICANCIE, now fully permitted by the Ecuadorian government, manages, trains and certifies this network of CBEs so that they all benefit fairly from the tourism industry. Going through them, rather than through privately owned lodges with absentee owners, offers direct benefits to both the community and to the traveler, who gets a more real-life experience.

Although different communities offer a slightly different emphasis, as well as different levels of comfort and exploration, between them, they are sure to provide what most conscientious and hearty travelers are seeking. Even better, connect several of the communities on one trip and have a wonderful overall experience. All accommodations are in traditional and basic, but comfortable, thatched-roof huts with clean beds and mosquito nets. Packages, at approximately $60 per person per day, include knowledgeable, trained local guides, all meals and transportation from Tena. Arrangements must be made ahead of time.

 For detailed descriptions of each of the community programs involved, read *Defending our Rainforest: A Guide to Community-Based Ecotourism in the Ecuadorian Amazon*, by Rolf Wesche and Any Drum, available in Quito bookstores and some gift stores or through **The Ecotourism Society** at www.ecotourism.org.

In Tena, contact **RICANCIE** at Av. 15 de Noviembre 772, ☎ 6-887-072; ricancie@ecuanex.net.ec, www.eduweb.com/schaller/TourInfo.html.

Jumandí Caves

Less than 15 miles north of Tena are the famous limestone Caves of Jumandí. Blanketed with local superstition, the caves are open to the public for a bit of muddy exploration. Don't expect to come out clean, and, unless you are an experienced spelunker, hire a local guide. If you really want to get into the thick of it, bring rubber boots and a head-lamp. New tourist facilities include a restaurant and swimming pool.

The caves are less than five miles north of Archidona on the Baeza-Tena Road (which meets with the Quito-Baeza Road) by bus or taxi and under an hour from Tena. Simply catch a bus from Tena heading to Quito and ask to be let off at the "Cuevas de Jumandí." Local guides in Tena can provide services, including transportation, rubber boots and lights for Jumandí and other less-visited limestone caves in the area.

Jungle Excursions

In addition to Jatun Sacha and the ecolodges listed below, various excursions into secondary and sometimes primary rainforest, mixed with "ethno-tourism" exist in the region around Tena and Misahuallí. As a population center for the relatively well-organized Quichua community, Tena also offers contacts for community-based ecotourism that is both less expensive for the traveler and of more immediate benefit to the local community. Keep in mind that on these excursions you will most likely learn more about culture, plant lore and agricultural customs than you will about wildlife. And the accommodations will be much more simple than the higher-end jungle ecolodges. Don't let this dissuade you, though, as these are truly unique and wonderful opportunities to get away from the resort-like places, to stay with families and learn about real life here in the Ecuadorian jungle.

Jatun Sacha Biological Reserve

The Jatun Sacha Biological Center for Field Research and Education was established in 1986 and now protects about 4,950 acres of tropical wet forest. Almost 80% of the reserve is primary forest and is one of the most biologically rich areas on earth. Jatun Sacha, which means "Big Forest" in Quichua, is a haven for biological conservation, research, education, community extension, and ecotourism in Ecuador. A private, nonprofit Ecuadorian foundation since 1989, the Jatun Sacha Foundation is now one of the two largest nonprofit conservation organizations in the country. The organization also co-owns and manages the Cabañas Aliñahui ecotourism lodge (see page 374) and conducts programs at two other stations in Ecuador. In addition, Jatun Sacha Foundation helped to fund and start up RICANCIE's community-based ecotourism project (page 363).

Above: The village of El Suspiro (Loma Alta)

Below: School children in El Suspiro

Above: The cloud forest near El Suspiro

Below: Giant tortoise of the Galápagos Islands

Above: The Galápagos Islands

Below: Sally Lightfoot crabs on Santa María (Floreana) Island

Above: Watch your step – stingrays on Santa María (Floreana) Island

Below: Galápagos sea lions, Punta Suárez on Isla Española

Evening accommodations in the Galápagos

Yellow land iguana, South Plaza Island, Galápagos

Above: Playful Galápagos sea lion pup

Below: Craters on the Galápagos, evidence of volcanic activity

Above: Another rough day for the author, Isla Española

Below: Blue-footed boobies on Isla Española

The lodging and research facilities are more suitable for students and researchers than they are for the general tourist. With shared baths, cold water, kitchen facilities, and electricity, they were designed for scientists and volunteers working on the reserve. Students are welcome to reside here as part of a volunteer program that may include anything from agricultural forestry to environmental education.

The forest itself is one of only a few contiguous intact expanses in the region. Although many of the larger, wide-ranging mammals no longer reside in this area, tapirs, monkeys, and a stunning array of birds continue to call the area home. Signed trails provide opportunities to explore; local guides are available upon request for an additional fee.

Jatun Sacha (www.jatunsacha.org) is about 14 miles east of the Río Napo bridge along the Ahuano Road. Their main office is in Quito at Pasaje Eugenio de Santillán N34-248 and Maurián, ☎ 2-2432-240, 2-2432-173, 2-2432-246, ☎/fax 2-2453-583. Or you can write to them at PO Box 17-12-867, Quito, mccolm@jsacha.ecx.ec. They also have an office in Tena, just north of the bus station.

AmaZoonico

This wildlife rehabilitation center provides an opportunity to see and learn about exotic animals not often found in the wild. The private reserve works with injured animals and wild pets in order to reintroduce them to their habitat. From several species of monkey (watch the zipper on your backpack – they'll take anything they can get their curious little hands on) to large cats and predators in flight, the animals here are diverse and well cared for. A visit to AmaZoonico is a real learning experience. Long-term volunteer programs are offered. Contact them c/o Angelika Raimann, Apt. 202, Tena/Napo, Ecuador, fax 00593-6-887-304, amazon@na.pro.ec, www.amazoonica.org.

Trips to AmaZoonico include a stay at, Liana Lodge, Cabañas Aliñahui and other lodges, described below.

■ Río Pastaza & the Southern Oriente

Excursions from Puyo

Puyo is the provincial capital of Pastaza, and about the only developed center in this largely untouched expanse of primary rainforest and indigenous territories. Bordered by Yasuní National Park in the north and the Río Pastaza and Peru to the south and east, most of the territorial rights to this land belong to the Quichua, with other indigenous groups claiming territories around the edges of the province.

Through an organization known as OPIP, the Organization of Indigenous Peoples of Pastaza, native people have claimed legal rights to this region and OPIP is actively pursuing the goal of maintaining it as a nature and culture reserve, including promoting community-based ecotourism (CBE) projects in local communities. These newly developed projects are, in some cases, the best chance for at least a couple of quickly disappearing cultures, including the last two remaining Záparo indigenous communities. **ATACAPI Tours** is the active ecotourism branch of OPIP, and operates in conjunction with the Puyo-based and Quichua-owned **Papangu Tours** to visit these remote communities (see *Tours & Tour Operators*, page 368).

Papangu trips range from day excursions to multi-day treks farther into the interior of the Oriente. Hiking through rainforest, visiting local Quichua communities, dugout canoe rides and fishing. Especially recommended is their three-day tour to **Chunchu Pamba Protected Forest**, though it is a bit more physically demanding than some of the more low-key trips. You have to be willing to rough it a bit.

Top 10 Things to Find in the Jungle

If you're in the jungle and want a treasure hunt, there are plenty of wonderfully exotic plants and animals to seek out. These are some of my favorites:

- Leafcutter ants – a whole line of them, usually walking right across your path carrying large leaves on their backs.
- Piranhas – you may be swimming with them!
- Howler monkeys – follow your ears, you'll hear them before you see them.
- A tarantula bigger than your hand!
- Stick insects.
- Oropendula nests – look up.
- A real vampire bat!
- Pink dolphins.
- A big vine to swing on, Tarzan-style.
- An anaconda snake, bigger than the vine.
- Lemon ants – you can eat them right off of the tree; mmm tasty!

Sangay National Park

The lower, eastern portion of Sangay National Park is one of the least-visited areas in the country. For the experienced navigator (or anyone with a good local guide), Sangay offers adventure at its finest. The park is enormous, encompassing more than 704,480 acres, with Volcán Sangay peaking out at 17,102 feet. From the southeastern entrance, expect limited trails, thick vegetation, plenty of rainfall, and abundant wildlife. The park center, just out of Macas in Proano, offers a number of facilities, as well as a base from which to arrange guiding services.

From Macas, head northwest to the village of **9 de Octubre**, where an overnight stay is required, before backpacking (with a guide) on trails into the park. Entrance costs about $20 and can be paid at the ranger station/education center in the village of General Proano, which is on the way to the village of 9 de Octubre. Camping is available and is the only way to visit Sangay in this region. Inquire with the rangers at the education center, where you can also look into more specific park information, but bring along a good map (IGM 1:50,000 *Volcán Sangay*).

Jungle Excursions Around Macas

The southeastern expanse of the Oriente (the region around Río Pastaza) offers incredible opportunities to explore virgin rainforest and indigenous communities in some of the most remote areas of the country. For now, these trips are for well-seasoned travelers and independent planners, although organized tours are gradually becoming available, especially through the likes of Canodoros and Kapawi Lodge (page 378), which offer visits to native Achuar communities.

From Macas there are also possibilities for trips into the land of the Shuar nation, an experience which should not be taken lightly. These people are historically very independent and aggressive in manner – only recently ending their practice of shrinking heads – and they're not necessarily accommodating to wandering gringos, who, by the way, don't stand a chance of surviving in the real rainforest without a knowledgeable native guide. Go with a Shuar guide if possible. There are several available in Macas, as well as at the **Shuar Federation**, headquartered in the village of Sucúa, about 15 miles south of Macas.

Lost in the Jungle or Jungle Comforts?

Ecuador's Oriente now offers the chance to visit even the deepest, most remote parts of the rainforest in relative comfort. The weather is warm and humid, but manageable. Simple accommodations are clean and more than adequate, especially when sipping on a cool *cerveza* while lounging in a hammock. Even hiking through the jungle is generally not too difficult. The reason for this level of comfort, however, can be summed up in one word: clearing. Lodges, trails and routes have been meticulously planned and developed either around naturally clear areas (the edge of an ox-bow lake, for example) or they have been cleared specifically for tourism.

Keep in mind that indigenous hunters and gatherers never had it so easy. Bushwhacking through undeveloped virgin rainforest the way traditional inhabitants did is enough to make you wish you were dead, and, in fact, most people left on their own would be dead in a very short time. The native jungle tribes depended on an intimate – almost spiritually and ecologically perfect – understanding of the land. The few groups left still depend on that.

Tours & Tour Operators

Many tour operators and community-based ecotourism organizations overlap with their services, I have listed them all together. In addition, most tours are associated with all-inclusive packages at ecolodges and are listed in the *Where to Stay* section, below.

In Tena, **Amorangachi Tours**, 15 de Noviembre 432, ☎/fax 6-886-372, is a respectable outfitter offering various multi-day excursions into the jungle and working closely with local people. Typical adventures include hiking, canoeing, staying at ecolodges, visiting local families, swimming, and panning for gold.

From Tena, **Senior Delfín Pauchi** (Casilla 245, ☎ 6-886-434/088, owner of Cabañas Pimpilala) is one of the better family enterprises, less than an hour from Tena. A Quichua native, Delfín is quite knowledgeable about the region. He incorporates jungle excursions with a stay at the cabañas, where you can meet his entire family. Delphín speaks only Spanish and Quichua, but his cultural and botanic knowledge is extraordinary. This is the place to visit for a genuine cultural experience.

The **Federación de Organizationes Indígenas**, FOIN, on the east bank of Río Pano, south of the footbridge, ☎ 6-886-614, organizes local communities to provide ecocultural guiding services and jungle excursions. FOIN helped fund and coordinate these efforts through RICANCIE (see page 363 and listing, below). FOIN can also recommend guides for visits to local caves and petroglyphs. This is a good option if you want to support organized indigenous community efforts for sustainable development, visit locals within their community, and see their day-to-day lives.

Community-based ecotourism in at least nine Quichua communities is offered by **RICANCIE**, an organization of Quichua communities – see page 363. Visiting local communities and working with locally trained guides is a great way to support their efforts and have a genuine experience. Packages to visit the communities, which are east of Tena toward Misahuallí, cost $60 per person per day, all-inclusive, and should be arranged in Tena. Note that guides typically speak Quichua and Spanish, but not often English. Contact them at ☎ 6-887-072. They are located at Av. 15 de Noviembre 777, Tena; www.eduweb.com/schaller/TourInfo.html.

Reportedly one of the best higher-priced community-based ecotourism packages, including transportation, lodging, guide services, and meals, is offered in conjunction with **Yachana Lodge**, located two hours downriver from Misahuallí. Their Quito office is at Baquedano 385 and Juan León Mera, ☎ 2-2566-035, 2-2503-275, ☎/fax 2-2523-777, www.yachana.org, info@yachana.com. Though I haven't visited Yachana Lodge, I look forward to your feedback on the lodge and its activities.

In Misahuallí, try **Cruceros y Expediciones Dayuma**, associated with Hotel Dayuma (see page 372), or in Quito at ☎ 2-2564-924, dayuma@hoy.net. Trips to their private reserve and cabañas are offered, as well as extended trips farther out into the Oriente, starting in Coca. **Ecoselva** (on the plaza in Misahualli, ecoselva@yahoo.es) is also recommended for custom-length multi-day excursions with knowledgeable guides.

Independent guides are plentiful in Misahuallí, and many are quite good. The best ones are licensed and are often associated with a Quito-based tour operator or a local community-based organization.

Central & Southern Oriente

In Puyo, try **Papangu Tours**, in conjunction with the **Organización de Pueblos Indígenas de Pastaza (OPIP)**, at 9 de Octubre and Atahualpa, ☎ 3-883-875, for multi-day, community-based ecotourism deep into the Pastazo region of *la selva*. **Amazonia Touring**, at Atuahalpa and 9 de Octubre, ☎ 3-883-219, visits nearby communities and runs trips into small pockets of jungle. Birding, botany and native lifestyles are the emphasis.

In the town of Macas, local excursions are available with **Aventura Tsunki Touring**, Amazonas and Domingo Comin, ☎/fax 7-700-464, tsunki@cue.satnet.net. They include a Shuar guide and English interpreter. **Tuntiak Expediciónes de la Selva**, in front of Hotel Peñon el Oriente, ☎ 7-700-185/082 provides local excursions, including trips into the jungle and Shuar Village. The **Shuar Federation**, ☎ 7-740-108, is in the small town of Sucúa and can arrange trips to traditional Shuar villages. It may take a few days to arrange, so don't just show up at a village unannounced. The Shuar you meet may have been "missionized" and dress in jeans and T-shirts in town, but their cultural history is of a fierce and aggressive people known for shrinking the heads of their enemies.

For trips into Sangay National Park, **Ikiaam**, 10 de Agosto, across from the bus station in Macas, ☎ 7-700-457, is recommended. Look around the main plaza in town for other outfitters.

Big river whitewater rafting is available on Río Upano and through the spectacular Namangosa Gorge with **ROW Expediciones**, an American-owned operator working in Macas, www.rowinc.com, info@rowinc.com. In Quito, ☎ 2-2239-224. Contact them in the US at PO Box 579, Coeur d'Alene, ID 83816, toll free ☎ 800-451-6034, ☎/fax 208-667-6506.

Ecotrek, in Cuenca, at Larga and Luis Cordero, ☎ 7-842-531, fax 7-835-387, offers trips into Cajas and Kapawi, in Ecuador's southern Oriente

Where to Stay

ACCOMMODATIONS PRICE SCALE	
Unless otherwise noted, prices are per room, up to double occupancy. Some prices are per person, particularly with all-inclusive packages, but these generally include meals, lodging, guide services and other amenities.	
$	Under $25
$$	$26 to $50
$$$	$51 to $100
$$$$	Over $100

■ From Baeza to Tena: Cloud Forest Lodges

 Near Antisana Reserve, about nine miles south of Beaza (43 north of Tena) and nestled in the lower eastern Cordillera of the Quijos Valley, **Cabañas San Isidro** lie at a comfortable 7,000 feet. Near the small town of Cosanga, beautiful scenery abounds in this veritable birders' paradise of montane humid forest. The converted dairy ranch hacienda offers comfortable lodging that is perched overlooking the valley. Cozy double rooms provide comforts, with hot water, private baths and electricity. Miles of trails offer easy exploration. A long bird list includes the renowned Andean cock-of-the-rock, easily accessible nearby where the males gather to put on mating displays. Spectacled bears, mountain tapirs, night monkeys, oncillas and pumas reportedly reside in the adjacent reserve. $$$ per person includes three meals a day and trail access, but doesn't include a bilingual naturalist guide. In Quito, Carrión N21-01 and Juan León Mera (pasaje), ☎ 2-2547-403, ☎/fax 2-2228-902, sanisidro@ecuadorexplorer.com, www.ecuadorexplorer.com/sanisidro.

☆ Also in the mid-elevation of the Eastern Cordillera is the **SierrAzul Cloud Forest Lodge**, offering a 6,175-acre primary cloud forest playground, located off the same road as San Isidro. In addition to the above mentioned opportunities associated with Cabañas San Isidro, the less expensive and more rustic SierrAzul offers a Spanish program in conjunction with local cloud forest conservation efforts, as well as incredible treks of up to 10 days from the Andes to the Amazon. Rooms are comfortable, with private and shared baths. As for birdwatching, SierrAzul is a highly valued destination lodge by many well-known international conservation, birding and educational groups. Their bird list is available online at www. sierrazul.com. There's radio communication only, as there are no phones here. Make arrangements in Quito at Joaquin Pinto 439 and Av. Amazonas, PO Box 17-1106398, ☎ 2-2564-915 or 2-2909-482, fax 2- 2907-870, sierrazul@access.net.ec.

☆ Immediately adjacent to San Isidro is **Yanayacu Biological Station and Center for Creative Studies**. Yanayacu, meaning "black river" in Quichua and named for the local river, offers rustic and down-to-earth facilities that cater mostly to self-sufficient groups. The station, which has kitchen access, running water, kerosene and candle lighting, is geared more toward tropical biology studies and personal growth activities, with volunteer opportunities offered at $210 per month. I haven't visited the station, but you can learn more about it at www.yanayacu.org/index.html, yanayacu1@hotmail.com.

■ Tena

Most accommodations in Tena are relatively inexpensive and cater to budget travelers.

The **Dayuma Hotel** (in Tena, call for directions, ☎ 6-584-964), offers simple yet agreeable accommodations. It seems to be quite popular with incoming jungle-bound gringos. Rooms are clean and comfortable and the restaurant is worth looking into even if you're not staying here. The hotel is associated with Cruceros y Expediciones Dayuma, a local tour operator (see *Tours & Tour Operators*, page 368). $

Well-recommended is the locally owned **Los Yutzos**, along Río Pano on César Rueda near Av. 15 de Noviembre. There is an Internet café across the street. $$

Hostal Traveler's Lodge, 15 de Noviembre 432, ☎ 6-886-372, is a popular budget choice operated by Amorangachi Tours (see *Tours & Tour Operators*, page 368). Simple but sufficient rooms include private or shared baths, and there's a good restaurant next door. The rooms downstairs near the office, however, are loud, as the television is *always* on. This is a place to meet young travelers, organize a tour, and gather helpful information. $

A step up in quality is **Hotel Mol Internacional**, at the north end of Tena on Sucre 432, ☎/fax 6-886-215. This is the nicest modern hotel near the town's center and is convenient for organizing trips and gathering supplies. Large, clean rooms include private bath and a balcony. $

An even better option is **Establo de Tomás**, ☎ 6-886-318, vía a San Antonio, a mile northeast of town along the river. Nice rooms are set on spacious grounds overlooking Río Tena. There's access to the river beach below, as well as a good restaurant, a bar, and a discotheque. $-$$

A bit closer to the "jungle" than Tena, in the vicinity of Puerto Misahuallí (the last-minute jungle-supply boomtown) is **Misahuallí Jungle Hotel**, across the river from town. Contact them in Quito, at Ramirez Dávalos 251 and Páez, ☎ 2-2520-043, fax 2-2504-872, www. misahuallijungle.com. Situated on a bluff overlooking the Río Napo, the lodge offers a peaceful setting with a great view from the open-air lounge, bar, and restaurant. Rooms with shared baths are in the main building. There are also comfortable cabañas, all of which include great views, private baths, electricity, ceiling fans, and screened windows. Several trails lead into the backcountry. Hire a guide for a chance to learn about the local forest. $$$

A less expensive choice in Misahuallí is **El Albergue Espanol**, on Arteaga. They work in conjunction with the Jaguar Lodge. The office in Quito is at Eloy Alfaro 3147 and Arosemena, ☎ 2-2453-703, alb-esp@uio.satnet.net. They offer a nice restaurant and views overlooking the river. $

■ Jungle Lodges Around Tena, Misahuallí & the Upper Río Napo

✪ **Cabañas Amorangachiñas** are located on Río Anzu, a tributary nearly 19 miles up the Río Napo from Misahuallí. Perched on a bluff 330 feet above the river, the spectacular hillside cabins offer great views in a relaxing environment. The open-air dining room is particularly interesting, with long benches looking out over the landscape below. You won't be staring at your neighbor while eating here. Between the cabins and the river is a parrot salt lick where, on clear mornings, you can see an amazing display of birds. Guided hikes into the surrounding area are through primary and secondary forests.

Central & Southern Oriente

Contact Cabañas Amorangachiñas through Patricia Corral, owner of Restaurant Cositas Ricas in Tena, ☎ 6-886-372. $$

☆ **Cabañas Cotacocha**. As you head down the Río Napo from Puerto Napo, the first quality tourist facility you find is Cabañas Cotacocha. Walking from the parking lot along the rock pathway, through the forest, and among enormous strangler figs, it becomes immediately obvious that the accommodations are in a great setting. Cabañas Cotacocha is nestled along the Río Napo in a rustic jungle environment that combines charm, comfort, and a relaxed atmosphere. Enjoy the afternoon in a hammock or chatting with other guests on the covered patio. The cabañas, while simple, are very cozy, with screened sides, comfortable beds, and clean bathrooms with hot water. Adding to the ambiance are candle and kerosene-lamp lighting, rather than electricity. Sleep to the soothing sounds of rain and insects, and don't be surprised by the small bats flying about in the evening. Informative local guides can be hired to explore the local forest. $$, meals included.

Located a few miles up the Ahuano road in Misahuallí. For reservations, contact Lizardo García 544 and Reina Victoria, Quito, ☎/fax 2-2541-527.

☆ **Cabañas Aliñahui**. Also known as the Butterfly Lodge, this is an excellent eco-resort located on a bluff above the Río Napo. The inspiring panoramic views of the rainforest, the Andes, and the surrounding snowcapped volcanoes are surpassed only by the region's rich biological diversity. Cabañas Aliñahui, which means "Good View" in Quichua, is co-owned by Jatun Sacha and the California-based Health and Habitat, a nonprofit organization that supports ecotourism, community development, conservation, and scientific research.

Panning for gold, visiting Jatun Sacha Station, and learning about the secrets of medicinal plants with a shaman are some of the package options available. You can enjoy an afternoon swim, take naturalist-led hikes into the local jungle, or visit the Conservation Center for Amazonian Plants of Jatun Sacha. Afterward, you can relax with the setting sun on vista porches that overlook the river below. At mealtime, savor exquisite Ecuadorian flavors as you dine in style. Double cabin-covered porch patios with cozy hammocks complement simple but comfortable rooms with shared baths. Set within a vast stretch of primary rainforest, this is the perfect place to enjoy the Amazon. $$$

Contact Cabañas Aliñahui through the Jatun Sacha Foundation in Quito, at Pasaje Eugenio de Santillán N34-248 and Maurián, ☎ 2-2432-240/173/246, ☎/fax 2-2453-583.

Jatun Sacha Research Station. Associated with volunteer work and scientific research, the research station isn't really equipped for the jungle-seeking tourist. See *Eco-Travel*, page 364, for more details.

☆ To get even farther away from the urban development, head down the river about half an hour to **Cabañas Anaconda**, on Anaconda Island. Here, peaceful surroundings may be close to civilization, but the natural atmosphere is far removed. The only noises are the flow of the river and the sounds of nature. The common dining area, bar, and lounge offer electricity and comfort in an attractive setting. The sleeping quarters are simple but comfortable and more than adequate. The island itself is a great place to poke around and watch for birds and butterflies, and the staff can organize various local excursions, depending on your special interests. Overall, this is good value and recommended if your goal is to just get away and relax in the Oriente. $$

Contact them through NAPATUR, Juan León Mera 1312 and Luis Cordero, Quito, ☎ 2-2547-283, ☎/fax 2-2545-426. Anaconda Island is located down the Misualli River, across from the village of Ahuano and Casa del Suizo.

Set in the village of Ahuano along the bank of the Napo, **Casa del Suizo** is a high-end, luxury jungle resort. A walled-in fortress of comfort, the Casa del Suizo stands in stark contrast to the surrounding community. This is the place to go if you are looking for elegance and luxury in a jungle surrounding. Although it seems a bit too refined for its location next to a very poor community, the resort is ideal for the well-to-do, comfort-seeking traveler.

The grounds offer individual and extremely nice cabañas, as well as hotel rooms in a main building. In all, the facilities can accommodate well over 100 people. They offer electricity and modern bathrooms with hot water, landscaped gardens, boardwalks, and relaxing patio views. The live-animal displays, however, are not what you would consider true wildlife viewing. The hotel also provides hiking and canoe excursions into the surrounding region, although the areas visited are fairly developed or disturbed. As is true at any high-end resort, the service and facilities are excellent. This is a great place to send the not-so-adventurous, comfort-seeking grandparents. $$$

Central & Southern Oriente

376 ■ Where to Stay

Contact their office in Quito at ☎ 2-2566-090, ☎/fax 2-2236-521, Julio Zaldumbide 375, and Toledo, sachalod@pi.pro.ec, www.casadelsuizo. com. The resort is a half-hour motorized canoe ride from Misahuallí and you will want to make arrangements in advance.

☆ Along the river about 45 minutes from Tena, **Cabañas Pimpilala** offers a unique jungle experience with a local Quichua family. This is a chance to get to know Delphin, a very knowledgeable and friendly native, and to learn about the wonders of the natural environment where he lives. Guests stay in traditional thatched-roof huts adjacent to Delphin's home. The cabañas are very basic, yet comfortable, with mattresses, mosquito netting, and toilets. $

Contact Delphin Paucha at ☎ 6-886-434, or make arrangements through Ríos Ecuador, ☎ 6-887-438, ☎ /fax 6-887-438; or, in Quito, ☎ 2-2558-264 or 9-730-215, info@Ríosecuador.com. The price of $35 per night includes transportation from Tena, all meals, accommodations, and a full day of guiding services.

☆ Continuing down the Río Napo, about 1½ hours from Misahuallí, is the **Hotel Jaguar**. On a bluff along the shore of the Napo, the modern hotel is set in a relatively undisturbed patch of forest. With an incredible view over the river below, the main building provides all the comforts and attractive décor you could desire. The lounge/bar, dining room, and terrace are all ideal for relaxing and reading a good book or soaking up the natural surroundings.

The Hotel Jaguar is less rustic than its simpler jungle counterparts, with white-plaster walls, cement walkways, and high-beamed ceilings. The rooms are quite nice – simple, but large – and offer modern bathrooms, hot water, and electricity during hours when the generator is running. The hotel's manager is friendly and exceptionally knowledgeable about the surrounding region. Don't hesitate to ask him questions. Full packages include meals and recommended jungle excursions. $

The address is Luis Cordero 1313 in Quito, ☎ 2-2239-400, 2-2230-552, ☎/fax 2-2502-682.

Yachana Lodge offers the highest-end community-based ecotourism project in the region. Built in conjunction with FUNDESIN, a not-for-profit organization that supports the local Quichua population, this project offers comfortable indigenous-style cabañas overlooking the Río Napo a couple of hours downriver from Misahuallí. Package tours include lodging, meals, guide services, transportation from Quito and cultural visits to local communities, where you can meet families and learn about local organic agricultural efforts. Guided hikes into the nearby rainforest are offered as well. Double rooms adjoin community bathrooms and family units complete with balcony and private baths are also available. This is a great opportunity to support local efforts. Packages cost $320 per person, less for students and children, for four days and three nights. $$$-$$$$

Their office in Quito is at Baqauedano 385 and Juan León Mera, ☎ 2-2503-275, ☎/fax 2-2523-777, info@yachana.com or inform@fundesin.org, www.yachana.com.

■ Puyo

In Puyo most accommodations are very inexpensive. On the higher end, **Hostería Safari**, located a few miles north of town on the road to Tena , ☎ 3-885-465, has been recommended for its location away from the main hustle of downtown. $$-$$$

Much less expensive, but still with private baths and hot water, television and fans (no air-conditioning), is the **Grán Hotel Amazónico**, in town at Marín and Atahualpa, ☎ 3-883-094. I can't vouch for the restaurant. $

Hosteria Turingia, Ceslao Marín 294 on the road to Baños, ☎ 3-885-180, turingia@punto.net.ec, is a popular stop for travelers. Just outside of town, these garden bungalows offer private baths and fans. There's a good restaurant. $-$$

■ Macas

If you're heading to the far southern stretches of the Ecuadorian Amazon, try **Hotel Peñon el Oriente**, Calle Domingo Comín 837 and Amazonas, ☎ 7-700-124, fax/☎ 7-700-450. Although the town is pleasant, there aren't many accommodation options here. The Oriente is probably the best choice in town. It offers a rooftop view and an enjoyable atmosphere; overall a good value. $

I've also heard that the **Manzana Real**, on 29 de Mayo, ☎ 7-700-637, is a good, inexpensive option, though every place in Macas is inexpensive. $

■ Jungle Lodges Near Macas

☆ Perhaps the finest operation in the entire country, **Kapawi Lodge** offers superior accommodations and ecocultural opportunities in a remote area of virgin rainforest. Kapawi, built in partnership with OINAE (the Achuar Indian Federation), maintains a solid relationship with local communities and extreme environmental and cultural sensitivity with regard to the facilities and operations. Tours include customized four- to eight-day trips at varying levels of physical activity. I highly recommend staying as long as possible. All tours involve canoe rides, jungle hikes, and visits to local Achuar communities. They can be tailored to match individual interests.

The lodge itself is absolutely first-rate, located along the southern stretches of the Río Pastaza before it joins to form the Amazon River. In fact, its comfort, charm, and appeal come as quite a surprise in such a remote section of the southern Oriente. Indigenous Achuar architecture and sustainable natural materials are used along with solar energy, biodegradable soaps, and biodigesting septic systems. The 20 double cabins are spacious and very cozy, with screened windows and large open terraces overlooking Kapawi Lake. State-of-the-art bathrooms are designed with the environment in mind. The luxurious common facilities include a comfortable lounge and bar, a dining room and kitchen, a conference room, and hammocks. And the food, which focuses on local cuisine, is out of this world. Even the refuse here is mulched into fertilizer for the organic garden. $$$$

Make arrangements through Canodros, Urbanización Santa Leonor. Manzana 5 Solar #10 (vía Terminal Terrestre), Guayaquil, ☎ 4-2285-711 or 4-2280-880, 4-2514-750 ☎/fax 4-2287-651, ecotourism1@ canodros.com.ec, www.canodros.com. In Miami, call toll-free ☎ 888-368-9929 or 305-662-2965. From Macas, a 50-minute flight over uncut Amazon rainforest to the Sharamentsa airstrip is followed by a 1½-hour motorized canoe ride to Kapawi.

■ Camping

 Sangay National Park offers camping with the entrance fee of $20, but a guide is highly recommended in this remote and rugged region. Bring everything you will need with you, as the infrastructure for travelers is virtually non-existent.

Several of the CBEs (Community-Based Ecotourism projects), as well as the higher-end ecolodges, offer camping excursion options on their package tours. Note that typically such tours will be all-inclusive. Unless you are a native of one of the local cultures or grew up in the jungle, camping on your own in the heart of the undeveloped parts of the Oriente will result in death.

Where to Eat

■ Puyo

 The best deal is **La Carihuela**, associated with a popular backpacker's hostal at Marín 576. It has a wide variety of tasty selections, moderately priced and very popular with foreign budget travelers. **Mesón Europa**, on Zambrano near the bus terminal, is about as high end as it gets in this part of the country, more expensive than La Carihuela. It serves tasty international dishes.

For indigenous cuisine native to this region, head to **Yana Puma**, at 9 de Octubre and Atahualpa. Tasty and cheap Amazonia-style meals are served in this bamboo restaurant. No, they don't serve puma.

■ Tena

The buzz of young travelers combines with clean conditions and tasty meals at **Cositas Ricas**, a restaurant associated with the Hostal Traveler's Lodge, 15 de Noviembre 432, ☎ 6-886-372. The menu includes both vegetarian and Ecuadorian options. Prices are cheap and portions are filling. The staff is friendly and will even track down a *cerveza* for you if there isn't a cold one on hand.

The restaurant at **Hotel Auca**, in the northern part of town along the river, also serves good local food. Prices are a bit higher than those at Casitas Ricas, but the atmosphere is more pleasant and less of a backpacker scene.

Chuquitos, on García Moreno by the plaza, caters to tourists, but is very popular with locals as well. Located on the main plaza, its ambiance is quite nice and its meals are typically Ecuadorian.

■ Macas

Your best bet is **Pagoda China**, on Amazonas and Domingo Comín. It's hard to imagine that a *chifa* takes the prize for best restaurant this far into the Ecuadorian Amazon. It's a bit more expensive than *chifas* elsewhere. More traditional dishes and café refreshments are served up across the way at **Café El Penon**. Otherwise, try **El Jardín**, centrally located on Calle Amazonas and Comín, which has been recommended but is a bit pricey.

The Galápagos Islands

There is no other place like these islands on earth! This unmatched archipelago is a world away from the mainland, yet it also helps define the identity of Ecuador. The Galápagos Islands captured the imagination of Charles Darwin and provided the catalyst for developing his theory of evolution, forever altering the written history of life on earth. Ever since the old pirate days, when the islands were referred to as the *Enchanted Islands*, the Galápagos have lured the inquisitive traveler with an unearthly beauty uniquely its own.

Lying more than 600 miles off the west coast of Ecuador, the Galápagos have evolved in relative isolation. The wildlife is majestic and friendly, with very little fear of people. Don't expect palm trees, white-sand beaches, and margaritas here. Expect jutting cliffs, volcanic moonscapes, emerald coves, and desert islands. Expect giant tortoises, swimming iguanas, friendly sea lions, and a rainbow of tropical fish.

Geography & Geology

The Galápagos are often called the **Islands Born of Fire**. The older exposed islands are approximately four to five million years old, created by underwater volcanoes that are still active today. Thus, the archipelago is relatively young and continues to evolve.

There are nearly 60 exposed landmasses that are currently named in the Galápagos. Thirteen are large islands, six are considered small is-

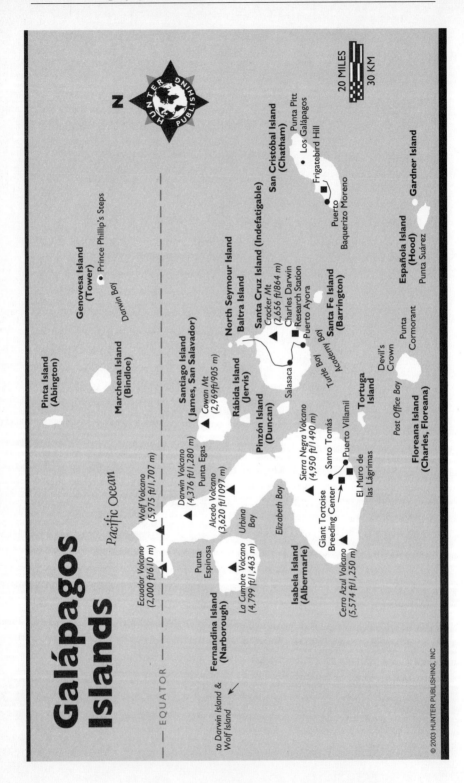

Galápagos Islands

Pacific Ocean

EQUATOR

to Darwin Island & Wolf Island

Fernandina Island (Narborough)

Ecuador Volcano (2,000 ft/610 m)

Wolf Volcano (5,975 ft/1,707 m)

Darwin Volcano (4,376 ft/1,280 m)

Punta Espinosa

Punta Egas

Alcedo Volcano (3,620 ft/1097 m)

La Cumbre Volcano (4,799 ft/1,463 m)

Urbina Bay

Elizabeth Bay

Isabela Island (Albermarle)

Sierra Negra Volcano (4,950 ft/1490 m)

Giant Tortoise Breeding Center

Santo Tomás

Puerto Villamil

El Muro de las Lágrimas

Cerro Azul Volcano (5,574 ft/1,250 m)

Pinta Island (Abington)

Marchena Island (Bindloe)

Genovesa Island (Tower)

Prince Phillip's Steps

Darwin Bay

Santiago Island (James, San Salvador)

Cowan Mt (2,969ft/905 m)

Rábida Island (Jervis)

Pinzón Island (Duncan)

North Seymour Island

Baltra Island

Santa Cruz Island (Indefatigable)

Crocker Mt (2,656 ft/864 m)

Charles Darwin Research Station

Puerto Ayora

Salasaca

Turtle Bay

Academy Bay

Santa Fe Island (Barrington)

San Cristóbal Island (Chatham)

Punta Pitt

Los Galápagos

Frigatebird Hill

Puerto Baquerizo Moreno

Tortuga Island

Devil's Crown

Punta Cormorant

Post Office Bay

Floreana Island (Charles, Floreana)

Española Island (Hood)

Punta Suárez

Gardner Island

20 MILES

30 KM

© 2003 HUNTER PUBLISHING, INC

lands, and more than 40 are islets. The largest is the 80-mile-long Isabela Island, with over half the archipelago's total land area. All told, the islands extend for more than 267 miles. It would take quite some time to visit them all.

Geologically, the Galápagos were formed as a result of the same process that created the Andes. In fact, the islands (and the Andes) are still being built, as plate tectonics dictate land formation here. The enormous underwater **Nazca plate**, as it moves slowly east toward the **South American plate**, passes over a hot spot in the earth's crust. Magma continues to rise from the core of the earth through the crust and creates volcanic islands. Currently, the islands are moving southeast toward South America at the rate of a couple of inches per year. Thus, the oldest of the Galápagos, **Isla Española** (over three million years old), is also the southeasternmost in the archipelago. Ultimately, the current Galápagos formations may join South America, but neither the currently exposed islands nor human beings are likely to be around to witness the meeting.

The majority of the Galápagos landmass lies well below the surface of the ocean and spreads east toward the mainland. There are additional underwater volcanic formations that were most likely exposed islands at one time, but which now lie deep underwater. Some are as old as nine million years and stretch well beyond the Galápagos toward the mainland.

Isla Fernandina and **Isabela** are the two youngest islands in the Galápagos chain, dating back only 750,000 years. In fact, much of the Galápagos chain is still being formed, and the region is considered to be one of the most volcanically active areas in the world. The land itself, formed from the volcanic basalt, consists of rounded cones and gentle slopes – very different from the jagged peaks of the Andes on the mainland.

Climate

The Galápagos are located directly on the equator, but are exposed to various natural cooling forces, resulting in a pleasant year-round temperature. From June through December, the cold **Humboldt Current** from Antarctica and the warm **equatorial current** from the north meet on the islands' shores to create a cool and misty season known as *la* *garua*. During this time, clouds condense over the islands and fall as mist in the highlands. The roughest, coolest, and foggiest months run from July through around October (though July and August are the busiest two travel months of the year). By January, the Humboldt Current weakens and trade winds from the southeast prevail, allowing a return of the warmer waters from the equatorial current and a more tropical climate. Cloudy and rainy weather (often with afternoon downpours) can occur from January through March, although the climate remains hot. Underwater viewing is at its best during this time. February is typically the hottest time here and it becomes progressively milder as May approaches.

History

■ Darwin & Natural History

The natural history of these islands is eminently curious and well deserves attention.
~ Charles Darwin, 1845

How did life in the Galápagos come to be? It had to start from scratch with some kind of boost from the mainland, which was over 600 miles away. Most likely, the archipelago was a resting place for early swimming, floating, and flying animals, as well as an accident destination for those thrown off-course. Plant seeds and insects arrived via bird feathers and perhaps, to a lesser extent, via long-distance wind drifts and natural rafts of driftwood or other vegetation. It is also likely that seeds passed through birds' digestive tracts. Certain plant species grabbed a foothold on volcanic earth and helped to form life-supporting soil. As the new habitat offered opportunities for colonizing species to adapt, the evolution of isolated communities began.

What happened next was first observed and perhaps best explained later by Charles Darwin after his famous visit to the Galápagos in 1835. During his five-week stay, the young naturalist observed, studied, and collected samples of various plants and animals, noting similarities with mainland relatives, but also seeing unique differences in physical and behavioral adaptations. His theory of evolution, however, was not born overnight. In fact, the young Darwin was devoutly religious, so questioning the Christian establishment was not easy for him. But what he saw forced him to think twice about the validity for him. But what he saw forced him to think twice about the validity of creationism. He had to entertain the notion that these differences between species may have been environmentally caused.

After returning home, Darwin spent years observing and performing genetic experiments while his theory evolved, although he did not use the term "evolution" during his work. Far from pushing his radical notions, Darwin kept his work largely to himself. It was only after similar ideas began to float about within the scientific community that Darwin quickly published his ideas. Ultimately, his observations resulted in one of the most far-reaching biological theories to date.

For more on Darwin and his theory of evolution, read his book *On the Origin of Species*.

■ Human History

Perhaps a surprise to some, Charles Darwin was not responsible for discovering the Galápagos Islands. Pieces of pre-historic artifacts were discovered here, leading scientists to believe that natives traveled to the islands to fish well before the **Spanish** arrived. This was quite a feat, considering the sailing vessels available at the time and the incredible distance from the mainland. The first recorded discovery was 300 years before Darwin in 1535 by **Tomás de Berlanga**, the Bishop of Panama. At the time, Berlanga was en route from Panama to Peru when forces of nature sent him way off course. Although it was an accidental discovery and obviously not a highlight of his journey (they left quickly), Berlanga did dub the island tortoises "Galápagos," after their resemblance to the Spanish horse saddle.

By the late 1600s the Galápagos became a hideout for **English** pirates, who had plundered Spanish ships full of treasure. As a result, the individual islands' original names were in English and it wasn't until Ecuador claimed them that Spanish names were given. Permanent settlements, however, did not occur for some time. By the late 18th century, **whalers** from the US and England used the islands as an outpost and had the greatest early affect on them. Whalers remained here for only a short time, until about the mid-1800s, but they devastated several of the endemic species and sub-species of the giant Galápagos tortoises, using their long-lasting meat as food on seafaring journeys.

The Famous Islands

The Galápagos Islands, over the course of a few hundred years, became some of the most famous islands on earth. They were referred to as enchanted, magical and even as haunted, partly because of the thick fog that often enshroud them. This was enhanced by the presence of pirates using the islands as a base for their exploits.The islands inspired Herman Melville in his *Benito Serreno* and *Las Encantadas*, both short stories within the collection, *The Piazza Tales*. By the time the first permanent settlers arrived, the Galápagos was hosting famous visitors and adventurers from across the globe.

Floreana became the first permanently inhabited island. The first occupant, a lone Irishman named **Patrick Watkins**, survived a brief occupancy beginning in 1807 after being expelled from his ship, though he lasted only two years before escaping back to the mainland. Shortly after Ecuador officially claimed the islands in 1832, they became home to Ecuadorian prisoners, guarded in a penal colony by **General José Villamil**. Eventually, Villamil was unable to maintain control over the prisoners, who mutinied. Several attempts were made to keep prisoners on Floreana over the years, but the extremely harsh living conditions on the islands forced most everyone away until continuous contact could be made with the mainland.

In 1929 a German doctor and his "disciple" left behind civilization and escaped to Floreana to live with the elements. Shortly thereafter, **Heinz and Margret Wittmer**, also from Germany and also hoping to start life anew, with their ailing son Harry, arrived in 1932. Along with a delusional baroness from Austria and her "workmen," this small community offered the beginning of Floreana's first continuous settlement. Others arrived shortly thereafter and the island became a brief port of call for luxury vessels. But, after all was said and done, only the Wittmers survived, and they are there to this day (see *Floreana Island*, page 413, for more).

At the same time as these settlers were making a home of Floreana, another settlement was growing on **San Cristóbal Island**, in modern-day Puerto Baquerizo Moreno, which was then and remains today the capital of the province of the Galápagos Islands and the seat of the provincial governor. Though the US and European countries vied for control over the islands as early as World War I, Ecuador kept them away until the next world war. In 1941, Ecuador allowed the US military to use Baltra Island first as a Naval Base, to protect the Panama Canal, and, subsequently, as an airbase. By 1959, the Galápagos were declared a national park, and their settlement and growth from then on was fueled by tourism. Today, by some accounts, 65,000 tourists visit each year, and over 15,000 permanent residents reside there.

Flora & Fauna

There are several ecological life zones in the Galápagos. The coastal and lowland areas offer little precipitation and include sandy beaches, rocky shorelines, mangroves, and salt-tolerant vegetation. Many seabirds, sea lions, crabs, and iguanas call these areas home. The next zone inland is the arid zone, with deciduous, drought-resistant vegetation. Cacti, land iguanas, Darwin's finches, and tortoises reside here. Higher up (650 to 2,000 feet), where there is more precipitation, is the *scalesia* zone, where a family of trees by the same name can be found. Here, *la garua* dampens the slopes of the higher mountains. This region is tremendously fertile, and much of it has been converted to agricultural and grazing land. Because of its isolation from the rest of the world, much of the flora in the Galápagos is found nowhere else on the planet. This is also true of the animals here.

In terms of wildlife, the Galápagos Islands are just as beautiful today as they were when Darwin visited more than 150 years ago. And as he pointed out so long ago, there are distinct variations among similar species on different islands.

As you hike on the islands, it is imperative that you stick to the trails. The creatures of the Galápagos already face significant pressures from eager and inconsiderate photographers and other tourists. Respect nature's privacy. You're certain to see plenty of wildlife without ever venturing off the designated trails.

■ Reptiles

 In addition to **lava lizards**, **nocturnal geckos**, and inconspicuous **Galápagos snakes**, you'll find the following reptiles in the Galápagos.

Giant Tortoise

Perhaps most famous of all the islands' inhabitants, and the namesake of the archipelago itself, is the giant tortoise. *Galápago* means "saddle," and refers to the tortoise's shell, or carapace. Although there is only one species of the giant tortoise, 14 subspecies, characterized by different carapace shapes, have existed throughout the islands at one time or another. Sadly, three of these subspecies are extinct while a fourth has only one tortoise – "Lonesome George" – remaining. Because the tortoise has few natural predators, humans are entirely responsible for their demise. Fortunately, efforts to repatriate decimated populations are well under way. You can visit Lonesome George and learn about current efforts for protection at the Charles Darwin Research Station on Santa Cruz Island.

How You Can Help

Founded in 1959, the **Charles Darwin Research Foundation** is the driving force behind the conservation of the Galápagos Islands. With the support of contributions, volunteers, scientists and educators, the Foundation has successfully contributed to the scientific understanding, preservation and education of the archipelago's land and marine ecology. There is no organization more deserving of support if your interest lies in helping to maintain this precious natural treasure. For more information, visit them online at www.darwinfoundation.org. In Quito, they are at Av. 6 de Diciembre N 36-109 and Pasaje California, Casilla (Postal Box) 17-01-3891; in Puerto Ayora, Santa Cruz Island, ☎ 5-526-147/148, galapagosinfo@darwinfoundation. org.

Pacific Green Sea Turtle

The Pacific green sea turtle resides here during a part of its life cycle. From November to January, breeding sea turtles are often observed swimming near shore. Between December and June, females lay eggs on the beaches and leave the future hatchlings to fend for themselves. The few young that reach the water may swim thousands of miles away, but they ultimately return to nest at the very same beaches where they were born.

Iguanas

There are three species of iguanas on the islands. One, the **marine iguana**, is the only seafaring lizard in the world. It takes to the ocean to feed on seaweed. Common along the rocky shores of most islands, marine iguanas tend to pile on top of each other as they lounge. The skin of a marine iguana is generally a scaly black (on males, the skin turns bright colors during mating periods).

The marine iguana's cousin, the **land iguana**, spends its entire life on land. There are two species: the Galápagos land iguana and the Santa Fé land iguana. Land iguanas are generally larger than marine iguanas and similar to each other in appearance, colored in shades of yellow. Both species feast primarily on prickly-pear cactus and live farther away from the spray of crashing waves than the marine iguana.

■ Mammals

Seals & Seal Lions

 Seals and sea lions represent the most noticeable of the few mammals that reside on the islands. The **Galápagos sea lion** is a subspecies of the California sea lion, and is distinguished from a true seal by its external ears and its use of front flippers for swimming. The sea lion is quite prolific throughout the islands; it is estimated that there are over 50,000 individuals. While it may be tempting to try to get a close-up photo of one of these adorable creatures, keep in mind that a saltwater sneeze from one of these beasts is about as disgusting as it gets. Also, don't be surprised if the dominant bull chases after you. They are particularly aggressive; snorkeling in a bull's territory is not advised.

The smaller **Galápagos fur seal** is endemic to the archipelago and is more active at night. It is characterized by thick, radiant fur – a prized commodity during the fur-hunting era of the 1800s. While the fur seal was at one point on the brink of extinction, its population today is fully recovered.

Whales & Dolphins

Several species of whales exist around the islands. Among them are the **humpback**, **minke**, **sperm**, **pilot**, and **killer whales**. Also common is the **bottle-nosed dolphin** and, to a lesser extent, the **spinner dolphin**. You won't have to search far and wide for these creatures – just look in front of your boat. They love to play in front of the bows of fast-moving vessels.

■ Fish

Several hundred species of fish circulate around the islands. Among the more noted are puffers, angelfish, surgeonfish, parrotfish, and triggerfish.

If your interest lies in snorkeling or diving, be sure to pick up a copy of *A Field Guide to the Fishes of the Galápagos* by Godfrey Merlin (1988, Libri Mundi, Quito) or *Reef Fish Identification – Galápagos* by Paul Humann (1993, New World Publications).

Sharks

Perhaps the most awe-inspiring of the sharks in the area is the **hammerhead**. As you're snorkeling on the water's surface, don't be surprised if you see the hammerhead's swift-moving silhouette just below. The endemic **Galápagos shark** and the **white-tipped reef shark** are other commonly sighted species. None of these is will bother swimmers and most guides know the best places to find them.

Rays

Just as incredible to witness, perhaps due to their sheer size and grace, are **giant rays**. Swimming among these majestic creatures is an experience not to miss. One species, the **spotted eagle ray**, can grow to over six feet long. Monster **manta rays**, which live farther offshore, can be seen jumping above the water's surface, crashing back down, and disappearing. It's an incredible sight and is actually an effort on their part to eliminate parasites from their backsides.

The shallow-water-dwelling **stingray** is the only species you really don't want to mess with. They are beautiful to behold, but often they rest along the bottom, hidden from view beneath the sand. The last thing you want to do is step on one. If a guide points out a sandy cove that is frequented by stingrays, swim elsewhere.

■ Crabs & Other Invertebrates

 The most photogenic of all the Galápagos invertebrates is the brightly colored **Sally Lightfoot crab**. Its unique design includes red legs and fore-pinchers, a yellow top, and a sky-blue underside. Standing out in stark contrast to the black volcanic rocks along the shoreline, the Sally Lightfoot's courtship dance is mesmerizing enough to hold a photographer in trance. **Ghost crabs**, too, are common on sandy beaches, and are fascinating to watch as they pop in and out of holes they make in the sand.

Tidal pools, which are great places to explore, are miniature ecosystems filled with a variety of colorful invertebrates. Barnacles, sea urchins, various snails, and sea stars (starfish) are just a few of the beautiful creatures that depend upon the eternal shift of the ocean tides.

■ Birds

Finches

 Darwin's finches, otherwise known as Galápagos finches, are perhaps the best known of all the wildlife in the Galápagos Islands. Although they are not brightly colored or exciting to witness, the finch's scientific and historical significance is fascinating. Darwin observed various species during his visit to the islands. Although he mistakenly identified them as warblers and other birds, he noted certain differences among populations. These physical and behavioral variations helped Darwin to formulate the modern theory of evolution.

Today, there are 13 endemic finch species living in the Galápagos. Among them are four species of ground finch, two species of cacti finch, three tree-finch species, and the woodpecker, vegetarian, mangrove, and warbler finches. Scientists speculate that every one of these varieties evolved here from a single ancestral species.

Galápagos Hawk

The only endemic raptor (predatory bird) that lives here is the Galápagos hawk. Dark brown in color, they can be seen soaring high over several of the islands. Breeding mates often include a large female and more than one male, each of which assists in rearing the young. Historically, the Galápagos hawk was hunted and their numbers were significantly reduced. Today, their population is bouncing back.

Boobies

For many, boobies are a highlight of any trip. Why? It may be because of their accessibility in large colonies that nest along the trails. More likely, though, it is their funny name in conjunction with the equally humorous "booby dance" that they perform during courtship.

Three species of boobies nest on the islands: the blue-footed, the red-footed, and the masked booby. Of the trio, the **blue-footed booby** is the most commonly seen. The blue webbed feet, face, and beak make for great photographs, particularly during the famous courtship dance. And they are not modest about their agenda. A zoom lens will do little to dissuade an active couple. Listen for the male's whistle.

The **red-footed booby** nests only on a couple of the smaller, more distant islands, and is, therefore, less observed by visitors (despite the fact that it's actually more common than the blue-footed booby).

The largest and least colorful of the three species is the **masked booby**, which is also common throughout the islands. A blackish, featherless "mask" surrounds its face and stands in contrast to the snow-white feathers on its body. The tips of its wings and tail are also black.

Each of the three species has evolved to occupy a slightly different ecological niche within the island ecosystem. All of them fish for food, but they do so in varying proximity to shore. The birds, with their sleek bodies and swift flight, are perfectly designed for dive-bombing schools of small fish.

Waved Albatross

To watch a giant waved albatross waddle up to the edge of a cliff, take a few steps, and plunge off is a fascinating sight. Its awkwardness is enough to make one wonder how the huge bird can leave the ground, let alone leap off a cliff and survive. Immediately, though, the bird rises back up to the cliff's edge, then elegantly and effortlessly drifts away. The waved albatross is, in fact, the only true "seabird" around, spending years at a time at sea. Lost sailors would be horribly mistaken to identify an albatross as a sign that land was nearby.

Up-close, the albatross is enormous, the largest of all the islands' winged creatures. Its courtship display should not to be missed, especially if you are visiting the Galápagos during the fall. (Forget about seeing an albatross around the new year holidays – the birds are all out to sea from the beginning of the year until about April.)

Española Island is the only permanent waved albatross nesting site in the entire world.

Frigate Birds

The pirates of the Galápagos are these enormous birds, of which there are two species, the **greater frigate** and the **magnificent frigate**. From above, these pterodactyl-shaped creatures look like something straight out of the age of dinosaurs. During courtship on land, the males inflate bright-red flaps of skin around their necks until they look like giant balloons. This colorful behavior is amusing to humans and great for pictures. Other Galápagos seabirds, however, don't particularly care for their airborne antics, as frigates literally steal fish from them in the air by aggravating them from above. Don't think of this as a character flaw, however. It is simply a matter of design. Frigate birds evolved so that they can't fish underwater. They are expert pilots and seem to be able to drift with the wind forever.

Penguins

The flightless **Galápagos penguin** is endemic to these islands and is the most northernmost penguin species in the world. If you happen to see a tuxedo shooting by just under the water's surface, it's a penguin. Underwater, they're as swift and graceful as any fish; on land, they're rigid and awkward.

More Winged Creatures

In all, there are dozens of bird species that reside in the Galápagos. Although it is beyond the scope of this book to detail them all, each is fascinating and well worth discovering. One of my favorites and the easiest to identify is the **brown pelican**. You won't have to go far to spot one, as they like to roost on the bows of yachts and can outstare even the most patient observer. The bright pink **greater flamingo**, by contrast, is found only in shallow, salty lagoons. Herons and egrets, such as the **great blue heron**, the snow-white **cattle egret**, the **lava heron**, and the **yellow-crowned night heron**, also call the Galápagos home. Common shorebirds include **American oyster-catchers**, **plovers**, **gulls**, **terns**, and **sandpipers**. Inland are owls, **pigeons**, **flycatchers**, **mockingbirds**, **warblers**, and **tanagers**, among others.

A great guide for birds is *A Field Guide to the Birds of the Galápagos* by Michael Philip Harris (Collins).

Conservation & the Environment

The Galápagos ecosystem has remained relatively intact compared to many other tropical tourist destinations, primarily due to international conservation efforts and the Ecuadorian government's realization of this national (financial) treasure. Nevertheless, significant environmental degradation has occurred over the last two centuries. Historically, the main direct assault against individual wildlife species was from hunting, while a more general attack on entire ecosystems continues from introduced plants and animals.

Darwin was fortunate to witness the abundance of giant Galápagos tortoises during his visit. Since then, whalers and colonists have decimated populations of the precious namesake animal. During the 19th and 20th centuries, well over 100,000 tortoises were killed for oil and meat, particularly for long seafaring voyages. Introduced animals, including goats, dogs, pigs, and black rats took their toll as well. Pigs destroyed tortoise nests to devour the eggs, rats ate hatchlings, and dogs could break through shells of tortoises that were up to several years old, while goats directly compete with tortoises for food.

In 1959 the Charles Darwin Research Station began an intensive protection, captive-rearing, and reintroduction program. This project has successfully returned many tortoises to their original islands. Unfortunately, the other major threat – that from introduced animals – persists, as eradication programs that focus on feral pigs, dogs, rats, and goats have had mixed success. Today, fewer than 15,000 tortoises survive and three (soon four) of the 14 subspecies are extinct.

The Galápagos land iguana met with a similar fate. Darwin wrote of this creature during his visit, "I cannot give a more forcible proof of their numbers, than by stating that when we were left at Santiago Island, we could not for some time find a spot free from their burrows on which to pitch our single tent." This particular colony is now extinct. The culprits were dogs, cats, pigs and goats. Emergency rescue efforts with other nearly decimated populations, again by the aid

of the Charles Darwin Research Foundation, have been relatively successful. Some of the wild dogs, goats, pigs and
cats have been eradicated or are now under an amount of
control.

Today, the greatest threats to life throughout the islands
are from human encroachment and habitat loss from agricultural expansion, primarily as it relates to tourism. The
majority of the population growth has occurred since tourism became popular in the 1960s and is directly or indirectly associated with the tourist dollar. In 1950, there were
1,346 inhabitants; by 1999 that figure had grown to 16,184.
This represents a 6.4% growth rate, higher than anywhere
else in Latin America or even Africa. Fortunately, the Ecuadorian government has recently implemented a moratorium on colonization in the islands and the population
hovers somewhere over 20,000 inhabitants today.

Agricultural expansion, particularly in the highlands of
Santa Cruz Island, has significantly reduced populations of
Darwin's finches. During a recent visit, my guide, a native
Galapaqueño, said that when he was young the finches
were everywhere near his home, but now they have disappeared. The mangrove finch, as well, has been reduced to a
few hundred individuals residing within the remaining
mangrove stands on Isabela Island. None of the species are
extinct – so far. Finally, increased and indiscriminate fishing continues to threaten marine ecosystems throughout
the islands.

Although the government regulates the number of tourists
and vessels allowed into the park, revisions are made and
loopholes are easily found. For example, a previous freeze
on the number of vessels allowed was manipulated when
yachts were reconstructed to accommodate more people
(the result is crowded conditions on all vessels). In addition,
there are several political figures involved in regulating the
islands, and often their incentives are at odds. The number
of tourists has increased from 11,765 in 1979 to as many as
66,000 by recent estimates. The National Park Service has
assured the International Galápagos Tour Operators Association that they will not further increase the number of
"cupos," or permits available to visitors.

The stress on wildlife and trail conditions from tourism cannot be overstated. A recent discussion with a couple of German "photographers" who were ignoring our guide's plea to
stay on the trail arose from a general misconception shared
by most tourists. Just because an animal does not fly away

or flee does not mean that it is not stressed. Studies actually show the opposite, revealing the animal has an accelerated heart rate and experiences a loss of vital energy reserves. Wildlife near the trails is much more used to human approach and therefore less bothered.

Keep in mind that Galápagos soils and vegetation are part of a fragile ecosystem. The accumulated effect of thousands of footsteps can cause much more damage than one lone drifter can begin to imagine. Remember, the problem is not with the 99% who are conscientious travelers, but with the 1% who are irresponsible. Environmental awareness and respect are the key to resolving these issues.

Getting Here & Getting Around

 TAME offers daily flights from mainland Ecuador to the Galápagos (Baltra Island) that depart early in the morning, as well as weekly flights to Puerto Baquerizo Moreno on San Cristóbal (although only a few tours begin here). From Quito or Guayaquil, the plane ride is typically purchased in conjunction with an island package tour. From Quito, the price is close to US$400 round-trip during peak season (student discount available) and a bit less during the off-season. Flights from Quito pass through Guayaquil and tickets from there are a bit less expensive. Make sure your flight is heading to the correct island. The TAME office in Puerto Ayora on Santa Cruz is located at Av. Charles Darwin near 12 de Febrero, ☎ 5-526-165. The TAME telephone number in Quito is ☎ 2-2430-555.

Upon arrival at Baltra Island, you must pay the $100 park entrance fee in cash. There will be shuttle buses waiting. If you are not meeting a representative of your tour operator here, take the bus to the ferry on the south side of the island and then catch the ferry across the channel (Canal de Itabaca) to the north shore of Santa Cruz Island. From here, a bus will carry you across the island to Puerto Ayora, where most tours begin. The total bus ride and ferry should only cost around $2.

Emetebe Avionetes flies daily between Baltra and Puerto Baquerizo Moreno on San Cristóbal Island (except Sundays), costing

Galápagos Islands

approximately $100 one-way. In Puerto Ayora, the Emetebe office is located on Av. Charles Darwin, above the post office, across from the port, ☎ 5-526-177. Inquire in Puerto Ayora about inter-island boat travel. Although it is more difficult to organize tours from San Cristóbal, it's a nice option if you have extra time.

Visitor Information

There are basically two ways to see the Galápagos. The first and more popular option is on a cruise package tour, where you travel between islands – ideally at night – and sleep on the vessel, while visiting the islands during the day. The other, less expensive option includes day excursions from Puerto Ayora on Santa Cruz and, to a lesser extent, Puerto Baquerizo Moreno on San Cristóbal Island. This option is more limited because of travel time between the islands, but may be better for budget travelers. See *Tours Operators & Travel Agents*, page 401, for more details.

■ Puerto Ayora

Puerto Ayora on Santa Cruz Island is the main hub for tourist activity in the Galápagos. It is a full-service town, complete with stores, restaurants, post office, communications services, and options for accommodations. The **Ministry of Tourism**, at Av. Charles Darwin, has island maps, with more information available next door at Capturgal, the Camera Provincial de Turísmo de Galápagos office. The Charles Darwin Research Station is also located here. The town is pleasant and small, with most everything you could require along its main street, including banks and Internet cafés. **Banco del Pacífico** is along Av. Charles Darwin near Pelican Bay and the **post office** is across from the docks. The **TAME** airline office is located at Av. Charles Darwin near 12 de Febrero, ☎ 5-526-165. **Emetebe**, ☎ 5-526-177, is also on Av. Charles Darwin, upstairs in the post office building. The **hospital** is at Av. Padre J Herrera and Darwin.

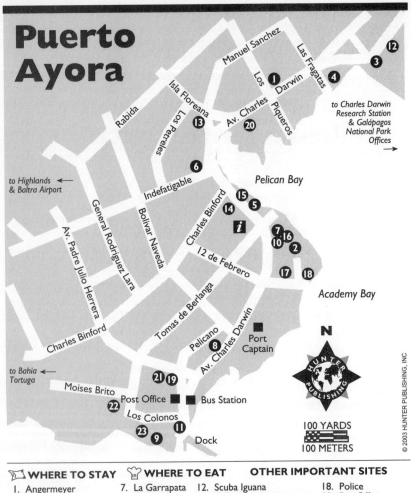

Puerto Ayora

to Charles Darwin Research Station & Galápagos National Park Offices →

to Highlands & Baltra Airport ←

Pelican Bay

Academy Bay

to Bahia Tortuga ←

Port Captain

Post Office

Bus Station

Dock

N

100 YARDS
100 METERS

© 2003 HUNTER PUBLISHING, INC

WHERE TO STAY
1. Angermeyer
2. Estrella de Mar
3. Galápagos
4. Red Mangrove Inn
5. SolyMar
6. La Peregrina B&B

WHERE TO EAT
7. La Garrapata
8. El Rincón del Alma
9. Salvavidas
10. La Panga
11. Toldo Azul

OTHER IMPORTANT SITES
12. Scuba Iguana
13. Galápagos Sub-Aqua
14. Moonrise Travel Agency
15. Banco del Pacífico
16. La Panga Disco
17. TAME
18. Police
19. Bus Office
20. Quasar Nautica
21. Galasam
22. Rolf Wittmer
23. Supermarket

■ Puerto Baquerizo Moreno

On San Cristóbal Island, this is another population center that also caters to tourism, albeit to a lesser extent. **Banco del Pacífico** is on the Malecón and 12 de Febrero, centrally located near the **post office**. **TAME**, ☎ 5-521-089, and **Emetebe**, ☎ 5-520-036, are both at the airport.

Puerto Baquerizo Moreno

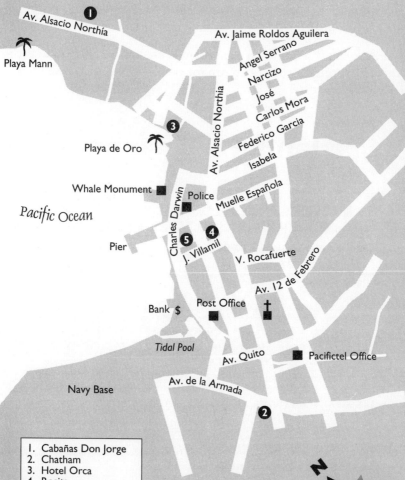

Av. Alsacio Northía ❶

Playa Mann

Av. Jaime Roldos Aguilera

Angel Serrano

Narcizo

José

Carlos Mora

Federico Garcia

❸

Av. Alsacio Northía

Playa de Oro

Isabela

Whale Monument

Charles Darwin

Police

Muelle Española

Pacific Ocean

Pier

❺ ❹

J. Villamil

V. Rocafuerte

Av. 12 de Febrero

Bank $

Post Office ✝

Tidal Pool

Av. Quito

Pacifictel Office

Navy Base

Av. de la Armada

❷

1. Cabañas Don Jorge
2. Chatham
3. Hotel Orca
4. Rosita
5. Iguana Net II & Tours

N

100 YARDS

100 METERS

HUNTER PUBLISHING

The **Ministerio de Turismo** is on Av. Charles Darwin near the southern end of Pelican Bay, ☎ 5-526-174, cptg@pa.ga.pro.ec. For information and updates on conservation, as well as responsible travel within the Galápagos, contact the **International Galápagos Tour Operators Association (IGTOA)**, in the US at ☎ 607-273-4321, igtoa@voyagers.com, www.igtoa.org. For special visits to the Galápagos Islands, including scientific research, contact the **Charles Darwin Research Station** in Puerto Ayora, ☎ 5-526-146, www.darwinfoundation.org, cdrs@fcdarwin.org.ec. You can reach the **National Park Service**, also in Puerto Ayora, for useful information, ☎ 5-526-189.

There is a small population center on Isabella Island in **Puerto Villamil**, though it doesn't cater to tourism, other than to the truly independent traveler.

Island Excursions

Most people visit the Galápagos with an organized tour, usually on a five- or eight-day cruise. Still, it is possible to blitz the islands on day-trips or stay for three weeks or longer. I find that an eight-day tour is just about right for the general traveler, as the first and last days involve arriving and departing.

> *Trips can be arranged and organized in Quito, Guayaquil, and Baños on the mainland. If you are coming to Ecuador and plan on visiting the Galápagos, you can book your trip at a lower cost in these cities than you can through travel agents abroad.*

There are literally dozens of cruise vessels represented by dozens of travel agents in Quito. Booking ahead during peak season, however, is advisable.

■ Tour Classes & Prices

Pre-arranged tours generally fall into three class categories, with the quality of the vessel roughly paralleling the quality of the guide and crew services. These prices do not include the US$100 in cash required as a park entrance fee or expenses for personal extras such as alcohol and bottled beverages.

Economy-class tours range from as low as $300 for a five-day tour to $600 for the better eight-day tours (about $50-$75 per day). Expect small, crowded boat conditions with minimal comforts, but plenty of young, budget travelers having a great time.

In the mid-range are **tourist-class vessels**, ranging anywhere from $500 to $1,200 for the very nice vessels (about $100-$175 per day). Most of these boats comfortably accommodate 16 passengers, plus crew, and offer a dining area, sun and shade decks, and small double cabins with tiny bathrooms (all cabins are small in the Galápagos, even on higher-priced vessels).

Luxury- or **first-class tours** cost as much as $2,800 (in the range of $200+ per day). These vessels range from sleek 12-passenger yachts to a monster 96-passenger cruise ship, complete with every amenity and top-notch guides.

If you are on a tight budget and have time to spare, or if you simply want a more customized trip, there are other options. **Budget travelers** can often find last-minute specials in Quito on tours that need to fill empty spaces. This, of course, means that you have to be ready to depart at any time (usually within a day or two of notification). Or you can fly to the Galápagos and try to arrange a tour from Puerto Ayora. This may take from one to several days or longer, depending on the season. The last person I spoke with who did this paid only $50 per day for the eight-day tour and had to wait only two days. Start asking around at your hotel in Puerto Ayora. You will eventually find something that works out. Don't depend on last-minute specials, however, during the peak travel months of December, July and August.

Finally, **day-trips** are available out of Puerto Ayora for as little as $40 per day. Much of the time on these tours, however, is spent traveling to and from sites. Therefore, the overall quality may be low. **Multiday, hotel-based trips** are also available and include a bit more flexibility.

■ Tour Operators & Travel Agents

Tour operators and travel agents are a dime a dozen, offering virtually anything you might be looking for. It is easy to walk into one of a hundred travel agents lining the streets around Avenida Amazonas in Quito and start asking questions. Give them your budget, time frame, and quality of trip desired and you will be on a plane to the Galápagos in the blink of an eye. Be sure to ask as many questions as it takes to make you feel comfortable with the product. Ask to see pictures of the vessel, and check with other travel agents to make sure you get a good deal.

It is obviously well beyond the scope of this book to detail the dozens of vessels that cruise around the islands. The most important thing to understand is that the quality of individual boats, crews, and guides changes constantly. Yachts fall into disrepair, are given facelifts, and are rebuilt on a regular basis. During a recent trip, for example, there was a beautiful new tourist-superior vessel, hardly a year old, half-underwater in the bay at San Cristóbal Island (this is not common, by the way). And a tour is only as good as its crew. There are a few companies (listed below) with consistently good reputations. Inquire about their boats with the travel agents or check with the South American Explorers Club (☎/fax 2-225-228, explorer@seac.org.ec) for the best and latest recommendations.

 A good listing and description of operators and boats can be found in *A Traveler's Guide to the Galápagos Islands* by Barry Boyce (Hunter Publishing).

For specials and last-minute tours from Puerto Ayora, try **Moonrise Travel Agency**, along the waterfront Av. Charles Darwin across from Banco del Pacífico, ☎ 5-526-402/3 or 526-348, sdivine@ga.pro.ec or sdivine@pa.ga.pro.ec. **Neptuno Tours**, also on Av. Charles Darwin, ☎ 5-262-246, offers good, inexpensive tours into the interior of Santa Cruz, as well as local snorkeling excursions. There are a couple of other last-minute booking agencies. Inquire around.

On the mainland is **Galasam (Economic Galápagos Tours)**, Quito, ☎ 2-2507-079/080, ☎/fax 2-2567-662; Amazonas and Cordero, in Guayaquil, ☎ 4-2312-447, fax 4-2313-351, office 1106, 9 de Octubre 424 and Córdova; www.Galapagos-islands.com. Galasam offers the best and most of the economy-class tours. Tours are on simple, small, and relatively crowded but clean vessels. All meals and drinking water are provided. Ask about the showers, as they may be little more than buckets of fresh water available for use on deck. Galasam also operates a new fleet of tourist-superior and luxury-class vessels worth looking into.

Rolf Wittmer of **Wittmer Turismo**, in Quito, Mariscal Foch E7-81 and Diego de Almagro, ☎ 2-2526-938 or 2-2563-098, ☎/fax 2-2228-520, rwittmer@tiptop.com.ec, www.rwittmer.com, is a true Galápaqueño. His family operates two tourist-superior/first-class sailing vessels. Rolf's trips emphasize the early human history of Floreana island, which his mother, Margaret Wittmer, wrote about in the book *Floreana* many years ago. Of German ancestry, Rolf is the first recorded native of the Galápagos Islands.

✫ **Ecoventura** is at Av. Colón E9-58 and 6 de Diciembre in Quito, ☎ 2-2507-408; in Guayaquil, Av. CJ Arosemena, ☎ 4-203-080, ecosales@ecoventura.com.ec. They offer a fleet of three 20-passenger first-class motor yachts, as well as live-aboard diving excursions. Vessels operate out of Puerto Moreno on San Cristóbal Island. Prices are moderate for a first-class vessel. Ecoventura has recently received a "green seal of approval" through an eco-certification program known as SmartVoyager – an honor it shares with Canodros.

✫ **Canodros** is based in Guayaquil (Urbanización Santa Leonor, Manzana 5 Solar #10 (Vía Terminal Terrestre), Guyaquil, ☎ 4-2285-711 or 4-2280-880, 4-2514-750, ☎/fax 4-2287-651, www.canodros.com, ecotourism1@canodros.com.ec. In Miami, call toll-free ☎ 888-368-9929 or 305-662-2965. They operate another first-class SmartVoyager-approved vessel. Canodros manages Kapawi Lodge, one of the best Amazon ecolodges, in conjunction with a local native community. Overall, they are a leader in responsible ecotourism. (See more about them on page 378.)

Eco-Certification in the Galápagos

SmartVoyager is a program that was developed jointly by Rainforest Alliance, an international conservation organization based in New York, and the Ecuadorian not-for-profit, Conservación y Desarrollo (Conservation and Development). According to their own description, the organization "minimizes the impact of tour boats in the Galápagos Islands by improving social and environmental conditions of boat operations. Operators that meet the program's standards are 'certified' and may use the SmartVoyager label in marketing. The label gives travelers the assurance that they are supporting operators who care about the environment, wildlife conservation, and the well-being of workers and local communities."

The process of eco-certification is long and expensive, which makes it difficult for tour operators without resources to be involved. The main focus is actually on the larger Galápagos cruise vessels, those that carry more than 16 passengers and can have the greatest negative impact. But these are the operators that have the resources to operate responsibly and some have taken the initiative to do so. To learn more about the program standards and the very real negative impacts of travel to the Galápagos and elsewhere, visit the website at www.rainforest-alliance.org.

Angermeyer's **Enchanted Expeditions**, in Quito, Foch 726 and Av. Amazonas, ☎ 2-2256-9960, ☎/fax 2-2256-9956, www.angermeyer. com, info@enchantedexpedtions.com, also offers well-recommended mid- to upper mid-range tours with quality service.

Galacruises is in Quito at J. Washington 748 between Amazonas and 9 de Octubre, ☎ 2-2556-036, seaman@uio.satnet.net, www. Galapagosseaman.com.ec. They operate the comfortable mid-range vessel called *Sea Man*. Freddie the *panga* boat driver is always good for a laugh.

Quasar Nautica-Galápagos Expeditions is in Quito, ☎ 2-2441-550, or in the US, ☎ 800-247-2925, Av. Los Shyris 2447, Edif Autocom, www.quasarnautica.com, qnautic1@ecnet.ec. They offer luxury-class yachts and sailing vessels with excellent guide and crew services. Inquire about their diving tours.

For first-class, luxury travel try **Metropolitan Touring** (they are as big as their name implies), in Quito at Av. República de El Salvador 970, ☎ 2-2464-780, ☎/fax 2-2464-702, www.metropolitantouring. com. Metropolitan offers some of the best vessels and tours in the Galápagos, but you pay for what you get. Although I would tend to question companies that bring such large numbers of people on a cruise to these delicate islands, Metropolitan seem to be one of the stronger proponents of conservation in the region.

Adventure Life, an American company, offers 10-day and seven-day all-inclusive Galápagos tours, as well as trips to the Andes and the Amazon rainforest. Contact them at ☎ 800-344-6118 or info@ad-venture-life.com. Their website, www.adventure-life.com, provides complete information.

Note that there are many "travel agencies" in Quito that are brokers for different tour operators and can search around to find availability among them. **Safari Tours**, admin@safari.com.ec, www.safari.com. ec, not only has one of the better up-to-date listings, but they are very helpful as well.

 Check out www.EcuadorExplorer.com for travel information on the Galápagos and Ecuador in general.

With regard to specific vessels, you can typically depend on those run by the recommended operators listed in this section, but check for references and make sure you know ahead of time what you will be getting. You can also check with the South American Explorers Club (☎/ fax 2-225-228, explorer@seac.org.ec) for yacht-specific comments and recommendations.

Island-by-Island

■ Baltra Island

 Flying from mainland Ecuador, expect to see nothing below but deep blue ocean for over an hour. As the airplane begins its descent, the jagged edge of a giant landmass meets the water's edge. Soon the island comes more into focus, dry and desert-like in appearance. Cacti seem to appear, but over 600 miles from anywhere? Welcome to Baltra Island and the Galápagos Archipelago.

Most travelers enter the Galápagos via the small airport at Isla Baltra, which was developed as a US airbase in the early 1940s to protect US interests from a perceived threat from Germany at the Panama Canal, as well as to prepare US forces en route to battle against Japan in the South Seas. In fact, Baltra was the largest military base in all of South America at the time, and created the first large-scale wave of immigrants from mainland Ecuador and surrounding countries. They built the infrastructure in record time. Now it is an Ecuadorian air base with only remnants of a bygone era.

Just a stone's throw north of Isla Santa Cruz, Baltra is a tiny island (10 square miles) that is primarily used as a point of arrival and departure for island tours. If you are on a prearranged tour, your host will probably meet you at the airport. Or follow the crowd from here to the shuttle bus, which takes you to the ferry that crosses over to Santa Cruz Island. Wait along the shoreline and watch as pelicans dive for fish nearby. Your wildlife viewing has already begun! Once on Santa Cruz, another bus or private transport will cross the island to Puerto Ayora, where most tours begin.

■ North Seymour Island

Isla Seymour is just north of Baltra and is often visited toward the end of a tour, before heading back to the airport on Baltra. This small island, about .75 square miles, offers a nice sample of Galápagos wildlife in one short hike. The magnificent frigate bird in courtship is the highlight. Males, with their bright red pouches inflated like balloons, offer great photo ops. Blue-footed boobies, sea lions, and marine iguanas are common here as well. The easy trail can take from 45 minutes to a few hours, depending on your level of curiosity.

Seymour Island offers no modern facilities and is accessible only as part of prearranged island tours, most of which stop here.

■ Santa Cruz Island

Chances are that your tour will begin here. A ferry from Isla Baltra provides transportation to the north side of Santa Cruz, and land transportation will continue to **Puerto Ayora**, where cruise vessels are docked.

Unfortunately, Santa Cruz Island is in grave danger as a result of continued development. In fact, it has the largest population of all the Galápagos islands, with over half of the archipelago's 20,000+ inhabitants. Its future will depend on a recent moratorium on immigration to the islands and effective regulation of agricultural expansion as well as other indirect impacts of tourism.

Puerto Ayora, the main town and focal point for tourism, lies on the south side of the island. Within walking distance is the **Charles Darwin Research Station**. Most tours stop by the station at some point during their visit. The walk from town to the research station passes through a unique "forest" of manzanilla, saltbush, and various cacti. Insects, which are relatively under-represented on the islands (compared to the mainland), abound in various shapes and sizes. Birders will enjoy Darwin's finches, flycatchers, and Galápagos mockingbirds.

The research station is important for understanding the magic of the Galápagos and its struggle to survive. At the main visitor's center are numerous exhibits that describe the archipelago's natural history, geology, historical issues, and conservation efforts. Slide shows are also presented here in several different languages. Farther along the main walkway is the tortoise conservation and rearing center. Learn about the natural history of the remaining endemic subspecies, as well as other ongoing projects. In addition, you can visit the center's tortoise incubation and repatriation facilities, where repopulating efforts continue at full speed. There are several small beaches nearby that are great for relaxing.

Back in town, the ocean-front street is a good place to pick up a souvenir or relax with a drink and a sunset view of Academy Bay. Prices here are a bit higher than on the mainland. Don't expect at the last minute to find an inexpensive, disposable underwater camera. They cost up to $25 here, compared to $15 in Quito. While you are lounging about near the shoreline, the wildlife – including marine iguanas, pelicans, and other shorebirds – may join you. *Pangas*, the little rubber motorboats, wait as water taxis at the pier to transport passengers between the island and their boats. Arrange to have a crew member pick you up, or take a water taxi for just over $1.

Just southwest of town lies another interesting sight – **Turtle Bay**, with one of the nicer beaches in the islands. Take the self-guided trail near the Pacífictel telephone office and walk for about 45 minutes to the white-sand beach. There you may find various seabirds, marine iguanas, and perhaps a shark or two.

In the interior of Santa Cruz, you can also explore the highland ecosystem. There are a few trailed areas worth inquiring about if you have an extra day or two on the island before or after a tour, including lava tubes, sinkholes, and a tortoise reserve. There are tours of eight days or longer that explore the highlands, so be sure to inquire if you are interested.

Puerto Ayora is the hub of tourist activity on the islands and has the best modern facilities. Plenty of shops, restaurants, and bars line the main waterfront. Most everything is located along Av. Charles Darwin – the main road adjacent to the water. Post and communications are also available here (see *Visitor Information*, page 397, for specifics).

On the north side of the island are a couple of visitor sites for boat tours that generally begin or end at the nearby Baltra Island (across the channel). **Las Bachas** offers a beach landing just west of the channel to Baltra Island. There is good swimming here, as well as a variety of wildlife that includes marine iguanas, crabs, and great blue herons. Pink flamingos are sometimes found in the lagoon. Farther west is **Caleta Tortuga Negra**, a small cove that provides a breeding ground for green sea turtles and is a habitat for reef sharks, rays and blue herons.

■ Española Island

A rocky shoreline and rising swells await your landing at **Punta Suárez** on Isla Española in the far southeast of the archipelago. One of the smallest of the "large" islands (23 square miles), Española offers a couple of visitor sights and various special treats. Immediately upon landing, you can walk among **sea-lion colonies** to get close-up photos of these adorable creatures. From here a short trail leads through colonies of **blue-footed** and **masked boobies**. There is no need to stray off the trail here – you may actually have to be careful not to step on them along the way! An assortment of dancing couples in courtship highlights the walk.

Colonies of **marine iguanas** also line the path and are about as immobile as the rocks they rest upon. And don't worry if a tiny black **Galápagos snake** crosses your path – it's not dangerous. A highlight toward the end of the trail is the colony of **giant waved albatross**. This is the only nesting place for this species; they arrive from March through December. At the edge of the sea cliff are spectacular views of the ocean, the rocky shoreline, and a giant blowhole that sprays water nearly 100 feet into the air.

On the northeast side of the island is **Gardner Bay**, where a white-sand beach and plenty of good swimming await. An offshore rock provides a great snorkeling opportunity.

Española Island offers no modern facilities and is accessible only as part of a prearranged tour. Reaching Española requires a long overseas passage, so the shorter tours with smaller boats are less likely to visit here.

■ Isabela Island

Isabela is a monster compared to the other islands. At 1,771 square miles, it makes up nearly three-fifths of the archipelago's landmass. Connected by five relatively young volcanoes, two of which are sometimes active, Isabela's sheer size makes it difficult to travel around and visit within the time frame of most tours, especially since the main sights are on the island's far west side. Few standard tours under two weeks in length visit Isabela, unless they skip the other major islands.

One of Isabela's main attractions is at **Urbina Bay**, about midway up the island's west coast. This uplifted plateau was underwater until 1954, as evidenced by embedded coral and other marine life. The area provides a good opportunity to see large marine iguanas, pelicans, flightless cormorants, sea turtles, and some of the few remaining **mangrove finches**. The impressive **Volcán Alcedo**, 4,144 feet high, is visible from here. If you have the time, do an overnight hike to the rim of the caldera. It offers active fumaroles and a spectacular view, and is the best place in the Galápagos to witness giant tortoises at home. Other overnight hikes include **Volcán Cerro Azul** and **Volcán Negra (Santo Tomás)**. All of these hikes require permits and a willingness to rough it. Inquire well in advance at the National Park office in Puerto Ayora, ☎ 5-526-189. Nearby is **Tagus Cove**, where early sailors often anchored. Look closely and you may spot their graffiti scratched into the side of the cliffs, as well as possibly the Galápagos penguin and flightless cormorant.

South of Urbina Bay is **Elizabeth Bay** (there is no place to dock here) and farther west is **Punta Moreno**. A dry landing is available, as well as a rough trail over lava flows and among brackish pools. Wildlife here is less abundant and diverse than on other islands that have been around longer. Nevertheless, pioneering species are evident, as well penguins and other shore birds.

The main "town" is **Puerto Villamil**, along the south coast of the island, and inhabited by a few thousand people, with the smaller village of **Santo Tomás** inland from here. You can arrange trips to the interior of the island from Villamil.

■ Fernandina Island

Fernandina Island, located midway along Isabela's western side, is the third-largest of the islands at 248 square miles. It is also the youngest island in the archipelago, characterized by beautiful lava formations and incredibly large populations of the endemic marine iguana. The visitors' arrival site, at **Punta Espinosa**, is on the northeastern tip of the island near **Tagus Cove**. In addition to the marine iguana, expect to see flightless cormorants, sea lions, and, if you're lucky, Galápagos penguins. Keep in mind that the volcano is still active.

Fernandina Island offers no modern facilities and is accessible only as part of prearranged island tours. It is reached via a long overseas passage that includes traveling around the enormous Isabela Island, so the shorter tours with smaller boats are less likely to visit here.

■ Genovesa (Tower) Island

Genovesa Island is farther northeast than any other island. None of the five-day tours and only some of the better eight-day tours visit Genovesa.

If you do manage to visit, however, you certainly won't be disappointed – especially if you are an avid birder. In addition to masked boobies, frigate birds, gulls, short-eared owls, and tropicbirds, there is also a large red-footed booby colony and an enormous colony of stormy petrels. The trail to the top of the cliff is known as Prince Phillip's Steps (El Baranco). It passes by various seabird nests and along the cliff's edge, where swarms of stormy petrels perform aerial acrobatics.

At **Darwin Bay** the scenery is spectacular, with rich green water surrounded by high cliffs and an abundance of marine life. A trail here follows the beach. This area and the lagoon just beyond the shore are great places to wander around and soak up the sea life. The bay itself offers snorkeling opportunities (hammerhead sharks frequent the area), although the water is a cloudy, olive-green color and may provide only limited visibility.

Genovesa Island offers no modern facilities and is accessible only as part of prearranged island tours. It is included on some of the eight-day or longer cruises.

■ Marchena & Pinta Islands

The 50-square-mile Isla Marchena is east of Genovesa and is one of the northernmost members of the Galápagos chain. Its distance from civilization, combined with its lack of official visitors' sights, makes Marchena one of the least-visited islands. It is a popular and renowned scuba diving destination for those wishing to get away from it all.

Marchena Island offers no modern facilities and is accessible only as part of a prearranged island tour. It may be included on some of the eight-day or longer cruises or as part of a specialized diving tour of the islands. Nearby is small Isla Pinta, which, likewise, is very rarely visited and only on longer specialized tours.

■ Plazas Islands

The tiny Plazas Islands, which are really just big rocks, sit off the eastern tip of Santa Cruz Island. South Plaza Island (32 acres) is easily accessible as a day-trip from Puerto Ayora. North Plaza Island is not open to visitors. South Plaza Island's trail, which begins at a rocky landing, follows the edge of a cliff and offers great views from above. A forest of opuntia cactus spreads across the small landmass and, combined with the reddish groundcover, provides habitat for the yellow land iguana. Various seabirds live here and are fun to watch from the edge of the cliff as they dance in the sky.

Plaza Island offers no modern facilities and is accessible only as part of prearranged island tours. It is included on most tours.

■ San Cristóbal Island

The easternmost (and fifth-largest) of all the islands is San Cristóbal. **Puerto Baquerizo Moreno** is the main entry point and is the provincial capital of the Galápagos. Some flights actually arrive on San Cristóbal and some tours begin here, although most begin in Puerto Ayora on Santa Cruz Island. The town is quite pleasant, with a laid-back atmosphere and unique Afro-Ecuadorian culture.

A short ride or walk from town provides the opportunity to see the islands' best and newest **visitor center**. Very modern and illustrative, it is well worth a visit to learn about the human and natural history of the islands. Everything is written in both English and Spanish, and the interactive approach to the displays makes it quite enjoyable.

Another short trail out of town leads to **Frigate Bird Hill**, where both the greater and the magnificent frigate birds are known to nest. The hill also provides good views of the bay. Northeast of town, past the village of **El Progresso**, is the highest point on the island, **Cerro San Joaquin** (2,930 feet); and, several miles farther, **El Junco**, a freshwater lagoon. Not many tours head out this direction, but the trail offers a good opportunity to view the inter-island life zones without the heavy traffic of Santa Cruz Island.

The tiny **Isla Lobos** is about an hour northeast of Puerto Moreno by boat. Although not as spectacular as some of the other stops, it is the site of the main sea-lion colonies of San Cristóbal. Swimming with sea-lion pups in the shallows is a tour highlight for many people.

Farther down the coast another hour or so is the sheer-rock outcrop of **Léon Dormido**, or "Sleeping Lion." This tiny island has been eroded in half, and boats can pass right through the center if the ocean is calm enough. Just circling around its massive vertical walls is exciting. There is no landing here, but boats will drift around while you snorkel between the rocks. The marine display is usually fascinating – there's a good chance of witnessing sharks or even a massive, spotted eagle ray.

Punta Pitt and **Turtle Bay** lie at the north end of San Cristóbal. Punta Pitt offers the chance to see all three species of boobies nesting in the same area (and the only place to see the nesting red-footed booby). Sea turtles are often found at Turtle Bay. Inland and a good hike away is **Los Galápagos**, one of the best places to witness the giant Galápagos tortoise in its natural environment.

Many tours do not have time for the four-hour round-trip hike into this area, so be sure to inquire if you are interested.

Puerto Moreno is one of two main towns in the Galápagos (the other is Puerto Ayora on Santa Cruz Island). Modern facilities include accommodations, restaurants, a tourist office, and even a bit of nightlife. Everything is located along the main street adjacent to the waterfront.

■ Santa Fé Island

Santa Fé Island, just two hours southeast of Santa Cruz and only nine square miles in size, is another popular destination for day-trips. The trail from the landing is a great way to see the giant and endemic **Santa Fé land iguanas**. There is excellent snorkeling here, or you can just hang out around the sea-lion colony and watch your fellow travelers flap around in the water.

Santa Fé Island has no modern facilities and is visited by most tours, particularly the shorter ones.

■ Santa María (Floreana) Island

South of Santa Cruz lies Isla de Floreana, site of the historical **Post Office Bay** and **Devil's Crown**. It is also the island with the most fascinating recorded human history outside of Darwin's voyage. Beginning in 1929, a few small groups of settlers decided to call Floreana home, including a German doctor and his partner, as well as the Wittmers (another German family), and an Austrian baroness with a couple of her lovers/servants. Trouble in paradise quickly arose as power struggles occurred and resulted in strange disappearances, hunting episodes with human prizes, and multiple suspected – but never proven – murders.

Margaret Wittmer

Margaret Wittmer, the first to successfully emigrate from Europe to the island and remain her entire life, wrote a book about those early days entitled *Floreana*, published by Moyer Bell Ltd. Publications (1990, first published in 1961). More like literary fiction than real life, it describes the harsh struggles to survive, visits from the rich and famous abroad, volcanic eruptions with US aircraft disappearing into a blazing inferno, a world war and an island war, to name but a few trials and triumphs. I highly recommend her story. Margaret Wittmer lived on Floreana until 2000, when she died at the age of 95. Her son Rolf, who was the first European Ecuadorian born on the islands, offers tours around the Galápagos, through his company, Rolf Wittmer Turismo (see Tour Operators & Travel Agents, page 400).

Post Office Bay, on the north shore of the island, is the main point of access. On the trail just off the beach is a junk pile of bones, debris, signs, and the historical post-office barrel. The barrel dates back to the late 1700s. Whalers would drop mail in the barrel and there it would sit until a passing sailor heading in the right direction would pick it up and deliver it. The tradition also played a major role in Margret Wittmer's account of *Floreana* and it continues today. Visitors are encouraged to drop a postcard into the barrel and look through the pile for anything that could be delivered close to home.

Continuing along the trail, you'll pass a decrepit fish-processing plant. Farther on is a lava tube that heads below ground and back toward the ocean. With a flashlight or headlamp and a good rope it is possible to scramble down the entry and into the tube. The passage eventually enters the water and walking becomes impossible. If you've brought your swimsuit, however....

Most tours spend time checking out the wildlife near shore on a *panga* (boat) ride. Expect to find sea-lion colonies, lava gulls, and pelicans. At **Punta Cormorant** there is an olive-green beach with a short trail that leads across a narrow section of the island. Along this trail is a small, brackish lagoon where bright pink flamingos and other lagoon feeders dwell. Sometimes there are dozens of flamingos here, but even if the flock is away there is still a good chance of witnessing a lone individual or two. Flamingos are very shy and nervous animals, so this is a good place to use your zoom lens.

At the end of the trail is a white-sand beach divided by black lava rocks. Here you'll find colorful Sally Lightfoot crabs dancing about and stingrays swimming in the shallows. It's a great place to swim, but watch your step near shore. Shuffle and slide your feet through the sand to avoid stepping on a stingray.

A *panga* ride from Punta Cormorant offers a special treat in the form of the **Devil's Crown**. This volcanic plug that pokes out of the water just offshore is a great place to see nesting and resting shorebirds. It is also one of the Galápagos' best snorkeling areas. The crater offers a small coral formation and numerous species of bright tropical fish, including the blue parrotfish, various triggerfish, and the pufferfish. For an extra-special rush, follow your guide's lead and look for sharks. You may be fortunate enough to spot the awesome hammerhead and white-tipped reef shark in one swim.

Floreana Island has few modern facilities and is accessible as part of most tours, particularly the shorter ones. There are a few places to stay near Black Beach on the western side of the island, including the Wittmer's guest house.

■ Santiago Island

Santiago, at 225 square miles, is the fourth-largest island and is usually visited only on eight-day tours. It is a favorite for many travelers due to the variety of wildlife found here. **James Bay**, on the western side, offers access to the island's most popular sight. From a landing at **Puerto Egas**, the rocky lava beach, local trails, tidal pools, and surrounding inlets are perfect for hours of exploration and wandering. The endemic fur seal, a nocturnal species, can be found lounging about in the shadows of the narrow inlets.

If you're looking for a workout, hike to the 1,291-foot summit of **Sugarloaf Volcano** for a spectacular view. Across James Bay is the brown sand of **Espumilla Beach**. There are also a couple of small lagoons where pink flamingos feed on occasion. Farther north is the scenic, cliffside **Buccaneer Cove**.

The island's other major sight, along the west side of the island, is **Sullivan Bay**. Fresh volcanic formations are the highlight here. A lava flow, dating back to the late 1800s, resulted in a variety of readily accessible volcanic deposits. *Pahoehoe* (pah-HOY-hoy) and *aa* (AH-ah) lava mix with a variety of funky swirls, bubbles, and other formations. This lava desert is also home to several pioneer plant species. A small penguin colony lives on the beach. Farther south is an offshore rock known as **Sombrero Chino**, so named because of its resemblance to a traditional Chinese hat. The channel between the land masses is popular for snorkeling.

There are no modern facilities on Santiago Island. Because of its distance from Santa Cruz Island, it is often visited on eight-day (or longer) tours.

■ Rábida Island

South of Santiago Island, a few miles away, is a much smaller islet, known as Rábida. There is a wet landing on the north side where sea lions lounge about. From here, there is a quick path leading to a salt lagoon with occasional flamingos looking for lunch. Beyond, you can walk to an overlook along a cliff edge, where marine birds dive about. There is also good snorkeling at the beach.

Adventures

■ On Wheels

Mountain Biking

There are limited opportunities to bike on Santa Cruz Island, either through an operator or by renting a bike in Puerto Ayora. Trips to the highlands offer a unique perspective of a different eco-zone than what most people see during their visit. Bikes available vary in quality, but tend to be sub-par. Inquire at the **Red Mangrove Inn**, Av. Charles Darwin and Las Frigatas, ☎/fax 5-526-564, for mountain bike rentals, or talk with the travel agencies in town. The Red Mangrove Inn also has motorbikes, kayaks and windsurf boards available for rent.

Mountain bikes and motorbikes can be rented from a few agencies in Puerto Ayora, including **Galápagos Discovery**, Padre J Herrera, ☎ 5-526-245, who also operate cycling tours in the highlands. Galápagos Discovery also rents surfboards.

■ On Horseback

There are few opportunities on the islands for horseback riding. If you are spending a few days on Santa Cruz, though, give it a try for a different experience here. Riding is done primarily on Santa Cruz's highlands. **Moonrise Travel**, Av. Charles Darwin, ☎ 5-526-348, ☎/fax 5-526-403, is the best agency to arrange for horseback riding on the island.

■ On Foot

Hiking

This is a part of any organized tour or day trip to specific islands. Trails are strictly regulated for foot traffic, and more often than not the hikes are little more than strolls, with plenty of wildlife viewing along the way. Nevertheless, they offer a perfect balance after spending a good amount of time on a boat traveling between destinations.

There are options for longer and overnight treks to a few of the volcanoes on the larger islands. There are also day-hikes available from the main towns, specifically Puerto Ayora and Puerto Moreno. See *Island Excursions*, page 400, for specifics on all-inclusive tours and *Adventures*, page 416, for information on hikes at each island.

■ Wildlife Viewing & Photography

Adventure travel is about experiencing life through the simple beauty of discovery, and this is epitomized in the Galápagos Islands. Although activities abound, most people come here for the overall experience, which includes general wildlife viewing and photography. Tour guides say to bring a roll of film per day. This may be enough if you are a less-than-enthusiastic picture-taker. However, anyone with an interest in wildlife and photography can easily shoot several times that amount. Fortunately for those ill-prepared to snap tons of pictures, there is usually an amateur photographer on board willing to sell an extra roll (but don't count on it).

As you learn more about the wildlife, you may hear of some secrets to help you take the best shots.

Photographers, especially, please take special considerations to stay on the trails and be respectful of your guides' requests. They do have full authority to remove you from a tour.

■ On & In Water

Snorkeling & Swimming

Snorkeling is readily available on tours and is a highlight for many visitors. The water remains a pleasant 72°F (22°C) from January to April, but can drop to a chilly 64°F (18°C) throughout the rest of the year. Although the snorkeling doesn't offer the sheer concentration of tropical reef fish as found at the Great Barrier Reef, for example, the variety of marine life is astounding. Nowhere else on earth can you witness a rainbow of tropical fish, awesome hammerhead sharks, giant sea rays, casual sea turtles, and lightning-fast penguins all in the same place. For a real treat, snorkel the shallows near a family of sea lions. They will swirl and twist in a dizzying display of underwater antics, especially the young pups, and will expect you to do the same or they may become bored and leave. Just watch out for the dominant bull as it patrols the territory and only swim where your guide recommends.

You can rent snorkel gear in Puerto Ayora on Santa Cruz Islands. Inquire with agencies in town (see *Tours Operators & Travel Agents*, page 401, for details).

Sea Kayaking

Although limited in the islands, sea kayaking around the more protected bays, coves and coastline of the Galápagos is an extremely pleasant way to skirt the water's edge at your own pace and discover the beauty of the islands. A few Galápagos vessels are equipped with sea kayaks, which makes for an added bonus during a tour. Inquire with agencies ahead of time to see if kayaks are included. In Puerto Ayora on Santa Cruz Island, a couple of places rent kayaks. Try the **Red Mangrove Inn** (see below).

Surfing

There is actually some decent surf at certain locations throughout the islands. Inquire with local agencies (below) on Santa Cruz and San Cristóbal Islands. Isabella Island also purports to have great waves, but finding a support network for surfing there is much more limited. **Galápagos Discovery**, Padre J Herrera, ☎ 5-526-245, rents surfboards, and windsurf boards are available at the **Red Mangrove Inn**, Av. Charles Darwin and Las Frigatas, ☎/fax 5-526-564. For more information on surfing, go to www.galapagossurf.com.

Diving

The Galápagos Islands have become world-renowned for scuba diving, primarily because the underwater life throughout the islands is, quite literally, found nowhere else on earth. From reef fish and penguins to sharks and sea turtles, the islands offer the adventurous diver a never-ending array of new experiences.

Although certification packages are available, this is not a destination for beginners. Currents can be strong and marine life can be intimidating. In addition, the water is cold during certain months, visibility may be low and most dives are boat dives. An intrepid underwater enthusiast, however, won't forget a trip here.

Diving is available on some organized cruises (bring your own equipment). A few tour companies specialize in diving, but they tend to be more expensive. Package dive cruises offer the benefit of visiting the islands on land, with up to three dives per day in addition. Some mid-range tours offer occasional diving, meaning you can pay extra – usually $75 – for a dive on any given day. Inquire ahead of time. The other option is day-trip diving out of Puerto Ayora and, to a lesser extent, Puerto Baquerizo Moreno on San Cristóbal Island. Obviously, distances traveled and, therefore, options available tend to be less with day-tripping, but equipment may be supplied. There are plenty of wonderful diving opportunities within a short distance of Santa Cruz and the central islands.

Dive Operators

Galápagos Sub-Aqua, on Av. Charles Darwin near Pelican Bay on Santa Cruz Island, ☎/fax 5-526-350, offers full diving services, including a week-long certification course that costs under $800. Daily dives with Sub-Aqua cost $75 for certified divers, $115 for non-certified divers. They also offer week-long hotel-based dive trips. In Quito, their office is on Amazonas and Pinto 439, Office 101, ☎ 2-2565-294, sub_aqua@accesinter.net, www.Galápagos_sub_aqua.com. ec.

Also on Santa Cruz Island is **Scuba Iguana**, at Hotel Galápagos, ☎ 5-526-497, info@scubaiguana.com, www. scubaiguana.com. The owners are recommended as being very knowledgeable about the best marine sites to visit. They also offer a full range of services, including day-long snorkeling excursions from Santa Cruz and equipment rental.

On San Cristóbal, try **Chalo Tours**, Malecón Charles Darwin and Villamil, ☎ 5-520-953, for boat tours, diving and snorkeling excursions and gear. They also offer island tours inland, as well as renting bicycles and surfboards. On Isabella Island in Puerto Villamil, try **Isabella Tours**, along the main plaza, ☎ 5-529-207, for tours and information, or **La Casa de Marita** (☎ 5-529-238, hcmarita@ga. pro.ec).

Strict environmental regulations apply in the Galápagos Islands and are strongly enforced by local diving guides and authorities. Your trip will end abruptly if you do not abide by them, so follow your guide's lead and familiarize yourself with the rules beforehand.

Where to Stay

ACCOMMODATIONS PRICE SCALE	
Unless otherwise noted, prices are per room, up to double occupancy. Some prices are per person, particularly with all-inclusive packages, but these generally include meals, lodging, guide services and other amenities.	
$	Under $25
$$	$26 to $50
$$$	$51 to $100
$$$$	Over $100

Mid-range to high-end accommodations on the islands are somewhat limited, as most people are here to see, well, the islands, which means spending time on a boat, rather than at a hotel. There are some options in Puerto Ayora on Santa Cruz Island and a few in Puerto Baquerizo Moreno on San Cristóbal Island.

■ Santa Cruz Island

Estrella del Mar, not to be confused with the yacht of the same name, is at Av. Charles Darwin and 12 de Febrero, near the waterfront, ☎ 5-526-427. This is one of the better budget accommodations, with different prices depending on whether or not the room has a balcony and ocean view. Comfortable rooms include private baths and fans. $-$$.

Hotel Angermeyer, Av. Charles Darwin and Piqueros, ☎ 5-526-277, ☎/fax 5-526-277, offers 22 refurbished modern rooms in a comfortable setting. An open-air lounge and bar area surrounds an attractively decorated poolside patio, although the pool itself doesn't offer much room for swimming. The food at the restaurant is not bad and the owners are quite friendly. Although not directly on the waterfront, the pleasant and relaxing ambiance makes this a good choice. $$$

Three hundred feet from the Charles Darwin Research Station is one of the best hotels in town, the **Hotel Galápagos**, ☎ 5-526-296, ☎/fax 5-526-330. The shaded grounds, waterside location, and great harbor views make this a favorite choice. The bar is perfect to sit with a drink and relax with the wildlife and a sunset view after a day out and about. And the Galápagos wildlife will more often than not be enjoying the patio session as much as you are. Local artisans decorated 14 comfortable rooms in maritime themes and native materials, and each has a private bath with hot water. There are hammocks and a relaxing ambiance in the common area and some of the best food in town is served at the restaurant. $$$$

A good budget choice with views of the bay is the **Hotel Sol y Mar**, along the waterfront, ☎ 5-526-281, ☎/fax 5-527-015. Another relaxing option, this hotel also offers the chance to enjoy breakfast in the company of the local wildlife with good views of Academy Bay. There are clean rooms with private baths, plus a recommended bar and restaurant and a friendly owner who can help you find a boat and arrange tours. $$

One of the best budget options in Puerto Ayora is **La Peregrina Bed & Breakfast**, on the main seaside street, Av. Charles Darwin, ☎ 5-526-323. This B&B offers a nice, family-run atmosphere at a reasonable rate. Five double rooms include separate baths and air-conditioning, and a dormitory is available for those really wishing to economize. The shaded porch is a nice place to enjoy a morning breakfast of fresh-cut tropical fruit, bread with jam, and coffee or tea. $

The **Red Mangrove Inn** is not far from the research station, at Av. Charles Darwin and Las Frigatas, ☎/fax 5-526-564, redmangrove@ecuadorexplorer.com, www.ecuadorexplorer.com/redmangrove. Situated at the water's edge, the peach-colored accommodations offer plenty of comfort for such a remote destination. Each double room has an ocean view, private, modern bath, and ceiling fans. There are tiled walkways and bathrooms, as well as attractively beamed ceilings, a Jacuzzi and a nice lounge/dining area. At the shore you can expect the company of marine iguanas basking in the sun, a colorful display of Sally Lightfoot crabs dancing about, and more. Ask about mountain biking, sea kayaking, and tours here as well. Overall, this is one of the nicest higher-end options. $$$

■ San Cristóbal Island

In Puerto Baquerizo Moreno, perhaps the best super-budget choice is **Chatham**, at Av. Northía and Av. de la Armada Nacional, heading toward the airport, ☎ 5-520-137. It is clean, comfortable, offers hot water and fans, is inexpensive, and it maintains a bit of atmosphere. Meals are available. $

Near Playa Mann, on Av. Northía, is **Cabanas Don Jorge**, ☎ 5-520-208, terana@ga.pro.ec. Playa Mann is the beach on the road heading north out of town toward the National Park Visitor's Center. Overlooking the ocean and popular swimming beach, the cabins here are comfortable but nothing special and are a bit more secluded than some of the other options. Rooms have hot water and fans, with meals available. $

Near Playa de Oro and a bit more centrally located, is the more expensive **Hotel Orca**, ☎ 5-520-233, pat@etnot.ecs.ec. Right on the water, Orca has been recommended as offering great seafood and extra amenities, such as air-conditioning. $$

■ Isabella Island

In Puerto Villamil, there are several options. **La Casa de Marita**, ☎ 5-529-238, hcmarita@ga.pro.ec, offers comfort with all of the necessary amenities, including hot water, air-conditioning and a travel agency for local excursions. $$

A better deal is the Swiss-operated **Isabella del Mar**, ☎/fax 5-529-125, Isabella@ga.pro.ec, www.hosteriaisabela.com.ec. Their amenities are similar to those at La Casa de Marita, but with more charm and a better price. Next door is **Ballena Azul**, under the same ownership.

■ Floreana Island

Probably the most famous of all the islands' accommodations is **Pension Wittmer** on Floreana Island, ☎ 5-520-150. In fact, it is the main attraction of the island. There is no real population base on Floreana but the history of the island is truly incredible, the foundation of which was laid by the Wittmer family and other adventurers. Expect comfort and complete isolation here. Though the electricity is on for only a few hours a day, rooms are comfortable, with private baths, hot water and meals included. Inquire around Puerto Ayora on Santa

Cruz for boat service to Floreana and make arrangements ahead of time. $$-$$$

■ Camping

Camping is not readily available on most islands within the Galápagos. Inquire at the National Park office in Puerto Ayora (☎ 5-526-189) about permits for camping on a few of the larger islands. Or check with the Tourism Minstry an Quito, Eloy Alfaro 1214 and Carlos Tobar, ☎ 2-2500-719/2507-555, ☎/fax 2-2507-564, www.vivecuador.com. The **Provincial Tourism Office**, Cámara Provincial de Turismo de Pichincha (CAPTUR), may be even more helpful, at Cordero and Reina Victoria in Quito near the Parque Gabriel Mistral, ☎ 2-2551-556. One popular option is hiking and camping on 3,688-foot **Volcán Alcedo** on **Isabela Island**. There are other overnight hiking and camping options available on the island as well. See Isabela Island, page 409, for details.

On **Santa Cruz Island** permits may be acquired to camp at **Tortuga Bay**, an hour walk from Puerto Ayora. Also, inquire with the **Red Mangrove Inn** about camping on their ranch in the highlands. The $60 rate includes two days, one night, meals and transportation.

Where to Eat

■ Santa Cruz Island

The food choices in **Puerto Ayora** are not bad, with the best available in the hotels. There are several other options in town, particularly along the main waterfront street, but these change hands and names frequently, as you might expect in a town dependent upon seasonal shifts of the tourism industry. It will be easy to find one with the right ambiance and flavor just by walking around.

For pizza and Italian food, try **4 Linternas**, just off of Av. Charles Darwin and 12 de Febrero. For everything from Ecuadorian and seafood cuisine to a hamburger and fries, there are several good choice along the waterfront street. From the southern end near the dock, try **Salvavidas** for set meals – breakfast, lunch and dinner – and atmosphere. With a view of Academy Bay is **Toldo Azul**, on Av. Charles Darwin. This open-air patio restaurant seems to be fairly popular and is close to all the waterfront activity near the *panga* pier. It serves good seafood. **Happy Tummy** is farther north and perhaps worth eating at for the name alone. Among the best in town is **La Garrapata**, right near the strange La Panga discoteque, but you will pay more for your meal.

For a bar ambience, yet serving food as well, try the adjacent **Joe's** and **Niño's**. I have not eaten at either, but they seem to pack in the crowds on occasion.

Just north of the bay along Av. Charles Darwin is **Rincón del Alma**, with good food and decent prices.

Keep in mind that all food and drink prices in the islands are higher than the mainland.

■ San Cristóbal Island

In **Puerto Baquerizo Moreno**, the Malecón (Av. Charles Darwin) offers a few choices, or you can head one block east along Av. Villamil toward the intersection of Hernandez. Among others, here you will find **Rosita**, one of the most popular restaurants in town. There are other less expensive options in the vicinity as well.

Shopping & Nightlife

■ Shopping

There are numerous **souvenir** shops all along Av. Charles Darwin in Puerto Ayora and its adjacent streets, most offering comparable quality. Prices are very inflated, and much of the stuff can actually be bought in Quito at a fraction of the cost. The best **supermarket** is across from the *panga* dock at the southern end of town.

■ Nightlife

As far as nightlife goes, follow your ears, and ask your guide and crew about the latest hotspots. There isn't anywhere very memorable, but then again most people don't go to the Galápagos for the human nightlife. A couple of places wax and wane with the tide of vessels anchored offshore for the evening. Nightlife can actually pick up around here, with "weekend" madness often occurring on a Wednesday (the night before tour turn-overs). Ask around or just listen for the latest popular bar, disco or salsa bar. There are a few.

Galápagos Islands

Appendix

Going Metric

To make your travels a little easier, here is a
chart that shows metric equivalets for the measurements
you are familiar with.

GENERAL MEASUREMENTS

1 kilometer = .6124 miles

1 mile = 1.6093 kilometers

1 foot = .304 meters

1 inch = 2.54 centimeters

1 square mile = 2.59 square kilometers

1 pound = .4536 kilograms

1 ounce = 28.35 grams

1 imperial gallon = 4.5459 liters

1 US gallon = 3.7854 liters

1 quart = .94635 liters

TEMPERATURES

For Fahrenheit: Multiply Centigrade figure by 1.8 and add 32.

For Centigrade: Subtract 32 from Fahrenheit figure and divide
by 1.8.

Centigrade	Fahrenheit
40°	104°
35°	95°
30°	86°
25°	77°
20°	64°
15°	59°
10°	50°

■ Learning the Language

If you enjoy practicing languages other than your own, you'll probably find that Spanish is easier than most. One of the main reasons for this is that it is very logical and has a lot of rules to guide your learning. Pronunciation is a joy, because in general the word is pronounced exactly as it looks – unlike English!

The syllable emphasis in Spanish is identified in one of three ways. If the word has an accent, the stress is on the accented vowel (dif-Í-cil). If the word ends in a vowel, an 'n' or an 's,' the stress is on the second-to-last syllable (her-MAN-o). Otherwise, it falls on the last syllable (est-AR).

DAYS OF THE WEEK

domingo	Sunday
lunes	Monday
martes	Tuesday
miercoles	Wednesday
jueves	Thursday
viernes	Friday
sabado	Saturday

MONTHS OF THE YEAR

enero	January
febrero	February
marzo	March
abril	April
mayo	May
junio	June
julio	July
agosto	August
septiembre	September
octubre	October
noviembre	November
diciembre	December

NUMBERS

un	one
dos	two
tres	three
cuatro	four
cinco	five
seis	six
siete	seven

ocho. . . . . eight
nueve . . . . nine
diez . . . . ten
once . . . . eleven
doce . . . . twelve
trece. . . . . thirteen
catorce. . . . . fourteen
quince. . . . . fifteen
dieciséis. . . . . sixteen
diecisiete . . . . seventeen
dieciocho. . . . . eighteen
diecinueve . . . . nineteen
veinte. . . . . twenty
veintiuno . . . . twenty-one
veintidós. . . . . twenty-two
treinta . . . . thirty
cuarenta . . . . forty
cincuenta . . . . fifty
sesenta . . . . sixty
setenta . . . . seventy
ochenta. . . . . eighty
noventa . . . . ninety
cienone . . . . hundred
ciento uno . . . . one hundred one
doscientos . . . . two hundred
quinientos . . . . five hundred
mil. . . . . one thousand
mil uno. . . . . one thousand one
mil dos . . . . two thousand
un millón . . . . one million
mil millones. . . . . one billion
primero . . . . first
segundo . . . . second
tercero . . . . third
cuarto . . . . fourth
quinto. . . . . fifth
sexto . . . . sixth
séptimo . . . . seventh
octavo. . . . . eighth
noveno . . . . ninth
décimo . . . . tenth
undécimo . . . . eleventh
duodécimo. . . . . twelfth
último . . . . last

CONVERSATION

¿Como esta usted?	How are you?
¿Bien, gracias, y usted?	Well, thanks, and you?
Buenas dias.	Good morning.
Buenas tardes.	Good afternoon.
Buenas noches.	Good evening/night.
Hasta la vista.	See you again.
Hasta luego.	So long.
¡Buena suerte!	Good luck!
Adios.	Goodbye.
Mucho gusto de conocerle.	Glad to meet you.
Felicidades.	Congratulations.
Muchas felicidades.	Happy birthday.
Feliz Navidad.	Merry Christmas.
Feliz Año Nuevo.	Happy New Year.
Gracias.	Thank you.
Por favor.	Please.
De nada/con mucho gusto.	You're welcome.
Perdoneme.	Pardon me.
¿Como se llama esto?	What do you call this?
Lo siento.	I'm sorry.
Permitame.	Allow me.
Quisiera...	I would like...
Adelante.	Come in.
Permitame presentarle...	May I introduce...
¿Como se llamo usted?	What is your name?
Me llamo...	My name is...
No se.	I don't know.
Tengo sed.	I am thirsty.
Tengo hambre.	I am hungry.
Soy norteamericano/a	I am an American.
¿Donde puedo encontrar...?	Where can I find...?
¿Que es esto?	What is this?
¿Habla usted ingles?	Do you speak English?
Hablo/entiendo un poco Español	I speak/understand a little Spanish.
Hay alguien aqui que hable ingles?	Is there anyone here who speaks English?
Le entiendo.	I understand you.
No entiendo.	I don't understand.
Hable mas despacio por favor.	Please speak more slowly.
Repita por favor.	Please repeat.

TELLING TIME

¿Que hora es?	What time is it?

Son las... . . . . It is...
... cinco. . . . . five o'clock.
... ocho y diez. . . . . ten past eight.
... seis y cuarto. . . . . quarter past six.
... cinco y media. . . . . half past five.
... siete y menos cinco. . . . . five of seven.
antes de ayer. . . . . the day before yesterday.
anoche. . . . . yesterday evening.
esta mañana. . . . . this morning.
a mediodia. . . . . at noon.
en la noche. . . . . in the evening.
de noche. . . . . at night.
a medianoche. . . . . at midnight.
mañana en la mañana. . . . . tomorrow morning.
mañana en la noche. . . . . tomorrow evening.
pasado mañana. . . . . the day after tomorrow.

DIRECTIONS

¿En que direccion queda...? . . . . In which direction is...?
Lleveme a... por favor. . . . . Take me to... please.
Llevame alla ... por favor. . . . . Take me there please.
¿Que lugar es este?. . . . . What place is this?
¿Donde queda el pueblo? . . . . Where is the town?
¿Cual es el mejor camino para...? Which is the best road to...?
Malécon. . . . . Road by the sea.
De vuelta a la derecha. . . . . Turn to the right.
De vuelta a la isquierda. . . . . Turn to the left.
Siga derecho. . . . . Go this way.
En esta direccion. In this direction.
¿A que distancia estamos de...? . . . . How far is it to...?
¿Es este el camino a...? . . . . Is this the road to...?
Es... . . . . Is it...
¿... cerca? . . . . near?
¿... lejos? . . . . far?
¿... norte? . . . . north?
¿... sur? . . . . south?
¿... este? . . . . east?
¿... oeste? . . . . west?
Indiqueme por favor. . . . . Please point.
Hagame favor de decirme . . . . Please direct me to...
   donde esta...
... el telefono. . . . . the telephone.
... el bano. . . . . the bathroom.
... el correo. . . . . the post office.
... el banco. . . . . the bank.
... la comisaria. . . . . the police station.

ACCOMMODATIONS

Estoy buscando un hotel... . . I am looking for a hotel that's...
... bueno. . . . . good.
... barato. . . . . cheap.
... cercano. . . . . nearby.
... limpio. . . . . clean.
¿Dónde queda un buen hotel? . . . . Where is a good hotel?
¿Hay habitaciones libres?. . . . . Do you have available rooms?
¿Dónde están los baños/servicios?. . Where are the bathrooms?
Quisiera un... . . . . I would like a...
... cuarto sencillo. . . . . single room.
... cuarto con baño. . . . . room with a bath.
... cuarto doble. . . . . double room.
¿Puedo verlo? . . . . May I see it?
¿Cuanto cuesta? . . . . What's the cost?
¡Es demasiado caro! . . . . It's too expensive!

■ Tourist Information

The **Ecuadorian Ministry of Tourism** (Ministerio de Turismo), at Eloy Alfaro 1214 and Carlos Tobar, ☎ 2-2500-719/507-555, ☎/fax 2-2507-564, www.vivecuador.com, handles issues related to promoting, managing and disseminating information about tourism in Ecuador.

South American Explorers, online at www.samexplo.org/, explorer@saexplorers.org, is one of the best sources of up-to-date information for travelers, such as the latest safety developments, recommended tour operators and Spanish schools. Their Quito Clubhouse office is at Jorge Washington 311 and Leonidas Plaza (mailing address, Apartado 17-21-431, Eloy Alfaro, Quito, Ecuador), ☎ 2-2222-5228, quitoclub@saexplorers.org.

■ Online Sources of Information

The **Latin American Travel Advisor**, toll-free ☎ 888-215-9511, www.amerispan.com/lata, LATA@pi.pro.ec, is an excellent source of up-to-date information regarding travel throughout Latin America, including Ecuador.

Ecuaworld, www.ecuaworld.com, is a comprehensive online source of background and travel information on the country.

Comparable is **www.ecuador.com**, a site operated by US-based Virtual Countries, Inc. as a clearinghouse for all Ecuador information.

One of the best Ecuador-based sources is **www.ecuadorexplorer. com**, a great guide for the latest travel information and tips.

Lanic Ecuador, www.lanic.utexas.edu/la/ecuador, offers academic research resources, including links to universities and institutions.

On the political front, **www.electionworld.org/ecuador.htm**, follows the latest Ecuadorian elections and political topics.

For information on the Galápagos Islands, visit **www. galapagosislands.com** or the Charles Darwin Research Station's site at **www.darwinfoundation.org**.

The **Ecuadorian Embassy** in Washington has a website at www.ecuador.org

For noteworthy news related to Ecuador and other Latin American countries, the *Miami Herald*, at **www.herald.com**, offers excellent coverage.

A major Ecuadorian newspaper, *Hoy*, is now online at **www.hoy. com.ec**. It is a great source of daily news (but you have to be able to read Spanish).

Also in Spanish is a major Quito-related newspaper online, *El Comercio*, at **www.elcomercio.com**, as well as Guayaquil's paper, *El Universo*, at **www.elcomercio.com**.

■ Recommended International Tour Companies

Ecuadorian Tour Companies

For recommended local tour operators and guides, see the appropriate regional chapters.

Birding

Borderland Tours, 2550 West Calle Padilla, Tuscon, AZ 85745, ☎ 800-525-7753/520-882-7650, www.borderland-tours.com, offers birding, natural history and cultural excursions.

Field Guides, 9433 Bee Cave Road, Building 1, Suite 150, Austin, TX 78733, ☎ 800-728-4953/512-263-7295, www.fieldguides.com, fieldguides@fieldguides.com, offers birding trips on the mainland and in the Galápagos.

Neotropical Journeys, at 3920 SE 14th Terrace, Gainesville, FL 32641, ☎ 877-384-2589/352-376-7110, www.njourneys.com, info@njourneys.com, has ornithologist- and naturalist-led trips.

Wings, ☎ 888-293-6443/520-320-9868, www.widdl.com/wings, wings@wingsbirds.com, has guided bird trips for over 30 years.

General Nature, Educational & Photography

Galápagos Travel, 783 Río Del Mar Boulevard, Suite 47, Aptos, CA 95003, ☎ 800-969-9014/831-689-9192, fax 831-689-9195, www.galapagostravel.com, info@galapagostravel.com, offers professionally led 11- and 15-day photography and natural history tours of the Galápagos Islands.

GEO Expeditions, 67 Linoberg Street, PO Box 3656, Sonora, CA 95370, ☎ 800-351-5041/209-523-0152, www.geoexpeditions.com, info@geoexpeditions.com, has been in the business of natural history tours of mainland Ecuador, the Galápagos Islands, and elsewhere for over 18 years.

Holbrook Travel, 3540 NW 13th Street, Gainesville, FL 32609, ☎ 800-451-7111/352-377-7111, fax 904-371-3710, www.holbrooktravel.com, travel@holbrook.usa.com, has specialized in Latin America and Africa for over 25 years. They emphasize natural history and photography, with a few trips to Ecuador.

Inca Floats, 1311 63rd Street, Emeryville, CA 94608, ☎ 510-420-1550, fax 510-420-0947, www.incafloats.com, info@incafloats.com, specializes in high end "nature and cultural adventures."

International Expeditions, One Environs Park, Helena, AL 35080, ☎ 800-633-4734, fax 205-428-1714, www.ietravel.com, intlexp@aol.com, is well known as a leader in general natural history and custom tours, as well as birding excursions. The focus is on the Galápagos.

Natural Habitat Adventures, 2945 Center Green Ct, Boulder, CO 80301, ☎ 800-543-8917/303-449-3711, www.nathab.com, info@nathab.com, brokers and charters high-end natural history and photography tours to the Galápagos, and is a big supporter of wildlife conservation organizations.

Mountain Travel-Sobek, 6420 Fairmont Avenue, El Cerrito, CA 64530-3606, ☎ 888-MTSOBEK (687-6235)/510-527-8100, fax 510-525-7710, www.mtsobek.com, info@mtsobek.com, is a global adventure travel company specializing in hiking, trekking, rafting, sea kayaking, wildlife and natural history tours.

Overseas Adventure Travel, ☎ 800-955-1925, www.oattravel. com, offers Galápagos and Amazon nature tours.

Voyagers International, PO Box 915, Ithaca, NY 14851, ☎ 800-633-0299/607-273-4321, www.voyagers.com, voyint@aol.com, leads natural history and photography tours to the Galápagos.

Wildland Adventures, 3516 NE 155th, Seattle, WA 98155, ☎ 800-345-4453/206-365-0686, www.wildland.com, info@wildland.com, offers tailored active (trekking) natural history tours.

Adventure Travel

Backroads, ☎ 800-GO-ACTIVE (462-2848)/510-527-1555, fax 510-527-1444, www.backroads.com, has high-end biking and multi-sport adventures.

Bike Hike Adventures, 597 Markham St., Toronto, Ontario M6G 2L7, Canada, ☎ 888-805-0061/416-534-7401, fax 416-588-9839, www.bikehike.com, info@bikehike.com, offers multi-sport adventures for the active outdoor enthusiast.

The World Outdoors, 2840 Wilderness Place, Boulder, CO, 80301, ☎ 800-488-8483/303-413-0938, www.theworldoutdoors.com, fun@ theworldoutdoors.com, offers the best moderately priced multi-sport adventures, including mainland (Andes) and the Galápagos.

Untamed Path, ☎ 800-349-1050/760-376-8851, www.untamedpath. com, info@untamedpath.com, is a small company specializing in small groups. They lead hiking, trekking and rafting adventures into the Andes and Amazon.

■ Environmental Groups

International

Conservation International, 1919 M Street, NW Suite 600, Washington, DC 20036, ☎ 800-406-2306/202-912-1000, www.conservation.org, inquiry@conservation.org, focuses on conserving biodiversity and human compatibility in biologically rich areas.

Earthwatch International, 3 Clock Tower Place, Suite 100, Box 75, Maynard, MA 01754, ☎ 800-776-0188/978-461-0081, fax 978-461-2332, organizes conservation expeditions, including coastal cloud forest projects.

People Allied for Nature, in New York, ☎ 212-279-7813, is a nonprofit organization dedicated to promotion of community-based tropical forest preservation. They worked with Earthwatch on a coastal cloud forest project.

The Nature Conservancy, 4245 North Fairfax Drive, Suite 100, Arlington, VA 22203-1606, ☎ 800-628-6860/703-841-5300, www.nature.org, comment@tnc.org, is a major international organization dedicated to preserving intact areas of natural land.

Rainforest Action Network, 221 Pine St., Suite 500, San Francisco, CA 94104, ☎ 415-398-4404, fax 415-398-2732, www.ran.org, rainforest@ran.org, "has been working to protect tropical rainforests and the human rights of those living in and around those forests" since 1985. They have actively supported indigenous rights and conservation in the upper Ecuadorian Amazon.

Rainforest Information Centre (RIC), PO Box 368, Lismore, NSW 2480, Australia, ☎ 61-2-66-213294, www.rainforestinfo.org.au, rainforestinfo@ozemail.com.au, is an Australian NGO (Non-Governmental Organization) founded in 1981 to protect the rainforests of the world and has also played an integral role in supporting Ecuadorian Amazon conservation efforts.

Ecuadorian Organizations

This is not a complete list. Other organizations are highlighted in the relevant chapters.

Acción Ecologia, Alejandro de Valdez 24-33 and La Gasca, Casilla 17-15-246C, Quito, ☎/fax 2-2230-676, verde@hoy.net, is an activist environmental watchdog group.

Andrate Ecological Foundation, García Moreno 804 and 9 de Octubre, Edificio Inca, Casilla 5800, Guayaquil, ☎ 4-2292-860, fax 4-290-740. Tropical dry forest reserve within the Churute Mangrove Ecological Reserve.

Center of Ecological and Cultural Study and Education (CIDECO), Los Corazónes 113, Otavalo, ☎ 2-2921-163. Focuses on environmental issues around Otavalo and the Imbabura Province.

Charles Darwin Foundation for the Galápagos Islands, Av. 6 de Diciembre N 36-109 and Pasaje California, PO Box 17-01-3891, Quito, ☎ 2-2244-803 or 2241-573, fax 2-2443-935, or in the Galápagos, Puerto Ayora, Santa Cruz Island, ☎ 5-526-147/148, www. darwinfoundation.org, galapagosinfo@darwinfoundation.org. An internationally renowned scientific and conservation organization dedicated to the protection of the Galápagos Islands.

Corporacion de Defensa de la Vida (CORDAVI), PO Box 17-12-309, Quito, elaw@cordavi.org.ec. An exceptional group of environmental lawyers skilled at using litigation for environmental protection and public interests.

ECOCIENCIA (Fundación Ecuatoriana de Estudios Ecológicos), Francisco Salazar E14-34 and Av. Coruña, Sector La Floresta, Quito, ☎ 2-2545-999, 2-2522-999, www.ecociencia.org/home.asp. This is a locally operated organization dedicated to the ecological study and conservation of Ecuador's natural regions.

Ecuadorian Council for the Conservation and Research of Birds (CECIA), La Tierra 203 and Av. de los Shyris, Casilla 17-17-906, Quito, ☎ 2-2464-359, cecia@uio.satnet.net. CECIA has gained a reputation for large-scale forest protection focusing on bird habitat, as well as creating valuable research projects.

ESTADE - Estructura y Administracion Del Estado (Studies on Structure and Government Administration), PO Box 17-17-8, Quito, ☎ 2-2447-740, fax 2-2467 830, www.estade.org, estade@estade.org. Focuses on environmental law and policy information dissemination, particularly with regard to mangroves and public policy.

Fundación Maquipucuna, Baquerizo 238 and Tamayo, La Floresta, Quito, ☎ 2-2507-200/201, fax 2-2507-201, roberto@ maquipucuna.org, or in the US, c/o Institute of Ecology, The University of Georgia, Athens, GA 30602-2202, ☎ 706-542-2968, fax 706-542-6040, usa@maquipucuna.org, www.arches.uga.edu/~maqui/. The foundation administers and works to protect the cloud forest around Maquipucuna, including sustainable community development and education projects in the region, as well as scientific research.

Fundación Natura, Av. Río Guayas 105 and Amazonas, Quito, ☎/ fax 2-2434-449, www.ecuanex.net.ec/natura, natura@natura. ecuanex.net.ec. This Ecuador's largest environmental organization, involved in a wide range of activities, including community development and natural resource management, biodiversity projects and urban ecology. Current projects are active throughout the mainland and Galápagos Islands.

Fundación Pro-Bosque, Bosque Protector de Cierro Blanco, Km. 15½, Vía a la Costa Guayaquil, ☎ 4-872-236, vonhorst@gu.pro.ec. They manage the protected forest of Cerro Blanco, near Guayaquil.

Jatun Sacha Foundation, Isla Fernandina 4378 and Tomás de Berlanga, PO Box 17-12-867, Quito, ☎/fax 2-2250-976 and 2451-626, www.jatunsacha.org, jatunsacha@ecuadorexplorer.com. This group works to combine scientific research, community development and environmental protection with ecotourism, primarily through volunteer opportunities at the three biological research stations it owns and manages.

Oilwatch, Casilla 17-15-246-C, Quito, ☎/fax 2-2547-516, www. oilwatch.org.ec, oilwatch@uio.satnet.net, is a watchdog group that focuses on the petroleum industry.

Fundación Rescate del Bosque Tropical – FURARE (Rainforest Rescue), Juan León Mera N32-33 and Carrión Edificio Zaldumbide 3er Piso, Quito, ☎/fax 2-254-1803, www.forestgarden.org/frresc.htm, forescue@uio.satnet.net.

■ Further Reading

Culture & History

Culture and Customs of Ecuador. Michael Handelsman, Greenwood Press, 2000. A wonderful overview of the people in this magnificent country, integral to understanding its unique cultural diversity.

The Conquest of the Incas. John Hemming, Pepermac/Harcourt Brace, 1993. An excellent overall account of this colonial period in Spanish Americas history.

Ecuador in Focus: A Guide to the People, Politics and Culture. Wilma Roos, et al. Latin America Bureau/Interlink Books, 1997. Covers all facets of Ecuadorian Society. A good overview.

Costume and Identity in Highland Ecuador. Laura M. Miller, Ann P. Rowe (Editor) et al., 1998. Examines costume and adornment of indigenous Ecuadorians as related to ethnic identity.

Two-Headed Household: Gender & Rural Development in the Ecuadorean Andes. Sarah Hamilton, University of Pittsburg Press,

1998. A study of indigenous Andean life based on several women and their families.

Ecuadorian Amazon

Head Hunters of the Western Amazonas. Rafael Karsten. AMS Press, 1976.

Savages. Joe Kane, Vintage Books, 1996. First-hand investigative journalist account of oil development in the Ecuadorian Amazon and its direct effects on the Huaorani natives. Very well done factual foundation that is also emotionally charged.

Amazon Crude. Judith Kimmerling. Natural Resource Defense Council, 1991. An in-depth investigation into the oil industry's impact on the Ecuadorian Amazon.

The Savage My Kinsman. Elisabeth Elliot, 1996. The remarkable story of the wife of a missionary who went to live with the very natives that murdered her husband in Amazonian Ecuador.

Crisis Under the Canopy: Tourism and Other Problems Facing the Present Day Huaorani. Randy Smith, 1996. A view on tourism in the Ecuadorian Amazon and its effects on indigenous groups, from the perspective of the country's premier expert.

Defending Our Rainforest: A Community-Based Ecotourism Guide in the Ecuadorian Amazon. Rolf Wesche and Andy Drumm, (a joint venture between the University of Ottawa, the British Embassy in Quito, Abya Yala, The Ecotourism Society, PROBANA and The Nature Conservancy). Mandatory for anyone wishing to support true community-based ecotourism in Ecuador.

Galápagos Islands & Nature

Galápagos: Islands Born of Fire. Tui De Roy, 1998. Written by a magazine writer and wildlife photographer, this is an excellent artistic overview of the many facets of the Galápagos Islands.

On The Origin of Species. Charles Darwin, 1859. The book that rewrote the history of life on earth and set the foundation for modern-day evolutionary biology.

Voyage of the Beagle. Charles Darwin, 1909. Account of his travels through South America.

Floreana. Margret Wittmer, Moyer Bell Limited, 1989. A wonderful historical account of the Galápagos' earliest permanent settler, complete with moving stories over the span of a generation.

Galápagos: A Natural History. Michael H. Jackson, University of Calgary Press/Academic & University Publishers Group, 1996. One of the best overviews of the natural history, geology, flora and fauna of the archipelago.

Galápagos: Worlds End. William Beebe, Dover, 1988. The story of a scientific expedition to study the island biology in the 1920s. Received rave reviews upon its publication.

A Traveler's Guide to the Galápagos Islands. Barry Boyce, Hunter Publishing, 2001. An in-depth guide to traveling in the Galápagos and an excellent complement to this guide book.

A Guide to the Birds of the Galápagos Islands. Isabel Castro, Antonia Phillips, A & C Black/Princeton University Press. A comprehensive bird guide with illustrations.

The Birds of Ecuador. Robert S. Ridgely & Paul J. Greenfield, Comstock Pub. Association, 2001. The best and latest guide to birds throughout the country, complete with detailed plates.

Reef Fish Identification: Galápagos. Paul Humann, editor, New World Publications, 1994. Great for the avid diver/snorkeler.

Ecology & Evolution of Darwin's Finches. Peter R. Grant, Princeton University Press, 1999. Meant for the evolutionary buff.

Flowering Plants of the Galápagos. Conley K. McMullen, Cornell University Press, 1999. A guide to the flora of the Galápagos, including over 400 species that call the archipelago home.

The Encantadas, or Enchanted Isles (part of *The Piazza Tales*). Herman Melville, 1856, Random House, 1996. Published after *Moby Dick*, *The Encantadas* reveals Melville's Galápagos Islands, part of a series of short stories.

Other

Two Wheels & A Taxi: A Slightly Daft Adventure in the Andes. Virginia Urrutia, Mountaineers Books, 1987. One grandmother's account of travel by bike and taxi through the Andes.

Ecuador Atlas Map. Ediquias, 2001.

Ecotourism in Ecuador

Nearly 650,000 foreign tourists visit Ecuador every year. Many are interested in nature and adventure travel in the less-developed sections of the country. Tourism is currently the fourth-highest earner of foreign exchange. It will continue to play a prominent and expanding role in Ecuadorian economics, as the top three earners of foreign currency (petroleum, bananas, and shrimp) either have limited reserves and/or are subject to fluctuating world-market prices. The importance of ecotourism as a sustainable-development tool cannot be overstated, though neither can its potential negative affects.

The United Nations declared 2002 as the International Year of Ecotourism (IYE) to highlight its contribution to conserving biological diversity and the sustainable use of natural resources, while promoting equitable community development in affected areas. Although it may at first appear to be lip service by the United Nations in an effort to "green" its image, the proclamation has resulted in global conferences on ecotourism and development, sharing of ideas and alliances and actions on many levels.

■ The History of Ecotourism

Charles Darwin was the catalyst for ecotourism in Ecuador, despite the fact that he lived well before the buzzword ever existed. After his visit in 1835, a wave of European tourists, from scientists to nature enthusiasts, traveled to the Galápagos. The Galápagos Islands National Park was officially established in 1959 to promote tourism, conservation, and biological studies. It put Ecuador on the map as an adventure-travel destination. By the mid 1970s, the discovery of oil in Ecuador's upper Amazon Basin resulted in new towns and roads being built. Meanwhile, photographers were already exposing the beauty of the indigenous Andean people. As a result, many more foreigners now visit the mainland of Ecuador than the islands.

■ Defining Ecotourism

Ecology is the study of the relationship between organisms and their environment. It is based on the concept of interconnectedness, the interdependence of all things, living and nonliving. The root "eco" stems from the Greek *oiko,* meaning home or environment. In its purest form, ecotourism is a tool that promotes community development, environmental preservation, education, science, and nature-based travel. In other words, it connects all the dots. At the absolute least, it is benign to the environment, while injecting money into the local economy in a responsible way. At best, it provides positive benefits to the affected communities. At worst, which is more often the case than not, it is a marketing buzzword used by anyone promoting tourism related to the environment, even if that tourism has a negative impact.

Often, those claiming that their operations abide by the definition of "ecotourism" do much more damage than good. In Ecuador's resort town of Baños, for example, there are more than 20 tour operators that market their businesses under the name of "ecotourism," without having any idea what that entails. On one jungle excursion, for example, the "white-water tubing" consisted of throwing sticks of dynamite downriver, then putting clients afloat in tubes to scoop up the dead, floating fish. This particular outfitter also dumped its trash directly into the forest adjacent to the waterway.

Ecotourism is a tool for community development as much as anything else. There is no justice in preaching about environmental preservation and responsible travel if Eduardo cannot feed his family. It is easy to forget about the effects of our actions while we're caught up in the magic of exotic lands.

Ecotourism Resources

The following organizations are leaders in supporting ecotourism and sustainable travel:

Ecotourism Australia (www.ecotourism.org.au) offers an international eco-certification program for tour operators, hotels and other organizations.

Planeta.com (www.planeta.com) is one of the best all-around clearinghouses for ecotourism-related topics in the Americas and public forums as they cover important events around the world and online.

The International Ecotourism Society (www.ecotourism.org) provides a membership-based forum for planners and operators, with publications related to ecotourism.

US-based **Sustainable Travel International** (www.travelwithoutatrace.org) promotes sustainability in the travel industry through a best-practice accreditation program.

The UK-based **Green Globe 21** (www.greenglobe21.com) also offers a contribution, identifying and placing a stamp of approval on those they consider responsible tourism operators.

The following questions (including ideas from Ecotourism Australia) are worth considering as you plan your trip:

- To what extent does tourism strengthen the conservation effort the places visited? Does it affect locals in a way that causes them to support preservation of their environment?

- Are locals benefiting financially from the tourist activity, directly or indirectly? Some outfitters build their own lodges and bring in their own (often foreign) guides and supplies. Many also fly clients directly into an area, operate the tour, and then leave immediately. Are locals receiving sufficient economic benefits as guides, cooks, crew, local supply dealers?

- Are the tour operators and accommodations efficient in the use of natural resources, such as water and energy? There are plenty of opportunities for lodges to use fast-growing, renewable, and sustainable building materials; rainwater showers; composting toilets; and solar electricity – or at least use candlelight and kerosene (which add to the ambiance anyway).

- Are the sensitivities of other cultures being respected? Are local customs considered? Are clients encouraged to dress modestly and leave jewelry at home?

- Is the outfitter or lodge involved in a recycling program?

- Who owns the hotels and ecolodges? Do they have good conservation ethics? Were locals displaced from their homes to make way for the project? Community-based lodges are more difficult to track down, but they provide the most benefit to the locals.

- Where does the food come from? Is there any program that includes organically grown food and ways to educate the locals about sustainable practices? Are you eating endangered species or beef from rainforest-grazed cattle that are encouraging local deforestation?

When researching or evaluating local outfitters, lodges, and services, think about the following:

- Are tour guides well versed in and respectful of local cultures and environments?

- Is there any involvement in current political and environmental issues, particularly in those of the local area?

Is there any networking with other stakeholders to keep each other informed of developments and encourage responsible practices?

■ Do they use catalogs and retail outlets to raise environmental awareness by distributing guidelines to consumers, as well as support ecotourism education/training for guides and managers?

■ Do guides ever intentionally disturb or encourage the disturbance of wildlife or wildlife habitats? Do they keep vehicles on designated roads and trails and abide by the rules and regulations of natural areas?

■ Does the tour operator ensure truth in advertising and maximize the quality of experience for hosts and guests?

While you're traveling, here are some ways to enhance your experience while being a responsible traveler:

■ Foster a true understanding of the natural and cultural environments visited, before, during, and after the trip. Read up on the community ahead of time, chat with the locals, and follow up on future progress.

■ Traveling by your own muscle power where possible has unsurpassed health benefits.

■ During any activity, stay on the trail and leave an area cleaner than it was when you found it.

■ Try not to disturb wildlife or wildlife habitats, as animals lose feeding and breeding energy when humans approach.

■ Familiarize yourself with local regulations.

■ Don't use soap or detergents in natural bodies of water.

■ When traveling, spend money on local enterprises.

■ Consider the implications of buying plant and animal products. Find out if they're rare or endangered, if they're taken from the wild, and if local authorities approve of the trade. Don't encourage illegal trade by buying products made from endangered species.

■ Provide feedback to tour operators, your travel agent, and government agencies (who manage the areas visited). Promote conservation from abroad after returning home.

■ Socioeconomic & Political Issues

It is important to note that conservation efforts such as creating parks and bio-reserves can no longer proceed independent of development projects. As human populations continue to rise and encroach upon the remaining natural environments, and as countries place increasing demands on natural resources, conservation and development efforts will continue to merge. This is where ecotourism comes into play.

Many of the heavy hitters in tropical conservation lie outside the realm of national and international government in the form of large-scale nongovernmental organizations (NGOs). They are extremely powerful, often funded by wealthy foundations and donors, and are serving agendas that may be out of touch with the local communities.

Big organizations may know statistics and have scientific knowledge of the field sites in question, but they may not have a sense of the environment at the local level. Often, they lack indigenous knowledge and fail to understand the natural relationship between locals and their environment. In addition, these organizations tend to address the affected natural resources from a point of view similar to that of foreign businesses and governments. In any case, the local impacts are often ignored or misunderstood.

Conservation efforts across the globe have failed because of this tendency to view the problems from thew outside, through filters that are incompatible with local conditions. Often, large reserves are created on lands that encompass indigenous peoples, whose rights are ignored. As a result, the local people are often displaced, not allowed to provide for their own families, and even viewed as a threat to biological diversity and nature-based travel. At the local level, communities are struggling simply to maintain their natural resource base while putting food on the table.

We need to build a bridge between community-level development/ conservation and large-scale foreign assistance. This must occur at all levels, from international financial institutions and unilateral government projects to NGO conservation programs, if we are to obtain true progress. At the micro-level, even within specific countries, socioeconomic, political, and environmental conditions vary dramatically. Fortunately, this realization has led to a growing number of success stories across the globe. Ecotourism development is playing a big role in these efforts.

Many proponents of economic growth in Ecuador view ecotourism as being at odds with other development strategies, such as resource extraction and the production of cash crops for export. In many cases this results in serious friction between environmental groups and scientists on the one hand, and industry on the other. Indigenous groups often get caught somewhere in the middle. Some are looking for jobs and the "better" life, while others are determined to preserve their cultural heritage and tradition. Tourism proponents and indigenous communities may also clash, depending on the circumstances. The indigenous Huaorani community in Ecuador's Amazonia is a perfect example.

The Huaorani are a nomadic forest people who reside in the region south of Coca and east of Tena and Puyo in Ecuador's Oriente. Conflict began in the 1970s, when the first oil companies began to extract from this region. During the early days of the petroleum industry there was a strong marriage between the government and business. As a result, the oil companies developed the region with little – if any – regard to the environment and local people. The early encounters between the Huaorani and oil workers ended in bloodshed on more than one occasion. The determined resistance of the Huaorani eventually forced some oil giants to withdraw from Ecuador, though only temporarily.

With roads having been developed, the tourism industry entered the country shortly thereafter. Unchecked tourism quickly became the single major catalyst for cultural degradation of the Huaorani. Abusive tour outfitters often lacked any more consideration than the oil companies. The Huaorani responded with demands of gifts and tolls for visiting their lands, and even went so far as to harass tourists for their belongings. Some confrontations between tour guides and the Huaorani became violent. As the situation deteriorated, the Huaorani became opposed to ecotourism in their homeland. Since then, however, outside organizations have worked with indigenous organizations to promote education and ecotourism within a monetary economy. It has taken years of hard work on everyone's part to develop a proper relationship, but success stories do exist. Although still a sensitive issue, now the nature and culture enthusiast can visit and stay with the Huaorani people.

■ Barriers to Ecotourism Development

In addition to direct competition with the oil industry, natural-resource development, and rapid colonization, ecotourism in Ecuador faces other challenges. Much of this has to do with marketing and management of the resources. As with other tropical "paradise" destinations, many foreign visitors explore the country via international tour operators. Their stay is often brief and targeted to specific popular destinations. In many cases this in-and-out form of travel injects little into the local economy. Community-based, family-run operations are often ignored. Ecuador has incredible opportunities for nature-based travel not offered by foreign tour operators. Local groups must work together to create a diversified product, target clients, and utilize pre-existing networks, such as travel agents, tour operators, and hotels throughout the country. These issues are discussed in much more detail on the www.planeta.com, in an article entitled *Tourism and the Future of the Maya Biosphere Reserve*, by Sharon Flynn and Juan Carlos Bonilla. It deals with current issues in Guatemala.

■ Time for Change – Bridging the Gaps

As tourism continues to play an expanding role in the Ecuadorian economy, so too must responsibility within the industry. Trends are heading in this direction, but a much more integrated approach is necessary. Concentrated efforts from all key players are required, including those of international NGOs, government policy makers, tour outfitters, local communities, and, ultimately, *you*, the educated traveler.

At one end of the spectrum, NGOs will continue to work with local communities, promoting nature-based tourism and alternative forms of sustainable development. The tour operator and the traveler, at the receiving end, must pressure the government and the public relations departments of businesses for increased protection of these precious natural resources. It is your dollar, your voice, and your responsible actions that can create the momentum necessary for change.

■ A Final Word on Education

Of perhaps more importance than simply visiting Ecuador's natural retreats is a true understanding of how to do so in a responsible manner. The educated traveler plays a major part in saving the rainforest. The protection of these precious resources depends on the appreciation and voices of people who cherish them. Locals already respect their natural environment, but often they must go against what they know is right as a matter of survival. They are more than willing to alter their current actions if the tourist dollar sends the proper signals.

The Ecuadorian government will continue to push nature-based tourism as a major source of foreign income, while simultaneously destroying the very areas they promote in the name of "economic development." It is up to the traveler to seek out information on responsible travel, to ask for it, to question outfitters and guides, and to spread knowledge. If the demand is there, so too will be the supply.

Index

Coast, 290-294; Central and Southern Oriente, 362-368; community-based, 335-337, 349; Galápagos, 394-396, 400-405; Guayaquil area, 312-314; national parks and reserves, 65-66; nature viewing, 69; North Coast, 259-264; Northern Highlands, 139-143; Quito area, 98-100; Quito South to Riobamba, 175-177; ratings, 70; Southern Highlands, 220-224; Upper Amazon Basin, 332-339; Western Slopes, 240-245

Ecuador, 4-32; climate, 18-19; cuisine, 29-30; currency, 43; customs and entry, 41-43; economy, 31-32; electricity, 54; flora and fauna, 19-27; geography, 16-18; getting around, 37-39; getting here, 34-36; government, 30; health and safety, 47-51; history and politics, 5-16; holidays and festivals, 57-59; information sources, 432-433; language, 54-55; leaving, 43; map, 3; people/culture, 27-28; provinces (map), 17; taxes and gratuities, 45; time zone, 54; travel information, 33-59

El Ángel, 130
El Ángel Ecological Reserve, 136, 142-143; camping, 149
El Boliche National Recreation Area, 181
El Cajas National Park, 221-222; camping, 229-230; fishing, 219; hiking, 217
El Corazón, hiking, 166
El Niño, 290
El Pahuma Orchid Reserve, 240-241, 247
El Relleno, sightseeing, 257
Embassies, 45-47
Entertainment, see Nightlife
Equator, 5
Equatorial monument, 89-90
Esmeraldas, 251; accommodations, 264-270; beaches, 255-256, 258; getting here and getting around, 253; restaurants, 270-271; sightseeing, 254-255; visitor information, 253-254
Española Island, 383, 408

Fernandina Island, 383, 409-410
Festivals, 57-59, 120, 160
Fish, 390
Fishing: Eastern Cordillera, 330; Salinas, 289; Southern Highlands, 219
Floreana Island, accommodations, 422
Frogs, 25

FUNDECOL, mangrove forest tours, 257

Galápagos Islands, 18, 381-427; accommodations, 420-422; adventures, 415-419; camping, 422-423; climate, 19, 34, 383-384; conservation, 388, 394-396; eco-certification, 403-404; excursions, 69-70, 400-405; flora and fauna, 387-396; geography and geology, 381-383; getting here and getting around, 396-397; history, 384-387; island by island, 405-415; map, 382; nightlife, 424-425; restaurants, 423-424; shopping, 424; visitor information, 397, 400
Gay and lesbian travelers, 56-57
Genovesa (Tower) Island, 410
Gualaceo, 212
Guandera Cloud Forest Reserve, 143
Guapulo suburb, 89
Guayaquil, 301-320; accommodations, 314-317; botanical gardens, 312; camping, 318; eco-travel, 312-314; flora and fauna, 303; getting around, 304-305; getting here, 304; history, 303; map (area), 302; map (central), 306; nightlife, 319-320; restaurants, 318-319; robberies, 307; shopping, 320; touring and sightseeing, 308-311; visitor information, 307
Guerilla activity, 333

Hang-gliding, 289
Health and safety, 47-51; malaria, 266
Hiking, 67; Baños area, 187-188, 190-191; Central and South Coast, 284-287; Central and Southern Oriente, 361-362; Galápagos, 416; Northern Highlands, 132-137; Quito area, 91-93; Quito South to Riobamba, 166-172; safety issues, 135; Southern Highlands, 216-217; Upper Amazon Basin, 330-332; Western Slopes, 238-239
Hitchhiking, 38
Holidays and festivals, 57-59, 120, 160
Horseback riding, 68; Baños area, 190; Central and South Coast, 287; Northern Highlands, 138; Pululahua National Reserve, 93; Quito South to Riobamba, 173-174; Southern Highlands, 219
Hot springs: Baños, 192; Baños/Cuenca, 207; El Salado, 192; Papallacta, 99-100, 132; Piscina de la Virgen, 192

Adventure Guides
from Hunter Publishing

"These useful guides are highly recommended." *Library Journal*

ALASKA HIGHWAY

3rd Edition, Ed & Lynn Readicker-Henderson
"A comprehensive guide.... Plenty of background
history and extensive bibliography."
(*Travel Reference Library on-line*)
Travels the fascinating highway that passes
settlements of the Tlingit and the Haida Indi-
ans, with stops at Anchorage, Tok, Skagway,
Valdez, Denali National Park and more.
Sidetrips and attractions en route, plus details
on all other approaches – the Alaska Marine
Hwy, Klondike Hwy, Top-of-the-World Hwy.
Color photos. 420 pp, $17.95, 1-58843-117-7

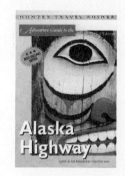

BELIZE

5th Edition, Vivien Lougheed
Extensive coverage of the country's political,
social and economic history, along with the
plant and animal life. Encouraging you to mingle with the locals, the author entices you with
descriptions of local dishes and festivals.
Maps, color photos.
480 pp, $18.95, 1-58843-289-0

CANADA'S ATLANTIC
PROVINCES

2nd Edition, Barbara & Stillman Rogers
Pristine waters, rugged slopes, breathtaking
seascapes, remote wilderness, sophisticated cities, and quaint, historic towns. Year-round adventures on the Fundy Coast, Acadian
Peninsula, fjords of Gros Morne, Viking Trail &
Vineland, Saint John River, Lord Baltimore's
lost colony. Color photos.
632 pp, $21.95, 1-58843-264-5

THE CAYMAN ISLANDS

2nd Edition, Paris Permenter & John Bigley
The only comprehensive guidebook to Grand
Cayman, Cayman Brac and Little Cayman. En-
cyclopedic listings of dive/snorkel operators,
along with the best dive sites. Enjoy nighttime
pony rides on a glorious beach, visit the turtle
farms, prepare to get wet at staggering blow-
holes or just laze on a white sand beach. Color
photos. 256 pp, $16.95, 1-55650-915-4

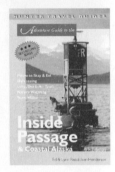

THE INSIDE PASSAGE
& COASTAL ALASKA

4th Edition, Lynn & Ed Readicker-Henderson
"A highly useful book." (*Travel Books Review*)
Using the Alaska Marine Highway to visit
Ketchikan, Bellingham, the Aleutians, Kodiak,
Seldovia, Valdez, Seward, Homer, Cordova,
Prince of Wales Island, Juneau, Gustavas,
Sitka, Haines, Skagway. Glacier Bay, Tenakee.
US and Canadian gateway cities profiled.
460 pp, $17.95, 1-58843-288-2

COSTA RICA

4th Edition, Bruce & June Conord
Incredible detail on culture, history, plant life,
animals, where to stay & eat, as well as the
practicalities of travel here. Firsthand advice on
travel in the country's various environments –
the mountains, jungle, beach and cities.
360 pp, $17.95, 1-58843-290-4

PUERTO RICO

4th Edition, Kurt Pitzer & Tara Stevens
Visit the land of sizzling salsa music, Spanish
ruins and tropical rainforest. Explore archaeo-
logical sites and preserves. Old San Juan, El
Yunque, the Caribbean National Forest, Mona
Island – these are but a few of the attractions.
Practical travel advice, including how to use the
local buses and travel safety. Island culture, history, religion. Color photos.
432 pp, $18.95, 1-58843-116-9

THE VIRGIN ISLANDS

5th Edition, Lynne Sullivan
A guide to all the settlements, nature preserves, wilderness areas and sandy beaches that grace these islands: St. Thomas, St. John, St. Croix, Tortola, Virgin Gorda and Jost Van Dyke. Town walking tours, museums, great places to eat, charming guesthouses and resorts – it's all in this guide. Color photos. 320 pp, $17.95, 1-55650-907-3

THE YUCATAN including Cancún & Cozumel

3rd Edition, Bruce & June Conord
"... Honest evaluations. This book is the one not to leave home without."
(*Time Off Magazine*)
"... opens the doors to our enchanted Yucatán." (Mexico Ministry of Tourism) Maya ruins, Spanish splendor. Deserted beaches, festivals, culinary delights. Filled with maps & color photos.

Other Adventure Guides include: *Anguilla, Antigua, St. Barts, St. Kitts & St. Martin; Aruba, Bonaire & Curacao; The Bahamas; Bermuda; Jamaica; Guatemala; Grenada, St. Vincent & the Grenadines, Barbados,* and many more. Send for our complete catalog. All Hunter titles are available at bookstores nationwide. or direct from the publisher. Check our website at **www.hunterpublishing.com**.

We Love to Get Mail

This book has been carefully researched to bring you current, accurate information. But no place is unchanging. We welcome your comments for future editions. Please write us at: Hunter Publishing, 130 Campus Drive, Edison NJ 08818, or e-mail your suggestions to comments@ hunterpublishing.com.